THELYPHTHORA
VOLUME I

TAKEN FROM MY LIBRARY SHELF
AND REPRINTED IN LIKE FORM
Original Fonts Version
Don Milton

All Text, Images, and Text Images
Copyright 2009 Don Milton
All Rights Reserved

Dedicated to the men who lost their lives, their livelihood, and their place in history because they chose the Bible, not custom.

Trust in the LORD with all thine heart;
and *lean not unto thine own understanding.*
In all thy ways *acknowledge Him, and He shall direct thy paths.*
Proverbs 3:5-6

ABOUT THE EDITOR/PUBLISHER

For the last ten years, Don Milton has pastored ChristianMarriage.com, an online ministry dedicated to providing theological answers to questions about marriage. Pastor Don has published numerous books on the topics of Courtship and Christian Marriage as well as Law & Justice. He recently published his own novel, The Prince of Sumba, Husband to Many Wives, and is currently working on a historical novel. He received his Bachelor of Arts in Linguistics from the University of Washington in 1987.

Don has a wonderful wife and three children. He would like to have more.

Other Books Published by Don Milton

Title	Author	Availability
Prince of Sumba Husband to Many Wives	Don Milton	Now
Exhortatory Address to the Brethren in the Faith of Christ	Martin Madan	Now
A Dialog on Polygamy	Bernardino Ochino Don Milton	Now
Letters to Joseph Priestley	Martin Madan	May 2009
Thelyphthora Volume II A Treatise on Female Ruin	Martin Madan	May 2009
Thelyphthora Volume III A Treatise on Female Ruin	Martin Madan	May 2009
Juvenal and Persius Volume I	Martin Madan	May 2009
Juvenal and Persius Volume II	Martin Madan	May 2009
John Milton on Polygamy	John Milton	May 2009
Many More Titles	Don Milton & Others	Fall 2009

To Purchase Books or to Contact Don Milton
Visit - DonMilton.com or write:

Don Milton
PO Box 10162
Scottsdale, AZ 85271-0162

ABOUT MARTIN MADAN

In 1746, thirty-five years before the Reverend Martin Madan wrote this book, he founded the London Lock Hospital. London Lock was the first voluntary hospital that treated venereal disease.[1] Shortly after Madan founded the Lock Hospital, the institution opened a new building and it became known as *The Female Hospital*. He then began to hold worship services in areas of the hospital *that afforded him the ability to preach as well as to lead a congregation in the singing of hymns* but soon it became crowded, so he set out to build a chapel. With donations from wealthy patrons he was able to build a chapel that seated up to eight hundred people.[2] This may not seem large compared with today's mega-churches but it's still a very large fellowship and it was one of the largest of his day. The wonderful thing about Madan's chapel was that it received enough in tithes to become a strong source of support for the hospital.[3] It was there that the singing of hymns first took hold as part of Christian worship.[4] The members of Lock Chapel sang from a hymnal that Madan, himself, had published. He published the hymnal as a benefit to future generations as well as to raise money for the hospital.[5] From the Chapel at the Lock, hymn singing spread quickly throughout the English speaking world with Madan's hymnal the standard. His mastery of musical worship brought thousands to the Chapel at the Lock and his hymns have brought many more thousands to a saving knowledge of our Lord.[6] In less than thirty short years from the first printing of Madan's hymnal, fully two thirds of the hymns sung, even in the parishes of the Church of England, had been lifted; *word for word, note for note, from Madan's own hymnal*. Madan's hymnal had in fact become the core of the Church of England's hymnal.[7] The Baptists' hymnal came out twenty five years after Madan's.[8] The hymnal that he published was called A Collection of Psalm and Hymn Tunes Never Published Before, the proceeds from which were for the benefit of the Lock Hospital.

Madan held the position of Chaplain at the Lock till the day he died. This was partly due to the fact that he eclipsed all of his contemporaries in promoting, as well as defending, the faith. It was Madan who defended Whitefield and the Methodists against the vicious satire of playwright, Samuel Foote, in 1760, (See his Exhortatory Address to the Brethren in the Faith of Christ at the back of this book) so it was not surprising that he continued to defend the faith and biblical morality till the day he went to be with the Lord."[9]

Four years after the publication of this book, Madan excoriated another group of rascals, the judges of England, for their inconsistency in rendering justice. In his seminal work, *Thoughts on Executive Justice*, he outlined the need for sure and swift punishment of criminals. After his death he was falsely accused of having favored hanging for theft, but he stated in the very book that they quoted out of context against him, that he agreed with the maxim that '*a less punishment, which is certain, will do more good than a greater [punishment], which is uncertain.*'[10] After another two years Madan defended the faith against Unitarian, Joseph Priestly in his *Letters to Joseph Priestley*. Another two years and Madan published his translation of Juvenal and Persius from Latin to English with copious explanatory notes. Today it remains unmatched in thoroughness.[11] On occasion Madan still preached at the Lock Chapel and yet he still found time to write dozens of letters excoriating those who would gamble on the horse races.[12]

Despite all these accomplishments, not to mention his many published sermons, Christian historians have failed to chronicle his ministry in their accounts of the great evangelists of the Eighteenth Century, not to mention the great legal minds of the Eighteenth Century. This and other books in this series, will attempt to correct that deficiency, a deficiency which has left an important part of Church history unrecorded; the transition from singing Psalms to singing hymns. And it was that transition that the Lord used to spark the great revivals of the hundred years that followed Madan's ministry. Prior to Martin Madan's successful promotion of hymn singing, there were only random cases of hymn singing. A church here, or a church there would allow hymn singing, and Christians at non-church venues as well as at dissenting churches sang hymns. However, it took the success of the Reverend Martin

About the Author - Martin Madan

Madan's chapel and its music to make it acceptable. The new hymn singing combined biblical concepts with calls to repentance into a moving form of worship. The hymn provides a way for biblical concepts to be presented in poetry set to music. Many lost souls have been deaf to all other forms of preaching, but have been converted by the hearing of a single hymn.

As you read this book, may you be blessed in knowing that its author was the man who polished some of the most famous words in today's hymnals, the man who composed and arranged the music behind many of those hymns, and the man who cared for and counseled the cast aside women of his time; Martin Madan, the Father of the Evangelical Hymnal.

The preceding *About Martin Madan* section as well as the following footnotes are used with permission, having been gleaned from Prince of Sumba, Husband to Many Wives, Chapter 12 - Martin Madan, A Memory of Love by Don Milton - Copyright 2009

1. "The first special hospital was the Lock Hospital near Hyde Park Corner, founded in 1746 by Martin Madan, who became its first chaplain."
A History of English Philanthropy
by Benjamin Kirkman Gray
London - P.S. King & Son, Orchard House, Westminster - 1905
 The following is an account of some of the types of patients that could be found at the Lock Hospital.
 "There are merit-mongers, among the most abandoned sinners. Two women were, some time since, admitted into the Lock Hospital, in order to be cured of a very criminal disease. Mr. Madan, who visited them during their confinement, laboured to convince them of their sin and spiritual danger, 'Truly,' said one of them, 'I am by no means so bad as some of my profession are : for I never picked any man's pocket, in my life.' The other said, 'I cannot affirm that I never picked a man's pocket; but I have this in my favour, that I never admitted any man in my company, on a Sunday, until after nine at night.'
The Works of Augustus M. Toplady page 168.
You will remember Toplady as the writer of that famous hymn,

About the Author - Martin Madan

Rock of Ages. He was a very close friend and admirer of the Reverend Martin Madan, having also preached at the Lock Chapel.

Good News from Heaven; or, the Gospel a Joyful Sound. At the Lock Chapel, near Hyde Park Corner, June 19, 1774. By the Reverend Augustus Toplady.

Recorded on page 375 of The Monthly Review Volume 52 1775

Madan wrote a tract concerning the sequence of events that led to the conversion of one such prostitute. Despite her conversion and new way of living, she soon died of the illnesses she acquired as a prostitute. This is chronicled in: *A Remarkable and surprising account of the abandoned life, happy conversion, and comfortable death of Fanny Sidney, a young gentlewoman, who died in London in April, 1763, aged 26 years.* By the Reverend Martin Madan

2. "The Lock Chapel was (officially) opened March 28, 1762" but the Reverend Martin Madan conducted services prior to that in other areas of the institution that afforded him the ability to preach as well as to lead the congregation in the singing of hymns.

Dictionary of National Biography - Edited by Sidney Lee - McMillan and Co. 1893 - Page 288

Through Martin's exertions a new chapel, capable of seating 800 persons, was erected in the garden of the hospital, he himself contributing 100 pounds.[100 pounds converts to $20,000 in today's U.S. dollars. University of Michigan conversion table.] It was opened on March 28, 1762 and by 1765 was entirely free of debt.

The Madan Family and Maddens in Ireland and England By Falconer Madan 1933 - Page 112

3. "In the case of the Lock Hospital, the musical movement coincided with the Evangelical. Its chapel was used not only by its inmates, but by a strongly contrasting *West End Evangelical congregation who rented sittings.*"

These rented pews helped pay for the expenses of the hospital.

The Princeton Theological Review - Volume XII - 1914

The Princeton University Press - Princeton, N.J. - Page 87

4. "He (William Romaine) held the extreme Calvinistic position as to the exclusive use of inspired words in Praise, and was able to impose his views upon his own congregation. But he could not

About the Author - Martin Madan

stay the rising tide of Hymn singing or make a breach between the Gospel and the Hymns of the Revival. *In Martin Madan the new Hymn singing found an effective sponsor.* The humorous and sturdy John Berridge was as early on the field as Madan, but less effective."
The Princeton Theological Review - Volume XII - 1914
The Princeton University Press - Princeton, N.J. - Page 73,74

5. In the preface to the Hymnal that the Reverend Martin Madan published, "The Collection of Psalm and Hymn Tunes sung at the Chapel of the Lock Hospital" Mr. Madan writes:
"I have at last, with no small care and trouble, completed this Book of Tunes for the use of the Chapel; and as the publication of them may be of service to the Charity, I must desire your acceptance of the Entire Copy, hoping that, by the sale of this Music, some addition may be made to your fund for maintaining and promoting the charitable work which you have undertaken."

6. The Church of England's hymnal began with Martin Madan's Collection of Psalms and Hymns (1760).
The New Schaff-Herzog Encyclopedia of Religious Knowledge by Johann Jakob Herzog, Philip Schaff, and others. Copyright 1909

7. In 1788, the publisher of the fifth edition of the Church of England hymnal, "appropriated fully two thirds of the contents of Madan's Collection."
The Princeton Theological Review - Volume XII - 1914
The Princeton University Press - Princeton, N.J. - Page 76

8. The first Baptist hymn-book was Rippon's (1787).
The New Schaff-Herzog Encyclopedia of Religious Knowledge by Johann Jakob Herzog, Philip Schaff, and others. Copyright 1909

9. It was Martin Madan who defended Whitefield and the Methodists against the vicious satire of playwright, Samuel Foote in his Exhortatory address to the brethren in the faith of Christ published in 1760

10. Thoughts on Executive Justice with respect to our Criminal Laws Published in 1785 - Page 63

11. A New and Literal Translation of Juvenal and Persius; with Copious Explanatory Notes, by which these difficult satirists are rendered easy and familiar to the reader. In Two Volumes.

About the Author - Martin Madan

By the Rev. M. Madan -Printed for the Editor, at Mr. Lewis's, No 157, Swallow-Street, Near Piccadilly MDCCLXXXIX (1789)
12. "It was formerly the abode of the celebrated [famous] Dr. Madan [Martin Madan], of whom we have given an account. During his residence here, [Birmingham, England] he interposed his authority as a magistrate, to prevent the introduction of illegal games into the town during the race week; he gave notice to those persons, who were in the habit of letting [renting] their houses for this purpose, that it was contrary to the laws of their country, and if they persisted in doing it, they must take consequences. Several tradespeople, who disregarded this notice, were sent to prison, which so exasperated the inhabitants, that they burnt his effigy, near the spot where the pump now stands."
Some Particulars Relating to the History of Epsom by Henry Pownall 1825
"I possess twenty-three letters from him to George Hardinge, Esq., M.P., July 9, 1789-March 14, 1790, [Against illegal gaming] written in good spirits and with some wit."
The Madan Family by Falconer Madan 1933
"Mr. Madan, however, the most respectable clergyman in the town, [Birmingham] preaching [1787-1789] and publishing... [against Priestley's Unitarianism] ...I addressed a number of "Familiar Letters to the Inhabitants of Birmingham," in our defence."
An Appeal to the Serious and Candid Professors of Christianity By Joseph Priestley - Page 105

THELYPHTHORA;

OR,

A TREATISE ON

FEMALE RUIN,

IN ITS

CAUSES, EFFECTS, CONSEQUENCES,
PREVENTION, AND REMEDY;

CONSIDERED ON THE BASIS OF THE

DIVINE LAW:

Under the following HEADS, viz.

MARRIAGE, ADULTERY,
WHOREDOM, and POLYGAMY,
FORNICATION, DIVORCE;

With many other INCIDENTAL MATTERS;

PARTICULARLY INCLUDING

An Examination of the Principles and Tendency of
Stat. 26 GEO. II. c. 33.

COMMONLY CALLED

THE MARRIAGE ACT.

IN TWO VOLUMES.———VOL. I.

THE SECOND EDITION, ENLARGED.

———What in me is dark
Illumine, what is low raise and support;—
That, to the height of this great argument,
I may assert ETERNAL PROVIDENCE,
And *justify* the ways of GOD to MEN.

MILTON.

LONDON:
Printed for J. DODSLEY, in Pall-Mall.
M.DCC.LXXXI.

Preparing for the Press—and speedily will be published,

THELYPHTHORA,
VOL. III.

I. Shewing by what *means,* and by what *degrees,* the *laws* of JEHOVAH concerning *marriage,* were *opposed* and *abrogated,* and a NEW SYSTEM invented and established by CHRISTIAN CHURCHMEN. Extracted from the most authentic *records,* from the earliest times of the CHRISTIAN CHURCH after the APOSTLES, to the *decrees* of the COUNCIL of TRENT, anno 1563, *inclusive.*

II. Observations on the foregoing uninterrupted SERIES of incontestible EVIDENCE, and the WHOLE applied to the subjects of this TREATISE.

III. The true ORIGIN and NECESSITY of MARRIAGE-CEREMONY.

With *many* other INCIDENTAL MATTERS.

CONTENTS OF VOL. I.

DEDICATION, — page i
PREFACE *to First Edition*, — v
——— *to Second Edition*, — xviii
INTRODUCTION, — — 1

CHAP. I.
Of MARRIAGE *as a* DIVINE INSTITUTION, — — 18

CHAP. II.
Of WHOREDOM *and* FORNICATION, — 46

CHAP. III.
Of ADULTERY, — — 57

CHAP. IV.
Of POLYGAMY, — — 74

CHAP. V.
CHRIST *not the* GIVER *of a New Law*, 300

APPENDIX TO CHAP. I.
Containing FARTHER THOUGHTS *on* Exod. xxii. 16, 17, — — 397

APPENDIX TO CHAP. II.
BUCER *on* CONCUBINAGE, — 401

ERRATA.

Page 22. n. l. 27. for a solemn contract—read *fidelity*.
 23. n. l. 5. ditto.
 67. l. 10. for very *feeble*—read comparatively *feeble* to what it once was, before the abolition of the writ *de hæretico comburendo*, 29 Car. II. c. 9.
 72. l. 11. for valiies—read vallies.
 79. n. l. 8. for *liver* on the *right* fide, and *heart* on the *left*—read *liver* on the *left* fide, and *heart* on the *right*.
 144. n. l. 15. for 161—read 152.
 207. l. 6 from the bottom, for τνη—read την.
 296. l. 2. n. after p. add 249.
 298. l. 28. after p. add 175—177.

TO THE

PRESIDENTS,

VICE-PRESIDENTS,

AND OTHER

GOVERNORS

Of those well-intended Charities, and beneficent Institutions

The *Asylum* — *Misericordia* — *Magdalene* — and *Lock-Hospital*.

THE AUTHOR of the following Treatise cannot fix on a more proper patronage for a work of this kind, than that of those noble and honourable persons, whose compassion on the miseries of the *female sex*, has led them to institute public charities for its preservation and relief.

As our laws are at present framed, women are exposed to *seduction, prostitution*, and *ruin*, almost

DEDICATION.

almoſt without controul;—they ſeem to be looked upon as lawful prey to the luſt, treachery, cruelty, and mean artifices of licentious and profligate men, who can ſeduce and then abandon them at their will.

That a want of good government among us in theſe reſpects, is one ſource of all thoſe evils, which your diſintereſted and humane endeavours are intended to prevent or remedy, is ſurely apparent on the ſlighteſt conſideration.

A ſyſtem of laws which leaves the horrid crime of *adultery* not only out of the liſt of its *capital puniſhments*, but even exempts it, as a *public* offence, from any animadverſion whatſoever in our courts of criminal judicature, muſt be attended with all thoſe miſchiefs that ariſe from the encouragement which impunity affords to vice.

The ſame may alſo be obſerved, with reſpect to the defenceleſs ſtate, in which the *weaker ſex* in general is left againſt the *ſtronger*; ſo that any man may ſeduce, and abandon at his pleaſure, the unhappy and deluded objects of his brutal appetite.

To

DEDICATION.

To exhibit a fyftem far different from this—to fet forth the *divine law* as the contrivance of *infinite wifdom*, for the fecurity, peace, prefervation, and protection of the *female fex*, is the purpofe of the following pages.—Were this to be made the bafis of our *municipal laws*, it would prove an adequate remedy for all thofe mifchiefs, which, in comparatively few inftances, can now only find a partial palliation, from benevolence like yours, but which muft, in general, be ftill the portion of thofe, whom GOD's law was formed to protect.

Many of you, my LORDS and GENTLEMEN, are members of the LEGISLATURE; and if, from what fhall be faid on the matters treated in this book, they fhould become the fubjects of your ferious confideration in your *legiflative* capacity, the author will gain one defirable end of his labours.

This furely muft be allowed—that, in point of fact, the alarming increafe of *female proftitution* and *ruin*, calls loudly for fome remedy: the *felf-evidence* of this, is the very foundation of thofe benevolent defigns, which distinguish the several public charities to which you so generously contribute.

Let Government adopt the *system* of heavenly wisdom, which adorns the pages of the SACRED VOLUME, and it will find a remedy in its own hands—what that *system* is, it has been the author's most serious endeavour to enquire, and to recommend it to all, but more especially to the consideration of those, whose care, expence, and vigilance, for the good of their fellow-creatures, has occasioned them the trouble of this address from

Their most humble servant,

And ardent well-wisher to their good designs,

THE AUTHOR.

PREFACE

TO THE

FIRST EDITION.

THE subjects of the following treatise, being of the utmost importance, have been considered with the most serious attention, and are laid before the reader on the highest authority, that is to say, on the authority of the *holy scriptures*.

Nothing less than this ought, or can, determine on the points herein treated, because they concern, not only the *present*, but *future* welfare of mankind: these, as taken in connection together, must depend, first, on *knowing*, and then on *doing* the will of GOD. What His *will* is, can only be known from the several revelations, or discoveries, which it hath graciously pleased Him to make of it, *by men, who spake not of themselves, but as they were moved by the Holy Ghost*. 2 Pet. i. 21.

To imagine that, without such revelation, mortals can understand, or know the mind and will of GOD, is an absurdity, even greater than to suppose we can know the thoughts of each other, without any declaration of them either by words or actions. But to admit the necessity of a divine revelation, to receive the scriptures as *that* revelation, and not to make them the only infallible *rule* and *guide*, in all matters which relate to the mind and will of God therein revealed, is, so far, to lay aside the revelation of God, to make it *void and of none effect*, and to place ourselves in no better situation, than if no such discovery of the mind and will of God had ever been vouchsafed us.

Thus we rob God of His honour, by slighting His *word*, and thus are people led to set up the determinations of human wisdom against it, and expose themselves to *be carried about with every wind of doctrine*, which the folly and superstition of *weak* men, and the wickedness and craft of *designing* men, may happen to invent.

By such means it has been, that so many errors of various kinds have found their way, in all ages, into the *church*, and have maintained their empire over the minds of men. Long *usage* has made them venerable—the prescriptive power of *custom* has given them establishment—and *both* these have prevailed on *human legislatures*, to afford them the awful obligation of their most solemn sanctions.

It cannot want many arguments to prove, that sundry *practices*, as well as *opinions*, which are found among the *heathen* nations, are abhorrent from all our conceptions of propriety, decency, and even humanity itself *.—All these have but one source—*They do err, not knowing the scriptures.*

Where

---

* I cannot forbear mentioning here that valuable, learned, and excellent work of *John Leland, D. D.* on the *Advantage and Necessity* of the *Christian Revelation*—wherein that author hath, with a strength of judgment, and depth of learning and erudition peculiar to himself, so proved his point, as to deserve the thanks of all who

know

Where *revelation* is received, yet if it be not adhered to as the *only* rule of *faith* and *manners*, and this unreservedly, the opinions and practices of men will be as wide from the mind and will of GOD, as those of the *Heathen* are. I might here instance in the opinions and practices of the *Pharisees* of old, as well as of many nations called *Christian*, in more modern days, and who are members of that *society* of professing *Christians* which insolently and exclusively styles itself—"THE "HOLY APOSTOLICAL and CATHOLIC "CHURCH"—amongst whom the most devout are worshipping a *wooden* god, which they call a *crucifix**, and a *breaden* god, which they call the *host*; and, besides these, they worship *saints* and *angels*, and *many such like things they do*. The foundation of all which is still one and the same—*They do err, not knowing the scriptures*; for though the *Papists*

know how to set a just value on the scriptures, as well as of those who would wish to do it. This valuable author says, "It is the mighty advantage of a *written revelation*, "that by an impartial consulting it, the deviations from "it may be detected, and things may again be reduced "to the original standard." Vol. i. p. 453.

* This invention of the crucifix, or image of Christ on the cross, is but old heathenism new vamped. *Maximus Tyrius*, a Platonic philosopher, who was master to *M. Antoninus*, says—"The divine nature stands not in "need of images or statues; but the nature and condi- "tion of man being very weak, and as far distant from "the Divinity as heaven is from earth, framed these "signs for itself, and attributed to them the names and "titles of the gods"—and he thinks that the legislators acted wisely in contriving images for the people. See *Leland*, vol. i. p. 338. The wise men and *philosophers* pleaded for images as necessary helps to human infirmity. Ib. 424.

have the scriptures, yet they do not adopt them as the only rule of *faith* and *worship*. *Their fear towards* God *is taught them by the doctrines and commandments of men**, If. xxix. 13. which take place of the mind and will of God, as revealed in His holy word.

Happy would it be, could *we*, reformed *Protestants*, clear ourselves of this charge in all respects!

To prove that we cannot, in some points of the utmost consequence, is the purpose of the following pages; which, while the *reader*

---

* Two of the articles in the famous creed of Pope Pius IV. are as follows:

XIII. I most firmly admit and embrace *apostolical* and *ecclesiastical* traditions, and all other observations and constitutions of the one *catholic and apostolic church*.

XIV. I do admit the holy scriptures in *the same sense* that *holy Mother Church doth*, whose business it is to judge of the true sense and interpretation of them, and I will interpret them according to the unanimous *consent of the fathers*.

The *Popish canon law* frequently affirms—that *the church is above the scriptures*.

Omnis quæ nunc apud nos est scripturæ authoritas ab ecclesiæ authoritate necessario dependet.—" All the authority " which we attribute to the scriptures, necessarily de- " pends on the authority of the church." *Pighius* de *Hierar. Eccl.* Lib. i. c. 2. *Eccius*, in his *Enchiridion de Authoritate Ecclesiæ*, maintains—*Ecclesiam esse scripturis antiquiorem, & scripturam non esse authenticam, nisi ecclesiæ authoritate.*—" The church is more antient than the " scriptures, and the scriptures are not authentic, save " by the authority of the church."

Hermannus goes farther, and affirms—*Scripturas tantum valere quantum valent Æsopi fabulæ, nisi accederet ecclesiæ testimonium.*—" The scriptures are no more to be va- " lued than *Æsop's Fables*, unless it were for the testi- " mony of the church." See *Hist. of Popery*, vol. i. p. 214.

peruses,

peruses, I could wish him to weigh in the *balance of the sanctuary*, to lay his *Bible* before him, and to call every argument, observation, and doctrine, to the strictest and most severe account, before that unerring tribunal. If he shall find any thing that is *wrong*, or detect any thing that is *false*, let him freely set it down to the *Author's* account. But whatever he shall find agreeable *to*, or clearly proved *by*, the *word* of GOD, let him not listen to the lying testimony of *prejudice* or *vulgar error* against it, but treasure it up in his mind, for the direction of his own *judgment* and *conscience*, in all situations and conditions of life.

If the *judgment* be mis-led or mis-informed, the more conscientious a man is, the farther will he be led into error, and the more firmly will he be attached to it; therefore it is well for us to listen to the counsel of the *wise man*—Prov. iv. 7. " WISDOM is the " principal thing, therefore get WISDOM; " and with all thy getting get UNDERSTAND-" ING."

As to differences, or even *errors*, (if *mistakes* about indifferent matters can be *so* called) where mere outward *forms* are concerned, and those of human invention, the *Author* desires *to think*, and *to let think*, and wheresoever the scriptures are *silent*, to be so too. He does not esteem it worth his while to expend a single drop of ink in such controversies. He does not suppose, that, had he lived in the second *century*, when the *Roman* and *Asiatic* Christians quarrelled about the keeping

keeping of *Easter*, and ran to such indecent lengths of animosity and discord, as might make the very *heathen* blush, he would have ventured a single scratch of his finger, to have had it decided whether it was to be held "on the fourteenth day after the first moon in the new year," or "on the same stated day in every year," or "on the first *Sunday* after the first full moon." All this rout was made to very little purpose: and had the *Author* been weak enough to have entered into the dispute, had he sided with the *Asiatics*, and been excommunicated by Pope *Victor* for his pains, it would not, according to his present notions, have given him a moment's uneasiness.

But where the peace and well-being (I had almost said the very *being*) of society are concerned, where disorders, of the most malignant kind, have infected the general mass, to the destruction of millions down to this moment, and threaten the destruction of millions yet unborn, and those chiefly from among the most defenceless part of the human species; when the lust, treachery, cruelty, and villainy of men, are let loose to ravage, as they can, on the weakness and credulity of helpless women; and when all this is apparently the effect of abolishing those parts of the *divine law*, which were evidently made to prevent it, and the introduction of a *system* of *human* invention is the means of its daily increase; too much cannot be said to point out the cause of the *disease*, and to lead to the *remedy*. The *former* is is from the substitution of the *wisdom of man*, in the place of the *wisdom of* GOD; the *latter* can only be discovered and rendered effectual, by restoring the *wisdom of* GOD to its due place in our esteem, and by making it, as it is found revealed to us in the scriptures, the *basis* of our *municipal* laws—the *line* of our conduct—the *rule* of our *obedience*.

Perhaps some may think, that there are *points* handled and discussed in this *book*, which had better been left under the clouds of obscurity which have long overwhelmed them, and hidden them from vulgar observation, lest disputes should be raised, and abuses committed by the perversions of the evil and licentious. It is written concerning the scriptures themselves, that, to some they are the *favour of life unto life**, and unto others the *favour of death unto death*. 2 Cor. ii. 16. And again—that the *unlearned and unstable wrested the epistles of Paul, as also the other scriptures, to their own destruction*. 2 Pet. iii. 16. As therefore there is nothing in this *book*, which is not to be found in those scriptures, as to the *points* above hinted at, the Author ventures it forth, confiding in Him who hath said—*As the rain cometh down, and the snow from heaven, and returneth not thither, but watereth the earth, and maketh it bring forth and bud, that it may give seed to the sower, and bread to the eater; so shall My word be, that*

---

* Haurit lethiferum bufo de flore venenum,
　Quo mel nectareum sedula promit apes.

At the same flow'r the *toad* and *bee* may meet,
That suck the *poison*—*this* exhaust the *sweet*.

goeth

goeth forth out of My mouth: it shall not return unto Me void, but it shall accomplish that which I please, and it shall prosper in the thing whereunto I sent it. If. lv. 10, 11.

He cannot be of the mind of *Synesius* the *Platonist*, who was raised to be a *Bishop* in the *Christian* church, but continued to be a determined *Platonist*; and had so far imbibed the spirit and doctrine of that school, as to declare his sentiments thus—" As darkness is " most proper and commodious for those " who have weak eyes, so I hold that * *lyes* " and *fictions* are useful to the people, and " that *truth* would be hurtful to those who " are not able to bear its light and splendor." And he adds—" If the laws of the church " would dispense with it, that he would " *philosophize* at home, and talk abroad in the " common strain, preaching up the general " and received *fables*." See note z, Leland, vol. ii. p. 344.

The antient philosophers had an *exoteric* doctrine—ἐξωτερικον—which they openly taught to the people; and an *esoteric* doctrine—ἐσωτερικον—which they taught privately to their select disciples, whom they let into the secrets

* *Maximus Tyrius* saith—that " a lye is often profit-" able and advantageous to men, and truth hurtful." So *Plato*, and others of the *philosophers*—the *Stoics* especially, who held that " a wise man might make use of a " lye for many conveniences and managements in life." See *Leland*, vol. ii. p. 220. Many of the early *Fathers* and *Christians* adopted the same principle, which has been called by the softer term of *pious fraud*, and would *lye* by wholesale—but this *only for the good of the church*—however, this has never been got rid of, as *Popery* can fully attest. See *Mosheim*, vol. i. p. 209.

of their fcheme. It was a maxim among them, that "it was lawful to deceive the people for the public good." Ib. 342—3. So the fect of *Foe* in *China*, have an *exterior* and *interior* doctrine with regard to a *future ftate*—they publicly preach it up to the people, but their *interior* doctrine rejects it. See Ib. 344, note z.

Such is human prudence and wifdom!— but the *divine wifdom* faith—*He that hath My word, let him fpeak My word faithfully.* Jer. xxiii. 28. *There is nothing covered that fhall not be revealed; and hid, that fhall not be known. What I tell you in darknefs, that fpeak ye in the light; and what ye hear in the ear, that preach* (κηρύξατε, *proclaim, publifh) upon the houfe-tops.* Matt. x. 26, 27. Comp. Mark iv. 21, 22. *Truth is like him that doeth the truth—it cometh to the light, that its deeds may be manifeft, that they are wrought in* God. *Error, like every one that doth evil, hateth the light, neither cometh to the light, left its deeds fhould be reproved.* John iii. 20, 21.

God never revealed any thing but that it fhould be known. When men want to conceal any part of divine revelation from the knowledge of others, it is too frequently with a purpofe of preventing the detection of fome errors in *human fyftems*, which, from fome finifter view or other, they dread the difcovery of. Thus the church of *Rome*, jealous of the light of fcripture, knowing that the whole dominion of *popes* and *priefts* over the underftandings and confciences of

the

the laity is founded in ignorance, keep, as far as they can, the scriptures out of their hands.

Others there are, who, from well-meant, but mistaken, zeal, for principles which they have been taught to *venerate*, dread that these should be attacked; as thinking the cause of *religion itself*, is involved with the *supposed truth* of what they are accustomed to believe. There can be no doubt, that when our *reformers* first attacked the POPE's *supremacy*, the worship of the *Virgin Mary*, the *celibacy of priests*, and other pious lyes and forgeries of the *church* of *Rome*, many devout and zealous people thought, that *religion itself* was, like *the ark* of old, 1 Sam. iv. 10, 11. about to be delivered into the hands of the * *Philistines*; and cried out, like *Micah*, when the *Danites* took away his *Levite* and his *Teraphim—Ye have taken away my gods which I made, and the priest—and what have I more?* See *Judges* xviii. 24.

If there be any thing in the *Bible* which ought to be *concealed*, it would be no very hard matter to prove, that it ought never to have been *revealed*. But as it often happens with private individuals, that they are afraid of looking too narrowly into the scripture, for fear of meeting with something to shake their preconceived opinions and prejudices;

---

* In 1547, Gardiner, Bishop of Winchester, said, "that he thought the removing images, was on design to subvert *religion* and the *state* of the *world*."—*Burnet*, Preface to Hist. Ref. vol. ii. p. 11.

so is it with all public and *national systems*. As these have been fashioned by *human* contrivance, they are not, for very obvious reasons, over-fond of too narrow a scrutiny on the single footing of *divine revelation*; lest, as they are formed like the *feet of the image* in *Nebuchadnezzar*'s dream, which were *part of iron, and part of clay*; so these being composed of the *heterogeneous* mixture of *divine wisdom* and *human contrivance*, a too curious investigator should, like the STONE *there* mentioned—*fall upon them, and break them to pieces.*

The Author of the following sheets professes himself a *Free-thinker*; not in the usual sense of that word, as what he has written must abundantly testify, but as an assertor of that right, which every reasonable creature is invested with, to *search, think,* and *judge* for himself. He therefore has endeavoured to lay some points, which he cannot but esteem of the utmost consequence, before the world, that others may exercise *their* privilege as the Author hath done *his*.

As for the *abuse* which any subject herein treated may be liable to—What is not *abused?* What in nature, providence, or revelation, has not been *abused* and perverted to some vile purpose or other? The very GOSPEL OF PEACE hath been *abused*, to sanctify fraud, violence, oppression, and persecution — to justify massacres, tortures, murders, even to men's *roasting alive* their fellow-creatures, and *thinking they did* GOD *service!* insomuch that,

that, were we to judge of the great HEAD of our *holy religion*, by the *abuse* which has been made of His authority, we should invert what He says, *Luke* ix. 56. and imagine, that He came *not to* SAVE men's lives, *but to* DESTROY *them*. Even the *grace of our* GOD has been, and *is* by many, *turned into lasciviousness*. (See Jude iv.) But what does all this prove? Nothing but the ignorance, perverseness, cruelty, and wickedness of human nature; and that *corruptio optimi fit pessima:* but it does not prove, that the GOD of heaven, who foresaw and foreknew such *abuses*, should not have revealed His *mind* and *will* to mortals; nor that *any part* of that revelation should be concealed, suppressed, or hidden from the eyes of men, for fear of its being *abused*. For this may be taken as a certain rule, that no *abuse* of the scriptures ever yet happened from a real understanding and knowledge of their contents, but from an ignorance, either in ourselves, or imposed on us by the design and artifice of others.

The grand question to be tried is, " whe-
" ther a SYSTEM, filled with *obligation* and
" *responsibility*, of men to women, and of
" women to men, even unto *death* itself,
" and this established by INFINITE WISDOM,
" is not better calculated to prevent the ruin
" of the *female sex*, with all its horrid con-
" sequences, both to the public and indivi-
" duals, than a SYSTEM of *human contri-*
" *vance*, where neither *obligation* nor *respon-*
" *sibility are* to be found, either of men to
" women,

THE FIRST EDITION.

" women, or of women to men, in inſtances
" of the moſt important concern to *both*, but
" more eſpecially to the *weaker ſex?*"

The whole of the evidence on both ſides is faithfully collected, and laid open, without any reſerve or diſguiſe, in this book—let every READER look upon himſelf as impannelled on the *jury*—let him impartially hearken to the *cauſe*—and a true *verdict* give according to the *evidence*.

PREFACE

TO THE

SECOND EDITION.

Notwithstanding the disadvantages under which this work has laboured, a *second edition* has long been called for, and now makes its appearance, in as expeditious a manner as the necessary delay of printing would permit.

The *author* would therefore fain hope, that the book has made its way by dint of that intrinsic *truth* which it contains—the *importance* of the subjects treated—the important *ends* proposed—and that conformity to the *oracles of* God, which it professedly makes the *basis* of its contents.

A work which militates against the received *notions*, long *customs*, and inveterate *prejudices* of mankind, can expect but little quarter from the world in general, and, of course, but little of that sort of *candor*, which is shewn to performances of *authors* who write on the *popular* side of a question. —This was fully experienced at the *Reformation*

mation—when *Luther*, and others, published against the ridiculous fopperies and gross villainies of *Popery*, they had *volumes* written against them, in which they were represented in every odious light imaginable.—They were " *heretics—antichrists—factors for the* " *devil*"—and, in short, all that was *bad*;—but the abuse of their adversaries had one good effect—it proved how much at a loss these were for fair argument, grounded on scripture-evidence, and how little able they were to meet their *opponents* with the *weapons* of a *spiritual warfare*. (See 2 Cor. x. 4.) Seldom does *abuse* serve any better purpose in *controversy*, than to create a very strong presumption, that those who *give* it have nothing better on their side, and therefore are in the *wrong*, and that those who receive it are, therefore, in the *right*.

With regard to the article of *abuse* of an *author*, if it be of the *personal* kind, let him set it down as so much gained; if it lights upon his *book*, let the book answer for *itself*, and if it cannot do *this*, let him set down the abuse which it meets with, as what it *deserves*.

Another expedient, which some *critics* have used to depreciate a work, is, to separate some given *subject* from the *rest*, destroy its connection with the main argument, and then, by selecting, in like manner, detached sentences or paragraphs, make these appear to their readers in a light not only different from

from the author's intention, but diametrically oppofite to his whole meaning.

Owing to this it has been, that the fubject of *polygamy* has been felected, and the *indifcriminate practice* of it faid to be recommended by the author of *Thelyphthora*. To guard againft this, in the plain and exprefs manner which he has done (vol. ii. p. 174—177. 288, and n. and 335, n.) he is forry to find was to little purpofe: thefe paffages were overlooked, whether intentionally or not, is to be left to thofe who beft know. However, let the whole that the author has written on the fubject be taken fairly and candidly together, and it will appear, that nothing more is faid, than is warranted by *fcripture, nature*, and *reafon*, and to prove that the *indifcriminate* prohibition of it in all cafes, however circumftanced—which is no where warranted by the law of God—is one fource of *public proftitution*—which, *Montefquieu* truly fays, " may " be looked upon as the greateft of misfor- " tunes in a popular ftate."

I know no book, the *Bible* itfelf not excepted, which may not be abufed by partial quotation;—and by that which is one confequence of it, *mifreprefentation*.—We may prove *atheifm* on *David*, as having faid, Pf. xiv. 1. *There is no God;*—a recommendation of *drunkennefs* from Pf. civ. 15. where he fays, *Wine maketh glad the heart of man*;—or we may fuppofe, that the prophet *Ifaiah*, and the apoftle *Paul*, meant to encourage the licentioufnefs of a *Sçavoir vivre* club—by faying
—*Let*

—*Let us eat and drink, for to-morrow we die.* If. xxii. 13. 1 Cor. xv. 32.

Something like the *difingenuoufnefs* which would attend fuch proofs as thefe, has attended the mifreprefentation of the author's treating *polygamy.*—He has maintained its forming a part of the *divine plan,* which was fo evidently calculated for the prefervation of the *female* fex from defertion and *proftitution*—but by a *part* only of what is faid on the fubject being taken, and placed in another point of view, he is accufed of recommending *polygamy* as an *indifcriminate practice,* to the fubverfion of the peace and domeftic happinefs of every family in the *kingdom*—an idea as foreign from his purpofe, as it was from the *Apoftle's* (1 Tim. v. 23.) to make *Timothy* a *winebibber* (οινοποτης)—See Prov. xxiii. 20. Matt. xi. 19.— when he exhorted him to — *drink no longer water, but* to *ufe a little wine for his ftomach's fake,* and his often *infirmities.* Thus *polygamy* is mentioned in no other light, throughout this treatife, but as * *expedient* in fome cafes, † *neceffary* in others, to prevent mifchiefs of an infinitely more deplorable kind, both to individuals in particular, and to the public in general, than can poffibly arife from every man's being obliged to keep, maintain, and provide for, as the fcripture has commanded, the women he *feduces*—but in order to this, its *lawfulnefs* muft be proved, for if it be difallowed of GOD—there is an end of all queftions upon the fubject, and we

---

* See vol. ii. p. 178.
† See Exod. xxii. 16. Deut. xxii. 28, 29.

must sit down contented under the present ruinous state of things, which is every day increasing the licentiousness of our men, the destruction of our *women*, and the * *depopulation* of the land.

As for partial and unfair representation, it has been an usual way of injuring arguments which do not easily admit of plain and fair answers.

Thus the *Papists* served *Erasmus*, on his publishing his " *Translation* and *Paraphrase* " on the New Testament." A great clamour was raised against him by the *faculty* of *divinity* at *Paris*, as before at *Basil*; and " *Natalis Bedda*, a doctor of divinity, who was
" at that time *Syndic* of the *faculty*, collected
" several propositions, which, as to the full
" import and general sense of them, were
" lame and imperfect, being separated from
" what went before, and from what fol-
" lowed after, and thereby might be taken
" in an ill sense; whereas, if they were red
" with what went before, and what fol-
" lowed after, it would be found they were
" found and orthodox." And thus at length a decree was passed against him, and " those
" doctors who were on the side of *Erasmus*,
" were obliged to hold their peace, lest, by

---

* We were lately told, in one of the public prints, how truly I cannot say, that—" a noble Lord stated in
" the House of Commons, with his usual accuracy, that
" the decrease of people in this country, within these
" last 90 years, has been ONE MILLION EIGHT HUN-
" DRED THOUSAND." Surely this must be an exaggeration—but yet it might be worth while to examine into the *increase* or *decrease* of the people.

" speaking

"speaking their thoughts freely, they should become odious, and their lives be made uneasy." See Du Pin, Cent. 16. p. 267—8. Eng. Transl.

What *Erasmus* wrote on the treatment which he met with from many quarters, on account of his publication, deserves our notice, as containing a proper admonition to those who *condemn*, because they read with *prejudice*; and to those who are *profligate* enough to *condemn*, without reading *at all.*

"Sic oportet ad librum legendum accedere lectorem, ut solet ad convivium conviva civilis. Convivator annititur omnibus satisfacere: & tamen siquid apponitur, quod hujus aut illius palato non respondeat, urbanè vel dissimulant, vel probant etiam, ne quid contristent convivatorem. Quis enim eum convivam ferat, qui tantùm hoc animo veniat ad mensam, ut carpens quæ apponuntur, ne vescatur ipse, nec alios vesci sinat?

"Et tamen his quoque reperias inciviliores, qui palam, qui sine fine damnent ac lacerent opus, *quod nunquam legerint.* Atque hoc sane faciunt quidam, qui se *Christianæ pietatis doctores* profitentur, & *religionis antistites*; cum sit plus quam *sycophanticum,* damnare quod nescias."

As I have too much reason to think that some of the *unlearned*, as well as the *learned*, stand much in need of being acquainted with the *above*, I will give it in *English.*

"A reader should come to the perusal of

"a book, as a courteous gueſt comes to a
"feaſt. The giver of the feaſt does his en-
"deavour to ſatisfy all; yet, if any thing be
"brought to table, which may not be
"agreeable to the palate of this or that per-
"ſon, they politely diſſemble their diſlike,
"or even *approve*, rather than *grieve* him
"who has invited them. For who could
"bear with that gueſt, who comes to the
"table only with a diſpoſition to find fault,
"and neither to partake himſelf, nor ſuffer
"others to partake of the entertainment?

"Yet you may find others more *uncivil*
"than theſe, who openly, and without end,
"will condemn and tear a work to pieces,
"which they have never red. And *ſome* do
"this, who profeſs themſelves *teachers of*
"*Chriſtian piety*, and *eminent* * *profeſſors* of
"religion. Whereas, to condemn that of
"which you are ignorant, is beyond the
"baſeneſs of the † *baſeſt informer*."

I could eaſily make ſome *ſtrictures* on the

---

* *Antiſtes* properly denotes a *chief prieſt*, *prelate*, or *biſhop:* but is alſo uſed for any man *eminent* among others. AINSWORTH.

Eraſmus probably uſed it in *the former ſenſe*. The author uſes it in the *latter*, for a *reaſon* which *ſome* of his *readers* have *more* cauſe, than he wiſhes they had, to ſee the propriety of.

† *Sycophanticum*, rendered literally, would afford no information to the *unlearned* reader; the term is therefore *paraphraſed*, in ſuch a manner, as to give an idea of the ſort of people which the *Greeks* called *Sycophants*, and, of courſe, what *Eraſmus* means by *Sycophanticum*. For the derivation and meaning of *Sycophants* among the *Athenians*, ſee *Chambers' Dict.*

above

above passage, but I forbear saying any more, than *Erasmus* has said for me.

I would recommend it, however, to all, who have, or shall criticise on this *work*, to be very certain they *understand* it; for I have a shrewd suspicion, that this has not been the case with *all* its *readers*; perhaps I might name some highly-respected characters, that have been *foremost* in very *unbecoming language* relative to *certain subjects* of it. If *those subjects* are *not* treated, in a direct consonance with the *law* of God, as revealed by *Moses*, they have my free liberty to say what they please; but otherwise, let them take care, lest their *wit, raillery,* and *pious sarcasms,* do not ultimately tend to vilify and ridicule the God *that made them*—let them beware, lest that question, once put on a very serious occasion, be not put to them, in *an hour* when they will find more difficulty, than they seem at present aware of, to answer it—*Whom hast thou reproached and blasphemed? And against whom hast thou exalted thy voice, and lifted up thine eyes on high? even against the* Holy One of Israel. 2 Kings xix. 22. Let them remember, that He will not only *convince the ungodly, of the hard speeches, which they have spoken against Him,* (Jude xv.) but, sooner or later, will *deal* with persons of a more *decent character,* and whose sayings have borne the *semblance* of *religious zeal, after their folly,* in that they *have not spoken of Him the thing that is right*. See Job xlii. 8.

As to the *Ladies,* who, I am told, are *ex-*
tremely

tremely difpleafed, I hope I have too much good manners, to prefume to enter into any controverfy with *them*; only I would recommend to them alfo, a very ferious attention to what is faid in the preceding *paragraph*—and to take great care, that their *objections* do not fall on HIM, who knew the fituation HE had placed them in, when HE made His *laws* for the protection of their *frail fifters* from ruin and deftruction.—They will, however, permit me to affure them, that if the *author* had found any thing in the *divine œconomy*, which tended to fupport the *pride* of one part of the *fex*, at the expence of the *ruin and proftitution* of the *other*, he would moft faithfully have declared it; and if his fair *readers* fhould *fearch the fcriptures* with an intent of finding fome fuch thing, he would very earneftly caution them, on *whom* they lay the *blame* of the difappointment which will moft certainly attend their enquiries.

The additions which have been made in this *edition*, are fuch, as tend to elucidate the paffages where they occur, and to fhew the refpect and attention, which the *author* moft gratefully pays, to any pertinent and candid obfervations, which have fallen in his way.

I now conclude this *Preface*, with the contents of a paper which I received from a very refpectable *Clergyman*, who was *candid* enough to let his *prejudices* fubmit to his *judgment*, and had *honefty* enough to *own it*.

The following *Queries* contain fo accurate an *epitome* of the work, and are fo much to the

the purpose, as to save the *author* the trouble of introducing them, with any farther remarks whatsoever.

"As the subject of a late publication, entitled "Thelyphthora; or, a Treatise on Female Ruin," &c. "is much misunderstood, and misrepresented by many people, who have, some of them, never read it at all, and the rest but partially, and not without prejudice, and therefore oppose it; 'tis judged best to send its opposers the following *Questions*, for them to answer: the doing of this, 'tis thought, will bring the matter to a point, enter upon particulars, and be a means to discover where, and with whom, *truth* is, and where, and with whom, *error* is.

"1. Are the mischievous, shocking crimes of whoredom, fornication, and adultery, got to an enormous and increasing height, in this land, and is the land defiled and deluged by them, or not? and is the frown, or curse of God upon the land, or is it not?

"2. Is it needful, and is it our bounden duty, to cry aloud against these God-provoking, and nation-ruining sins, and to seek a remedy against this monstrous evil, or is it not?

"3. Is there any thing destructively horrible in the lives, and any thing shockingly dreadful in the deaths of abandoned women, alias, common prostitutes, or is there not?

"4. What

" 4. What *number*, how many thousands are there of these miserable creatures in our land? and have they any evil effect on the male sex, or not?

" 5. Do our laws, as they now stand, hinder this ruinous evil, or do they not? and *can* they, or *can* they *not*?

" 6. Do our laws encourage, or discourage, honourable marriage, or celibacy? encourage, or discourage population?

" 7. Do our laws, in any cases, put asunder those, whom GOD has joined together, and keep together those, whom He has ordered to be put asunder, or do they not?

" 8. Is there any *remedy* at all spoken of in GOD's word, against the great evil of lewdness; and if there be, what is that particular remedy?

" 9. Does GOD, in His word, order, that whores, adulterers and adulteresses shall be *put to death*, or does He not? See Leviticus xx. 10. Deut. xxii. 21, 22.

" 10. In particular instances of some persons injuring others, does GOD, in his word, enjoin any *recompence* that the injurers and offenders shall make the injured, or does He not?

" 11. Are some of our laws, in this land, framed upon the Divine laws, in the above-mentioned particular, and do they inflict punishment on some transgressors and offenders, in any cases, according to the spirit of the divine laws, or not?

" 12. Is

" 12. Is there any *particular* recompence
" that GOD, in his word, orders an *unmar-
" ried* man to make a virgin whom he has
" defiled, or is there not? and if there be,
" what is it? See Exodus xxii. 16, 17.
" Deut. xxii. 28, 29.

" 13. Is there any particular recompence
" that a *married* man is enjoined to make the
" virgin, whom he has defiled, or is there
" not? If there be, what is it? Is the vir-
" gin, in the above case, to receive a recom-
" pence, and the virgin, in this, to receive
" none, and to be abandoned? See the above
" scriptures.

" 14. Is our marriage-ceremony, in the
" church, so of the essence of marriage as to
" *constitute* marriage; and, therefore, none
" are married in GOD's sight, but what are
" joined together, by a priest, with that ce-
" remony?

" 15. Is the marriage of the people called
" *Quakers*, in this land, marriage *in* GOD's
" *sight?* and also according to our laws?

" 16. Were the marriages performed by
" justices of the peace, in the last century,
" for eighteen years together, marriages in
" GOD's sight, and according to our laws?

" 17. In what way, or by what form, were
" all those people of old joined together,
" whose marriages are recorded in scripture-
" history?

" 18. In what way, or by what form
" were Christians married for upwards of a
" thousand

"thousand years immediately after the birth
"of Christ.

"19. Was our church marriage-cere-
"mony the consequence of Pope Innocent
"the 3d, putting marriage, as a sacrament,
"into the hands of Popish priests, or was
"it not?

"20. What reasons can be assigned for
"GOD's permitting so many people, and,
"particularly, some of his distinguished
"saints of old, to live allowedly in the
"practice of *Polygamy*, and to die, with-
"out ever reproving them, calling them
"to repentance, (if it was a *sin*) and with-
"out their ever expressing any sorrow for
"it, and shewing any evidences at all of
"their repentance? And if GOD's word be
"the rule of our conduct, and if the ex-
"ample of these saints be written for our
"learning, what are we to learn from them,
"respecting their polygamy?

"21. If these saints of old lived and died
"in *sin*, by living and dying in the allowed
"practice of *polygamy*, what is the *name* of
"the sin? By what term is it to be distin-
"guished? Was it adultery? or, whore-
"dom? or, fornication? Was their com-
"merce licit or illicit? What command-
"ment did they sin against? Were they
"adulterers, whoremongers, or fornicators?
"What does the scripture-history of the
"lives and deaths of these saints teach us to
"call this their practice?

"22. Were

"22. Were Hannah, and Rachel, and (after Uriah's death) Bathſheba, whores or adultereſſes; or, were they lawful and honoured wives? How are they ſpoken of, and how were they treated, as the ſcripture-hiſtory informs us?

"23. Were Joſeph, Samuel, and Solomon, baſtards, or honourable legitimate ſons? In what character were they ſpoken of and treated? Did GOD ſhew favour to them, or diſlike of them?

"24. Were not Hannah, Rachel, and Bathſheba, whores, or adultereſſes; and Joſeph, Samuel, and Solomon, baſtards, according to the *laws of our land?*

"25. Are there any things unſcriptural, as well as impolitic, in the late act of Parliament for the preventing clandeſtine marriages, and if there be, what are they, and why? And why did half the Houſe of Lords, ſave one ſingle voice, move for a *repeal* of this act?

"26. In what way can a ſtop be put to theſe following ruinous, deteſtable, horrible, and national evils; namely, brothel-keeping, murdering of infants by ſeduced women; pregnant virgins committing of ſuicide; medicine-taking to procure abortion; the venereal diſeaſe; ſeduction; proſtitution; whoredom; adultery; and all the deplorable evils accompanying and following the miſchievous ſin of lewdneſs in this land? If GOD's law reſpecting the commerce of the ſexes, was obſerved, and

"if

"if the laws of our land were to enforce that, might we not expect His blessing on such means used to accomplish so needed and desirable an end?

"27. On supposition that polygamy be a practice disallowed of GOD, is the *other* part of the scheme for preventing the horrible evils of lewdness in our land, scriptural and practical, or not?

"28. Is the design and aim of the book to hinder lewdness, and its deplorable effects, or not?

"After these questions are answered, not in a trifling, superficial, and merely specious and declamatory manner, but in a full, plain, fair, scriptural, and reasonable manner; and the answers are open and honest, free from paltry subterfuge, and all deceiving equivocation, and reservation, and all the answers are founded on truth and facts, we shall then notice what the *consequences* will be of such a right mode of answering these questions; and so find out, whether the arguments in "Thelyphthora" be scriptural, reasonable, and defensible, or not; whether the scheme in that book has a good or a bad tendency; whether to be reprobated, or received; and whether the friends and abettors of it are friends or foes to their country? the cause of GOD? the temporal, spiritual, and eternal welfare of their fellow-creatures?"

THELYPHTHORA.

INTRODUCTION.

TO call in question the truth of long-received *opinions*, is a sort of employment which *few* chuse to be engaged in; not only from the natural indolence and supineness of the human mind, but from the reception which such attempts are likely to meet with from the *generality*, who are always jealous of whatsoever may seem an attack on *principles* which have the sanction of *antient custom*; and from thence, even of *laws* themselves, for their support.

We need but look * back to the times of the *Reformation*, in order to see this abundantly

---

* If we carry our researches into the history of the Heathen world, we shall find that it was an established maxim adopted by *Plato*, and in which all the other *philosophers* without exception concurred, that " every " nation should worship the gods according to the esta- " blished laws and customs, to which also every private " person in his own practice ought to conform." By this artifice of the *devil* (who is emphatically styled the " *god of this world*, that *blinds the minds of men*," 2 Cor. iv. 4.) not only the Heathen world, but a great part of the *Christian* world, hath been enslaved in chains of error

dantly verified. Our *Reformers* no sooner began the salutary work of enquiry after *truth*, and its infallible consequence, the detection of error, than the whole *Christian world*, so called, was in arms against them. *Councils* were summoned, *synods* held, and their sentences were, in substance, what that of the " *men, brethren,* and *fathers,*" of the *Jews* was against that supposed *innovator, Paul* of *Tarsus*, when they said, " *Away with such a fellow from the earth, for it is not fit that he should live.*" Acts xxii. 22.

When *Paul* and *Silas* were apprehended, and carried before the magistrates at *Philippi,* the charge against them ran in the following terms :—" *These men, being Jews, do exceedingly trouble our city, and teach customs which are not lawful for us to observe, being Romans,*"

But why was it not *lawful* for the *Romans* to observe what *Paul* had been teaching? Because of the contrariety of the *Roman* laws

and delusion. On the footing of this maxim it was, that when *Socrates*, who was the wisest of the *philosophers,* attempted to awaken his countrymen to a more rational and spiritual sense of *divine things* than they had been accustomed to, he was accused at *Athens* by *Anytus* and *Melitus*, that " he did not believe those to be gods " which the city believed, and that he introduced other " new gods"—for this he was put to death. How many *Christians* have been put to death on a similar principle, let the annals of those declare who are now crying, *How long*, O LORD, *holy and true, dost thou not judge and avenge our blood on them that dwell on the earth!* Rev. vi. 9, 10.

So *Cicero* binds it as a duty upon the people " to fol-" low the religion of their ancestors." Cic. de Leg. lib. ii. c. 8.—*ritus familiæ patrumque servanto.*

and superstitions to GOD's word—for a like reason, the *Reformers* taught things which it was not *lawful* for the subjects of this kingdom *to observe*, because the system of the laws of church and state were opposite to the *Bible*—and, as far as they are so still, so far will a writer against them be deemed no better than a *troubler of the land*, and a teacher of *customs which it is not* LAWFUL *for us to observe*. He likewise stands fair for being called one of those, who would *turn the world upside down*. See Acts xvi. 20, 21. xvii. 6.

Had not *Luther* quarrelled with *Pope Leo* X, and brought himself into difficult and dangerous circumstances, it is not impossible but that the light of that great *reformer* had remained hidden under the * *bushel* of *monkery*. However, it pleased GOD to order it otherwise, and, in his gracious providence, to over-rule *Luther*'s situation, for the investigation and promulgation of the *faith once delivered to the saints*. Jude 3. This extraordinary man was led to search, think, and judge for himself; and (drawing his *artillery* from the inexhaustible *arsenal* of the *holy scriptures*) first to † attack, and then to overthrow,

* Matth. v. 15.
† I would observe, that *John Wickliffe*, an *Englishman*, educated at *Oxford* in the reign of Edward III. has the honour of being the first person in *Europe* who publickly called in question, and boldly refuted, those doctrines, which had passed for *certain* during so many ages. Guth. Gram. vol. i. 247. For this he was sorely persecuted during his life; and after his death, his bones, which had been buried forty-one years, were dug up

throw, *errors*, which had been received as the moſt ſacred *truths* for ages, and which had been maintained, by every ſupport, which the credulity and ſuperſtition of mankind, aided by laws and powers *eccleſiaſtical* and *civil*, could give them.

From whence I would infer, that no *opinions* or doctrines whatſoever, receive any *concluſive* proof of their truth, from the ſuffrages of men, however wiſe, learned, or however ſupported by human *maxims, cuſtoms,* or *laws*. To take it for granted, that truth muſt be where there are theſe ſupports, is at once to give up our privilege of enquiring and judging for ourſelves; and, if ſo, we might as well have been born without *reaſon* and *judgment* as with them. Upon ſuch a principle as this, a *Mohammedan* has as good * a reaſon for the truth of the *Koran*, as we have for the truth of the *Bible*; for the *former* hath as much the *cuſtoms* and *laws* of *Turkey* for

---

and burned. This by a ſolemn decree of the council of *Conſtance*. See Fox's Martyrs, vol. i. 529. He was the firſt tranſlator of the New Teſtament from the *Latin Vulgate* into *Engliſh*. He died about 1387. Jortin Rem. vol. v. p. 479—80.

* So had the antient *Heathen* for the truth of their ſyſtems. Many of the *philoſophers* actually reſolve all *moral* obligations into merely *human laws and conſtitutions*; making them the *only* meaſure of right and wrong, good and evil: ſo that if the people had a mind to be inſtructed what they ſhould do or forbear, they ſent them to the laws of their ſeveral countries, and allowed them to do whatſoever was not forbidden by thoſe laws. *Leland,* vol. ii. 81, 82. *Plato* is for people's "worſhip-
" ping the gods appointed by the laws of the ſtate, and
" in

for its support, as the *latter* has those of *England*. "*Idolatry* at *Pekin* (says a late writer) *Mohammedism* at *Constantinople*, *Popery* at *Rome*, and *orthodoxy* at *Westminster*, will be all equally right. The earth will turn round in *England*, and stand still in *Italy*; and our holy religion will be true in *Europe*, but an arrant falsehood throughout all the continent of *Asia*." *Humanum est errare*, is too true respecting *every* man and *all* men, as fallible creatures. *Churches* and *councils*, as well as other communities *, are therefore

---

" in the manner there prescribed." Ib. p. 119. note p. So before him *Pythagoras*,

'Αθανάτους μεν πρῶτα Θεὺς ΝΟΜΩ ΩΣ ΔΙΑΚΕΙΤΑΙ Σεβϑ.——

First the immortal gods, *as is by law ordain'd*, Worship.

When *Erasmus* was about to publish his edition of the New Testament, he was sorely abused, for presuming to amend the *text*, by correcting some blunders in the commonly-received readings—and, in his account of the arguments of his opposers, says, among others, *Quidam hic nobis tradunt Lesbiam regulam, ut id habeatur pro recto, quod vulgo receptum est*. " Some here lay down for me the *Lesbian* rule, that, " that should be esteemed *right*, which is commonly received." At this rate, how unprofitably does a man pass his time in endeavouring to instruct himself, with the hope of instructing others?

* " By paying little deference to *general councils*, few inconveniences arise, compared with those which inevitably follow a blind and tame submission, in points of faith, to human decisions, and to *public wisdom*, as some of our controversial doctors have loved to call it, which may be *public folly*.

" *Public wisdom* is a mere *Proteus*; and, not to consider it in *Pagan* or *Mahometan* countries, amongst the *Jews* it once was the *wisdom* of *Ahab* and *Jezebel*, " and

therefore liable to be miſtaken, as is modeſtly confeſſed by the Church of *England* in her 21ſt *article*, " Of General Councils."

" When they be gathered together (foraſ-
" much as they be an aſſembly of men
" whereof all be not governed by the Spirit
" and word of God) they may *err,* and
" ſometimes *have erred* in things pertaining
" to God. Wherefore things ordained by
" them as neceſſary to ſalvation have neither
" ſtrength nor authority, unleſs it may be
" declared that they are taken out of the
" Holy Scriptures."

The writer of the following pages would humbly hope, that, having ſo venerable an authority for calling in queſtion the truth of certain matters, which are moſt *aſſuredly believed amongſt us,* he ſhall not be deemed impertinently contentious, if, touching ſome points, he differs from the generality of his countrymen, who, contenting themſelves with *notions* and opinions *received by tradition from their fathers,* have never thought of looking after the foundations on which they are grounded, and have therefore miſtaken the *fallible* authority of men like themſelves, for the divine and *infallible* authority of *truth itſelf.*

That our *brothels* are filled with *harlots,* our ſtreets with *proſtitutes,* and our land with

---

" and afterwards of *Annas* and *Caiaphas*. It ſets out
" with a great ſhew of religion, it begins with the
" *Goſpel according to St. Matthew,* and it often ends *in*
" *the Goſpel according to Mr. Hobbes."* Jortin Rem,
vol. ii. p. 193—4.

impurity,

impurity, is too dreadfully true. *Magdalens, Asylums,* and all the kind and benevolent interpositions of public charities, however we may suppose them, with respect to some few individuals, to answer their benevolent designs, are inadequate to the cure of so crying an evil. A tree is not to be destroyed by plucking off a few leaves, or by cutting away here and there a branch; nor can so general an evil, as we have spoken of, be reformed by so partial, so precarious a remedy, as, from the nature of things, it is in the power of the best disposed, as matters are now constituted amongst us, to administer.

The *ax must be laid to the root*—this is the divine wisdom. The truth is, that the evil above mentioned, as all others, arises from the neglect and contempt of the divine law, and the substitution of human * laws in its stead. The wisdom and goodness of God, which He has shewn in the provision graciously made for the protection and defence of the *weaker* sex, from the villainy, treachery, and cruelty of the *stronger*, are disregarded. God's laws are laid aside, for that system of baseness and barbarity, which per-

---

* This *practice* exactly harmonizes with the *principles* of Lord *Bolingbroke*, who concludes a very horrid sentiment on the *commerce* of men and women, with these words:—" *Increase and multiply* is the law of na-
" ture. The manner in which this shall be executed,
" with the greatest advantage to society, is the *law* of
" man." Here this matter is left wholly to political considerations and human laws, without any *divine law* to restrain or regulate it.

mits men, with impunity, first to *seduce*, and then to betray, to infamy, want, misery, disease, and even death itself in many instances, thousands and tens of thousands of unhappy women, who (were the laws of Heaven regarded, as they ought to be, and made the foundation of our *municipal* laws) instead of becoming nuisances, and reduced to the state of *Devils* * incarnate, might have been the comforts of their families, the delight of their friends, the ornaments of civil society.

As to what shall be advanced on these, and on the other subjects of the following discourse, the *author* is not wild enough to imagine that, what he has to say, will meet with any better reception than *that book* does from whence he takes his authority; or that any person who does not regard the *Bible* so far as to pay an implicit regard to its sacred

---

* This expression will not be thought too strong, when the appendages, and concomitant-vices of *prostitution* are considered; such as *profane cursing* and *swearing*—*blasphemy*—*obscene* talking—*drunkenness*—*lying*—*thieving*—and even the *unnatural crime* mentioned Rom. i. 26. This is so *frequent*, as even to have become *common*. When such are the gradual consequences of eradicating every principle of *modesty* and *virtue* from the *female* mind, how ought that *law* to be reverenced, which was ordained of Heaven for their protection! *Montesquieu*, L'esprit des Loix, vol. i. Liv. 16. c. 12. observes, that " there are so many evils attending the loss
" of virtue in a woman, the whole soul is so degraded
" by it, and so many other faults follow upon it, that,
" in a popular state, *public incontinence* may be regarded
" as the greatest of misfortunes."

dictates,

dictates, will be in the least persuaded by what will be offered: much less that there will be any alteration in our *national system of laws*, 'till, *as* a nation, we practically adopt, as we certainly profess to believe, and as it is evidently *true*, that GOD is to make laws for man, and not man for GOD; or, in other words, that the *world* is to conform to the *Bible*, and not the *Bible* to the *world*.

It is now long since Christ charged the *Jewish Rabbies* with *making void the law of God through their traditions, and teaching for doctrines the commandments of men*, hereby proving themselves the children and followers of those of whom he complains Is. xxix. 13. *This people draw near me with their mouth, and with their lips do honour me, but have removed their heart far from me, and their fear towards me is taught by the precept of men.* Human nature is * just the same *now* that it was *then*, and the same leaven has run through *human systems*, more or less, to this hour.

Our laws concerning *marriage*, especially since the famous *marriage-act*, are full

---

* " August 1, 1543, the *Parisian* divines assem-
" bling the people by the sound of a trumpet, published
" five-and-twenty heads of *Christian doctrine*, proposing
" the bare conclusions, and determinations, without add-
" ing reasons, persuasions, or grounds; but only pre-
" scribing, as it were by authority, *what they would
" have believed.* These were printed, and sent through
" all *France*, confirmed by the *King's* letters, under most
" grievous punishments against whomsoever spake or
" taught otherwise." Brent. Hist. Coun. Trent. 105.

of this, and hence in part arises the mischief complained of. By substituting a human *ceremony* of *man's invention,* in the place of the *only* ordinance of marriage which GOD ever instituted or revealed, we have reduced the most solemn of all ties to a sort of *civil institution,* the most sacred of all obligations to a mere *civil contract;* and where the *latter* can be avoided, the *former* is as *totally* vacated, as if it had never been.

By GOD's express command from *Mount Sinai,* where the laws concerning *moral* good and evil, were eternally and unalterably fixed, no man could *take* a *virgin* and then abandon her. *He shall surely endow her to be his wife.* Exod. xxii. 16. And again, Deut. xxii. 29. *She shall be his wife;* BECAUSE HE HAS HUMBLED HER, *he may not put her away all his days.*

Will any say—" these laws are * antiquated?" I answer, " they are as unchangeable as the GOD that made them." His *law* is His *will,* and therefore can no more *change* than Himself. *The strength of* ISRAEL *is not a man that He should repent* נחם change his *mind, opinion, or purpose.* 1 Sam. xv. 29. *I am* JEHOVAH, *I change not,* is the character

---

* We read in the memoirs of the great *Scriblerus,* that one of the *philosophical works* of that *profound* genius was intitled, " A complete digest of *the laws of Na-*
" *ture,* with a review of those that are *obsolete* or re-
" *pealed,* and of those that are ready to be *renewed* and
" put in *force.*"

which

which he records of himself, Mal. iii. 16; and to shew that he hath stamped the same *unchangeableness* upon his *laws*, he says, Deut. iv. 2. *Ye shall not* ADD *unto the word which I command you, neither shall ye* DIMINISH *ought from it, that ye may keep the commandments of the* LORD *your* GOD. And again, Deut. xii. 32. *What thing soever I command you, observe to do it, thou shalt not* ADD *thereto nor* DIMINISH *from it*.

Now, I do take it for granted, that He, who, speaking to the people of *Israel*, calls himself THE LORD YOUR GOD, is also THE LORD OUR GOD. *Is he the God of the Jews only? Is he not also of the Gentiles? Yes—of the Gentiles also*. Rom. iii. 29. For which very evident reason, I do conclude, that both *Jews* and *Gentiles* are equally subject to those laws which the LORD THEIR GOD once revealed and established for the *moral* government of the world: and therefore (as we may learn from the testimony of the *Apostle* of the *Gentiles* under the New Testament, Gal. iii. 10. as well as from *Moses* under the Old Testament, Deut. xxvii. 26.) *Cursed is every one, that continueth not in* ALL *things which are written in the* BOOK OF THE LAW, *to do them*.

These laws therefore stand on the same footing with what we usually call the *Ten Commandments*—and are no more subject to *decay* or *alteration* than *they* are. I say they stand on the same footing, because they were equally delivered by GOD to *Moses*, on the

same

same divine *veracity*, the same awful, and indisputable *authority*, and are guarded by the same tremendous *sanction*.

That the merely *ceremonial* laws are *waxed old*, and *vanished away*, Heb. viii. 13. is certain, because they were only established for the *time then present*, Heb. ix. 9. to point out, and prefigure *things to come*. They had their end and accomplishment in CHRIST, and of course their utter abolition. This, so far from arguing any *change* of mind or will in GOD, is one of the highest and most illustrious proofs of the uniformity, and consistency, with which he has laid down, carried on, and perfected the same one design from the beginning.

But the *moral* laws which respect the wellbeing of society, the prevention of disorder, confusion, and all other appendages of *moral evil*, must endure, as long as the objects to which they relate endure on the face of the earth. When *St. Paul*, Gal. iii. 10. and Rom. x. 5. cites the sanctions of the *moral* law from the Old Testament, he shews very clearly, that it still remains as an invariable rule of conduct, from which all the people of GOD, whether *Jews* or *Gentiles*, are equally forbidden to depart.

Can any person therefore, in his sober senses, imagine that it was *unlawful* in the sight of GOD (because expressly by a *positive* law forbidden) *three thousand* years ago, to take a virgin and then abandon her, but that now it is *lawful*? or, because there is no law of
this

this land against it, it is therefore less offensive in the eyes of GOD, than at the instant He forbad it? or that GOD's law is only binding on the consciences of men, where it has the sanction of human * institutions to inforce it? If it be *time* which wears out the malignity of such an evil, or the obligation of the divine law against it, we may as well imagine that other crimes stand in the same predicament, and the most atrocious violations of the security and happiness of mankind, will have a *prescriptive* innocence to plead in their excuse.

That all such reasonings are not only without foundation, but directly opposite to the *divine truth*, we learn from that *truth itself*, which hath assured us, that " *it is easier for heaven and earth to pass, than one tittle of the law to fail.*" And that we may be assured He stamped the most permanent authority on that law, and particularly on that part of the law of which we have now been speaking, He adds, in the very next words—" *Whosoever putteth away his wife, and marrieth another, committeth adultery; and whosoever marrieth her that is put away from her husband, committeth adultery.*" This is no *new* law enacted by our blessed *Saviour* on the subject,

---

* We may say of human laws, ceremonies, and institutions, which interfere with the obligation of GOD's ordinances or commandments, as *Henry* II. King of *France* said of the *papal* dispensations, that—" they are
" not able to secure the conscience, and are nothing
" but a shadow cast before the eyes of men, which can-
" not hide the truth from GOD."

but an application and explanation of that very law which he had, immediately before, said,—" could never fail," and which was given to *Moses* at mount *Sinai*. See *Luke* xvi. 17, 18.

When our Lord in his sermon on the mount, as recorded by *St. Matthew*, is about to explain the *moral* law, and vindicate it from the false glosses which the *Scribes* and *Pharisees* had put upon it, he prefaces his explanation with these remarkable words— " *Verily I say unto you, 'till heaven and earth pass, one jot or one tittle* (one, even the most seemingly inconsiderable part of a single letter) *shall in no wise pass from the law, till all be fulfilled.*" ἕως ἂν παντα γενηται. *Until all things be done.* Which, with the learned *Dr. Hammond* on Matth. v. 18, I would thus paraphrase: " 'Till the world be destroyed, and
" all things come to an end, no one least
" particle shall depart from the law, or
" be taken away, or lose its force and ob-
" ligation." " *Whosoever, therefore,* saith Christ, ver. 19, *shall break one of these least commandments, and shall teach men so, he shall be called the least in the kingdom of heaven; but whosoever shall do, and teach them, the same shall be called great in the kingdom of heaven.*" After such a testimony as this to the * *immu-*

---

* The Psalmist saith, Ps. cxix. 89.

לעולם יהוה נצב דברך בשמים
For ever O *Jehovah!* is *settled* thy word in the heavens

I must therefore declare it, not only as my *opinion*, but as a fixed article of my *faith*, that a single *atom* of the *moral law* can never be changed—*nor will God alter the thing that is gone out of his lips.* Ps. lxxxix. 34.

tability

tability of the divine law, it would hardly be decent in me to attempt an addition to its force, by any further arguments.

I will therefore now proceed to examine the subjects proposed, which I shall do singly on the authority of GOD's word; and this, not by detaching one text here and there from the rest of the sacred scriptures; but by examining carefully the *whole* throughout, *comparing spiritual things with spiritual,* 1 Cor. ii. 13. and thus allowing the word of GOD to be, what GOD doubtless intended it should be, the *best comment* upon *itself*.

Nor shall I venture to rest any one point on the authority of even the best * *translations*, but constantly have recourse to the *original scriptures*, being desirous to follow that sensible maxim, that " nothing should " be received in proof, but on the best tes- " timony which the nature of the thing will " admit of." If, in matters of *civil* property, " a copy will not be admitted in " evidence, where the original can be come " at," how much doth it behove us, in matters of *eternal concern,* to have the best evidence for our determinations? *Satius est petere fontes quam sectari rivulos.*

I have endeavoured to clear my imagination of all *worldly* systems, and *human inventions*

---

* Whosoever reads the strictures *on*, or rather *against*, the sacred scriptures, of that ignorant and malicious reviler of them, *M. de Voltaire*, may see how he has been led into his mistakes by some of the *Latin* and *French* translations.

what-

whatsoever, whether *Popish* or *Protestant*, and to allow no authority more modern than the sacred scripture, *less* weighty than inspiration itself, to amount to a proof of what is *true* or *false*. As for the writings of primitive * *fathers, Christians*, &c. the whole rabble of *schoolmen*, together with the decrees of *councils, churches, synods*, &c. a man, who wishes to know the *truth*, should no more receive a matter of *doctrine* on their authority, than he should a matter of *fact* on the testimony of a *Popish* legend. Nay, I will

---

* These were but *fallible men*, like ourselves, at best; and if we consider the strange opinions which are to be found in their writings, we must acknowledge them to be very faulty. Though they have been so mutilated, changed, interpolated, and corrupted, by the various *sects* who have wanted their testimony to speak for them, that it is difficult to know what is *genuine*, and what is not. I remember to have met with the following dismal, though short account, of the writings of the *fathers*,—" Scatent erroribus tum veterûm tum recenti-" orum hæreticorum." " They abound with the errors, " as well of the old, as of the more modern *hæretics*." Burnet observes, that " there was a great mixture " of *sophisticated stuff*, that went under the *antient* " *names*, and was joined to their *true works*, which " critics have since discovered to be *spurious*." Hist. Ref. p. 30. 2d edit. vol. i. The *apostle*, Tit. i. 14. warns us against *Jewish fables*; we should be equally careful of *giving heed* to those which seem to bear a *Christian* stamp.

We might as well recommend a *young man* to the study of so many volumes of *news-papers* to make him an accurate *historiographer*, as to the study of the *fathers* to make him a *sound divine*. How far they may make him a *rotten* one, may be seen in the *Life of Dr. Clarke*, by *W. Whiston*, p. 143, 151, 155.

go farther and say, that the * dying words, and unshaken constancy of *saints, martyrs,* and *confessors,* ought to prove no more than that " they themselves believed what they " said," unless the *holy scriptures* bear testimony to their opinions.

However clear the *spring* is, yet, when it divides itself, flowing from the fountain-head into different channels, it will naturally present to the *eye* the *colour,* and to the *palate* the *taste,* of the different soils through which it may happen to take its course. I have therefore found little encouragement to rest any thing on the authority of *commentators;* who, being prejudiced by education, influenced by custom, and misled by others that have gone before them—instead of *thinking* as the *Bible speaks,* too frequently make the *Bible* speak as *they think.* The conclusion of the matter therefore ought to be—*To the* LAW *and to the* TESTIMONY! If. viii. 20.

---

* Much has been built on the constancy with which the *martyrs* suffered—but when we find people dying with equal constancy for opposite opinions, nothing is conclusively proved on either side, but that each believed his own tenets.—See Burnet's Hist. Ref. vol. ii. p. 112. 3d edit. the case of *Joan* of *Kent,* and of *George Van Pare,* a *Dutchman.*

It is a dangerous thing to build our faith on *equivocal* testimony, instead of the ONE INFALLIBLE EVIDENCE of GOD'S WRITTEN WORD—which can neither *lye* nor *deceive;* and against which there can lie no appeal, to any *other writings* in the world, nor to any *other testimony* of any kind whatsoever.

CHAP. I.

Of MARRIAGE as a Divine Institution.

WHEN the great and all-wise Creator had formed man upon the earth, *male and female, He blessed them, and said unto them, Be fruitful and multiply, and replenish the earth.* Gen. i. 28. This command was to be fulfilled in a way of GOD's own appointment; that is to say, by *the union of the man and woman* in *personal knowledge of each other.* This is the only † *marriage-ordinance* which we find revealed in the sacred scriptures. Wherever this *union* should come to pass, though *two* distinct and independent persons before, they now were to become as *one. They shall be one * flesh,* Gen. ii. 24. and so

---

† By this expression, I would be understood to mean, *that by which* the parties become *one flesh* in GOD's sight, so as *not to be put asunder*. See Matth. xix. 5, 6.

* לבשר אחד —*as one flesh*—ἐις σαρκα μιαν, Gr. Test. The Hebrew ל prefixed, hath often this sense. See Josh. vii. 5. Lam. i. 17. So the *Greek* preposition ἐις, which answers to it. Compare 2 Sam. vii. 14. with Heb. i. 5. where the לבן and לאב of the Old Testament, are rendered by ἐις πατερα and ἐις υιον in the New Testament; and clearly evince the names of *Father and Son* to be *œconomical* names of *office* in the covenant of redemption, not descriptive of an inferiority and subordination in the persons of the GODHEAD. Compare Luke i. 35.

Also היה with ל, and a noun following, denotes some change of condition, state, or quality, and signifies —*to become*. Gen. ii. 7. 24. xvii. 4. Exod. iv. 4. & al. freq.

indissolubly

indissolubly *one*, as to be inseparable. *What God hath joined together, let not man put asunder.* Matt. xix. 6.

That this *oneness* arose from this *act* of *union*, and from the command consequent upon it, that *they should be one flesh*, is evident from the *Apostle*'s reasoning, 1 Cor. vi. 15, 16. *Know ye not that your bodies are the members of* CHRIST? *Shall I then take the members of* CHRIST, *and make them the members of an* * *harlot? God forbid! What, know ye not that he that is* JOINED *to an harlot is* ONE BODY? *for two,* saith he, *shall be* ONE FLESH.

This question of the Apostle's—*Know ye not that he that is joined to an harlot is one body?* and what follows, being taken together, have a plain reference to what *Adam* said, Gen. ii. 24. and seems very fully to determine, not only the strictness of the *marriage-union,* but *that* which constitutes it in the sight of GOD. In all which there is not the least hint, or most distant allusion, to any *outward* rite or ceremony administered by any person whatsoever; but the whole is made to rest simply and only in the

---

* πορνη, from περνημι, or περναω, *to sell*. A *whore,* a woman who prostitutes her body for *gain.* So the Latin *meretrix* is from *mereor,* to *earn, get money:* and our *English* word *whore,* from the German *huren* (Dutch *hueren*) to hire. Thus *Ovid.* lib. i. eleg. 10.

Stat *meretrix* certo cuivis *mercabilis* ære,
Et miseras jusso *corpore* quærit opes.
     See *Parkhurst*'s Gr. Lex.

personal † union of the *man* and *woman*. It is this *alone* which, according to the *Apostle*, makes them *one flesh*.

If

† It may be presumed, that in what *Adam* said, Gen. ii. 23. he had an immediate reference to her formation out of a *part of himself*; but that there was also an allusion to the personal *union* of the *male and female*, in what he says, ver. 24. is clearly proved by the *Apostle's* argument, 1 Cor. vi. 16; otherwise his citing this passage of Gen. ii. 24. would have been nothing to the purpose to shew that *this* makes them *one flesh*. The Hebrew רבק באשתו is rendered by the LXX, ΠΡΟΣΚΟΛΛΗΘΗΣΕΤΑΙ, προς την γυναικα αὐτȣ, in Matt. xix. 5. ΠΡΟΣΚΟΛΛΗΘΗΣΕΤΑΙ τη γυναικι αὐτȣ. Let the *reader* compare all this with the *Apostle's* ὁ ΚΟΛΛΩ'ΜΕΝΟΣ τῇ πόρνῃ, and it will be very easy to see that the same *idea* runs through the whole; which is, that those who are *thus joined*, are *one body*, and pronounced by GOD—*one flesh*. This will appear still the more evidently, if we consider OUR LORD's expression, as represented by the *Evangelist*, Matt. xix. 6. where he uses the word ΣΥΝΕΖΕΥΞΕΝ, hath *joined*, or *yoked together*, as the *effect* of the *cause* expressed by Προσκολληθήσεται. All this will appear still more evidently, if, with the accurate *Ar. Mont.* we translate ודבק באשתו, *& adhærebit* IN UXORE SUA.

A very candid critic on *Thelyphthora*, asks, " how the " above idea (of κολλώμενος) is reconcileable with the " context, in which the same word is applied to the Lord " —Ὁ κολλώμενος τω κυριω, He that is JOINED *to the Lord*," &c.? It is a pleasure to me to give a candid question as candid an answer.

The *idea* contended for, where κολλώμενος is made use of as denoting the union of a *man* with an *harlot*, cannot be the same with that where it denotes the union of the believer *in one spirit with the Lord:* the *one* is evidently a *carnal* idea, the other as evidently *spiritual*; yet the *marriage-union* is emblematical of the *spiritual* union between CHRIST and the believer, as to the strictness and indissolubility of the union itself, and many other particulars, which the reader may find, Eph. v. 22—33. where (v. 31.) the *Apostle* quotes Gen. ii. 24. and expresly assimilates it to the union of CHRIST *with the church*, v. 32. Thus

are

If the licentious and temporary union with an *harlot*, makes a man to become *one body*, and *one flesh* with her, we may suppose that the sin of *fornication* receives no small share of its malignity, from the abuse thereby committed of the *ordinance* of *marriage* as established by God: as entering into it without any intention of abiding by it, but merely to gratify a transient lust, and that with a woman who departs from one to another, as gain or evil desire may lead her. Nevertheless the *Apostle*, on the authority of Gen. ii. 24. says, that *he that is* JOINED *to an harlot*, is *one body*, and *one flesh* with her, by being engaged in *that ordinance*, of which these things are declared, in the passage referred to, to be the inevitable consequences.

From what has been said, it appears, that *marriage*, as instituted of God, simply consists (as to the essence of it) in the *union* of the *man* and *woman* as *one body*; for which are *earthly* things made use of to teach us *heavenly* truths; and indeed in this dark and imperfect state of *mortality*, this is the *only* way by which we can become acquainted with them; they are therefore made use of for this gracious purpose, throughout the whole *Bible*.

The *Apostle* is shewing, in this place of 1 Cor. vi. the horrid inconsistency of *believers*, who, in a *spiritual* sense, are *joined to the Lord*, (compare John xv. 5.) and become *one spirit* with him, (so that their very bodies are *temples of the Holy Ghost*, ver. 19.) taking those *bodies* from the *sanctified* use (see 1 Thess. iv. 4, 5.) to which they ought to be dedicated, and *joining* them in carnal commerce with an *harlot*, by which they become *one body*, and of course *one flesh*, with her.—This is not glorifying God in *their bodies, and in their spirit, &c.* ver. 20. but a profanation and defilement of *both*.

plain and evident reason, no outward forms or ceremonies of man's invention, can add to or diminish from the effects of *this union* in the sight of God. What ends these things may serve, as to civil purposes, I shall not dispute: but I cannot suppose that the * matrimonial-

* Our marriage-ceremony, or form of *solemnization* of *matrimony*, was settled by *Archbishop Cranmer*, and twelve others, in the reign of Ed. VI. *i. e.* about 232 years ago, or 1548 years after the canon of scripture was closed, and is certainly the method by which the *civil contract* is established among us, provided it be administered agreeably to a subsequent act of *parliament* (26 G. II. c. 33.); but how far must the mind be gone in superstition and prejudice, to suppose, that a human ceremony can controul or alter the fixed and determinate *laws* of *Heaven*, or have the least influence on what *does* or *does not* make the parties *one flesh* in God's sight! Grot. de Jur. lib. ii. c. 5. § 8. saith—Conjugium naturaliter esse existimamus talem cohabitationem maris cum femina, quæ feminam constituat quasi sub oculis & custodia maris. Nam tale consortium & in mutis animantibus quibusdam videre est. In homine vero, qua animans est utens ratione, ad hoc accessit fides, qua se femina mari obstringit. Nec aliud, ut conjugium subsistat, natura videtur requirere.

We account marriage to be naturally such a cohabitation of the *male* with the *female*, as may place the female, as it were, under the eye and custody of the *male*; for such a fellowship [or intercourse] is to be seen among certain brute animals. But as to man, as he is an animal having the use of reason, to this (natural conjunction) has acceded a solemn contract, by which the female binds herself to the male. Nor does nature seem to require any thing else for the subsistence of marriage.

Gronovius notes on part of the above passage, as follows, viz.

Custodia maris.] Videtur addendum, procreationis, & mutui auxilii causa.

The

trimonial-service in our church, or any other, can make the parties more *one flesh* in the sight of God, supposing them to have been *united*, than the *burial*-service can make the corpse over which it is red more dead than it was before.

Supposing they have not been *united*, they are not *one flesh* in the sight of God, by any virtue in the words of the service, any more than a piece of *wafer* becomes *flesh and blood* by a Popish priest's consecration. It is not *man*, but God, which makes the *twain one flesh*; neither is it *man's ordinance*, but God's *institution*, which brings that to pass. If this be not so, why, notwithstanding the words of the service, does incapacity, inability, or impotency, in either party, render all that has been done *null* and *void*? See Burn, Eccl. Law, vol. ii. p. 39.

By observing the *outward* ordinance, the intention of the parties is publickly recognized, and they are pronounced *man* and *wife* in the sight of the world; but they are not so in God's sight, unless by anticipation, as it were, with respect to the mutual promises made to each other, which the sacred scriptures call *betrothing* or *espousing*; but the

---

The custody of the male.] It seems there should be added—for the sake of procreation, and of mutual help.

Accessit fides.] Tacite significat fidem quam dat maritus uxori non esse a natura, sed ab instituto.

Acceded a solemn contract.] Here is tacitly signified, that the faith which the *husband* pledges to the *wife*, is not from nature, but by (positive) institution.

C 4   contract

contract is then, and only then, *complete* in the fight of God, when the only ordinance which He has appointed has paffed between them; and therefore it is very properly ftyled —*the confummation.*

As to the perfon celebrating the marriage —the place where—the manner how; it is very certain, that thefe things are wholly of human invention, and therefore not only various in different parts of the world, but alfo in the fame country. We have amongft us *Jews, Papifts, Quakers*; all thefe obferve an outward form or ceremony different from each other. As for the church of *England*, we have differed from ourfelves; for the fame ceremony which would have conftituted a *legal* marriage before the 26th of the late King George II. will not do it now, unlefs certain circumftances, introduced and infifted upon by act of parliament, be obferved.

But the *all-wife Legiflator of the univerfe* hath not left His divine inftitutions on fo vague, fo precarious, fo uncertain a footing. *But fee,* faid He to *Mofes, that thou make all things according to the pattern fhewn thee in the mount.* Heb. viii. 5. We find every particular, down to the very pins in the tabernacle, every *rite* and *ceremony,* even to the minuteft circumftance, exactly delineated and revealed. But we find no *marriage-fervice,* or *religious ceremony of an* * *outward* kind, fo much

---

* As for the manner of celebrating marriage, *Mofes* has left no direction about it. We do not find it accompanied

much as mentioned. The business of *marriage*, by which I understand, the parties *actually* becoming *one flesh* in GOD's sight, was left as at first ordained, to the one simple *act* of union. A conclusive proof this, that nothing else is of *divine* institution; consequently, that nothing else is essential to constitute a marriage in the sight of GOD, but that *this* is.

Should the *Reader* retain the least doubt of the truth of what has been said, or be under any difficulty in understanding what is meant by those words—*They shall be one flesh*, we may refer to a very clear explanation of the matter, not only by reviewing St. *Paul*'s words, 1 Cor. vi. 15, 16. but also by considering more minutely what is meant by those passages mentioned before, from the law of *Moses*; but as the *texts* are not cited at length, I will here set them down as they stand in the places referred to.

Exod. xxii. 16, 17.

If a man entice a maid that is not betrothed, and lie with her, he shall surely endow her to be his wife. If her father utterly refuse to give her unto him, he shall pay money according to the dowry of virgins.

By this passage, as from many others in the sacred scriptures, it appears, that fathers, during the minority of their daughters, as in every other instance (see Numb. xxx. 3, 4, 5.) so in the business of contracting marriage,

companied with any religious ceremony, such as going to the Tabernacle or Temple, offering sacrifices, or even that it was performed by or before a *priest*. See Ant. Univ. Hist. vol. iii. p. 145.

had

had a negative in their own power: therefore *if a woman being in her father's house in her youth*, i. e. being under age, as we term it, *betrothed* or *espoused* herself to a man, the *former* by * *verba de futuro,* the *latter* by *verba de præsenti,* as the *civilians* speak; both which were held so sacred, that *defiling* either a *betrothed* or *espoused* woman was a species of *adultery,* and to be punished with death: —yet if the father withheld his consent, neither the *betrothing* nor *espousals,* nor any contract arising from them, could lawfully be carried into execution. But in the passage before us, matters were gone too far to be recalled. The man had not only *enticed the maid,* but had actually *lain with* her; and therefore GOD commands that *he shall* SURELY endow her לו לאשה *sibi in uxorem.* Mont. *for his wife.* For now the primary institution took place, *they shall be one flesh;* and what GOD *had joined together* (by pronouncing them *one flesh)* man could not *put asunder.* Therefore the 17th verse doth not say—" If the *father utterly refuse to give her unto him,* such marriage shall be *null* and *void;* but—

---

* Spousals *de futuro* are, according to our ecclesiastical law, a mutual promise, or covenant of marriage, to be had afterwards; as when the man saith to the woman—" I will take thee to my wife;" and she then answereth, " I will take thee to my husband."—Espousals *de præsenti* are a mutual promise or contract of present matrimony; as when the man doth say to the woman —" I do take thee to my wife,"—and she then answereth—" I do take thee to my husband." 2 Burn 16.

if—

if—or—* *though the father utterly refuse to give her unto him, he shall pay money according to the dowry of virgins.* Which is but explanatory of what goes before, he *shall* SURELY *endow her to be his wife*, by paying מהר *the dower*, into the hands of the father *after becoming one flesh* with her, as he ought to have done, and was usually done, *before*-hand. מהר is supposed to be a *dowry* or portion which the husband paid into the hands of the bride, or her father, as a kind of purchase of her person. This is, to this day, the practice of several † *eastern* nations; and this was not to

---

* So אם is often rendered, as in *Judg.* xiii. 16. Pf. xxvii. 3. Isa. x. 22. Jer. xv. 1. Lam. iii. 32. & al. freq.; and so I think it ought to be understood here, (however I may differ from the *Talmudists*) in order to make this verse consistent with the preceding, where it is said— מהר, ימהרנה *endowing* he shall *endow her*, &c. as well as to avoid the very great difficulty of supposing that such an action as *enticing the maid, lying with her,* and *then leaving her* on the father's refusal, was of no higher consequence than paying a *small* sum of money; for the כסף, or *silver* paid, amounted to very little, and rather seems to be payable as an acknowledgment of the contract, than any thing else. See Nold. Heb. Part. אם, No. 13. translated by *quamvis*—*although*:—where the reader will find many authorities.

† See Parkhurst's Heb. Lex. sub voc. מהר.

Tacitus L. de Mor. Germ. mentions such a custom among the *Germans*. Dotem non uxor marito, sed uxori maritus offert, intersunt parentes & propinqui, ac munera probant: In hæc munera uxor accipitur, hoc maximum vinculum, hæc arcana sacra, hoc conjugales Deos arbitrantur. " The wife doth not bring a dower
" to the husband, but the husband to the wife; the pa-
" rents and relations are present, and approve the gifts.
" On these gifts the wife is accepted; this is the chiefest
" bond: these are sacred mysteries, with which they
" think

to be withheld becaufe the hufband had married the woman either *without* or *againſt* the father's confent. In ſhort, the man was not to take advantage of his own wrong. But, אִם * *whether* the father refufed or *not*, the dowry muſt be paid according to law, and thus the contract be publicly ratified.

Having feen what was to be done where a man *enticed a maid,* and took actual poffeffion of her, *againſt* the father's *confent*; let us next fee what was to be done when a man took a maid, without even the father's *knowledge*; not by a feduction or enticement, but on a fudden and unexpected interview, by meeting her without any previous intent.

Deut. xxii. 28, 29.

If a man find a damfel that is a virgin, which is not betrothed, and lay hold † on her and

" think the Gods are married." This was called among the *Romans—coëmptio nuptialis,* and was reciprocal, as well on the woman's fide as on the man's. To this Virg. Georg. I. l. 31. feems to allude:

Teque fibi generum *Tethys* emat omnibus undis.

* This is alfo one fenfe of the Hebrew particle אִם *an—utrùm—whether* or *not—*of which *Noldius* gives many examples. See Nold. p. 65. No. 2. edit. 1734. It is to be remarked, that *Noldius* has not mentioned Exod. xxii. 17. as an example of any of the fenfes here given, viz. either as *fi—quamvis—*or *utrùm*.

† The word וּתְפָשָׂהּ feems here to be rightly rendered by *lay hold on her—Prendra* Fr.—*take her.*—The *Jewiſh* doctors conſtrue this into that fort of *violence* and *conſtraint,* which we call *a rape*. But this is fpoken of at ver. 25, where the word חזק is ufed; which is a much ſtronger expreffion than תפש *to take,* or *lay hold on*; and fo our tranflators have (ver. 25.) obferved, in their tranflating

and lie with her, and they be found; the man that lay with her shall give unto the damsel's father fifty shekels of silver, and she shall be his wife; BECAUSE HE HATH HUMBLED HER, *he may not put her away all his days.*

The word *shekels* is not in the original, but inserted by our translators; in the passage of Exod. xxii. 17 there is the same word כסף *silver*, or *silver-money*; there it is said in general, *according to the dowry of virgins.* Here it is said כסף חמשים Quinquaginta argenteos, *fifty pieces of silver-money.* By comparing the two passages, we may therefore look upon this as the assessment of

translating והחזיק by—*force her.* That this is the true idea of the word, may be seen by comparing 2 Sam. xiii. 11, 14. when *Amnon* commits a *rape* on *Tamar.* The word תפש does not necessarily signify violence, which חזק does. *Omnis significatio est vehementia, fortitudo. Calasio,* sub voc. This place of Deut. xxii. 28. is rather to be understood of " defiling a maid, that being " occasionally *laid hold on*, did presently yield, not be- " ing solicited before-hand, and drawn to it by de- " grees. But Exod. xxii. 16. speaks of such as did " *entice a maid*, with promise of marriage, and then de- " filed her." *Clark.* The two passages taken together shew, that in neither case shall the man *abandon* the *virgin* he hath *taken.* We must conclude there is a reason for using different words at ver. 25, and ver. 28, in the *Hebrew* text, though the LXX. translate them both by βιασμενῶ—probably תפש is a more general word than חזק, and signifies *laying hold on*, or *apprehending*, whether by *violence* or otherwise. Among the *Athenians*, if a man had *ravished* a young woman (so she were freeborn) he was fined 1000 *drachmæ*, and, besides that, was obliged to *marry* her, unless it could be made appear, she had taken something of him in consideration. *Rous*'s Archæol. Atticæ, 199.

the usual *dowry of virgins* paid to the father. It was to be paid in *this* case as well as the *former*, for in *both* the father's consent was precluded; but in no case was he to be defrauded of the מהר or *dowry*. This was as much to be paid when his daughter was taken *against* his consent, as when *with* it, and so when taken *without* his knowledge and consent, as in this latter case. But on whatever account the money was to be paid, it alters not the point in question, for, saith God, *She shall be his wife*, or *woman*—Fr. *Elle lui sera pour femme*—BECAUSE HE HATH HUMBLED HER, *he may not put her away all his days*. This is clearly explanatory of the *original* institution—*they shall be one flesh*, and what *God hath joined together* (by pronouncing them *one flesh) let not man* (either the parties themselves, or any human power whatsoever) *put asunder*.

I should rather chuse to let the scripture answer for itself, than appeal to human authority for its explanation. I will only here just observe, that I am by no means singular in my views of these things. Our *ecclesiastical* courts have proceeded on this principle, have called this *personal intercourse*, previous to any *outward* ceremony, a *marriage de facto*, and have compelled the parties to a public recognition of it *in facie ecclesiæ*, in the *face of the church*. See *Blackstone*'s Comment. vol. i. 435, 439:—and in *Burn*'s Ecc. Law, Tit. *Marriage*, there is this remarkable passage, " Nor was he or she to be dis-

"missed or absolved, if those spousals *de fu-*
"*turo,* by reason of *carnal knowledge,* or
"some other *act* equivalent, did *become ma-*
"*trimony.*" By this it does appear, that,
in the judgment of our *canon law,* if a man
had promised a woman to marry her at a *fu-*
ture time, and in the mean time *lay with her,*
or used the *freedoms of an husband* with her,
such promise did, by such acts, become *ma-*
trimony.

So sacred have our *canonists* esteemed this
act, that where one of the parties have forsaken the other, and married another than
the person to whom they have been *thus*
joined, the *ecclesiastical courts* have pronounced
sentence of divorce, with regard to the *second*
marriage, *causâ precontractûs,* by reason of
precontract. With what authority will appear by-and-by.

In Bacon's Abr. vol. iii. p. 574, we find
the following case :—A. contracts himself
with B. and after marries C. B. sues A. on
this contract in the spiritual court. There
sentence is given that A. shall *marry* and *co-*
habit with B. which he does accordingly.
They are *baron* and *feme,* without any * divorce between A. and C; for the *marriage* of
A. and C. was a mere *nullity* †.

That

---

* In the time of H. VIII. an act was passed, that marriages solemnized and consummated should stand good,
notwithstanding any *precontract* that had not been consummated. But this was done only to gratify the *King,*
and therefore in the next reign (2 Ed. VI.) this act was
repealed.

† The law since 26 Geo. II. c. 33. is quite the reverse, the *precontract* between A. and B. would be a
nullity,

That I am not singular in my opinion, respecting the one divine ordinance of *marriage*, will also appear from the remarkable statute of Henry III; which, as it is very short, I will transcribe.

"To the king's writ of bastardy, whether
"one born *before* matrimony may inherit in
"like manner as he that is born *after* ma-
"trimony: all the *bishops* answered, that
"they would not nor could not answer to it,
"because it was against the common order
"of the church. And *all* the *bishops* in-
"stanted the *lords*, that they would con-
"sent, that all such as were born * *before*
                                                "matrimony,

nullity, and the *marriage* between A. and C. *valid*. Such are the liberties which mortals have presumed to take with the *ordinance of Heaven*. But this cannot alter either the *thing itself*, or God's views of it.

* " *Constantine*, to discourage *concubinage*, and to
" encourage *matrimony* in persons who lived together in
" that way, ordered, that if a man married his *concubine*,
" the children which he had by her before *marriage*,
" should become legitimate. But the *church* meddled
" not with these distinctions of the civil laws, but re-
" garding only the law of nature, approved *every con-*
" *junction* of one man with a woman, if it was with one
" woman and perpetual; and the more so, because the
" holy scriptures employ the name of *wife* or of *concu-*
" *bine* indifferently.

" The first council of *Toledo*, A. D. 400, hath this
" canon, He who with a *believing wife* hath a *concubine*,
" is excommunicated: but if his *concubine* is in the stead
" of a *wife*, and he adheres to her alone, whether she
" be called *wife* or *concubine*, he is not to be rejected
" from communion." See Jortin Rem. vol. ii. p. 294, 295; who adds—" This canon shews that there were
" *concubines* approved by the church."

I would here add, that *Austin*, *De fide & oper.* c. 19. says—" If a *concubine* should profess to know no other
                                                        " man,

" matrimony, as to the succession of inhe-
" ritance, should be legitimate, as well as
" they that be born *within* matrimony, for so
" much as the *church* accepteth SUCH TO
" BE LEGITIMATE. And all the *earls* and
" *barons* answered with one voice—that they
" would not change the laws of the realm,
" which hitherto have been used and ap-
" proved."

Here was a strong push made, that the ordinance of GOD should be in some measure recognized, as to its scriptural import and validity, in our municipal laws; but human wisdom forbad it!

In antient *Rome*, there were three kinds of marriage, distinguished from each other by the names of *confarreation, coëmption,* and *use*.—the last of these came very near to the simplicity of the divine institution. It was,

" man, although she should be dismissed from him to
" whom she is subjected, it may well be doubted whether
" she ought not to be admitted to receive baptism." So that it appears very plainly, there was a time, when the conjunction of the man and woman did not depend, for its validity and lawfulness, upon human ceremonies and inventions.

In how many matters, as well as in many of the above circumstances, hath the *church* (as it is called) changed it's notions of things! I have often thought, that if *Methuselah* had begun his long life with the æra of the *Christian church*, and had lived his 969 years in the *Christian* world, his life must have been a very miserable one, unless, like the *vicar of Bray*, of famous *versatile* memory, he could have changed with the times, and have held at least as many different opinions as he was years old.

when the accidental living together of a man and woman had been productive of children, and they found it neceffary or convenient to continue together; when, if they agreed on the matter between themfelves, it became a valid marriage, and the children were confidered as legitimate.

By the firft law of the 12th table, relative to *marriages*, it is declared, that " when a " woman fhall have cohabited with a man for " a whole year, without having been three " nights abfent from him, fhe fhall be " deemed *his wife*." By which it appears that the *Romans* confidered living together, or *conjugal* cohabitation, as the very effence of matrimony. *Broughton* Hift. Lib. tit. *Marriage*. This may be reckoned one inftance, in which, to the difgrace of *us Chriftians, the Gentiles, which had not the law, did, by nature, the things contained in the law.* Rom. ii. 14.

According to the laws of *Scotland*, cohabitation with a woman for fome time, and openly acknowledging of her as a wife, confirms the marriage, and renders it valid in law. Mem. of *Cranftoun*, p. 30. So where a man and woman have lived together 'till they have children, if the man marry the woman, even upon his death-bed, all the antinuptial children become legitimated, and inherit the honours and eftate of their father.

The cafe is the fame in *Holland*; with this difference only, that all the children to be legitimated, muft appear with the father and mother in the church, at the ceremony of
their

their marriage. See the *History of Women*, by *W. Alexander*, M. D. vol. ii. p. 252, 267.

Our system in *England* is very injurious and cruel, as it destroys one grand inducement to matrimony, where a man and woman have lived together and had children, by stamping bastardy on the issue without remedy. Whence so inhuman a plan should be derived into the common law of the realm, cannot well be devised; but it must be supposed to have commenced in some of the darkest ages of ignorance and barbarism; for at the latter end of the twelfth century, *Pope Alexander* III. made a constitution, that " children born " before the solemnization of matrimony, " where matrimony followed, should, to all " intents and purposes, be as legitimate as " those born after matrimony." By which it should seem that the institution of *Constantine* had been totally laid aside; also, that the *church* thought very differently of marriage, from what it did in the fourth century. See before, p. 31, note.

Upon the whole, it may be concluded, that such laws as are above mentioned, would never have been thought of, unless the proposers and framers of such schemes of *post-legitimation*, had been convinced, that the *conjugal cohabitation* of the man and woman was a lawful marriage in God's account, consequently the issue legitimate in His sight: therefore they were willing to reconcile matters as well as they could, between *human invention* and *divine institution*.

Having,

Having, I trust, established this truth, that where a man and a virgin are united by the *communication of their persons* to each other, they become *one flesh* in the sight of GOD, so made by his express command, insomuch that the man *may not put her away all his days*; it follows, that they are *indissolubly* united, beyond the power of *disunion* by any human authority whatsoever.

It is the contempt of this law, this primary law of nature, or rather of the GOD of nature, established from *the beginning*, and afterwards enforced and explained by the positive laws above-mentioned, which lies at the root of the evils complained of. For, *if a man* כי איש which is the scripture's way of saying *any man, every man*, without distinction (for GOD makes none in the texts we have been considering, nor in any other) was deemed the *husband* of the *virgin he lay with*, and was obliged to make a public recognition of it, as enjoined by GOD so to do, without any liberty to *put her away all his days*; if the law of the land was as positive as to this, as the law delivered from GOD to *Moses* above-cited, we should see a wonderful change in the manners of the people, as well as a stop put to the daily ruin of innocent girls. Would the *great* and *opulent* debauch their tenant's or labourer's daughters, of their own servant-maids, if they knew that this put it into the power of such poor creatures to claim their *seducers* as their *husbands?* Certainly not, at least not in one instance of ten thousand where

it

it now happens. Muft we not fuppofe, that the great and merciful Creator enacted His laws for the protection of the * *weaker* fex againft the *ftronger*, as well as for the prevention of *confufion and every evil work*, which muft enfue from men and women's coming together and parting ὡς ἄλογα ζῶα Φυσικά (as the *Apoftle* fays) *like natural brute beafts which are without reafon?* As therefore a contempt of the laws of Heaven, is evidently the caufe of the evil, it is as evident that nothing but reftoring their due *refpect and efficacy* can ever cure it.

How great an impediment to matrimony doth this alfo prove, among the profligate and licentious part of mankind? (which, as the world goes, I do not fuppofe to conftitute a very fmall part of it)—for if men can gratify their paffions, and indulge their love of variety, without the leaft danger of much further trouble than it cofts them to feduce a poor unwary girl, they will hardly bind them-

---

* The *Atheift* and *Hobbift* deny any principle of *right* or *natural juftice* before the invention of *civil compact*, which, they fay, gave being to it; and accordingly have had the effrontery to declare, that a *ftate of nature was a ftate of war*. See Pope's Works, quarto, 1769, vol. i. p. 534—5, note.

This feems to coincide with the *vulgar* notion, of throwing the *marriage-union* on an human *outward* ceremony, or *civil compact*, without which the fexes *are in a ftate of war*, and each to make what depredations they can on the other: little adverting to the wife and holy provifion which the CREATOR ordained againft this, long before *civil compact*, arifing from *marriage-ceremony*, was invented, or exifted.

selves to the painful œconomy of a family-life, or confine themselves to the attention and concern which a family must require.

In every point of view, the contempt of GOD's law is very shocking; but be it remembered, that, though we have no municipal law to enforce its obligation, it ought to be binding and obligatory on *every man's conscience in the sight* of the divine *law-giver*.

There is no *statute* which punishes the defilement of our neighbour's wife, though it is a *capital* offence by GOD's law, and punished with the *death* of *both* the parties; yet surely none will say, that it is the less criminal before GOD: or, because the seventh *commandment* has no human municipal law to enforce its rigour, that therefore the consciences of individuals are under *less* obligation to observe it, or have more liberty to transgress it, than if it had.

But it sometimes happens, that a man having *enticed a maid*, &c. lives with her for a season, and then turns her off for another, not perhaps without making *some* provision for the *first*, and the conscience of the man is salved by this piece of *generosity*, as it is called. But the law of GOD is directly against such a proceeding—*He shall* SURELY *endow her to be his wife*, saith the *most High*: and the reason given for this, can never alter nor cease, because the *act* from which it arises can never be recalled. The law of GOD therefore as much remains in force against *such* a *putting away*, as against *theft or murder*.

It

It is not unusual for women *so put away*, to marry other men, nay, sometimes they are portioned by the *seducer* for this very purpose. This fashionable way of getting rid of women, includes in it *many* crimes. First, It is a breach of that positive law—*He shall surely endow her to be his wife*—and again—*She shall be his wife; because he hath humbled her, he may not put her away all his days.* Secondly, It is therefore a species of unlawful, forbidden *divorce.* It is, thirdly, *adultery* in the woman *so* put away to marry another. And, fourthly, *He that marrieth her that is put away committeth adultery.*

We never allow any thing to be *adultery* except the *outward ceremony* has passed; but God's positive commands are not subject to the controul of *human invention.* It would be a solecism in philosophy, to talk of setting the *sun* to the *dial,* and not the *dial* to the *sun;* it is as great a one in divinity, to argue, that the law of God is to be accommodated to the law of man, and not the law of man to the law of God.

Let us suppose for a moment, that, as it is said to have been the case amongst the *Spartans, theft* was not to be looked upon in a scandalous point of view, but * rather allow-

---

* *Aulus Gellius,* lib. xi. c. 18. tells us, out of an antient lawyer, that the old *Ægyptians* held all manner of thefts to be lawful, and did not punish them. *Diodorus Siculus* mentions this law among them, that they who live by robbery were to enter their names, and bring what they stole to the *priest,* who mulcted the man that was robbed, a fourth part, and gave it to the thief. See *Patrick* on Gen. xlvi. 34.

able and commendable, if done so dextrously, as that the persons were not detected in the fact; Would this shake the authority of the *eighth commandment*, or be pleadable before God as a justification of the *thief? Consider the work of God, that which is crooked cannot be made strait, and who can make that strait which he hath made crooked?* Eccl. i. 15. vii. 13.

From what has been said, I think it may be fairly concluded:

1.

That *marriage* is a divine institution, and, as such, to be abided by as revealed to us by its holy and blessed author.

2.

That those who look upon it merely as a *civil contract*, and therefore subject to the alteration and controul of men, have different views of it from those given us in the scriptures.

3.

That a woman's *person* cannot be separated from her *self*; wherever she bestows the *one*, the *other* is bestowed also.

4.

That when she delivers her *person*, and consequently her *self*, into the possession of a man, she is (if not betrothed to another) by *that* act, inseparably united to him, so indissolubly joined, that she cannot leave him, nor may he put her away all his days.

5.

That if these truths were received, as they are indeed the truths of God, millions of of women (especially of the lower sort) would be saved from ruin; for, being protected, received, and provided for as GOD's law enjoins, as the *wives* of those men who first enticed them, they could not be turned out upon the wide world, with the loss of reputation, friends, and consequently all power of helping themselves, but by ways too dreadful to think of!

Before I conclude this point, I must desire not to be misunderstood, as if I meant to undervalue or despise *human ordinances*; they have excellent use, and, in this mixed state of things, are necessary to maintain that order and decency, which are so necessary for the regulation of the outward actions of men. I would rather infer their use and necessity, than doubt of either. When I say that the *marriage-service of the church*, doth not constitute a marriage in the sight of GOD, I say true; because by finding no such *service* in the *Bible*, and that marriages were had and solemnized without it, I therefore conclude *that* cannot be *it* which constitutes a marriage in the sight of GOD; for, if so, we must suppose that people before the invention of such service, were not *married at all*, but lived in *sin*; which is absurd and impossible. That *some* service, or ceremony, is expedient, for many good and laudable purposes, must be allowed—as, for the public recognition of the mutual engagement of the parties to each other—to ratify their union as to inheritances,

heritances, and many other laudable ends of *civil* fociety; and as none can live together as *man* and *wife*, without offence, unlefs they * *fubmit to the ordinance of man*, it ought, where it poffibly can, *to be fubmitted to for the Lord's fake.* 1 Pet. ii. 13.

But it is a great *abufe* of fuch things, to put them in the place of the inftitution of GOD; fo that *this* is of no force or validity in GOD's fight without the other. Hence it is, that, men thinking they are not *married*, unlefs by a *prieft* in a *church*, take advantage of their own villainy, and thus *feduce* women, and *put them away* at their pleafure; whereas GOD's law binds them, in the *firft inftance*, and declares the bond *indiffoluble*. So that, as to the purpofes of the divine inftitution, if a thoufand *priefts* were to read a thoufand

---

* This golden rule of 1 Pet. ii. 13. appears by the context, to relate to that obedience which we owe to the *civil* powers. But then the laws of *civil* government muft not be inconfiftent *with*, or repugnant *to*, the law of GOD, for if they be, we muft not *fubmit* to them, but rather *fuffer* than *obey*. When *Nebuchadnezzer* fet up his *golden image*, the three children of *Ifrael* would not obey the king's *decree* to worfhip it; they chofe rather to endure the *fiery furnace.* Dan. iii. 17, 18. So Daniel vi. 10. And as it is with *civil*, fo is it with *ecclefiaftical* ordinances of men; thefe muft be confonant with GOD's word, otherwife we muft act as the *apoftles* did, *Acts* iv. 19. Men may make laws for the public recognition of a *marriage* in the *fight of the world*; but to ordain in what *marriage* fhall confift in the *fight of* GOD, is out of their jurifdiction, and depends folely on the appointment of GOD's *own* law.

services over the parties, thefe cannot add to, nor diminish from their union before GOD, which, as in His fight, is created by the Almighty *fiat*—*they shall be one flesh.* This furely muft be as evident, from the whole tenor of the fcripture, as that the pouring water on a perfon, or dipping him in water, in the name of the *Bleſſed Trinity*, is the complete divine ordinance of *baptiſm*, though no *act* is done, or *word* faid, befides.

There are no where in the *Hebrew* of the Old Teftament, or *Greek* of the New Teftament, any fpecific names for *married perſons*, fuch as the *Engliſh* words *huſband* and *wife*—but איש and אשה *man* and *woman*—So Ἀνηρ and γυνη, which alfo fignify perfons of the *male* or *female* fex in general; but when coupled with pronouns poffeffive, as אישה *her man*—אשתו *his woman*. Ὁ ἀνηρ σου, *thy man*—ἡ γυνη ἑαυτȣ, *his woman*, they then denote the *marriage-relation*: but *how* that relation is entered into, fo as to become indiffoluble on both fides, hath already been fhewn; to which we may add fome obfervations on the word בעל which we tranflate *huſband, married.* See Gen. xx. 3. בעלת בעל *maritata marito*. Mont.; literally, according to our idiom, *married to an huſband.* Ifa. lxii. 4. וארצך תבעל & *terra tua erit maritata*. Mont.; *and thy land ſhall be married*. Now בעל fignifies *to have*, or *take poffeffion*, or *authority over*, as a participal noun—Ὁ ἐχων—he *who hath*.

Hence

Hence it signifies *to marry*, to *take possession of a woman*, to *have her*, as we say. See Deut. xxiv. 1. xxi. 13. In *Niph*, to *be married*, taken *possession of as a wife*. Isa. lxii. 4. with liv. 1. See *Parkhurst*'s Heb. Lex. בעל. So *Calasio*. " Significat dominium, magisterium, domi-
" natus est, habuit, possedit ut dominus,
" maritus fuit, rem habuit cum muliere."
" It signifies dominion, the place or office
" of a ‡ master or governor." " As a verb,
" he governed, had, *possessed*, as a † lord or
" master, he was married, or, *had to do with*
" *a woman*." By all which, taken together, it appears that this *last* circumstance is *that* which *brings* her into the possession, and reduces her under the *dominion* of the man, according to that of Gen. iii. 16. latter part. See Deut. xxii. 29, where it is expressed by ענה *Compressit eam*. Mont.; *He hath humbled her*. English translation. Surely this affords an additional and conclusive proof, that a man's *taking possession of a woman* in the sense above-mentioned, is in the language of scripture *marrying her*, or making her אשתו *his woman*.

This appears also from Deut. xxiv. 1, where the word בעל, according to *Pagninus*, is used in this sense—

‡ Our English word *husband* hath this *idea*, according to *Johnson*—" *Hosband*, master, Danish; from *house* and *bonda*, *Runic*, a master." See Dict.

† The *husband* is called, Exod. xxi. 3. בעל אשה *mulieris dominus*, Mont. *Lord of a woman*, *Maritus*. marg.

כי יקח איש אשה ובעלה
eâ cum coierit & fæminam vir ceperit fi.
Pagninus. Mont. Marg.

Here the *taking* the *woman*, and *lying with her*, moſt clearly appears to make her the *man's wife*, as the reſt of the verſe and the three following demonſtrably ſhew.

Biſhop *Patrick*, on this place, obſerves, that " the *Hebrew* Doctors make a difference
" between theſe two : underſtanding by *tak-*
" *ing a wife*, eſpouſing her to be his wife,
" and by *marrying her*, his completing the
" contract by *lying with her*." The former ſignified by יקח׳ the latter by בעלה.

There is another word which denotes a *wife*, *viz.* שגל—from the root שגל—which in Kal. ſignifies to *lie carnally with a woman*. See Deut. xxviii. 30. alſo Pſ. xlv. 9. Neh. ii. 6. in both which latter places we have tranſlated it *Queen*; but this it does not ſignify, in any other ſenſe, but as the King's *wife*. Ar. Mont. renders it by *conjunx*—a *yoke-fellow*, or *wife*; συγκοιτος—*Aquila*. See that learned and uſeful work, *Parkhurſt's* Heb. & Eng. Lex. ſub voc. שגל.

I ſhould now proceed to conſider *marriage*, or *matrimony* as it is called, in another point of view, namely under *civil* conſiderations, and, as ſuch, an object of *human laws:* but before this can be done in a proper manner, ſome incidental points muſt be fully underſtood and diſcuſſed. Therefore the ſubject of *matrimony*, as a *civil* contract controulable by *human* legiſlature, muſt be deferred for a ſeaſon.

CHAP.

CHAP. II.

Of WHOREDOM *and* FORNICATION.

WHEN GOD, the CREATOR and LORD of all, was pleased to ordain and establish the means by which His creatures were to *increase and multiply, and replenish the earth,* in which primary command His *reasonable* creatures were equally interested with the brute part of the creation, and in some respects, if we consider *this* world as connected with *another,* infinitely more, and therefore the command was particularly addressed to them, Gen. i. 28.—it could not be but that the *act,* whereby mankind was to be propagated, must be totally *innocent* in itself: otherwise it could not have been consistent with the state † of *innocence*

---

† We are told, Gen. i. 31. that GOD *saw every thing that He had made, and behold it was* טוב מאד *very good.* We cannot, consistently with this account of things, doubt that every endowment of the human nature, whether of body or mind, came under this description; consequently, that those *desires* which were necessary to lead man to the propagation and continuance of his species, were without any evil whatsoever. We cannot sufficiently abhor the folly and blasphemy of *Jerome* and some others, who say, that " *Adam*'s desire to *know* his " *wife,* was the first sin which made GOD repent that " He had made man, and was the occasion of turning him " out of *Paradise.*" Coitús præmium mors—says *Jerome* contr. *Jovinian.*

No inconsiderable difficulty awaited this scheme, which arose from the question—" How then was the world to " be peopled, if not by natural generation?" But this was easily solved, by imagining that " the *earth* would " have been supplied with *men,* as the *heavens* are with " angels,

cence in which man was when *marriage* was firſt ordained. But that this *act*, innocent in itſelf as any other function of the body, might be kept within due bounds of *order* and *decency*, and all confuſion and diſorder avoided; God enacted certain † *poſitive* laws for this very purpoſe, to confine within ſuch bounds as ſeemed good to Himſelf to limit, that *natural*, but *violent* paſſion, which, for the great purpoſe of propagating the *human ſpecies*, was made an *inſeparable* adjunct to the *human frame*.

Thoſe who imagine that this appetite is in itſelf *ſinful*, either in the *deſire* or *act*, charge God *fooliſhly*, as if He could ordain the *increaſe* and *multiplication* of mankind by an *act* ſinful in itſelf: an abſurdity little ſhort of *blaſphemy*! *Sin*, we are told, on the moſt infallible authority, *is the tranſgreſſion of the law*, 1 John iii. 4;—and *where no law is, there is no tranſgreſſion*, Rom. iv. 15:—when

" *angels*, by the immediate creative power of God,
" without the interference of any *generation* what-
" ſoever." See *Du Pin's* Eccl. Hiſt. Eng. Tranſ. Cent. 5.
p. 31, where *St. Chryſoſtom* delivers himſelf to this effect.

When ſuch monſtrous opinions can have been maintained by thoſe who, in their day, were looked upon as *fathers of the church*, let it warn thee, Reader, againſt ſearching for truth any where but in the bleſſed word of God; dread as much to leave it for an inſtant, as a blind man would dread to walk amidſt pits and precipices without a guide, or a mariner to ſail among rocks and ſhoals without a pilot. Remember what the Pſalmiſt ſays, *Pſ.* cxix. 105. *Thy word is a lamp unto my feet, and a light unto my path.*

† *Conjunctio maris cum fœminâ, per quam propagatur genus humanum, digniſſima res eſt legum curâ.* Grot. de Verit. lib. ii. § 13. " The conjunction of the *male* with " the *female*, by which the human race is propagated, is " a matter moſt worthy the care of laws."

therefore this act is done agreeably to GOD's will, it is like all *other* acts so done, *good* and *not evil*. In order to make it *evil*, it must be done against some precept of GOD's law, otherwise it is as innocent as satisfying our *hunger* with *eating*, or our *thirst* with *drinking*. These may become *sinful* by their *abuse or excess*; so may the *other*; but in *itself*, and in its *lawful* use, it is as perfectly *innocent* as the two *former*.

We have observed before, that where a man and woman become *personally* united to each other, they are *one flesh*, and are forbidden to *put each other away*. This is the *ordinance of marriage, and the *only* one which is revealed in the scriptures; therefore we may call it the *only* one which GOD ever ordained.

But when men *corrupted their ways upon the earth*, Gen. vi. 12, this ordinance of *marriage*, sanctified by GOD's *blessing*, Gen. i. 28, and ratified by His own *express command*, Gen. ii. 24, was, as every other *divine* institution, corrupted, perverted, and abused; and men, to satisfy their desires at as cheap a rate as possible, without the incumbrance of a wife and family, or confining themselves to the sober duties of maintaining, taking care

---

* Unless we agree in defining the terms made use of, no argument can be properly understood, or satisfactorily concluded. I would therefore here repeat, what I have already said—"that, as in GOD's sight, by *marriage-ordinance* I mean, *that*, by *which* the parties become *one flesh*—and by *marriage*, the *actually becoming so*." This *was, is*, and ever *must be* one and the same, in all *ages, times*, and *places*, however mankind may differ about the adventitious circumstances of *human ceremony*—whether *Jewish, Popish, Protestant, Mahometan*, or *Heathen*.

of, or providing for their houſeholds, choſe to have intercourſe and commerce with women, like *brute beaſts*, for the ſake of mere appetite, and then to leave the women for the ſervice of the next comer. Something of this ſort may not improbably be the meaning of Gen. vi. 2, where it is ſaid, that *they took them* נשים *women of all which they choſe.* For though this word, in certain connexions, denotes what we call *wives* (as Deut. xxi 15.) yet it ſignifies primarily the *female ſex*, or *women in general*. Such traffic was offenſive to God, an abuſe of His *ordinance*, (ſee 1 Cor. vi. 15, 16.) and tending to deſtroy the *marriage-obligation*, not only by rendering the bond which was created by it ineffectual, but by inducing mankind to deſpiſe it, and ſet it at nought. All *genealogies* muſt be confounded, inheritances obſcured, and relationſhip itſelf deſtroyed; for who could aſcertain theſe things, ſo neceſſary to the exiſtence of all civil ſociety, in the commerce with *harlots? Confuſion*, and every *evil work*, muſt enſue; and therefore the all-wiſe *Governor of the univerſe* forbad *whoredom* and *fornication* on pain of death *temporal* and *eternal*. See 1 Tim. i. 8, 9, 10.

The *Hebrew* word זנה is particularly appropriated to this offence in the Old Teſtament, as πορνεια is in the New Teſtament; and we ſhall never find it mentioned but with the divine *abhorrence*. We have no law to enforce the puniſhment which God annexed to it, or to treat an *harlot* or *whore* as a *capi-*

tal offender; but it is nevertheless offensive to GOD, and will now, as ever, meet with marks of His displeasure. *Know ye not,* faith *Paul,* 1 Cor. vi. 9, *that the unrighteous shall not* inherit *the kingdom of* GOD? *Be not deceived, neither fornicators, nor idolaters, nor adulterers,* —&c.—*shall inherit the kingdom of* GOD.

So odious is *whoredom* in GOD's fight, that it is not only said to defile the parties who are guilty of it, but the very *land itself* was said to be *defiled* thereby, Jer. iii. 9. Though this *text* may perhaps primarily relate to *idolatry*, which is *spiritual whoredom*, yet it serves to shew the malignant nature of *whoredom*; otherwise this would not be made use of, as *adultery* is in the same verse, in a figurative sense, to denote the other.

GOD expressly commanded, that there should *not be a whore of the daughters of Israel, Lev.* xix. 29. *Deut.* xxiii. 17; and ordained, that a woman *playing the whore*, if the daughter of a common person, should *be stoned to death, Deut.* xxii. 21. but if the daughter of a *priest*, she was to *be burned with fire, Lev.* xxi. 9. I mention these things as proofs of the sinfulness of an act, innocent in *itself*, when committed against a divine positive law. No human power or custom can alleviate its guilt, or make it less offensive to GOD than His word has made it; the person's conscience that thinks otherwise is sadly deceived.

Though what has been already said may serve as a definition of this offence, yet, to save the
Reader

Reader the trouble of looking back, as well as to be still more explicit upon the subject, I would define זנה, or *whoredom*, to be " a wo-
" man's *giving* her person to a man, without
" any intent of *marriage*, but either for the
" mere gratification of *lust*, or for *gain* or *hire*,
" and departing from that man to others for
" the *same* * purposes." This is being what the *Hebrew* scriptures call זונה, an *harlot* or *whore*. See Gen. xxxviii. 15, 16. The radical idea of the Hebrew זנה seems to be, to *encompass, encircle, infold, enclose*; and denotes *unlawful embraces* between the *sexes*. Hence we render it, *to commit whoredom*. See Parkh. Heb. and Eng. Lex. sub voc.

As *whoredom* is generally used in our translation, as denoted by the word זנה, and seems rather appropriated to signify the *woman's* share in the offence; so the term † *fornication*, which is expressed by the same word in the original, seems to be the name given

---

* After reading the above, it is hardly to be conceived with what eyes people have red this book, and yet charge the *author* with giving no definition of *whoredom*.

† Our English word *fornication*, seems to be derived from the Latin *fornix*; which literally signifies *an arch or vault in houses*—and by a *metonymy*—a *brothel-house*, because these were in *vaults* under ground. Ainsworth. Hor. Epist. 14. l. 21, 22. says to his *steward*—

―――― *Fornix* tibi, & uncta popina;
Incutiunt urbis desiderium, video.

" For well I know, a tavern's greasy steam,
" And a vile *stew*, with joy your heart inflame."
FRANCIS.

Hence the haunters of those places were called *fornicators*. See *Johnson's* Dict. Hor. Sat. lib. i. Sat. 2. l. 30, 31.

to the offence which the *man* commits in such *illicit* commerce. Though this observation may not hold in all cases, yet it is the best reason which occurs to me, for our using *different* words, to denote an offence of the *same* kind.

I readily confess, that the revival of God's antient laws against *whoredom*, amongst us, would be very dreadful, and indeed *unjust*, unless the whole consistent scheme which God has laid down was *all* to be revived together. The women, under God's law, could *force* their seducers to take them as their wives; or rather were deemed so *actually* married, as not *to be put away*. A woman had but to summon her *seducer* before the *judges*, to prove the fact against him, and their sentence, which must have been according to the law, must have been obeyed on *pain of death*. Deut. xvii. 12. Unless this were (as it ought to be) the case among us, it would be oppressive, unjust, and cruel to the last degree, to punish women with death, for being, by the treachery and villainy of men, forced into a way of life (however abhorrent in itself, or culpable) which is the natural, and, in most instances, the inevitable consequence of their being deserted by those who ought to have protected them, but against whom they have no remedy, or means to make them act the just and honourable part.

Under this head of *forbidden* lewdness, I would mention the practice of taking an *harlot*

lot to *keep* for a time, and then, when pleasure or conveniency prompts, dismissing her. This is usually called *keeping a mistress*; but as there is no intention of *marriage*, and this is only done for the *mere* gratification of *lust*, it is not only a very evil example to others, and a defiance of the laws and good order of society, but doubtless comes under the *condemnation*, as it must be ranked under the description, of *fornication* and *whoredom*.

This was not the situation of the פילגשים or † *concubines* amongst the *Jews*; these seem to have been looked upon as *wives*, though, in some respects, of an inferior rank. They were so far considered as *wives*, that the man who took them had such a propriety in them, as to make it a very great offence, if not *adultery* itself, to violate them; as appears in the case of *Jacob*'s concubine *Bilhah*. *Reuben*, the eldest son of *Jacob*, had lain with her; and

---

† *Dr. Johnson*, in his Dictionary, makes a *concubine* signify—" a woman kept in fornication, a whore, a " strumpet:" but no such meaning of the word פילגש is to be found in the scriptures. It is greatly owing to such interpretations of words which are used in our *translation*, that we are led to have very false conceptions, not only of words, but of whole passages, in the sacred volume.

So the word *adultery*—instead of keeping to the unvaried use of the Hebrew נאף, we make it signify every thing which our ideas have annexed to the *English* term *adultery*. At this rate, the truth of scripture can never be fixed, but must alter with the languages into which it may happen to be translated, or with the ideas which change of times, or opinions, may affix to certain words in those languages.

Jacob, Gen. xlix. 4. *calls* it " *going up to his
" bed and defiling it.*" For this crime *Reuben*
was disinherited, and put from the right of
the *first-born*. Compare Gen. xlix. 3, 4. with
1 Chron. v. 1.

Though the children of the *concubine* did
not inherit as the children of the wife in most
cases, yet in one very remarkable one we find
they did, and that by the disposal of GOD
Himself. *Leah* and *Rachel*, are called the
wives of *Jacob*; *Bilhah* and *Zilpah* were his
concubines (as may appear from Gen. xxxv.
22.); yet the children of *these* inherited the
land of *Canaan* equally with the children of
the *former*.

I confess myself not master enough of the
subject, to define exactly the difference between אשה a *wife*, and פילגש a *concubine*, in
all respects; neither have I been fortunate
enough to meet with so precise a definition
in any author, as to warrant a determination
of the question. What I have found upon
the subject, I submit to the Reader, in the
notes below †, and in the *appendix* to this
chapter,

---

† The authors of the Univ. Hist. (vol. iii. p. 141.) call
the נשים *wives* of the *first rank*, and the פילגשים *wives* of
the *second rank*; " which last, say they, though most
" versions render by the word *concubines, harlots*, and *pros-*
" *titutes*, yet in none of those places of scripture where
" the word is used, which are about thirty-six in num-
" ber, is any such sinister sense implied." However,
they state a two-fold difference between *these* and the
wives of the first rank. " First—that the *latter* were
" taken with the usual ceremonies, and the *former* with-
" out.

chapter, which he will see at the end of this *volume*.

This is certain, no mark of disapprobation is set upon *concubinage* in the scriptures, though they speak so severely against *whoredom*; which, to me, is an evident and conclusive proof, that there is some specific difference between them. Indeed we find the owner of the *concubine* called *her husband*; she *his wife*. So the text, *Judges* xix. 1. A certain *Levite* took to him פילגש אשה *uxorem pellicem*. Mont.; *a wife concubine:* and in

" out. Secondly, with respect to their authority, and
" the honour paid to them and their children."

This is very clear, that the sacred *tongue*, made use of by the *Holy Ghost* in the scriptures, makes distinctions, which amount to demonstration of there being no foundation for confounding the פילגשים with *whores* or *harlots*. The words אשה and פילגש are sometimes used for the same person. See Gen. xxv. 1. 6. (xxx. 4. with xxxv. 22.); but פילגש and זונה are never thus used.

Calasio defines פילגש as—*Ancilla unita & addicta viro absque scriptura*, i. e. *contractu dotali & sponsalibus*. " An
" handmaid united and devoted to a man, or husband,
" without writing—*i. e.* without any contract for dower
" or espousals."

Busbequius expressly affirms, " that a *wife* is distin-
" guished from a *concubine*, in *Turkey*, merely by a
" *dowry*, which seems also to have been the distinction
" among the *Jews*." See *Outlines of a new Commentary on Solomon's Song*, (a most ingenious and excellent work) p. 21. written by an *author* to whom the world is highly indebted, for " *Observations on divers passages of scrip-*
" *ture*," in two *volumes*—a work, which, by laying before us the *manners* and *customs* in the *East*, elucidates the scriptures of the Old Testament beyond any other comment that has yet appeared. It may be truly said of *Mr. Harmer*, that he has the happy art of making " dark
" things plain," in a way, which, at the same time that it *instructs*, highly *entertains* the reader.

verse 3. he is called אישה *vir ejus*. Mont.; *her husband*, as we translate it. So the Fr. of D. Martin, *son mari*; and this translation seems to be very proper, because, the damsel's father is called, ver. 4. his (the Levite's) חתן *father-in-law*; and ver. 5. the Levite is called חתנו *his* (the damsel's father's) *son-in-law*; each of these relations by marriage being expressed by the word חתן. Surely this affords a conclusive proof, that the *concubines*, in those days, were in some sense *wives*; but, in what sense, it may be very difficult to determine exactly. The root חתן signifies to *contract affinity by marriage*. Gen. xxxiv. 9. Josh. xxiii. 12. In this last passage, the LXX render it by ἐπιγαμίας ποιεῖν, to *make marriages*. So that though we cannot state the precise difference between the *wife* and the *concubine* in every particular, yet there was too great a similarity between them, not to be both widely different from what we call a *kept mistress*, in whom the man claims not a jot more property, than in an horse hired for a day's journey, nor is more care or concern usually taken about them, when once the fancy or humour of the *keeper* leads him to resolve upon dismission.

The remedy of this mischief depends on that of the others which have been mentioned; all must stand or fall together.

CHAP.

CHAP. III.

Of ADULTERY.

I COME now to consider an offence against the positive precepts of GOD, which is of the most malignant kind, that of *commerce between the sexes*, where the woman is the *wife*, consequently the inviolable and unalienable property of *another man*.

This is truly and properly *adultery*, and described in the *seventh* commandment by a word, which, throughout the whole *Hebrew* scriptures, is confined to that single idea. Hence it is, that it is used, in a figurative sense, to denote the turning from GOD to the worship of *idols*. GOD calls himself the *husband* of His church; the church is represented under the figure of a *spouse* or *wife*; therefore, apostatizing from JEHOVAH to *idols*, is called, in a spiritual sense, *adultery*, Is. liv. 5. * *Thy Maker is thine husband.* Jer. iii. 14.

---

* The words in the original are בעליך עשיך in the plural number, *thy husbands, thy makers*; then follows, *Jehovah Sabaoth* IS HIS *name*. Surely here, as in Eccl. xii. 1. and in many other passages, the careful reader must see a *plurality* of persons in *Jehovah* openly revealed. To imagine, as many do, that this fundamental of *true religion* was reserved to the days of the *New Testament*, is one of those consequences of ignorance with respect to the Hebrew scriptures, under which *we Christians* content ourselves.

Turn,

Turn, O backsliding children, for I am married to you. Then GOD complains, ver. 20. *Surely as a wife treacherously departs from her husband, so have ye dealt treacherously with me, O house of Israel, saith the Lord of hosts.*

It is the misfortune of ours, as of all arbitrary languages, to want † precision; so that when

---

† One great reason of which is, the aptness of such languages to acquire new meanings by length of time. This is remarkably the case with ours; for instance, the word *knave* formerly meant *a boy*—*a male child*—then a *servant boy*, and by degrees, *any servant man*. In some old English translations, I am told, that Παυλος δȣλος Ιησȣ Χριsȣ, is rendered, Paul a *knave* of Jesus Christ. These meanings are obsolete, and now it signifies a *petty rascal*, a *scoundrel*, a *dishonest fellow*. See *Phillips*'s Dict. and *Johnson*. So the word *lust*, which now generally, if not only, carries with it an idea of something *filthy* and *unlawful*, was used by the translators of the *Bible* to signify *lawful* desire, (Deut. xii. 15. xiv. 26.) as well as that which is evil. In *Phillips*'s Eng. Dict. 6th edit. 1706, the word *lust* is thus defined—" unlawful passion or desire—wantonness—leachery"—so that its signification of *desire*, in a *good sense*, is totally excluded. But this cannot affect the import of the Hebrew אוה, or the Greek ἐπιθυμια. Dr. *Johnson* (Dict. sub voc.) defines it by, 1. *Carnal desire*—2. *Violent* and *irregular desire*. See Ps. xxxiv. 12. Prayer Book Translation. Other instances of such mutation might be given. But this cannot be the case with the *Hebrew* language; if it could, it must cease to be the word of GOD, and become the word, the uncertain word, of man.

In short, it would amount to a creation of *new laws*, which still must vary with the new use of words, and thus, from time to time, create *new offences*, in proportion to words acquiring new meanings. But the *mind* of GOD hath been graciously delivered to us in a language as unchangeable and fixed as *itself*. Therefore, what the *words* meant when recorded by the *sacred penmen*, they mean to this hour, and will mean for ever—for which when we speak of *adultery*, we include in it every idea which is usually affixed to the word by *custom*, whether right or wrong. There is a * precision in the *Hebrew* language peculiar to itself; every word is derived from some fixed *root*, or is itself that *root*, which has a fixed and determinate meaning; and though the word branch itself into ever so many different, and seemingly contradictory senses, yet the original idea contained in the *root* will always circulate, as the same sap from the root of a tree, will always flow through the stem to the several branches, be which very conclusive reason, it is impossible that any word of the Old Testament can acquire a new meaning under the New Testament. Wherefore the word נאף *adultery*, can never admit of any other meaning or construction, than it received in the books of *Moses* and the *prophets* — what that was, will appear in the sequel.

How arbitrary languages have always been subject to change, by their being governed by fashion and custom, we may learn from *Horace:*

<pre>
          ——Mortalia facta peribunt,
Nedum sermonum stet honos, & gratia vivax.
Multa renascentur, quæ jam cecidere: cadentque
Quæ nunc sunt in honore vocabula; si volet usus,
Quem penes arbitrium est, & jus & norma loquendi.
</pre>

<pre>
  All *things* shall perish, and shall words presume
  To hold their honours and immortal bloom?
  Many shall rise, that now forgotten lie,
  Others, in present credit, soon shall die,
  If custom will, whose arbitrary sway,
  Words, and the forms of language, must obey.
                                         FRANCIS.
</pre>

* The *Hebrew* language is worthy its *omniscient author*, equally free from *deficiency* or *hyperbole:* not so the *modern* languages; they have indeed *letters* to form *sounds*, but the words they compose are *arbitrary, uncertain,* and frequently *false.* Hutch. Abr. p. 41.

they

they ever so many. From the want of such precision in our language, we are apt to fix meanings to the words of scripture, which, when considered in the original, they will not bear: and in few are we more mistaken than in the meaning (the scriptural meaning) of the word *adultery*.

The words of the seventh commandment are—לא תנאף—which we very properly translate—*Thou shalt not commit adultery*. But what is the true meaning of the word נאף *adultery?* The only certain way to know this, is to consider its uniform signification throughout the whole *Hebrew Bible*; and whoever doth this, will find that it is never used but to denote the defilement of *a* * *betrothed*

---

* The learned authors of the *Ant. Univ. Hist.* vol. iii. p. 137. rightly observe, that " adultery was punishable " with death in both parties, whether they were both " married, or only the woman." But, they add—" We " cannot affirm the punishment of a married man to " have been the same, who *committed adultery* with an " *unmarried woman*." This *solecism* of " a married " man's *committing adultery* with an *unmarried woman*," arises from the popular and improper ideas which are annexed to the English word *adultery*, and from not attending to the single and only idea annexed to the Hebrew נאף throughout the *Bible*. Consistently with this, *Anthonius Matthæus*, the civilian, affirms, that " adul- " tery cannot be committed between a *married* man and " an *unmarried* woman." This is certainly true; because no trace of such an use of the word is to be found throughout the *Bible*.

And indeed, the fixing a determinate meaning to the word נאף *adultery*, was of the utmost importance, for every man who committed *adultery* was guilty of a capital crime, and liable to be punished with *death*.—This was,

trothed or married woman; except in the *figurative* fenfe above mentioned, with refpect
to

was, therefore, too ferious a matter to be left in a ftate of uncertainty, refpecting what did or did not conftitute the offence.

What *Wetstein* fays on Mark x. 12. is worth attending to on this point.—*Potiora fuiſſe jura mariti quam uxoris inde manifeſtum eſt, quia uxor jure & conſuetudine Judæorum erat in manu ac poteſtate viri. Porro uxor cum juvene rem habens, adulterii erat rea et morte punienda: non item vir rem habens cum innupta; quod etiam apud veteres Chriſtianos obtinuit.*

Baſil. Can. 21. Εαν ανηρ γυναικι συνοικων, επειla μη αρεϑεις τω γαμω, εις πορνειαν εμπεση, πορνον κρινομεν τοιᵘτον—ου μεν]οι εχομεν κανονα τω της μοιχειας αυ]ον υπαγαγειν εϰκλημα]ι, εαν εις ελευθεραν γαμu η αμαρlια γενη]αι —ο μεν]οι πορνευσας uκ αποκλει⸱ησε]αι της προς την γυναικα αυ]ʓ συνοκησεως, ωςε η μεν γυνη επανιον]α απο πορνειας τον ανδρα αυ]η παραδεξε]αι, ο δ'ε ανηρ μιανθεισαν των οικων αυ]ʓ ατοπεμ↓ει. Και τɤ]ων δε ο λοϳος ου ραδιος, η δε συνηθεια ɤ]ω κεκρα]ηκε.

"From hence it is manifeft, that the laws which re-
"lated to the hufband were more eligible than thofe
"which related to the wife, becaufe, by the law and
"cuftom of the *Jews*, the wife was in the *hand*, and
"under the power of the hufband. Moreover, a wife
"having to do with a young man was guilty of *adultery*,
"and to be punifhed with death. But it was not fo
"with the hufband who had an affair with an unmar-
"ried woman, which alfo obtained among the antient
"*Chriſtians*."——*Baſil*, Can. 21. "If a man cohabiting
"with a wife, afterwards, not pleafed with marriage,
"fhould fall into *fornication*, we judge fuch an one a
"*fornicator*.—We have not any *canon* (or rule) to bring
"him under an accufation of *adultery*, if the fin fhould
"be with a woman free from marriage—nor indeed fhall
"he that (thus) committeth fornication, be fhut out
"from cohabitation with his wife: fo that the wife fhall
"receive the man returning from *fornication* to herfelf,
"but the man fhall fend away from his houfe a defiled
"wife. The reafon of thefe things is not eafy to con-
"ceive, but thus hath the cuftom prevailed."

It

to *idolatry*, where the *same* idea is exactly preserved.

In *Lev.* xx. 10. we have an accurate and clear explanation of the significant word נאף as well as of the commandment where it is found. *If a man commit adultery with his neighbour's wife, the adulterer and adulteress shall surely be put to death.* What is here called *committing adultery with his neighbour's wife*, is called, Ezek. xviii. 11. *defiling his neighbour's wife*; and Prov. vi. 29. *going in to his neighbour's wife.* If we turn to Deut. xxii. and consider the exposition of the *seventh* commandment which *Moses* was directed, by the *Holy Spirit*, to deliver to the rising generation, before their entrance into *Canaan*, from ver. 13. to ver. 29. inclusive, we shall find this idea uniformly preserved * throughout. See also Lev. xviii. 20.

So

It is to be observed, that *Basil* lived in the fourth century. If the above rule was of so long standing, as to be called συνηθεια, a *custom*, it proves demonstrably, that the very early *Christians* did not consider *adultery* as relating to any thing but to the *defilement* of a *married woman*, and of course, that the interpreting the New Testament so as to rank *polygamy* with *adultery*, is a much more *modern* invention than is usually supposed.

* נאף " Mæchatus est, adulteravit, adulterium com-
" misit. *Prov.* vi. 32. per *metaphoram*—Idola coluit. *Jer.*
" iii. 9. Differt a זנה quod generaliter *scortari* significat, ut liquet ex Oseæ iv. 14. at hoc verbum non
" nisi in *nuptam* competit. Mercer in Pagn.
" R. Solomon Jarchi notat dici tantum de *nuptâ.*"
Leigh's Crit. Sacr.

נאף " To commit *adultery* with matrons. See Litt. Dict. Mæchor. to *adulterate*, to *commit adultery* [with a
" married woman] Prov. vi. 29, 32—34. Metaphori-
" cally,

So strict is this law with regard to this offence, that it even reaches to the defilement of a *betrothed* woman, who, in GOD's sight, is reckoned as the man's *wife* to whom she is betrothed. *If a man be found lying with a woman married to an husband, then they shall both of them die, both the man that lay with the woman, and the woman; so shalt thou put away evil from Israel.* Deut. xxii. 22. By these latter words we are taught, that the sin or adultery, like that of *murder*, was not to be looked upon merely as a personal offence, which was of no further consequence than to the parties committing it, but, if not punished as GOD commanded, brought guilt upon the very land itself, which could only

"cally, to *worship idols*, Jer. iii. 9. It differs from "זנה, which signifies *whoring* in general, as is plain "from *Hosea* iv. 14. But this word *only* belongs to in- "continency with a *married woman*.

"R. Solomon *Jarchi* observes, it is only used where a "*married woman* is concerned."

Aben Ezra thinks, that it signifies all *illicit commerce*, even *whoredom*—"But I see, saith *Grotius*, on Exod. "xx. 14. that this word is taken by the *Hebrews* in the "sense of *adultery* only, and so it is translated in this "and the other places where it is used, by the Greeks, "Latins, and other interpreters." See Leigh, ib. and margin.

The LXX always render it by μοιχευειν and μοιχᾶσθαι.

However, not to rely on the faithfulness of *translators*, the accuracy of *lexicographers*, or the wisdom of *commentators*, either critical or explanatory, we must have recourse to the *word itself* in the original; and if we find, that in all its connections throughout the *Hebrew* scriptures, it never is used but in *one single sense*, we are not warranted to put *any other* upon it.

be

be *put away* by the punishment of the offenders. Then follows ver. 22. *If a damsel that is a virgin be betrothed unto an husband, and a man find her in the city and lie with her, then shall ye bring them both into the gate of that city, and ye shall stone them with stones that they die: the damsel, because she cried not, being in the city; and the man, because he* HATH HUMBLED HIS NEIGHBOUR'S WIFE.

Such is the law of THE MOST HIGH against *adultery*, or the *defilement of a man's wife*. Yet it is not the object of our *municipal* law as any *public* offence whatsoever. The injured husband may bring a civil action for private damages; but neither the *adulterer*, nor the *adulteress*, can be indicted or punished, * as a *public* offender, by any one *statute* throughout

---

* " In the year 1650, when the ruling powers found
" it for their interest to put on the semblance of a very
" extraordinary strictness and purity of morals; not only
" *incest* and wilful *adultery* were made capital crimes,
" but also the repeated act of keeping a brothel, or com-
" mitting fornication, were (upon a second conviction)
" made felony without benefit of clergy. But at the re-
" storation, when men, from an abhorrence of the hypo-
" crisy of the late times, fell into a contrary extreme of
" licentiousness, it was not thought proper to renew a
" law of such unfashionable rigour. And these offences
" have been ever since left to the feeble coercion of the
" *spiritual court*, according to the rules of the canon law;
" a law which has treated the offence of incontinence,
" nay even *adultery itself*; with a great degree of tender-
" ness and lenity; owing perhaps to the celibacy of its
" first compilers. The *temporal courts* therefore take no
" cognizance of the crime of *adultery*, otherwise than
" as a private injury." *Blackstone*, vol. iv. p. 64. Id. vol. i. 433.

Bishop

throughout our whole code of laws. How far this is seen to be for the comfort of society, and the honour of a *Christian* nation, let others determine; I can only say, that, if the law of GOD (which by the way is as clear and positive a law as can be conceived) took place, we should hardly hear of such daily offences against it, as now disgrace, dishonour, and defile the land. Such however is the *consistency* of our *statute laws*, such their *conformity* to the law of GOD, that they make a man a *felon*, and, but for the *benefit of clergy*, liable to suffer *death*, if he have *two* wives of *his own*; but he may seduce and debauch as *many wives* of *other people*, as may fall in his way, and he is free from punishment, except, as I said before, by way of *civil* action for the wrong done to the husband.

It is said, indeed, that " * our law considers marriage in no other light but as a *civil contract*, and leaves the holiness of the marriage-state to the *ecclesiastical* courts;" but surely in a *Christian* land, " the holiness of the marriage-state" ought to be an object of the *municipal* laws, as of infinitely greater consequence to the *public*, and to the

---

Bishop *Burnet*, in his history of the Reformation, speaking of the state of the church before that period—saith—" The unmarried state both of *seculars* and *regulars* gave infinite scandal to the world; for it appeared that the restraining them from having *wives of their own*, made them conclude that they had a *right* to *all other men's*: and the inferior *clergy* were no better, &c." See *Crit. History of England*, p. 141.

* Blackstone Comm.

peace and welfare of society, than many other offences, which are properly deemed objects of their utmost severity. For what are the consequences of *adultery*, even in a temporal view? *All* its evils cannot be reckoned—but only to mention a *few*:—It must introduce a total confusion as to the offspring, a defeating of rightful heirs, an utter obscurity as to family descents and pedigrees; for where *adultery* is, no man can know his own children, or even ostensible brothers and sisters ascertain their relation to each other: for which, as well as for many other wise causes, doubtless it was (as well as to preserve the sanctity of the marriage-institution) made *capital* by the DIVINE LAWGIVER. This we may humbly presume to be the case; for this offence is introductory of that kind of disorder, which must, in the very nature of it, tend to destroy every bond of *civil* and religious society, and make the world, in a moral sense, a mere *chaos*.

Why then is *adultery*, notwithstanding it is so condemned by the positive law of GOD, so frequently, so shamelessly, so openly practised? It is because the law of GOD being disregarded in the conscience, and not enforced by the laws of the land in all its terror, its importance is not adverted to: for though outward laws may not reach the heart, yet, they frequently, by restraining the outward actions of men, may lead them to view such offences in a different light, than when there is no punishment attending them.

Such

Such is the depravity of mankind, that we find the saying of the *Preacher* generally true: *Becaufe fentence againft an evil work is not executed fpeedily, therefore the heart of the fons of men is fully fet in them to do evil.* Eccl. viii. 11. *Impunity* begets security; and this muft produce and multiply *tranfgreffion*.

As to thofe reliques of the *Pope*'s tyranny in this country, commonly called the *ecclefiaftical courts* *, their power is but very *feeble*; for which I and every free Proteftant ought to be thankful. This fort of *imperium in imperio*,

---

* An inftance of the oppreffion of thefe courts, and the tyranny they exercife where they can, may appear from the following cafe:—*Ann Jenkinfon* was prefented at the *primary* vifitation of the *Archbifhop of York*, 1777, for *fornication*, fhe being with child by C. D. a *fingle man*. The cafe was, that the man had *promifed* her *marriage*, not only privately to herfelf, but alfo before the *Juftice*, when fhe fwore C. D. to be the father of the child. He foon after married another woman. The *fpiritual* court proceeded againft the *poor girl*, thus abandoned by the man, and without ever *citing* her, fent an *excommunication* down, which was *red* and *returned* accordingly. Another was *cited* on fuch an account, but could not take out *her penance*, becaufe fhe could not pay a certain *fum of money* which was demanded: fo that it is poffible fhe may alfo have been *excommunicated*.

The late Mr. *Shenftone*, in his works, vol. ii. p. 258. 4th edit. gives feveral definitions of the word *church*. Among others is the following, viz.—" A body of peo-
" ple who too frequently harrafs and infeft the *laity* ac-
" cording to law, and who conceal their *real* names un-
" der that of a *fpiritual court*."

No man, fays Bifhop *Burnet*, was more fenfible of the abufes of the court called the *fpiritual court*, than Archbifhop *Ufher* was. No man knew the beginning and progrefs of them better, nor was more touched with the ill effects of them. Life of Bifhop *Bedell*, p. 85.

which excludes trials by *juries* in criminal matters, and substitutes paper depositions in the place of *vivâ voce* evidence, is too abhorrent from every principle of our free constitution to be endured; and I am astonished, that at the Reformation, their very *being* was not annihilated, as that of the *star-chamber* was afterwards, 16 Car. I. These * *courts*, however, have cognizance of the crime of *adultery*, for which they can set the offender on a *joint stool* in a *white sheet*, under title *Penance*; unless, under title † *Commutation*, he

---

* In antient times, the *King's* courts, and especially the *Leets*, had power to enquire of and punish *fornication* and *adultery*; but by 13 Ed. I. Stat. 4. called the statute of *circumspecté agatis*, these matters were turned over to the *ecclesiastical courts*. See 1 *Burn*, 662, 663. Also 2 *Burn*, 144, 145.

† All this wicked traffic of *penance* and *commutation* was originally derived from the doctrine of *indulgences*; concerning which, *Tetzel* and his associates, when describing the benefit of *indulgences*, and the necessity of purchasing them, a little before the *Reformation*, thus express themselves:—" The efficacy of indulgences is so
" great, that the most heinous sins, even if one should
" *violate* the *mother of* GOD, would be remitted and ex-
" piated by them, and the person freed both from *pu-*
" *nishment* and *guilt*. For *twelve-pence* you may redeem
" the soul of your father out of *purgatory*."

Tetzel was sent into *Germany*, in the time of *Leo* the *Tenth*, with a large cargo of *indulgences*, which he disposed of for the raising a sum of money for the *Pope*. *Tetzel* affirmed, that he could not only pardon *sins past*, but also *sins to come*; whereupon a *German* gentleman bought *such* a pardon of him, and afterwards robbed *Tetzel* of the money. *Tetzel* threatening him, the other said, he had *bought his pardon*, declaring *that* was the sin which he determined to commit. To which *Tetzel* could not reply.

or she can buy off their sin and shame with a *sum of money*. See 1 Burn. Ecc. Law, 663, quarto. Whatever be the cause, most certain it is, that the crime of *adultery* daily increases amongst us, insomuch, that one would think many of the *British ladies*, once famed for their modesty, chastity, and sobriety, either never red their *Bibles* at all, or else only that edition of it which was printed by the company of *Stationers*, in the reign of *Charles* the *First* (and for which Archbishop *Laud* fined them severely in the *star-chamber)* wherein they printed the *seventh* commandment without the word *not*, so that it stood, *Thou shalt commit adultery*.

But if in reading the *Hebrew Bible* we restrain the word נאף *adultery* in the *seventh* commandment, to the *married woman* only, and to the *man who defiles her*, do we not leave the man, who, having *one wife*, takes *another* *, out of its reach? I answer—It is not

---

* The wise, holy, uniform, and connected scheme of GOD's *moral* government, with respect to the *commerce of the sexes*, has *two* principal ends in view. The *one*, to prevent all *confusion of issue*—the *other*, to secure the *female sex* from that which must lead to it. Therefore a woman's going from *one man* to *another* is in all cases made a *capital offence*, and punishable with *death*. On the other hand, no man could *take* a woman, and then wantonly *forsake* her. This, being apparently the source of * *adultery* and *prostitution*, is positively forbidden. The law which forbids this, though conceived in *general* terms, without any limitation or exception, must, in some cases, fail of the provision it has made for the above purposes,

* Matt. v. 32.

not for us to judge in this matter, but by the rule of GOD's word; if *that* brings such a case within the reach of the *seventh commandment*, or of any one interpretation of it which is to be found in the *book of that law*, then such a man is *condemned:* if otherwise, he is *free—For where there is no law, there is no transgression.* Rom. iv. 15. *And sin is not imputed (ελλογειται, reckoned, charged, brought to account) where there is no law.* Rom. v. 13.

By the *book of the law*, I mean the *Pentateuch*, or *five* books of *Moses*, delivered by GOD himself to that eminent *servant* and *prophet* of the MOST HIGH, and by him committed to writing, and delivered to the people. To the *book of this law* the great *apostle of the Gentiles* evidently refers, Gal. iii. 10. where he says, *Cursed is every one, that continueth not in all things which are written in the* BOOK OF THE LAW, *to do them*. Our LORD's forerunner, *John* the *Baptist*, declared THE LAW *was given by Moses, John* i. 17. There is therefore *no* law but that which was given by GOD to *Moses*, nor was any *new law* enacted after the canon of the *Pentateuch* was closed by the death of *Moses*. The distinction and difference of *moral good* and *evil* were then un-

---

without the allowance of *polygamy*; as, where the man *taking* the woman was *married before*. It is therefore necessary for us to enter deeply into this question; which I shall endeavour in the next *chapter*, not on the precarious footing of *popular prejudice* and *vulgar opinion*, concluding that we are wiser than the inhabitants of more extensive parts of the globe; but on the firm basis of *divine revelation*, concluding that GOD is *wiser* than *man*.

alterably

alterably fixed, and the nature of *both* invariably to remain the fame. *What God doeth, it shall be for ever; nothing can be put to it, nor any thing taken from it: and God doeth it that men should fear before Him.* Eccl. iii. 14.

As I am fully perfuaded, on the moſt mature deliberation, that taking from GOD's law in *some* points, and adding to it in *others*, are the chief caufes of the evil complained of, with regard to the ruin of *one* fex, by the luft, cruelty, treachery, and perfidy of the *other*; I ſhall examine the ſubject before us the more freely: not ſuppoſing that *polygamy*, being made *felony* by that fanguinary ſtatute 1 Jac. I. c. 11. is therefore *sinful* in the fight of GOD, any more than that *adultery* is *innocent* before Him, or one jot the more fo, becauſe our ſtatute-book has ordained no puniſhment for it whatſoever. Nor does its being looked upon with deteſtation and abhorrence in this part of the world, any more prove the *unlawfulness* of *polygamy* in the fight of GOD, than the approbation and practice of it in other more extenſive parts of * the globe, can prove its
lawfulness.

---

* The *pride* and *self-importance* ſo natural to fallen man, are the true reaſons why people of all climes and countries are apt to imagine themſelves in the *right*, and all others who differ from them in the *wrong*. The *Turk* deſpiſes the *Chriſtian*, becauſe he is not a *polygamiſt*, the *Chriſtian* in his turn abhors the *Turk* becauſe he *is*—what ſhall decide between them? *Cuſtom, uſage, prejudice of education, national belief*, municipal laws—have as much to plead on one fide as on the other: theſe may ſay——

Non noſtrum inter vos tantas componere lites.

lawfulness. All must stand or fall by GOD's own revelation of His *own* will, in His *own* law. To suppose that His law can be different in different parts of the world, which he *hath made,* and *upholds with the word of His power;* or that His one uniform jurisdiction doth not equally and invariably extend over all His reasonable creatures; is to think of Him as the poor idolatrous, ignorant *Syrians* did—*The* LORD *is God of the hills, but he is not the God of the valies.* 1 Kings xx. 28.

Near akin to this, is the supposition that GOD can change his mind, and be of one mind in the *Old Testament,* and of another in the *New Testament;* if so, He may now have changed His mind again, and neither of these

---

The only decisive appeal which can be made, must be to the *Hebrew* scriptures, unless we are to suppose that the Great Moral Governor of the *universe* had no *mind* or *will* concerning the matter, or that he left his church and people in the dark for four thousand years together, touching an affair of such infinite consequence. As for imagining that he left the adjustment of *marriage* to the days of the New Testament (which is a popular notion amongst us) having suffered the *Jews* to live in ignorance and error concerning it for so many preceding ages—this is as false in point of fact, as if it were said, that they lived without any *revelation* at all. As surely as the writings of *Moses* contain the law of GOD, so surely was the law of *marriage* adjusted and settled in the minutest particular. Among other reasons why this must necessarily have been the case, is that very conclusive one, which arises from the dependence of the lawfulness of the *issue* on the lawfulness of the *marriage,* and of course the preservation of true *genealogy* throughout the whole *Jewish* dispensation; a matter in which our dearest and eternal interest is concerned.

books

books contain a single syllable which can be depended upon; so that after all the pains we can take to acquaint ourselves with the *divine* mind and will, we may be as utter strangers to them as the savages in *America* are.—But when we search the indelible records of truth, we find that the attribute of *unchangeableness* shines, with a distinguished lustre; *I am Jehovah*, saith He, *I change not.* Mal. iii. 6. GOD is *one*—His will is *one*—therefore *this*, no more than *Himself*, can know any alteration, diminution, or change. What was *law* * at the *beginning* will be *law* to the *end*; and therefore what that *law* is, as touching the point in question, I will now proceed, with the confidence which the love of truth inspires, and with a proper disregard for the fallacious and unscriptural reasonings of men, in the freest manner to consider.

---

* This is true even of the *ceremonial law*, as to its *meaning* and *substance*. It cannot be less true of the *moral* law, which is founded in the relation which mankind bear to GOD and each other, and therefore must be as *immutable* as that *relation* is.

CHAP.

CHAP. IV.

Of POLYGAMY.

I PROMISED the *Reader*, that the proofs for what I advance should be drawn from the *word* of GOD; and, for my own sake, as well as that of the *truth*, I find myself more especially bound to keep this promise, with respect to the subject before us: for if I were to go to *human* authorities, I should wander into such an endless labyrinth of difference and contradiction, as to lose sight of every thing but fruitless * disputation.

---

* Fruitless indeed! For the great *Puffendorf*, B. vi. c. 1. § 17. says—" Whether or no this practice be re-
" pugnant to the *law of nature*, is a point not fully set-
" tled among the learned." He then gives the arguments on both sides, " leaving the decisive judgment to
" be passed by the reader." So that upon the footing of *human wisdom—adhuc sub judice lis est*. The author therefore only considers it on the footing of the *divine law*, conceiving it impossible to determine its *lawfulness* or *unlawfulness* in GOD's sight by any thing else. According to this law will all men be judged at the last day: therefore, to appeal to any other, in matters of conscience, is absurd to the last degree. There is no other principle or means of discovering the mind and will of GOD touching this, or any other religious truth, no other rule or measure of judging and determining any thing about it or concerning it, but only the *writing* from whence it is taken, it being wholly of divine revelation, and that revelation being only expressed in that writing. See Dr. Owen on the Scriptures, p. 18.

That

That the mifchiefs which muft inevitably attend *polygamy* on the *woman*'s fide, do not accrue from it on the part of the *man*, is very clear: and on this principle, we may account for the total difference which is put between them in the *divine law*—the *one* punifhed with *death*, the *other* not fo much as mentioned in a *criminal* light. So far from being prohibited or condemned by the *law*, we find it *allowed, owned,* and even *bleffed* of God: and in no one inftance, amongft the many recorded in fcripture, fo much as *difapproved*.

By *polygamy*, I would be underftood to mean *, what the word literally imports, the *having* and *cohabiting with more than one wife at a time*. Whether taken *together*, as feems to be the cafe of king *Jehoafh*, 2 Chron. xxiv. 3. or firft *one* and then *another*, as Jacob, Gen. xxix. 28. or David, 1 Sam. xxv. 43; it was *this* which was *allowed* of God, confequently practifed by His people. The *putting away* or divorcing *one* woman, in order to take *another*, was as much forbidden in the Old Teftament as in the *New*. God fays, Deut. xxii. 29. *She fhall be his wife; he may*

---

* *Polygamy*, ftrictly fpeaking, is of two forts; either when one woman promifcuoufly admits of more hufbands than one, or when one man is at the fame time joined in marriage to more than one woman—The former of thefe is too abhorrent from *nature, reafon,* and *fcripture,* to admit of a fingle argument in its favour, or even to deferve a moment's confideration. The author therefore, by the word *polygamy*, only means the *latter*, throughout this treatife.

not

not put her away all his days. So before, ver. 19; and again, Exod. xxi. 10. *If he take him another wife, her food (i. e.* of the *first wife) her raiment, and her duty of marriage, he shall not* * *diminish.* Putting away or *divorcing* a *first,* in order to take a *second,* is a palpable breach of these laws, and therefore treated by the great and infallible *interpreter* of them as a heinous offence against GOD, it being a breach of that obligation, laid upon the man, to confider his wife as *one flesh* with himself, and, as such, to cleave to her for life, as *bone of his bone, flesh of his flesh,* Gen. ii. 23; which our LORD cites, and reasons upon, to prove the abomination of such a proceeding, as absolutely contrary to the original institution of the *marriage-bond.*

This, however, was the common practice of the profligate *Jews* of that day, who abused the liberty of *divorce* permitted by *Moses* in certain cases, to the most licentious purposes, so as to make *marriage* little better than a pretence for gratifying their lusts, divorcing *one,* in order to take *another,* and thus profaning the holy ordinance of GOD, by giving it no higher place in their esteem, than as a means of indulging their depraved appetites. A monstrous practice! against which CHRIST's discourse, *Matth.* xix. 4, &c. is levelled, not against *polygamy,* as considered simply in itself. If we interpret this passage

---

* לא יגרע —not *withhold—withdraw— keep back*—ἐκ ἀποςερησει, LXX; much less shall he *put her away.*

as such an explanation of God's law *from the beginning*, as will serve to prove all *polygamists* are * *adulterers*, we must condemn a large generation of God's dearest servants and children; and instead of believing that *all these died in faith*, Heb. xi. 13. we must say, that many of them died in a state of *unbelief* and *disobedience*; and instead of looking for *Abraham, Jacob, David*, &c. in the kingdom of *heaven*, we must look for them in the kingdom of *Satan*; for *his* they were, and *him* they served, if *polygamy* be an offence against the law *from the beginning*, under which these people lived and died, without the least repentance, or any signs of it, as *adulterers, fornicators,* and *whoremongers*. That is the infallible † consequence of the common interpretation of this passage; for Christ does not ground the authority of what He declares on any *new law* which he was introducing, but on an explanation of God's *law* from *the be-*

---

* *Adultery* is marked as a mortal sin, Gen. xx. 3. in the history of *Abimelech* king of *Gerar*; and *polygamy* therein stands as utterly distinguished from it—this in the judgment of Jehovah *himself*. Comp. Gen. xxvi. 9, 10, 11. See post.

† *For sin is the transgression of the law.* 1 John iii. 4. *All unrighteousness* (i. e. *all unconformity to the law*) *is sin.* 1 John v. 17. *The soul that sinneth, it shall die.* Ezek. xviii. 4. *The wages of sin is death.* Rom. vi. 23. *Whoremongers and adulterers God will judge.* Heb. xiii. 4. The weak arguments which have been made use of to excuse the *sin of polygamy*, as some call it, in the *patriarchs*, and the Old-Testament *saints*, will be fully considered and exposed in this chapter.

ginning,

ginning, revealed first to *Adam*, afterwards recorded by *Moses*, that it might be transmitted to all succeeding generations, as the one rule of faith and practice, for all those to whom God's word should come, to the end of the world. *Neither with you only*, saith *Moses* to the people (then present at the re-publication of God's law, Deut. xxix. 14, 15.) *do I make this covenant and this oath, but with him that standeth here with us this day, before the* Lord *our* God, *and also with him that is not* (or *those* who *are* not) *here with us this day*, i. e. with all succeeding generations, till time shall be no more.

Therefore Christ, so far from altering, changing, or destroying the law delivered from God by *Moses*, enters a *caveat* against such a supposition (Matt. v. 17.) *Think not that I am come to destroy the law or the prophets; I am not come to destroy, but to fulfil: for verily I say unto you, 'till heaven and earth pass, one jot or one tittle shall in no wise pass from the law, 'till all be fulfilled*—ἕως ἂν πάντα γένηται—*until all things be done.* Hammond. And again (Luke xvi. 17.) *It is easier for heaven and earth to pass, than one tittle of the law to fail.* This not only stamps *unchangeableness* upon the *law*, but upon its *import, sense*, and *meaning*, as *one* and the *same* throughout all ages and generations, as an invariable rule of life for the members of God's *visible church* upon earth, even to the least *jot* or *tittle*.

Notwithstanding,

Notwithstanding, as this passage of Matt. xix. is the chief ground on which that absurd position is built, that "*Polygamy*, though " allowed under the *law*, is forbidden un- " der the *gospel*;" or, " though permitted " under the Old Testament, is * forbidden

---

* The notion that *marriage* under the *New Testament*, is different from what it was under the *Old Testament*, which, as will appear in a *third volume* of this work, is true genuine *Popery*, reminds one of *Moliere's Medecin malgrè lui*, where SGANARELLE is setting forth his profound *medical* and *anatomical* knowledge; as an instance of the *last*, he places the *liver* on the right side, and the *heart* of the *left*.——GERONTE says —*On ne peut pas mieux raisonner sans doute. Il n'y a qu'une seule chose qui m'a choqué. C'est l'endroit du* foye *& du cœur. Il me semble que vous les placez autrement qu'ils ne sont. Que le cœur est du côté gauche, & le foye du côté droit.*

SGANARELLE. *Oui cela estoit* AUTREFOIS AINSI: *mais nous* AVONS CHANGE' TOUT CELA, *& nous faisons maintenant* LA MEDICINE D'UNE METHODE TOUTE NOUVELLE.

GERONTE. *C'est ce que je ne sçavois pas, & je vous demande pardon de mon ignorance.*

SGANARELLE. *Il n'y a point de mal, & vous n'estes pas obligé d'estre aussi habile que nous.*

" GERONTE. One cannot, doubtless, discourse bet-
" ter on the subject.—There is but one thing that has
" displeased me—I mean the situation of the *liver* and
" the *heart*.—It seems to me, that you place them other-
" wise than they are—that the *heart* is on the *left* side,
" and the *liver* on the *right*.

" SGANARELLE. Yes, it was formerly so; but we
" have changed all that, and now-a-days we practise
" *physic* after a *method entirely new*.

" GERONTE. That I did not know, and I ask your
" pardon for my ignorance.

" SGANARELLE. There's no harm done.—You are
" not obliged to be as skilful as *we* are."

" under

" under the *New*" (as if there could be a law in the New Testament contradictory to that in the Old Testament) it may be worth our while to consider the matter more minutely.

The question put by the *Pharisees*, Matt. xix. 3. is not, " whether it be lawful to " marry *two wives* at a time, or to take *one* " to *another?*" but—" *Is it lawful for a man* " *to* PUT AWAY *his wife for every cause?*" The question concerns *divorce*, and *divorce only*. When we consider *who* it was that was to give the *answer*, we may be certain of its entire pertinence to the *question*. It follows (ver. 4, &c.) *He answered and said unto them, Have ye not read, that He which made them at the beginning, made them male and female, and said, For this cause shall a man leave father and mother, and cleave unto his wife, and they twain* (i. e. the *man* and his *wife*) *shall be one flesh? wherefore they are no more twain, but one flesh. What therefore* GOD *hath joined together, let not man put asunder.*

With so close, so apposite, so conclusive an answer, grounded on the *old* marriage-institution, not on any *new* dispensation; they ought to have been satisfied that *divorce* was *unlawful*. But they urge him farther, and (ver. 7.) *said unto him*—*Why did Moses then command to give a writing of divorcement, and put her away? He saith unto them, Moses, because of the hardness of your hearts,* SUFFERED *you to put away your wives, but from the beginning it was not so* (i. e. that *men* should *put away* their *wives*). *And I say unto you, that whosoever shall put away his wife, except it be for fornication, and shall marry another, committeth adultery; and he who marrieth her which is put away, committeth adultery.*

This last is the verse which has made the difficulty; for if this were meant to condemn *polygamy*, it amounts, so far, to a *contradiction*, or rather *repeal*, of the *old law*, which permitted it; and then more than a *jot or tittle* has passed from the law. If it means that it was *always sinful*, and against the law of GOD, it condemns, as was before observed, all that ever practised it, and falls heavy on some of the greatest saints, that are recorded in scripture as patterns of *faith, holiness,* and *obedience.*

This difficulty, like many others in the scriptures, can only be solved, by attending to the character of the speaker, the peculiar circumstances of the persons spoken to, and the particular occasion on which the words were spoken; for want of this, we are apt to interpret the scriptures more by *sound* than *sense*, and thus make them *speak* what they never *meant* ‡.

‡ You then whose judgment the right course would steer,
Know well each *antient*'s proper character;
His fable, subject, scope of every page;
Religion, country, genius of his age:
Without all these at once before your eyes,
Cavil you may, but never *criticise*.
Ess. on Crit.

VOL. I.

The *Jews*, at the time of their dispute with Christ on the subject of *divorce*, were fonder of *tradition* than of the scriptures, and of the teachings of their *rabbies*, than of the law of God; insomuch that Christ charges them (*Matt.* xv. 9.) with *teaching for doctrines the commandments of men:* and (*Mark* vii. 9, 13.) with *rejecting* and *making the word of God of none effect, through their tradition.* There were several famous *rabbies*, whom they highly reverenced, but particularly *Shammah, Hillell,* and *Akiba.*

* The school of *Shammah* taught, that a man could not be lawfully divorced from his wife, "unless he had found her guilty of some "action which was really infamous, and con- "trary to the rules of virtue." But the school of *Hillell* †, who was *Shammah*'s disciple, taught, on the contrary, that " the least rea- " sons were sufficient to authorize a man to " *put away his wife.* For example—if she " did not dress his victuals well, or if *he* " *found any other woman he liked better.*" *Akiba* was still more indulgent than *Hillell,* for he affirmed that " it was sufficient cause for
" a man

If such requisites are necessary for judging properly of the *shallow* productions of mortals, how much more are those abovementioned necessary, that we may judge aright of the *deep things of* God.

* See *Cruden,* under *divorce.*

† *Shammah* and *Hillell* are supposed to have lived about an *hundred years* before the destruction of the *second temple.* Some say they were cotemporaries with *Herod* the Great. See Ant. Univ. Hist. vol. x. p. 429, 469.

"a man to *put away his wife*, if she were not agreeable to her husband."

Josephus and *Philo* shew very sufficiently, that in their time the *Jews* believed *divorce* to be lawful on every trivial cause. That the *Pharisees* had learnt to explain the toleration of *Moses* in a like extensive manner, may be gathered from the question which they put to our SAVIOUR. The above observations may therefore serve as a key to the scripture under consideration. The *Pharisees* (who asked, whether it *was lawful for a man to put away his wife for every cause?*) seem to have been deeply tinctured with that position of *Hillell*, and to have adopted that particular cause of *divorce* mentioned by him, that of *seeing a woman they liked better*, so *putting away one* whom they liked *less*, in order to take *another* whom they liked *more*. Against this CHRIST may be understood to level his answer—*Whosoever putteth away his wife, except for the cause of fornication, and marrieth another, committeth adultery,* &c. not as condemning *polygamy* in itself, against which there *was no law,* but under the particular circumstance

---

Of *Akiba* it is said—*Circa ea tempora vixit*—"he lived about those times." Athan. Vinc.

Dr. *Owen* on the scripture, p. 227, makes him *armourbearer* to the Pseudo-Messias *Barchochab*, in the days of *Adrian*; when, in the pursuit of a design to restore their temple and *worship*, the *Jews* fell into a rebellion against the *Romans* all the world over. This was about the year 135. From these different accounts, it seems probable that there was more than one person of the name of *Akiba*, or, as some call him, *Aquiba*.

of unlawful *divorce* to effect it, against which the law of GOD was from *the beginning*. Such a thing was not contained in *Moses's permission*, nor mentioned therein, but was contrary to the very *institution* of *marriage*; and, as our LORD shews clearly, ver. 4, 5, 6, virtually forbidden by the very words of it. It was as unlawful for a *man* to put away or *divorce* his wife for *another woman*, as for a *woman* to put away or *divorce* her husband for *another man:* the *marriage-bond* being *equally* binding as to the matter of *putting away*. We may also observe, that though the *saints* of GOD, of whom we read so much in the Old Testament *, practised *polygamy*, yet they did not put away *one wife* in order to make room for

"* The example of the *Heathens* and *Mahometans* may indeed be of no great force in the argument for *po-* *lygamy*, because it appears that those people are guilty of many violations of the law of nature; but the *polygamy* of the *fathers* under the *old covenant*, is a reason which ingenuous men must confess to be unanswerable." See *Puffendorf*, lib. vi. c. 1. § 18.

Some have thought, that the examples of *Abraham*, *Jacob*, and the other Old-Testament saints, are too far removed into antiquity, to serve as proofs for the lawfulness of *polygamy*.—But did ever any one object to the history of *Cain*, as an example of the criminality of murder, or of GOD's thoughts on that subject? or does the *Apostle*, in the epistle to the *Hebrews*, scruple to recapitulate, by *name*, those heroes of antiquity, who did such mighty works by the power of faith, as examples to us? In short, doth he not assure us, Rom. xv. 4. *That* WHATSOEVER THINGS *were written afore-time, were written for our learning?* But what can we *learn* from either the *precepts* or *examples* of *old time*, if we are to suppose that GOD has changed his mind upon the subjects which they hold forth to us?

another.

another. This was as directly forbidden them by the law of GOD, delivered by *Moses*, as by CHRIST, on the authority of that law, to these *Pharisees*.

Here I would observe, that our translators of the *Bible* seem to have paid too much attention to the *Scribes* and *Pharisees*, in the rendering the passage referred to for the justification of their doctrines about *divorce*. The *Pharisees* say, *Moses* COMMANDED *to give a writing of divorcement, and put her away*. Thus the *rabbies* construed *Deut*. xxiv. 1, &c. in the *imperative* mood; and we, by doing the same in our translation of that passage, have justified their misinterpretation, and even justify the *divorced woman's* going to be *another man's wife*. *She may go*, and *be another man's wife*; so we translate, verse 2. No marvel, if this be the case, that CHRIST is supposed to *condemn* something which was before *allowed*; whereas the whole passage is suppository or *hypothetical*, and only introductory of that positive law, ver. 4. The whole should be rendered thus, if we would avoid the absurdity of supposing *Moses* to *command*, what GOD positively forbad, and to consign a *married woman* into the arms of an *adulterer*, in the very face of the *seventh* commandment, by saying, "*She may go and be another man's wife*." ver. 2. This would be establishing ‡ *adultery* by a solemn law.

The

‡ The learned *Dr. Whitby*, in order to get rid of this consequence, is for supposing, that these divorces dissolved

The *Hebrew* text should be rendered—*When, (or if) a man hath taken a wife, or woman, and married her, and it come to pass that she find no favour in his eyes, because he hath found some uncleanness in her, and* (IF) *he write her a bill of divorcement, and give it in her hand, and send her out of his house, and she shall have departed out of his house, and* (IF) *she go and be another man's wife, and* IF *the latter husband hate her,* (here we explain the ו by an IF, why not before?) *and write her a bill of divorcement,* &c. or *if the latter husband die, which took her to be his wife, her former husband, which sent her away, may not take her again to his wife after that she is* DEFILED, *for that is abomination before the* LORD, *and thou shalt not cause the land to sin, which the* LORD *thy* GOD *giveth thee for an inheritance.*

Thus the *Greek* * interpreters express the sense of these four verses, and the *Vulgar Latin*,

solved the *bond* of *marriage*; but this is directly contrary to what CHRIST asserts, for his whole argument shews, that nothing can do this, but *adultery* in the wife. The *Doctor* was certainly led into this mistake, by our wrong translation of the passage, in *Deut.* xxiv. 1—4.

* To the testimonies here mentioned, for this interpretation of the *Hebrew* text, we may add that of the learned *Buxtorf*; who observes, that in the words of *Moses*, Deut. xxiv. 1—4. (see Jer. iii. 1.) this one prohibition only is contained,—" *That a man shall not receive* " *again to his bed, a wife which he hath once put away*"— but that the custom itself of *putting away wives*, is, in that place, neither approved by *Moses*, nor plainly condemned, but left as it were indifferent. And the observation of our *Saviour*, that this *permission* was given by *Moses, because of the hardness of their hearts,* sufficiently makes

Latin, yea, and the *Chaldee* paraphrase may be so understood. So *Tremellius* renders the words, and *Vatablus* explains them, *Scripseritque ei libellum repudii & dederit Ei in manu, ejeceritque,* &c. IF *he shall have written her a bill of divorce,* &c. " This is not an absolute sen-
" tence," saith *Vatablus,* " but ought to be
" joined to the words following, which shew
" that IF such things happened, that IF a
" man divorced his wife, and IF another took
" her, the former husband might not take
" her again, she having been *defiled.*" Which proves the same thing contended for by our LORD, in His discourse with the *Pharisees,* that those *permissive divorces,* which, says He, *Moses permitted,* ἐπέτρεψεν —not, as the *Pharisees* would have it, ἐνετείλατο, *commanded*—made *no* difference as to the *marriage-bond* in the *sight* of GOD. The man who *put away his wife,* for no other cause than marrying *another,* which was the practice of these people, committed a great sin, not only by not *cleaving to his wife,* as GOD had commanded, but by *putting her away* for *another woman,* and thus *causing her to commit adultery* with another man. See Matt. v. 32. And in this sense, as *accessary* to his divorced wife's crime,

---

makes it appear, that the *Mosaical* indulgence doth not amount to an approbation, but signifies only a bare toleration, or connivance, exempting from *civil* punishment. See *Puffend.* b. vi. c. 1, § 23.

So *Clark* on Matth. xix. 8. intimates, that " *Moses*
" permitted divorce to prevent a greater civil mischief.
" He did so far allow of it, as to exempt them that did
" it from any *civil* punishment, but still it was a transgression of the *moral* law, and so a sin against GOD."

might himself be said to *commit adultery*. But more of this hereafter.

If those *divorces* could have operated, as a *dissolution* of the *first* marriage, she would not have been DEFILED by marrying another man; but this not being the case, she was DEFILED* in the sight of GOD, when put away by *unlawful divorce*, as when she went to another man without *any divorce*. Very striking are the words of Jer. iii. 1. *They say, If a man put away his wife, and she go from him, and become another man's, shall he return to her again? shall not that land be greatly polluted?*—But where is any thing like this said of *polygamy*? That *polygamy* was practised throughout all ages of the *Jewish* œconomy, cannot be denied. It is equally evident, that it was the deliberate, open, avowed, and wilful practice of the most *holy* and *excellent of the earth*, of *Abraham*, the *father* of the *faithful*, the *friend of* GOD, If. xli. 8. as well as of the most illustrious of his children; and this, without the least *reproof* or *rebuke* from GOD, or the most distant hint or expression of his displeasure, either by *Moses*, or any other of the prophets. No trace of *sorrow*, *remorse*, or *repentance*, touching this matter, is to be found in any one instance, and therefore many *commentators* are at a loss to maintain the *sinfulness* of *polygamy*, but at the expence of *scripture, reason, and common sense.*

---

* The word (Deut. xxiv. 4.) which we translate *defiled*, is טמא. The same word is used, Ezek. xviii. 6, 11, 15. for *violating another's wife*.

Some

Some say—"It was a *sin*, but GOD * allowed it for the *hardness of their hearts.*" That *Moses* suffered (ἐπέτρεψεν, permitted, tolerated) *divorce,* so far as not to exact the outward punishment of it in certain cases, is evident from the *supposed* circumstances in *Deut.* xxiv. 1, &c. But this was in order to avoid worse mischief amongst the wicked and profligate part of the community, such as mal-treating, beating, or even killing their *hated* wives. This is what we may suppose, in part at least, to be meant by our LORD, when He says— *Moses, because of the hardness of your hearts, suffered you to put away your wives.* This is said of *divorce,* not of † *polygamy,* as plainly appears by the words of the text. And herein *Moses* seems to have acted more as a *politician,* than as a *lawgiver*—by *permission,* not

---

* The idea of JEHOVAH's allowance of *sin,* and that for ages together, is placing him, in point of holiness, purity, and justice, below the notion which the heathen had of their gods—*Homer* says——

Οὐ γὰρ χείλια ἔργα θεοὶ μάκαρες φιλέουσι. Odyss. Ξ. ver. 85.
  Yet sure the gods their impious acts detest,
  And honour justice, and the righteous breast.
    Pope. See Ps. v. 5.

† The learned authors of the *Universal History,* vol. iii. p. 137, observe, that *Moses,* among other things, "was forced to indulge them (the *Jews*) in *polygamy.*"—But what could this have to do with *Abraham, Jacob,* and those who lived before *Moses?* It is evident that *polygamy* was practised by the holiest of the saints, ages before *Moses* existed; therefore, ascribing the practice of it to an *indulgence* of *Moses,* is as great a mistake, as ascribing the original of *circumcision* to the *law* of *Moses.* Comp. Gen. xvii. 10—14. with John vii. 22.

by *commandment*, like that of *Paul*, 1 *Cor.* vii. 6. It is not said—GOD *suffered it*—but —*Moses suffered you to put away your wives:* but, CHRIST adds, *from the beginning it was not so*—i. e. that men should *put away their wives.* Here is not the least hint about *polygamy.*

Can we suppose, however, that GOD suffered *Abraham, Jacob, David*, and others of His saints, to break His law, and this for the *hardness of their hearts?*—If they had *hearts of stone*, who ever had an *heart of flesh?* Ezek. xi. 19. Do not reason and common-sense start back at *such* a supposition?

Others have as absurdly said, "that, GOD, "being the sovereign, has a right to *dispense* "with his own laws, and having ‡ done this, "*polygamy* was no sin."

‡ The elaborate *Noldius*, after long arguments upon the subject, pro and con, of his own and other people's, which may all be seen Heb. Part. Annotat. 225. concludes—*Sanctos veteres polygamos* non peccasse coram Deo, quia habuerunt *dispensationem specialem & extraordinariam.*—" The *old saints*, who were *polygamists*, did not "sin before GOD, because they had a *special and extraor-* "*dinary dispensation.*" But, 1. Where is such a *dispensation* recorded? 2. The very supposition of such a thing is as absurd as it is profane; more becoming the character of a *Pope of Rome*, than of the HOLY GOD. 3. The idea of a *special and extraordinary dispensation* to some, and leaving others under the *guilt* of sin, seems to be borrowed from the speech of one of the doctors *(Soto)* at the famous council of *Trent*, who said, " The antient *fa-* "*thers* had *many wives* by dispensation, and the others, "who were not dispensed with, did live in perpetual "sin."—*Hist. of Council of Trent*, Eng. Transl. by *N. Brent*, p. 671. This directly militates against the *universality*

We find particular occafional inftances of God's difpenfing with the rigour of His laws on certain emergencies, and for particular purpofes—as in David's eating the *fhewbread, which it was not lawful for any but the priefts to eat.* Alfo in fome other inftances which might be mentioned. But where do we find a *total* fufpenfion of one of the commandments of the *moral* law for ages together? If it was as great a fin for a man to have *two* wives, as for a woman to have *two* hufbands, why fufpend it on the part of the *man,* and not on the part of the *woman?* Why invariably ordain punifhment on *one* fide, and not on the *other,* if each was equally finful againft the law itfelf? *Doth* God *pervert judgment? Or doth the Almighty pervert juftice?* Job viii. 3. God *is no refpecter of perfons.* Acts x. 34. *He accepteth (i. e.* with undue and partial favour) *no man's perfon.* Gal. ii. 6. *As many as have finned in the law, fhall be judged by the law.* Rom. ii 1 , 12. Nor is it conceivable that the righteous Judge of all fhould Himfelf depart from the rule laid down for his *vice-gerents,* the *judges of*

---

fality of the law, Deut. xxi. 15, which is conceived in as general terms as poffible, and moft clearly fuppofes that *any man* might have *two wives.* The *Levirate,* or *law,* Deut. xxv. 5, 6. which *Noldius* calls a *difpenfation* for marrying the brother's wife, contrary to Lev. xviii. 16. is very improperly called fo, it being a *pofitive commandment,* eftablifhed for a *particular purpofe,* and both the law itfelf, and the reafon of it are there fet down. This is not the cafe with *polygamy,* for there is no law which prohibits it, nor any to eftablifh a *partial* allowance of it.

the

the earth, (*Deut.* i. 17.) *Ye shall not respect persons in judgment.* No other account then can consistently be given of the matter, than what may be gathered from the uniform and unvaried use of the word נאף—*adultery*—in the *seventh* commandment, as relating to the *wife*; that is to say, as forbidding *polygamy* on *her* side, but not to the *husband* as forbidding *polygamy* on *his*.

Others would make the wife, holy, great, and good men, who were *polygamists*, wholly *ignorant* of the law, as to the true meaning thereof, and say—"*The times of ignorance* God *winked at*"—wresting this text *(Acts* xvii. 30.) which speaks of the blind *Gentiles*, who were without the *written law of* God, and making it relate to the *Jews*, to whom *were committed the oracles of* God. *Rom.* iii. 1, 2. But, waving this, was ABRAHAM, that *prophet*, Gen. xx. 7. whom God, from the familiar intercourse He had with him, calls *His* * *friend?* (If. xli. 8.) —was *Jacob*, who spake with God *face to face* (Gen. xxxii. 30.) *ignorant?* Could MOSES, the sacred penman and expounder of the law, be *ignorant?* so *ignorant*, as not to know its true meaning? Could

---

* GOD saith, *Gen.* xviii. 19. *Shall I hide from Abraham that thing which I do?—for I know him, that he will command his children and his houshold after him, and they shall keep the way of the* LORD, *to do justice and judgment.* How Abraham could teach others to *keep the way of the* LORD, and yet be *ignorant* of it himself, cannot easily be conceived. *If the blind lead the blind, both shall fall into the ditch.* Matt. xv. 14.

DAVID

DAVID be *ignorant*? If so, to how little purpose was his *study in it all the day long*? Pſ. cxix. 97. Are we to ſuppoſe *Solomon* ignorant, to whom GOD ſaid—*Lo, I have given thee a wiſe and underſtanding heart, ſo that there was none like thee before thee, neither after thee ſhall any ariſe like unto thee?* 1 Kings iii. 12. See 1 Kings iv. 29, &c. Comp. Matt. xii. 42. Luke xi. 31. Such a ſolution of the matter will more eaſily prove the *ignorance* of ſuch commentators, than their aſſertions prove *ignorance* in the holieſt and wiſeſt men that ever lived under the light of the Old Teſtament, where alone GOD's law is to be found, and on the authority of which the whole New Teſtament can only * ſtand. The *kings of Iſrael* were expreſsly commanded to write a copy of the law with *their own hand*; it was to be *with them*, and they were to *read in it daily*. Deut. xvii. 18, 19. The *Prieſts* and *Levites* could not be *ignorant*; for their *lips were* to *keep knowledge*, and the people were to *ſeek the law at their mouth*. Mal. ii. 7. As for the *people*, they not only *heard* the law conſtantly, but were commanded to write it

---

* *Ignatius*, Epiſt. ad Philadelph. c. 8. introduces a *Jew* ſaying—'Εαν μὴ ἐν τοῖς ἀρχαίοις εὕρω ἐν τω 'Ευαγγελίω ȣ πιϛεύω—niſi invenero in antiquis (vaticiniis) Evangelio non credo: which I heartily aſſent to, thus paraphraſed—" What I do not find in *Moſes and the pro-* " *phets*, I'll not believe in the *goſpel*." But there is no danger of this, no hazard of being put to ſuch a trial; for certainly the New Teſtament faith *none other things than Moſes and the prophets did ſay ſhould come to paſs*. Acts xxvi. 22. See Rom. xv. 4. Luke xxiv. 44, 45.

upon the very *door-posts of their houses. Deut.* vi. 9. Whatever else, therefore, their *polygamy* proceeded from, it could not be derived from *ignorance*. They could not be *ignorant* of the *seventh* commandment; and supposing that many of them, like their descendents in later times, lost sight of its *spiritual intendment*, yet the meaning of its *outward letter* they could hardly be at a loss for, especially as they must observe its uniform and unvaried use throughout the whole of their scriptures. If, therefore, *polygamists* sinned against the *seventh* commandment, they did it with their eyes open; and whosoever can believe that such men as we have mentioned, could do this without any scruple before-hand, or sorrow afterwards, or the least sign of repentance, must believe more than, for their sakes, and the sake of thousands of GOD's saints (who though not mentioned as *polygamists*, doubtless were so) I could wish even to surmise, or than is in the least consistent with the account which we have of them in the holy scriptures.

I shall only observe farther on this head, of attributing the practice of *polygamy* by the Old-Testament saints to *ignorance*, that we must charge *ignorance* on GOD's high-priest *Jehoiada*, who stands recorded, 2 Kings xii. and 2 Chron. xxiv. as one of the wisest, best, and greatest characters that ever lived, as likewise one of the most exemplary promoters of GOD's honour, and a chief instrument of the reformation of religion in *Judah*, in the reign of of king * *Jehoash*. If so, our charge of *ignorance* will not stop here, but even reach the *Spirit of* GOD *Himself.* For He says, that *Joash did right in the sight of the* LORD *all the days of Jehoiada the priest,* 2 Chron. xxiv. 2. or (as it is 2 Kings xii. 2.) *all his days, wherein Jehoiada the priest instructed him;* and yet we are told, ver. 3. that *Jehoiada took for him* TWO WIVES, *and he begat sons and daughters.* On whom shall the commentator fix *ignorance?* On *Jehoiada* the high-priest, for teaching his pupil king *Jehoash* to be a *polygamist*, by taking for him *two wives?* or on *Jehoash*, who received them, and *cohabited with them?* or on the *Holy Ghost*, who bears testimony to the *rectitude* of king *Jehoash's* conduct, *all his days wherein Jehoiada the priest instructed him?*

The learned Bishop *Patrick*, on 2 Chron. xxiv. 3. says, that "*Jehoiada* did not take "these *two wives* for the king, but for him-"self." Supposing it to be so, the proof of the lawfulness of *polygamy* in *Jehoiada's* opinion is equally strong. But this sense of the *Bishop*'s will hardly arise from the position and construction of the *Hebrew* text: for it does not stand in the order of our translation —*And Jehoiada took for him two wives*—so as to make *him* the relative to *Jehoiada*; but

And	brought	to him	Jehoiada	two	wives
Et.	tulit	ei	Jehoiada	duas	uxores
† וישא		לו	יהוידא	נשים	שתים

Mont.

So

---

* Called JOASH also, 2 *Chron.* xxiv.

† The verb נשא certainly signifies to take a wife for *one's*

So that the לו—*to him*—stands as the relative to the chief subject of the preceding verse, which is evidently king *Jehoash*, whose history the sacred penman is here recording, as a part of which this action of *Jehoiada*'s is here related.

The *Bishop* is conscious of a difficulty in his interpretation, arising from a constant tradition of the *Jews*, that the *high-priest* was to have but *one wife* at a time, which was founded on *Lev.* xxi. 13, 14. This he endeavours to get rid of by saying—" It is not certain that " *Jehoiada* was *high-priest*, for he is every " where called *Jehoiada the priest*, and but " once only (ver. 6.) the *chief*."—But this is no argument at all against his being *high-priest*, for *Abiathar*, who was *high-priest*, is no where called so in the Old Testament, but always *the priest*; so his father *Ahimelech*, as the *Bishop* himself observes on 1 Sam. xxi. 1; so *Eli the priest*, 1 Sam. ii. 11; *Zadoc the priest*, 1 Kings iv. 2. 1 Chron. xxix. 22; and even *Aaron* himself, *Pf.* xcix. 6. The title of ראש—the *chief*, or *head*, which is given to *Jehoiada*, ver. 6. signifies certainly more than " the chief of one of the courses of priests." —His having apparently the conduct and management of every thing * relating to the temple, his anointing *king Jehoash* (comp.

---

one's self—but it also signifies to *take* or *bring* a wife *for another*. See Ezra ix. 2, 12. Neh. xiii. 25; in which passages the word נשא is used in both these senses.

* As well as the entire management and command over all the *Priests* and *Levites*. See 2 Chron. xxiii. 4—8.

1 Kings i. 45.) and many other circumſtances related of him, beſpeak him plainly to be no leſs than high-prieſt; and therefore the word ראש—*chief*, or *head*—denotes this here, as it does that *Seraiah* was † high-prieſt, 2 Kings xxv. 18. For all which reaſons it ſeems clear, that *Jehoiada* (who had before married *Jehoſhabeath*, the ſiſter of king *Ahaziah*, 2 Chron. xxii. 11.) took not theſe *two wives* for himſelf, but for king *Joaſh*.

Theſe things are too plain not to force conviction on the minds of many; therefore it is that they have ſaid with the learned author of the "*Hiſtorical Library*"—" Poly-" *gamy*, though not expreſsly *allowed*, is " however *tacitly implied* in the law of Moſes." This is going farther than thoſe I have mentioned, but yet does not come up to the matter. For if it be forbidden by the *ſeventh* commandment, or by any other law, it is as contradictory to ſcripture to ſay, that it was *tacitly implied*, as that it was *expreſsly allowed*. This laſt is the truth; it was *expreſsly allowed*, and that by GOD *Himſelf*: a direct proof this, that it was not forbidden by the *ſeventh* commandment, or by any other law, unleſs we can ſuppoſe the all-wiſe GOD to be ſo inconſiſtent with Himſelf, as to *forbid*, and yet *allow*, the ſame thing under the ſame circumſtances.

---

† That *Seraiah* was deſcended in a right line from *Eleazar* the ſon of *Aaron*, appears 1 Chron. vi. 4—14. and of courſe ſucceeded to the *high-prieſthood*. As ſuch he is regiſtered. Ibid.

VOL. I.   H   Some

Some have found out, that "*polygamy* was allowed for the more expeditious peopling of the world."—Suppoſing it is a mean of increaſing *population (which by the way will admit of great doubt) yet where was the uſe of this amongſt the *Jews*, when, before their

---

* This common notion, or rather *vulgar error*, is adopted by *St. Auguſtine*, De Civ. Dei, lib. xvi. c. 38. where, ſpeaking of the antient *polygamy*, he ſays it was lawful—*Quoniam multiplicandæ poſteritatis cauſâ plures uxores lex nulla prohibebat.* "Becauſe, for the ſake of multiplying *poſterity*, no law forbad many wives."—Thus thought many of the *fathers*, and the *Romiſh* church in general, till the doctrine of *diſpenſations* was introduced; then they ſaid it was a *ſin*; but GOD gave a *diſpenſation* to ſome to practiſe it—thus artfully making the *Holy* GOD a diſpenſer with *ſin*, and ſetting an example for the *Pope*'s firſt *making ſins*, and then *diſpenſing* with them. But let us ſuppoſe ten men and ten women—can it be imagined, that if theſe ten women are each ſeverally married to one *man*, they are not likely to have as many children as if they were all married to one of the men? *Porter*, in his Obſervations on the *Turks*, ſays, p. 292, that the number of children in *Turkiſh* families is not what the idea of *polygamy* ſuggeſts; that they have not, in general, ſo many children as are found in common families of *Chriſtians and Jews*—He even uſes this as an argument againſt *polygamy*. On the other hand, many have contended for the permiſſion of *polygamy* as "a ſpeedier means of peopling the world; it appearing, that in *polygamous* countries, people abound more than in others that are *monogamous*." But I take the real ſtate of the caſe, upon the whole, to be this; wherever there are the moſt *married women*, there the increaſe of the people will be the greateſt. *Polygamy*, therefore, as tending to increaſe the number of *married women*, muſt certainly tend to *population*. But then we are to ſuppoſe, that women who are married under *polygamous* contracts, would not otherwiſe be married at all; for in no other view can *polygamy* be ſaid to increaſe *population*; in this it certainly muſt.

entrance

entrance into *Canaan*, they were as the *stars in heaven for multitude?* Deut. i. 10; and yet *polygamy* did not cease after their entrance into the *promised land*.

As for all *popular* arguments against *polygamy*, which the wisdom of this world has invented, and believed as so many certain conclusions on the side of truth, they equally apply against the wisdom and holiness of GOD in *allowing* it, as against those who *maintain* it: therefore, as *He will be justified in His sayings, and clear when He is judged*, Rom. iii. 4. the best answer which can be given, for the present, is that included in the awful question of the *Apostle*, Rom. ix. 20. " Nay but, " O man, who art thou that repliest against " GOD?" Though this immediately relates to another point, yet it is applicable to all the vain reasonings of men against the dispensations of *Providence*, either in the *natural* or *moral* world. Which said reasonings, when thoroughly canvassed, and set in their true light, will appear to be neither more nor less, than the pleadings of human *pride*, on the behalf of human *ignorance*. Our prejudices and our opinions reciprocally affect each other, and, upon examination, they will usually be found as much alike as the *image* and the *mold* it is cast in.

" Go wiser thou, and in thy scale of sense,
" Weigh thy opinion against *Providence*—
" Call imperfection what thou fanciest such,
" Say, *here* He gives too little—*there* too much—

" Snatch from His hand the balance and the rod,
" Rejudge His justice, be the GOD of GOD.

> "In pride, in reas'ning pride, our error lies,
> "All quit their sphere, and rush into the skies;
> "And who but wishes to invert the laws
> "Of *order*, sins against th' ETERNAL CAUSE.
> "All this dread *order* break—for whom?—for thee?
> "Vile worm! Oh madness! pride! impiety!
> "Go teach ETERNAL WISDOM how to rule,
> "Then drop into *thyself*—and be a *fool*.
> "From pride, from pride, our very reas'ning springs—
> "Account for *moral*, as for *nat'ral* things:
> "Why charge we *Heaven* in *those*, in *these* acquit?—
> "In *both*, to *reason right*, is to *submit*."
> Essay on Man.

In fewer, but in still more forcible and humbling words, doth *Paul* express himself to the *self-wise* among the *Corinthians*—and in *them* to *us*—1 Cor. iii. 18, 19.—*Let no man deceive himself*—*If any man among you seem to be wise in this world*—εν τω αιωνι τȣτω—like the philosophers, *politicians*, and *rabbies* of the *age*, (GUYSE) *let him become a* FOOL *that he may be wise*—*for the wisdom of this world is* FOOLISHNESS *with* GOD.

Though it be beside my design, in this treatise, to consider the subjects thereof on any other footing than as they appear in the scriptures; yet I will so far depart from my purpose, as to take notice of a *popular* argument *against polygamy*, which, in the minds of some learned and considerate men, has been of such importance, as to outweigh all that could be said *for* it. It is this—" The *males*
" and *females* brought into the world are
" nearly on a balance, only allowing a little
" excess on the side of the *males*; whence it
" follows, that nature intends only one wife
" for

"for the same person; if they have more,
"some others must * go without any." This
argument,

* So must it be even upon the principle of *monogamy*; for if, according to these calculators, there be more *males* than *females*, it is not possible that *every* man can have a *wife*; some *must go without*. However, a departure either way from the original proportion of *one male* and *one female*, destroys all arguments which can be drawn from thence against *polygamy*; for the precedent which this might otherwise have been, being departed from by the *Creator* himself, it of course ceases with respect to his creatures. Major *Grant* observes, that a little excess on the side of the *males*—" is to make up for the extraor-
" dinary expence thereof in *war* and at *sea*"—to which others have added, as a consideration also, " the labo-
" rious and dangerous employments in which men are
" engaged, and women are not." As for *war*—it is written—*Whence come wars and fightings among you? Come they not hence, even of your lusts* (ἡδονῶν, the desires after sensual gratifications) *which war in your members? Ye lust and have not, ye kill and desire to have, and cannot obtain*, &c. James iv. 1, 2. So *Plato* in his *Phædo*, § 10. Edit. Cantab. 1673, p. 88. και γαρ πολεμυς και στασεις και μαχας ѕδεν αλλο παρεχει η το σωμα και αι τѕ̃ѕ επιθυμιαι. " For nothing but the body and its lusts (or evil de-
" sires) *produce wars, seditions, battles*." Can it be reasonably supposed, that the *Almighty*, whose gracious command is—*Thou shalt love thy neighbour as thyself*—is directed, in the proportion of *males* and *females*, by the most horrid and fatal proofs which men are daily giving of their enmity to Him and each other! and that more men than women are born into the world on this account?

These *wars*, together with the extension of commerce, and the calls of numberless artificial wants which luxury has introduced, certainly expose the lives of men to the dangers of the *sea*. But who hath required this at their hands?—Let an *Heathen* give the answer:

> *Nequicquam* Deus *abscidit*
> *Prudens oceano dissociabili*
> *Terras, si tamen impiæ*
> *Non tangenda rates transiliunt vada.*

Audax

argument, plausible as it may seem, wants one essential to *solidity*, which is *truth*. For saying

> *Audax omnia perpeti*
> *Gens humana ruit per vetitum nefas.*
> HOR.

> GOD hath the realms of earth in vain
> Divided by th' unhabitable main,
> If ships profane, with fearless pride,
> Bound o'er th' inviolable tide.
> No laws, or human or divine,
> Can the presumptuous race of man confine.
> FRANCIS.

GOD *hath made man upright, but they have sought out many inventions,* saith *Solomon,* Eccl. vii. 29. To imagine that the providential dispensations of the ALL-WISE GOD, are to be accommodated to *these,* or regulated by them, is surely too absurd to bear an argument.

As for " laborious employments, many of which are " attended with danger, and which usually fall to the " share of the *males,*" let as many of these be selected as can be deemed *necessary,* and then, against them, let us set —the many diseases to which *females* are peculiarly liable, and to which *men* are *not*—let us add to these the peril of child-birth, and then, this last supposed *reason* for more males being born than *females,* will be as groundless as the two former.

I should imagine, that no opinions whatsoever, however false and absurd, are without having *reasons* given for them. Nor is it to be doubted, that a *Ptolemaist* would give as many reasons for the *sun*'s going *round the earth,* as a *Copernican* would for the *earth*'s going *round the sun.*

The following question is said to have been once laid before a certain very learned body :—Take a tub of water weighing one ton weight—into which put a *salmon* of thirty pounds weight ; Why will not the tub be heavier than before the fish was put into it ? The fact being taken for granted, produced many *wise* reasons for it ; but none were thought *so wise* and adequate, as—*Corpora non gravant in loco suo*—therefore the *fish* being in its *place* or proper element, lost its power of adding any thing to the weight of the tub of water. At last, it was proposed to

saying which, I will, by way of justification, transcribe a few paragraphs from *Dr.* Forster's "*Observations during a Voyage round the World*"—published 1778. This ingenious author, who seems to be a most strenuous *monogamist*, after speaking of "Monogamy established in the isles of the *South Sea*," very candidly says—"But here I find myself obliged to confess, that I am not as yet persuaded of the great and universal argument for *monogamy*, viz. the *equal proportion of women to men*; as, in my opinion, it is not clearly proved that this just proportion holds place in all countries and climates. On the contrary, I am of opinion, that the constitution of food and climate, and the prevailing custom of marrying many wives, have, by length of time, produced a considerable disparity between the numbers of men and women; so that now, to one man, several women are born. This observation is really confirmed by fact; for *all* the voyagers unanimously agree, that among all the *African* nations *polygamy* is customary; nor has any one observed that there are men among these nations *without wives*, for every one is matched to *one* or *more* females." Here he refers to *Bosman*'s "Description of the coast of *Guinea*," "who likewise," says

to weigh the tub, both with and without the fish; when, to the confusion of all their reasonings, the matter ended as the reader may conceive.

the Doctor, "expressly declares, that the
"number of women *much* exceeds that of
"the men."—"When a *polygamous* nation
"lives in the neighbourhood of *monogamous*
"nations, there is always a probability that
"the women necessary for so many men
"who have *more* than one wife, are obtained
"by stealth, force, or by commerce from the
"neighbouring nations; but in *Africa*, all
"the nations are *polygamous*; every man is
"*married*, and has *more* than *one* wife. He
"cannot procure these wives from the neigh-
"bouring tribes where the same custom pre-
"vails: it is therefore, in my opinion, a
"clear and settled point, that the women
"born among these nations must be more
"numerous than the males.

"Though the colonists at the *Cape of
"Good Hope* are *monogamous*, I observed, in
"the various families of the town and coun-
"try, the number of * females to prevail."
—"It has been observed † in *Sweden*, more
"females

---

* *Kempfer*, on numbering the people of *Meaco*, in the kingdom of *Japan*, found the *females* to exceed the *males* in the following proportion:

 Females, 223,573
 Males,   182,072
    ―――――
    41,501 more *females* than *males*.
Spirit of Laws, vol. i. p. 373.

† How far this observation may hold good in this kingdom I know not—but, being lately on an occasional visit to the *vicar* of a country village, I had the curiosity to look into the parish register of births; I took ten years in the latter part of the last century, viz. from 1670 to
            1679,

"females than males have been born during the latter part of this century—it is reported in the kingdom of *Bantam*, even *ten* women are born to *one* man;" and refers to " Lord *Kaimes*'s Hift. of Man, vol. i. p. 176." *Montefquieu*, Spirit of Laws— Eng. Tranf. 4th edition, octavo—vol. i. p. 374. mentions this—" I confefs," fays he, " if what hiftory tells us be true, that at " *Bantam* there are *ten* women to *one* man, " this muft be a cafe peculiarly favourable to " *polygamy.*"

From all this it appears to me, that, unlefs we can find that GOD delivered to *Mofes* as many different laws to govern the actions of His reafonable creatures, as there are different parts of the globe inhabited by them, fo as that there is one law for the inhabitants of *Afia* and *Africa,* and another for thofe of *Europe,* this fort of arguments, drawn from the outward appearances of things in different parts of the world, proves nothing on either fide of the queftion, but the exceeding ignorance of mankind as touching the acts and difpenfations of that INFINITELY WISE BEING, whofe *judgments are unfearchable, and His ways paft finding out!* Rom. xi. 33.

The beft and faireft, and indeed the only way to get at the truth, on this as on every

---

1679, inclufive, and there appeared to have been born in that fpace 19 more *males* than *females.*

In the fpace between 1770 to 1779, inclufive, the number of *females* born exceeded that of the *males* by 27.

other

other occasion where religion is concerned, is to lay aside *prejudice*, from whatever quarter it may be derived, and to let the *Bible* speak for itself. Then we shall see that *polygamy*, notwithstanding the *seventh* commandment, was allowed by GOD *Himself*, who, however others might mistake it, must infallibly know His own *mind*, be perfectly acquainted with His own will, and thoroughly understand His own *law*. If He did not intend to allow *polygamy*, but to prevent or condemn it, either by the *seventh* commandment, or by some other law, how is it possible that He should make laws for its *regulation*, any more than He should make laws for the *regulation* of *adultery*, *theft*, or *murder*? How is it conceivable that He should give the least countenance to it, or so express His approbation of it, as even to *work miracles* in support of it? For the making a woman *fruitful* who was naturally *barren*, must have been the effect of * supernatural power.—He *blessed*, and in a distinguished manner *owned* the issue—and declared it legitimate to all intents and purposes. If this be not *allowance*, what is? As to the *first*, namely, his making laws for the *regulation* of *polygamy*, let us consider what is written, Exod. xxi. 10. *If he (i. e.* the husband) *take him another wife* (not—in so doing he sins against the *seventh* commandment, recorded

---

* Pf. cxiii. 9. *He maketh the* barren woman *to keep house, and to be a joyful mother of children.*

in the preceding chapter—but) *her food, her raiment (i. e.* of the firſt wife) *and her duty of marriage, he ſhall not diminiſh*—לא יגרע—he ſhall not *ſubtract* or *withold,* ἐκ ἀποϛερῃσει, LXX. Compare 1 Cor. vii. 5. Here God poſitively forbids a *neglect,* much more the *divorcing* or *putting away* the *firſt wife,* but charges no *ſin* on taking the *ſecond.*

2dly. When *Jacob* married *Rachel* ſhe was *barren,* and ſo continued for many years; but God did not leave this as a puniſhment upon her for marrying a man who had *another wife.* It is ſaid, *Gen.* xxx. 22. that God *remembered Rachel, and* God *hearkened unto her—and opened her womb—and ſhe conceived and bare a ſon —and ſaid,* God *hath taken away my reproach.* Surely this paſſage of ſcripture ought to afford a complete anſwer to thoſe who bring the words of the marriage-bond, as cited by Christ, Matth. xix. *They twain ſhall be one fleſh,* to prove *polygamy* ſinful; and ſhould lead us to conſtrue them, as by this inſtance, and many others, the Lawgiver Himſelf appears to have done; that is to ſay, where a woman, not *betrothed to another man,* unites herſelf in *perſonal knowledge* with the man of her choice, let that man's *ſituation* be what it may—*they twain ſhall be one fleſh.* How otherwiſe do we find ſuch a woman as *Rachel,* united to *Jacob,* who had a wife then living, praying to God for a bleſſing on her intercourſe with *Jacob,* and God *hearkening unto her, opening her womb,* removing her barrenneſs, and thus, by miracle, *taking away her reproach?*

reproach? We also find the offspring legitimate, and inheritors of the land of *Canaan*; a plain proof that *Joseph* and *Benjamin* were no *bastards*, or born out of lawful marriage. See a like palpable instance of GOD's miraculous blessing on *polygamy* in the case of *Hannah*, 1 *Sam.* i. and ii.—These instances serve also to prove, that, in GOD's account, the *second* marriage is just as valid as the *first*, and as obligatory, and that our making it *less so*, is contradictory to the divine wisdom.

3dly. GOD blessed and owned the issue. How eminently this was the case with regard to *Joseph*, see Gen. xlix. 22—26; to *Samuel*, see 1 Sam. iii. 19. It was expressly commanded, that a *bastard*, or son of a woman who was with child by * *whoredom*, should not *enter into the congregation of the* LORD, *even to his tenth generation.* Deut. xxiii. 2. But we find *Samuel*, the offspring of † *polygamy*, ministring to the LORD in the tabernacle at *Shiloh*, even in his *very childhood, cloathed with a linen ephod before* ELI *the priest.* See this whole history, 1 Sam. i. and ii. Who then can doubt of *Samuel*'s legitimacy, consequently of GOD's *allowance* of, and blessing on *polygamy?* If such second marriage was in GOD's account *null and void*, as a sin against the *original law* of marriage, the *seventh* commandment, or *any other* law of GOD, no mark of *legitimacy* could have been found on

---

* ἐκ πορνης. LXX.
† See Appendix, N⁰ 1. vol. ii.

the

the issue; for a *null* and *void* marriage is tantamount to *no* marriage at all; and if no marriage, no legitimacy of the issue can possibly be. Instead of such a blessing as *Hannah* obtained, we should have found her and her husband *Elkanah* charged with *adultery*, dragged forth and *stoned to death*; for so was *adultery* to be punished. All this furnishes us with a conclusive proof, that the having *more* than *one wife* with which a man cohabited, was not *adultery* in the sight of God; or, in other words, that it never was reckoned by Him any sin against the *seventh* commandment, the *original marriage-institution*, or any *other law whatsoever*.

4thly. But there is a passage (Deut. xxi. 15.) which is express * to the point, and amounts to a demonstration of God's allowance of *polygamy*. *If there be to a man* שְׁתֵּי נָשִׁים—TWO WIVES—(Compare Gen. iv. 19. 1 Sam. i. 2. xxx. 5.)—the ONE BELOVED, *and the* ONE HATED, *and they have borne him children, both the* BELOVED *and the* HATED—*and if the first-born be to the* HATED, *then it shall be, when he maketh his sons to inherit that which he hath, that he may not make the son of the beloved first-born before the son of the hated, which is indeed the first-born, by giving him a double portion of all that he hath; for he is the beginning of his strength, and the right of the first-born is his.*

* " Herein is a law, tacitly implied at least, for a man " to have two wives." Ant. Univ. Hist. vol. iii. p. 141.

On the footing of this law, the marriage of *both* women is equally *lawful*, God calls them both *wives* (for so the word נשים must be rendered in this place, as the context shews plainly) and He can't be mistaken, if He *calls them so* they certainly *were so*. If the *second* wife bore the first son, that son was to inherit before a son born afterwards of the * *first* wife. Here the issue is expressly deemed *legitimate*, and inheritable to the *double portion of the first-born*; which could not be, if the *second* marriage were not deemed as lawful and valid as the *first*.

The *wisdom of this world*, as at present constituted, would say—the man was an *adulterer*—the *second* wife an *adulteress*—our law would make the man a *felon*—our *ecclesiastical* courts would pronounce the *second* marriage *null* and *void*—the issue would be *bastardized*—and our *devout* people would lift up their hands and eyes, and deem the whole a monstrous piece of wickedness! Which view of the matter is most agreeable to the *mind* and *will* of God, must be left to the *judicious* reader to determine.

Dean *Delaney*, who cannot venture to deny absolutely that this text relates to *polygamy* —yet, in a note, endeavours to get rid of its evidence, by saying, that " this one expres-
" sion—*her's that was hated*—see our transla-
" tion—makes this law appear rather to be un-

---

* This could not happen where there were *two wives* in *succession*.

" derstood

"derstood of the children of two *successive*
"wives."—But the *Hebrew* runs thus—והיה
הבן הבכר לשניאה—*and the first-born son be to the
hated*—so that the stress laid on the words of
our translation, *her's that was hated*, is good for
nothing. See Reflections on *Polygamy*, p. 56.

The learned *Dr. Rutherforth* has also taken
no small pains, to get rid of the conclusive evidence of this text in favour of the divine allowance of *polygamy*. That learned professor,
in his lectures which he red at *Cambridge*, on
Grotius de Jure, found this *text*, in the plain
and obvious meaning of the *Hebrew*, by no
means conformable to the position which he
had laid down, that *polygamy* was contrary to
the *law of nature*; he therefore is for supposing the *two wives* to have been in *succession*,
and that the *first-born* was the son of the *first
wife*. See *Institutes of Natural Law*, b. i. c. 15.

But it is very extraordinary, if this were
the case, that it should not be so expressed.
This is a point of too much consequence, to
be established on words, which do not carry
that meaning, and no other, on the face of
them: so far from it, the only terms used in
the description of the *women* are—" *The one
" beloved—and the one hated*,"—who can say
which was *which?*—consequently, presume to
determine, of *which wife* the *first-born* was, in
point of time?

Dr. *Rutherforth*, as well as Dr. *Delaney*,
in his treatment of all *scriptures* which oppose his *law of nature* scheme, puts one in
mind of *Kolben*'s account of the *Rhinoceros*—
" This

"This creature, in order to get at his prey,
"marches towards it in a *right line*, tearing
"his way very furiously through all oppo-
"sition of trees and bushes. When he is
"upon the march, he is heard at a great dis-
"tance, forcing his way through thick bushes,
"and snapping of trees."

As for *Grotius* and *Puffendorf*, they both allow that the *Jewish* law permitted *polygamy*, as they both declare; and both mention this text as one proof of it. See *Grot. de Jure*, lib. ii. c. 5. § 9. Marg. *Puffend.* lib. vi. c. 1. § 16.—The like may be said of the great *Mr. Selden, Bishop Patrick*, and every other learned *commentator*, who had not a very *interesting reason* for imitating *Peter Kolben's Rhinoceros* above-mentioned.

One particular occasion of this law seems to have been, what had happened in the case of *Leah* and *Rachel, Jacob's* שתי נשים—*two wives*—*the one beloved* and *the one hated*.—See Gen. xxix. 30, 31. *Reuben was the first-born* of *Leah*—*Joseph* of *Rachel*. *Jacob* disinherited the son of the *hated*, and gave the *right of the first-born* to the son of the *beloved*—but this was not a mere act of *caprice*, and undue *preference*, against the law of inheritance, upon account of *Jacob's* partiality to *Rachel*; but an act of *justice*, on account of *Reuben's* crime, who had gone up to *his father's couch*, and defiled his *concubine Bilhah*.—He therefore disinherited him, as a punishment, and the *birth-right* thus became *Joseph's*, who
was

was the *first-born* of *Jacob* by *Rachel*. See 1 Chron. v. 1, 2.

As this might have been made a precedent among the *polygamous Jews*, and what had been an act of *justice* in *Jacob*, made use of to justify an indulgence of undue partiality for *one wife* before *another*, to the *disherison* of the *first-born*, and to the overturning the sacred rights he was invested with, as a *type* or *figure* of *Him that was to come*—who, as the great *antitype*, is *styled*, " the *first-born* of *every* " *creature*." Col. i. 15.—therefore this law seems to have been made, and stands as an irrefragable proof of the lawfulness of *polygamy*; because it stands as a proof, not only of the *allowed* practice of it, but of the *legitimacy* of the *issue* in the sight of GOD; which is evinced to demonstration in the above case of *Joseph*, who could not have inherited the *right* of the *first-born*, on any other principle.

Simeon was the next son of *Leah*, but could not take the inheritance, not being the *first-born* of his mother—but *Joseph* was, and therefore, as the only *legitimate heir*, took the birth-right, on the *disherison* of *Reuben* the first-born of *Leah*.

But farther. To say that *polygamy* is sinful (for if it ever *was* it certainly *is*, and if ever it *was not* it certainly *is not*, unless some positive law hath made an alteration, or unless good and evil change their nature by length of time, like the fashion of our cloaths) is to

VOL. I.   I   make

make God the *author of sin*; for * not to forbid that which is evil, but even to countenance and promote it, and this uniformly for ages together, is being so far the *author* of it, and accessary to it in the highest degree. —And shall we dare to *say*, or even to *think*, that this is chargeable on HIM who *is of purer eyes than to behold evil, and who cannot look on iniquity?* Hab. i. 13. God forbid!

When HE is upbraiding DAVID, by the prophet *Nathan*, for his ingratitude towards His *Almighty benefactor*, (2 Sam. xii.) He does it in the following terms: ver. 8. I GAVE ‡ THEE *thy master's house*, and thy
MASTER'S

---

* *Puffendorf*, b. vi. c. 1. § 16. observes, that the *Mo-*
"*saical* law was so far from forbidding this custom, that
"it seems in several places to suppose it;" and refers to
Deut. xxi. 15. xvii. 16, 17. and 2 Sam. xii. 8.

‡ When *Esau* met *Jacob* with his wives and children, he asked—*who are those with thee?* and *Jacob* said—*The children which* GOD *hath* GRACIOUSLY GIVEN *thy servant.* Gen. xxxiii. 5. Now, can we suppose that GOD'S gracious gifts are peculiarly bestowed on acts of rebellion against His positive laws? Yet we must either suppose this, or that *Jacob's polygamy* was no transgression of the law.—See Gen. xxx. 16, 17, 18, another remarkable instance of GOD'S special blessing on *polygamy*.

The mention of *Esau* reminds me of a remarkable part of his history. He took *two wives*, both *Hittites*, idolatresses—*which were a grief of mind unto Isaac, and to Rebekah.* Gen. xxvi. 34, 35. But whence arose this grief of mind in *Esau*'s parents? Not on account of his *polygamy*, but because he had married *heathen women*, as is clear from xxvii. 46: therefore *Jacob* is sent to *Padan-Aram*, that he might not take a *wife* of the *daughters of Canaan*, but of his *mother's family*; and when *Esau* saw that the daughters of Canaan pleased not Isaac his father, he
went

[115]

MASTER'S WIVES INTO THY BOSOM, *and I gave thee the house of* ISRAEL *and* JUDAH, *and if that had been too little, I would moreover have given thee such and such things.*

Can we suppose GOD giving *more wives than one* into DAVID's *bosom*, who already had *more than one*, if it was *sin* in DAVID to *take* them? Can we imagine that GOD should thus transgress (as it were) His own commandment in *one* instance, and yet so severely reprove and chastise DAVID for breaking it in another? Is it not rather plain, from the whole transaction, that DAVID committed

---

went and took a wife of the daughters of Ishmael, unto the wives which he had—but we hear of no lamentation of *Isaac and Rebekah*, over this *fresh act of polygamy*. As for *Jacob*, we read of his return out of *Syria* with no less than *four wives*—that when he came to *Mahanaim*, and heard of *Esau*'s approach, he rose up that night, and took his two *wives*, and *his two women-servants* (called also *his wives*—See Gen. xxx. 4, 9. and his *eleven sons, and passed over the brook Jabbock.* Gen. xxxii. 22.' And *Jacob was left alone, and there wrestled a man with him,* &c. This *man* is called אלהים ver. 30. GOD ; in Hof. xii. 4. מלאך *an angel*; and ver. 5. the *Lord God of Hosts*—which, all put together, shews us, that it was not a *mere man*, nor *created angel*, but מלאך יהוה the *angel* JEHOVAH—*the messenger of the covenant*, Mal. iii. 1. who appeared often in an human form under the Old Testament, in token of His *future incarnation* under the New Testament, even *the man, the* GOD-*man* CHRIST JESUS—He who is represented by commentators as ranking *polygamy* with *adultery*, Matt. xix. 9. But what was his conduct towards *Jacob?*—Doth He reprove Him for the *sin of polygamy*, in which he was living? No—*He said, Thy name shall no more be called Jacob, but Israel; for as a prince hast thou power with* GOD *and with men, and hast prevailed*—*and he* BLESSED *him there.* Comp. Deut. xxvii. 26. and Gal. iii. 10.

I 2   *mortal*

mortal sin in taking another *living* man's wife, but none in taking the widows of the *deceased* SAUL? that therefore, though the law of GOD condemned the *first*, yet it did not condemn the *second?*

This passage of 2 *Sam.* xii. 8. is so conclusive a proof of GOD's allowance of *polygamy*, that writers on the other side of the question have not been able to get rid of it, but by a downright corruption of the text. Instead of the plain, obvious, and literal meaning of the word חיק—which signifies the " *breast* " or *bosom*, from the *throat* to the *pit of the* " *stomach*," have construed it into *power*, and would tell us that " GOD gave SAUL's *wives* " into DAVID's *power*, as a *sovereign*, not in- " to his *bosom* as an *husband*."

" Take this expression in its strongest and " most strict sense" (says the late reverend and learned * *Dean Delaney*, in a book called " Reflections on *Polygamy*," printed at London, 1737, under the name of *Phileleutherus Dubliniensis*) " as where *Sarai* tells *Abram* " that she had *given her maid into his bosom*, " (Gen. xvi. 5.) what more can be meant by " it, than that she gave her into his *power?*" We have but to look at the whole context of

---

* This *Reverend* gentleman is so candid as to tell us, —" that he has ventured to differ from all the commen- " tators he ever met with, in the sense of *every text re-* " *lating to this point*,"—i. e. of *David's polygamy*.—So that, by his own confession, he stands *alone*, in his interpretation of *every text* upon the subject. See Reflections on *Polygamy*, p. 3.

that passage, and this learned man's question receives a full and explicit answer, and his whole argument an absolute refutation. Gen. xvi. 1. &c. *Now* SARAI, ABRAM'S *wife, bare him no children, and she had an handmaid, an* ÆGYPTIAN, *whose name was* HAGAR; *and* SARAI *said unto* ABRAM, *Behold now the* LORD *hath restrained me from bearing, I pray thee* GO ‡ IN UNTO MY MAID, *it may be that I may* OBTAIN CHILDREN BY HER. *And* ABRAM *hearkened unto the voice of* SARAI: *and* SARAI, ABRAM'S *wife, took* HAGAR *her maid, the Ægyptian, and gave her to* ABRAM *to be* HIS WIFE (לאשׁה) *and* HE WENT IN UNTO HAGAR, *and she conceived; and when she saw that she had conceived, her mistress was despised in her eyes: and* SARAI *said unto* ABRAM, *My wrong be upon thee; I* HAVE GIVEN MY MAID INTO THY BOSOM, *and when she saw that she had conceived, I was despised in her eyes; the* LORD *judge between me*

---

‡ The sequel of this chapter seems to afford, to every candid mind, a very conclusive proof, that this proposal of *polygamy* to *Abram* by his wife *Sarai*, was not *sinful*, neither *Abram's* complying with it in the least displeasing to GOD; for on *Hagar's* departure from *Sarai*, on account of *hard usage*, ver. 6. the *angel of the* LORD recommends it to her to *return*, and promises *to multiply her seed exceedingly, that it should not be numbered for multitude*—tells her *she should bear a son*—בן—which promise was fulfilled, ver. 15. Now, for all this to happen, in support *of*, and as a blessing *upon*, a *polygamous* marriage, if such marriages were *sinful*, and of course abominable in the eyes of GOD, is, I freely own, past every notion which I have conceived of the *scripture-character* of the *holy* GOD of *Israel*. See Gen. xvii. 20.

and thee. This scripture is too plain to need any comment. I will therefore, after observing that חיק no more signifies *power,* than it signifies an *horse,* only add, that if SAUL's *wives* had not been given into DAVID's *bosom,* in the plain and * usual sense of that expression, the circumstance itself could not have afforded that striking aggravation, so beautifully intimated in *Nathan*'s parable, of the *rich man's sparing to take of his own flock, and his own herd, to dress for the way-faring man that was come unto him, but taking the poor man's lamb, &c.*

The learned *Dean,* as well as some other commentators on this famous passage, go still farther, and tell us, DAVID could not enjoy these widows of SAUL as *wives,* because in so doing he would have committed *incest,* they being *mothers-in-law* to MICHAL, SAUL's daughter, who was DAVID's wife. But where is such an union forbidden? I have carefully examined the degrees of *affinity* and *consanguinity* wherein marriage is forbidden, and do find a man must not marry his *own mother-in-law,* (Lev. xviii. 8.) but as to his *wife's mother-in-law,* there is not a trace of such an impediment. As for MICHAL's *own mother,* she, if living, must be put out of the question. See Lev. xviii. 17.

These things being considered, the observations of such commentators evaporate into

---

* Deut. xiii. 6. אשת חיקך—*uxor sinus tui.* Mont.—*The wife of thy bosom.*

just

just what NATHAN's parable and remonstrance must do, supposing such criticisms to be true; that is to say, into—nothing at all. DAVID's ingratitude to GOD, and to his * WORTHY URIAH—were not so marked by NATHAN, because DAVID had a number of women whom he could *not enjoy*; but because he might have *enjoyed* them whenever he pleased: therefore his taking URIAH's *wife* was the more inexcusable, and his rebellious ingratitude against GOD, who gave him so many women *into his bosom*, the more aggravated.

These truths have not failed universally in their influence, but have forced themselves into the consciences of some; who, not being able to resist their conviction, have confessed that " *Polygamy* was *allowed* of GOD to " the *Jews*, but yet it is † *forbidden* to Chris- " tians"—which is just as true as if it was said, that " the people under the Old Tes- " tament were *men* and *women*, but *Chris-* " *tians* ‡ are not; for to suppose that the

human

---

* 2 Sam. xxiii. 39.

† *Polygamy* is prohibited among *Christians*, but was allowed, by *Divine appointment*, among the *Jews*. Chambers, Tit. *Polygamy*.

‡ Or to say with *some of the* antient fathers, who were *wiser* than the scriptures, that the *crescite & multiplicamini* of the Old Testament has nothing to do with *Christians* under the New Testament—Quia hodie, repleto mundo, non tam necessarium quam olim; and again—hoc dictum pertinere ad tempora ante *Christum*, non ad nos qui alio vivimus ævo—mundum jam non desiderare illud *crescite & multiplicamini*. " The com- " mand

human species is changed, is not more abfurd, than to fuppofe a change either of the *original* defign of God in the inftitution of marriage, or of the fenfe and meaning of the *feventh* commandment, as forbidding or condemning that *now*, which was not forbidden or condemned, either by the one or the other, for fo many ages *before*. As for the pofitive law of the *feventh* commandment, it is attended with fuch pains and penalties in the breach of it, that it is impoffible but that fome inftance of God's difapprobation of *polygamy* muft have been met with, had that been within the meaning of it; otherwife the abfurdity muft follow, of fuppofing a fufpenfion of this law for 1500 years after it was ordained of God, delivered to *Mofes*, and by him to the people at *Mount Sinai*—and all this for the indulgence of *mortal fin* in *one* fex, while it was punifhed with death in the other.

In the firft place, I would obferve in general, that *polygamy*, in its proper fenfe, as practifed under the Old Teftament by the people of God; that is, the taking *two wives together at once*, or *one to another*, and *cohabiting with both*, is not fo much as * men-

---

" mand—*Be fruitful and multiply*, &c. is not neceffary,
" as once it was, becaufe the world is filled with peo-
" ple.—That belonged to the times before Christ,
" not to us who live in another age—the world now
" wants not that—*Increafe and multiply*."

* Unlefs incidentally, 1 Tim. iii. 2. 1 Tit. i. 6. where nothing is faid, either good or bad, as to the matter itfelf in general.

tioned

tioned any where, that I can find, from the *first* chapter of *Saint Matthew* to the *last* of the *Revelation of Saint John*, inclusive: therefore it cannot be said to be * *condemned*. The famous passage in Matt. xix. which has been already considered, and will be more fully hereafter, certainly relates to † *divorce*, and, properly speaking, not to *polygamy*; for this, simply considered, does not come in question. The people there, so far from intending *polygamy*, meant nothing less, for they meant to have but *one wife at a time*; else why were they for *divorcing one*, in order to take ‡ *another?* Their sin was this, not the *taking* and *cohabiting* with *more than one* at a time. They imagined themselves *totally free* from the *first*, before they married the *second*.

The New Testament was not to introduce a *new law* concerning this, nor any thing else. Nothing is to be found there which was not in the Old Testament, only as to the *manner*; the *matter* is one and the same. Otherwise, how could *Paul* derive any strength to his argument, Gal. iii. 10. by citing the sanction

---

* Judge *Blackstone* says, very gravely—Comm. vol. i. p. 436.—" *Polygamy* is condemned by the law of the " *New Testament.*"

† So our *translators* undoubtedly thought; for in the summary of the contents printed at the head of the chapter, they only say—" CHRIST answereth the Pha-" risees concerning *divorcement.*" ver. 3—10. So Mark x. 2. " *Touching divorcement.*"

‡ Here the word ἄλλην, Matt. xix. 9. is supposed to signify *another* (i. e. *any* other *woman*) according to our translation. But that this may not be the sense of it, see after.

of the *old* law, to prove the neceffity of *falvation by grace?* If the law be in a fingle inftance altered, or changed in one fingle point, how can it be faid by an infpired *apoftle* of CHRIST—*Curfed is every one that continueth not in* ALL THINGS *which are written in the book of the law to do them?*—which, as it never had, fo it never can have but one fenfe and meaning; and our LORD fhews, that it not only condemned the *act*, but the very *thought* of *adultery*. Did it only begin to do this, when CHRIST faid, *Whofoever looketh upon a woman to luft after her, hath already committed adultery with her in his heart**? Matt. v. 28. (but then this muft mean fuch a woman † as

adultery

---

* *Per γυναικα autem intelligitur uxor alterius.* "By the word γυναικα—*woman*—the wife of another is underftood. 2 Sam. xi. 2, 3, 4. Job xxxi. 1, 7. Prov. vi. 27. Ecclus ix. 7, 8, 9. xxvi. 9. Sufan. viii. 9, 32." See Wetft. on Matt. v. 28.

† The word γυνη—like the Hebrew אשה—is certainly a general term, and fignifies *a woman*, as diftinguifhed from a man; and in this fenfe it is ufed *Matt.* xiv. 21. *Acts* v. 14. & al. freq.

But this cannot be the fenfe of it here; for if it be finful to *look* with *defire* on any *woman* whatfoever, then it would be finful for a man to *defire* his own wife, to whom he is actually married, or a virgin to whom he is contracted; and this would lead us into all the abfurdities of the antient *mifogamifts*, who held *marriage itfelf* to be *finful*.

In this place, therefore, it certainly means a *woman* confidered as *related to a man*; and that, whether be*trothed* or *efpoufed* only (See Matt. i. 20, 24. Luke ii. 5.) or that hath cohabited with her hufband, (Luke i. 5, 13, 18.) for with no other can *adultery* be committed; and it is very evident that *our Saviour*'s difcourfe is on that fubject; as forbidden and condemned by the *feventh commandment*, which He is explaining.

Γὺν

adultery could be committed with, suppofing the *thought* brought forth into *act*). And does not the Old Teftament fay the fame thing? What

Γύνη in the New Teftament, like אשה alfo in the Old Teftament, is the term made ufe of to denote a *married woman*—when *others* are defigned, we meet with κοραστον, a damfel, Fr. *damoifelle*—παρθενος, a *virgin*—χηρα, a widow—but I believe it would be difficult to find a fingle paffage in the New Teftament, where γυνη is ufed neceffarily to denote an *unmarried woman*. μεμέρισαι ἡ γυνὴ ᵏ ἡ παρθένος, 1 Cor. vii. 34. Afterwards the παρθενος is called αγαμος—the γυνη, γαμησασα.

For want of fuch diftinction, fome *commentators*, by letting their *own* imaginations loofe, have filled thofe of many *readers* with matter of fore diftrefs and bondage of confcience, as if the *defire* after any *female* whatfoever, came within what they call the *fpiritual* import of the *feventh* commandment.

I once knew a gentleman, who often affured me, that he never approached *his own wife*, without finding a fecret uneafinefs in his mind, left he was doing wrong. He was a great admirer of what are called *fpiritual expofitors*. Thefe are, too often, a fpecies of *commentators*, who, neglecting the fcriptural fenfe and meaning of the *original*, wander into every conceit which a warm, or perhaps a wild imagination may fuggeft, from the found of words in a tranflation. Some inftances of this have been given in this work, and as many more might be given, as would furnifh ample materials for a work by itfelf.

N. B. Let every man be fure he underftands the *original letter*—before he *prefumes* to defcant upon the *fpirit* of it; or he will bewilder himfelf and his readers; and what is worfe, be fetting forth many things as the *word* of GOD, which are not fo.

Such people there always were.—Among the *heathen*—*Democritus oculos fibi eruit, quòd mulieres fine concupifcentia afpicere non poffit. Sed nihil aliud fecit, quam quod fatuitatem fuam urbi manifeftam fecit.* Tertull, in Apologet.—
" *Democritus* plucked out his eyes, becaufe he could not
" behold women without concupifcence. But he did nothing elfe than expofe his folly to the city."—

What else is the meaning of the *tenth* commandment, which says, *Thou shalt not covet thy neighbour's wife?* or of Prov. xxiv. 9.

The
Among the *Jews*, we read of a sect of *Pharisees*, who were called *Talpæ* or *Moles*, because they walked about with their eyes shut or blindfolded, lest they should behold a woman; and, says my author—*sæpe in muros impegerint & sanguis profusus fuerit*—" They often got bloody noses " by running against walls." See Christoph. Gerson, in Talmud. p. 24.

We are told of a *Jesuit*, called *Alphonsus Rodicius*, who, though he served at the mass 44 years, and had given absolution to thousands, had never beheld the face of a woman in all that time. Geneal. Mar. 31 Oct. p. 577.

Another was so *pious*, and so avoided the sight of all women, that he would not even see his *own mother*. Ib.— To what does this amount?—A delusion of the Devil— an arraignment of the wisdom and holiness of the CREATOR in our formation, by condemning as evil, those appetites, which He hath implanted in our nature, for the purpose of incitement to marriage, and, of course, to the continuance of the human species. To avoid such errors, one safe rule may be laid down, viz. That no *desire* is, or can be *unlawful*, but where the object of it is *unlawful* for us to possess. Let us keep to this, and then we shall not be whittling away the strong, noble, manly sense of scripture, into the ridiculous whims and fancies of visionaries and enthusiasts.

Notwithstanding the length of this note, I cannot help taking notice of a text, which is supposed to be the ground of the *Talpæan* austerity above-mentioned, and which is as likely to be abused to the purposes of *self-righteousness*, as that of Matt. v. 28. It is that of *Job* xxxi. 1. *I made a covenant with mine eyes, why then should I think upon a maid?* Job is asserting his integrity with respect to many circumstances of his life and conversation, and among the rest, with regard to fleshly incontinence; and this chapter begins with—*I have made a covenant with mine eyes*.—ומה אתבונן על בתולה—*Et quid considerabo in virgine.* Mont. Our translation is near enough the original, to give us the sense of it; however, that *sense* must be interpreted according to the analogy of the *divine law*, and not according to the mere *sound* of

the

The thought of foolishness is sin? The word זמת which we translate *the thought*, signifies the words; for *Job* (ver. 2, 3.) shews us, that he means to express a very grievous offence, such as excludes from *all portion of* GOD, and *inheritance in the kingdom of heaven* (Comp. 1 Cor. vi. 9.) and which bringeth *destruction on workers* of such *iniquity*. This is sufficient to make it impossible that *Job* can speak the truth, if nothing more is meant than is literally expressed. In the first place, *Job* had made no such *covenant*, &c. *as not to think on a maid*, for he had married one. Secondly, this can be no sin, simply considered in itself; for if so, men must plunge into sin, or there must be an end of the world; which but ill agrees with—INCREASE and *multiply*, &c.

Some have therefore construed this to mean, that *Job* was content with *one wife*, and verged not towards *concubinage* or *polygamy*.—Neither of these were forbidden or condemned by the *law*, but, as has been shewn at large, practised openly by the greatest *saints*, and allowed and blessed of GOD; therefore cannot answer to ver. 2, 3.

For which reasons this text is very difficult to interpret agreeably to the analogy of faith, unless the word בתולה—*maid*, or *virgin*—be taken here, for what it certainly imports elsewhere, בתולה ארשה—*virgo desponsata*—a *betrothed* or *espoused virgin*, who still was called בתולה. See Joel i. 8. and perhaps Jer. ii. 32. Comp. If. lxi. 10. latter part. See Deut. xxii. 23, 24, 25.

That *Job* should not suffer himself to *think* on (i. e. so as to *desire*) such a one, is of a piece with what he says, ver. 9, 10, 11, 12; for such a one was, in the eye of the law, *another man's wife*. Deut. xxii. 23, 24. So that *Job* is not to be understood as making *transgression where there is no law*, like the *Talpæ* and the *Jesuit* above-mentioned; but as protesting his innocence with respect to *adultery*, in every sense of the word, as not suffering himself to *look on*, so as to *lust after*, a *virgin betrothed*, much less to commit *actual adultery*, by *defiling his neighbour's wife* ver. 9, 10, 11, 12.

Solomon *Jarchi* construes the passage very liberally indeed, or rather *paraphrases* it thus, viz. "*I made a covenant*, &c. that I would have no knowledge of any man's wife." See *Chappelowe* on Job, vol. i. p. 425.

a *wicked*

a *wicked imagination, prava aut mala cogitatio.* Mont.—*an evil thought.* The *law is spiritual,* says *Paul, I had not known lust* (i. e. known it to be *evil)* except the law had said, *Thou shalt not covet.* Rom. vii. 7. Therefore, when our *Saviour* preached on the *Mount,* He did not make, ordain, or publish any *new law,* nor did he make the law more *spiritual* than when published at *Mount Sinai;* but He set it forth, and vindicated it from the false glosses of the *Scribes* and *Pharisees,* who, in their teaching, dwelt on the *outward* letter only, throwing a veil of obscurity over its *spiritual* sense and meaning. The *seventh* commandment was just as *spiritual* under the Old Testament as under the *New*. The very thought of *adultery* in DAVID, was as sinful as it would have been in *Saint Paul.* How then can it be imagined, that the commandment against *adultery* meant not as much in the times of *Moses* and the *prophets,* as in the days of CHRIST and His *Apostles?* or, in other words, as much under the Old Testament as under the *New?* How can it be thought to condemn any thing amongst *Christians,* which it did not equally condemn amongst the *Jews? Whatsoever things the law saith, it saith to them that are under the law* (whether *Jews* or *Christians)* that every mouth may be stopped, and all the world become guilty before GOD. Rom. iii. 19. If then the law ever condemned *polygamy* as *adultery, whoredom,* or *fornication,* it certainly does it *now*; but, as hath

hath been shewn, it never did condemn it in any one instance, not only *from the beginning*, by any construction put on the *original marriage-institution*, but also for 1500 years together after the giving the law at Mount *Sinai*; therefore it never has condemned it since: for CHRIST gave no *new* meaning to this or any other of the commandments, but only vindicated and restored the *old*. What *was* murder is *now* murder—what *was* theft is *now* theft—what *was adultery* is *now* adultery—and what *was* none of these, *is* still none of these.

GOD's *law* is His *will*, and His *will* is His *law*; a change of *one* must infer a change in the *other*, and either of these a change in HIMSELF: an idea which is wholly irreconcileable with the *scripture-character* of GOD, *with whom there is no variableness, neither any shadow of turning. James* i. 17.

Men may cobble, and vamp, and alter, and repeal laws, and indeed it must be so, as mischiefs, which escape all human prescience and foresight, must daily arise; but it cannot be so with OMNISCIENCE. *All things are present and open to Him. Heb.* iv. 13. He ordained the propagation of mankind—*He blessed them*, and said *unto them, Be fruitful, and multiply, and replenish the earth.* Gen. i. 28. He made the woman, and *brought her to the man*, and said—*A man shall cleave to his wife,* Gen. ii. 22, 24. (by which expression, according to St. *Paul*'s * interpretation, 1 Cor. vi. 1 ɔ,

---
* See before, 19, 20, and note.

vi. 15, 16. is meant the act of † copulation or *marriage)* and *they shall be one flesh*—thus creating between them so indissoluble a bond, as never to be divided more. Though these words were spoken immediately by ADAM, yet, doubtless, he spake under the influence of the *divine Spirit*, as may appear from CHRIST's manner of applying the words, Matt. xix. 4, 5. and may therefore, as what MOSES and the *prophets* spake under the same holy influence, be styled —" *The word* of GOD." The circumscription and regulation of the whole was provided for by fixed, determined, and immutable laws, calculated for all times, places, and ages of the world, wherein He should be pleased to make them known. These laws, on the establishment of the church, on its deliverance out of ÆGYPT, were given to MOSES, and enforced and explained by him, and the subsequent *prophets*, under the immediate command and teaching of GOD; and continue, like the *holy Lawgiver Himself*, one and the *same* for ever. Who *may* marry together, and who may *not*—what is a lawful marriage in GOD's account, and what is not so, was not left to the uncertain or presump-

† This is the literal import of דבק באשתו—*agglutinatus erit in uxore sua*. Mont. (See before p. 20. note,) ill expressed by—*shall cleave to his wife*.—The *verb* Προσκολληθήσεται, LXX. Matt. xix. 5. and Eph. v. 31.—and the *participle* Κολλωμενος, 1 Cor. vi. 16.—are in the *passive voice*.—— For the *Author's* idea of the word *marriage*, see before, p. 48. note.

tuous

tuous determinations of mankind, but immutably fixed by *written laws* of God. To these it is our bounden duty to conform, and to say to all subsequent inventions of men, as well those which forbid marriage entirely, as those who would put *asunder those whom* God *hath joined together*, under pretence of greater purity and holiness, as the angel did to Peter, Acts x. 15. *What* God *hath cleansed, that call thou not common or unclean.*

I have mentioned the law being explained by the *prophets*. These were extraordinary messengers which God raised up, and sent forth under a special commission; not only to *foretell things to come*, but to *preach* to the people, to hold forth the *law*, to point out their defections from it, and to call them to repentance, under the severest terms of God's displeasure, unless they obeyed. Their commission, in these respects, we find recorded, Is. lviii. 1. *Cry aloud, spare not, lift up thy voice like a trumpet: shew my people their transgressions, and the house of Jacob their sins.* This commission was to be faithfully executed, at the peril of the *prophet*'s own destruction, as appears from the solemn charge given to *Ezekiel*, chap. iii. 18. *When I say to the wicked, Thou shalt surely die, and thou givest him not warning, nor speakest to warn the wicked to save his life, the same wicked man shall die in his iniquity, but his blood will I require at thine hand.*

These *prophets* executed their commission very unfaithfully towards God and the people, as well as moſt dangerouſly for themſelves, if *polygamy* was a ſin againſt GOD's law; for it was the common practice of the * whole nation, from the *prince on the throne* to the *loweſt of the people*; and yet neither ISAIAH, JEREMIAH, nor any one of the *prophets*, bore the leaſt teſtimony againſt it. They reproved them ſharply and plainly for *defiling their neighbours wives*; as *Jer.* v. 8; xxix. 23.— in which fifth chapter, we not only find the *prophet* bearing teſtimony againſt *adultery*, but againſt *whoredom* and *fornication*, ver. 7. for that they aſſembled themſelves by *troops in the harlots houſes*. Not a word againſt *polygamy*. How is it poſſible, in any reaſon, to think that this, if a ſin, ſhould never be mentioned as ſuch, by GOD—by † MOSES—or any *one* of the *prophets*?

Here I may particularly mention *Elijah* the *Tiſhbite*, who could with truth ſay of himſelf, 1 Kings xix. 10. קנא קנאתי—*zelando zelatus ſum*. Mont. Which emphatical reduplication we tranſlate by—*I have been* VERY JEALOUS *for the* LORD OF HOSTS. This holy man was fired with zeal for GOD's law, and was a moſt faithful and undaunted reprover of ſin, even to the very face of *king Ahab*

---

* *Joſephus* calls it πάτριον—which anſwers to what we mean by the word *national*.

† Moſes mentions all the ſins of the *nations* of *Canaan*, as warnings to the *Iſraelites* not to be guilty of them; but their *polygamy* is no where mentioned or condemned, nor are the *Jews* warned againſt it. See *Lev.* xviii. 3, 24, &c.

(who

(who at that time reigned in *Ifrael*, and was doubtlefs a *polygamift*, by his having *feventy fons*) yet not a word is faid about his *polygamy*; which could hardly have been omitted, had it been a fin againft either the *primary* law of marriage, or the *feventh* commandment. The fame zeal which led *Elijah* to tell *Ahab*, that *he and his father's houfe had troubled Ifrael, by forfaking the commandments of the* LORD, *and following Baalim*, muft furely have led him to reprove *Ahab*'s polygamy, had that alfo been a *forfaking the commandments of* JEHOVAH. The fcripture, 1 Kings xvi. 31. ftrongly remarks, as an aggravation of *Ahab*'s fuperlative wickednefs, that he married an *idolatrefs*, contrary to Deut. vii. 3. Had his *polygamy* been contrary to *Exod.* xx. 14. this would hardly have efcaped the reproofs of the prophet *Elijah*, who did not forget *Jezabel*, and the *prophets which ate at her table*. 1 Kings xviii. 19.

We may alfo obferve that *Ezekiel*, ch. xxii. fets down very particularly the fins of *lewdnefs*, which the *Jews* were addicted to in his day, ver. 10, 11. but not a word of *polygamy* is there to be found.

Although it be true, that none of the *prophets before the captivity* mention it as a *fin*, yet did not MALACHI, after the *return from the captivity*, fpeak of it, and in very fevere terms *condemn* it? thus clofing the canon of the Old Teftament with a moft awful reprehenfion of it? Mal. ii. 14, 15.

As this famous paſſage is taken for granted to be a condemnation of *polygamy* under the Old Teſtament, let us examine it, and we ſhall find that it does not even relate to the ſubject: if it did, it would be very ſtrange, that ſo material a point ſhould eſcape *all* the *prophets* that went before him, *Moſes* himſelf not excepted. This ſingle circumſtance ſhould make one ſuſpicious of the common interpretation given to this portion of ſcripture by the general run of *commentators*, who, miſtaking the *ſound* of the words for the *ſenſe* of the text, have followed one another like ſheep, who keep the ſame track, only becauſe others have gone before them. The words, as they ſtand in our tranſlation, are theſe— THE LORD *hath been witneſs between thee and the wife of thy youth, againſt whom thou haſt dealt treacherouſly: yet ſhe is thy companion and the wife of thy covenant. And did not He make one? yet hath He the reſidue of the ſpirit. And wherefore one? That He might ſeek a godly ſeed. Therefore take heed to your ſpirit, and let none deal treacherouſly againſt the wife of his youth; for the* LORD GOD *of* ISRAEL *ſaith, that he hateth* PUTTING AWAY.

The *laſt* words are a key to the reſt, and ſhew, that the inſtance in which they *dealt treacherouſly with their wives*, was *putting them away*; and this, in order to take *heathen* women in their room. This is manifeſt from ver. 11. JUDAH *hath dealt treacherouſly*, and 'n abomination is committed in ISRAEL and \RUSALEM; for JUDAH *hath prophaned the holineſs*

holiness of the LORD *which he loved, and hath married the daughter of a strange god.*

EZRA *, who lived about this time, hath recorded the fact at large, and fully explains the matter; *chap. ix.* 1. *The people of* ISRAEL *and the priests have not separated themselves from the people of the lands, for they have taken of their daughters for themselves, and for their sons, and the holy seed have mingled themselves with the people of those lands.*

Ver. 10. *And now, O* LORD, *what shall we say after this? for we have forsaken thy commandments, which thou hast commanded by thy servants the prophets,* saying, *The land which ye go to possess is an unclean land,* &c.

Ver. 12. *Now therefore give not your daughters unto their sons, neither take their daughters to your sons,* &c.

Chap. x. 2. *We have trespassed against our* GOD, *and have taken strange wives of the people of the land. Now therefore let us make a covenant with our* GOD, *to put away all the wives, and such as are born of them,* ver. 3.

The *putting away* these heathen women was a *duty*, and this by the positive law of GOD. For GOD having, as it were, forbidden the *banns* in express words (Deut. vii. 3.) their marriages were absolutely null and void *ab initio*; they could contract no valid marriage whatsoever with them, and therefore must *put them away*. This affords us a strong proof of the *lawfulness* of *polygamy*, where the

† See also *Nehemiah* xiii. 23—29.

woman was not excepted againſt, as by the law above mentioned, or by ſome other: for if this were otherwiſe, we ſhould hear of *putting away* all but the *firſt* in all caſes. GOD would not have ſuffered any marriage which was contrary to the *ſeventh* commandment, any more than thoſe which were contrary to *Deut.* vii. 3. When we compare EZRA and MALACHI together, we find by the *former*, that the *Jews* took *heathen women for their wives*; and by the *latter*, that they not only did this, but *put away* their *Iſraelitiſh* wives for *that very purpoſe*. This is plainly what ver. 14. calls *dealing treacherouſly* with their wives, their divorcing them for this *unhallowed* purpoſe. There the *prophet* uſes the like arguments againſt them as he had before uſed, ver. 10. with regard to their *dealing treacherouſly with their brethren—Have we not all one father? hath not one* GOD *created us? why do we deal treacherouſly every man againſt his brother, by profaning the covenant of our fathers?* When they put away their *Jewiſh* wives, and married the *heathen* idolatrous women, they *profaned the covenant of their fathers*; that is, that command of GOD delivered to their fathers, not only in the *original* inſtitution of marriage, which forbad *putting away*, but alſo that poſitive law, Deut. vii. 3. which forbad marriage with *heathens*. They *dealt treacherouſly with their brethren*; that is to ſay, with the *parents* and *relations* of their unjuſtly-*divorced wives*, who gave them their *daughters* or *ſiſters* in marriage, to *abide* with them, not

to

to be *put away*. They *dealt treacherously also with their wives*, in *putting them away*.—Therefore the *prophet* reproves them, and calls them to repentance by the following considerations, ver. 14, 15; which I will endeavour to lay before the *reader* in a paraphrase suitable to the literal and true meaning of the *original* Hebrew, and conformable to the *analogy* of divine revelation, as delivered to us by Moses and the *prophets*. Then it will appear, that these distinguished servants of God were not guilty of concealing, disguising, or dissembling the truth; nor God Himself capable of suffering His *seventh* commandment, as well as the *original institution of marriage*, to be transgressed, not only with impunity, but *allowance*, uniformly through so many ages, or of leaving His church and people utterly ignorant of His mind and will touching so important a matter, for all that time,

ולא אחד עשה—*Et ne unus fecit?* Mont.— *And did not one make?* Here our *commentators*, misled by our *translators*, and these by the vulgar error of the *sinfulness* of *polygamy*, tell us, that " these words signify God's making
" but *one woman* at the beginning; He had the
" *residue of the spirit*, and therefore could
" have made *more women* for Adam if He
" had pleased." One misfortune attending so ignorant a comment, is, that the word אחד cannot signify *one woman*, unless, among other changes, *women* were of the *masculine* gender under the Old Testament, though of the *feminine* under the New Testament;

tament; for אחד is certainly of the *masculine* gender—אחת is the feminine—See Judges ix. 53.—אשה אחת—*mulier una.* Mont. & al freq This, besides an undue transposition of the words, is, I take it, a conclusive reason for saying they mistake the passage. It is not—*Did not he make One?*—but—*Did not One* make?* like ver. 10. *Have we not all* ONE *Father? Did not* ONE GOD *create*
" *us?* Did not *One,* or THE ONE, make
" both you and your *Jewish wives?* Did
" He not form both of you—(see Deut.
" xxxii. 6.) *naturally* of the same seed of
" *Abraham—spiritually* by the same holy dis-
" pensation and ordinances?—At ver. 14. it
" is said—והיא חברתך—*she is thy companion,*
" or associate—ואשת בריתך—and *a wife,* or
" woman, *of thy covenant*—i. e. a partaker
" with thee in the *covenant* made with *Abra-*
" *ham* and his seed after him. So the *prophet*
" Zech. ix. 11. where GOD says to the *daugh-*
" *ter of Zion*—As for thee.—בדם בריתך—*In*
" (or by) *the blood* THY COVENANT *I have*
" *sent forth thy prisoners,* &c. where בריתך—
" *thy covenant*—compared with the context
" in this place of *Malachi,* clearly determines
" the meaning to be as above, and it stands
" here as opposed to the *daughter of a strange*
" GOD, ver. 11.—ושאר רוח לו—And *He hath*

---

* If the attentive reader will compare the אחד—*one,* in this place, with אל אחד—*one* GOD, ver. 10. surely he must see, that the same *Almighty Person* is meant. There he is said to *create*—here to *make.* Comp. Gen. ii. 3. latter part.

" (or

" (or hath He not ?) the *remainder of the Spi-*
" *rit*—Hath He not the same *power* He ever
" had ?—Is His hand shortened at all, so
" that He cannot complete your restoration
" if He pleases, or punish you still more se-
" verely, if you continue disobedient to His
" commandments ? *Spirit* is here used for
" *power**, mighty, but especially *irresistible*
" *power*; as Ps. cxxxix. 7. Is. lix. 19. Is.
" lxiii. 14. Is. xxxiv. 16.—ומה האחד מבקש
" And what did THE ONE *seek?* זרע אלהים
" —*a* † *seed of* GOD—*an* ‡ *holy seed* (see Ez-
" ra ix. 2. compare ver. 14.) therefore *take*
" *heed to your spirit*—that is, your *temper—af-*
" *fections*"—as רוח is very often applied, (see
Numb. xiv. 24. 1 Sam. i. 15.) " *and none of*
" *you deal treacherously against the wife of thy*
" *youth*, (whom thou hast married when a

---

* So the *power* of the *Spirit* is often used for the *Spirit itself.* Comp. Is. xxxii. 15. Luke xxiv. 49. Acts i. 8. See also *Judges* xiii. 25; xiv. 19; xvi. 17, 20. Rom. i. 4. with 1 Cor. vi. 14. & al. freq. In an old edition of the *Bible*, printed in the year 1615, there are short notes added in the margin; and in the note on the word *Spirit*, in this text, it is explained to mean *power and virtue*.

† Et quid Unus quærit nisi semen DEI. *Vulg.*

‡ This can have nothing to do with *polygamy*, because, if it had, we should have hardly found it *allowed* of GOD, and practised by his saints; or, in fact, have found some of the most distinguished and blessed men that ever lived, the offspring of *polygamous* marriages; witness holy *Joseph*, and the prophet *Samuel*. Besides all this, we may observe, that the *Jews*, who are in this place of *Ezra* emphatically styled *the holy seed*, were descended from the *twelve sons* of *Jacob*, half of which were born under *polygamy*.

" virgin)

"virgin) by *putting her away*, and *taking* "these *idolatresses; for I the* LORD *hate putting away.*" The confideration of the relation they stood in to JEHOVAH—He their common Father—they His profeffing *children*, was one argument againft their feparating—another was, that, as the LORD fought a *godly feed* in their offspring, by their being devoted to Him in their earlieft infancy, then brought up in the *nurture and admonition of the* LORD, this defign would be defeated by their taking *idolatrous* women, who, inftead of devoting the children to JEHOVAH, would be for bringing them up to the * *worſhip* of their *idols*, and an *ungodly feed* be the confequence. See *Deut.* vii. 3, 4. Laftly, GOD had forbidden *divorce* from the beginning, (fee Gen. ii. 24.) for He *hateth putting away* at any rate; but how much more to fee His own profeffing daughters *put away*, that His own profeffing fons might *marry the daughters of a ſtrange God?* This was indeed *doing an abominable thing which* GOD *hated.* Jer. xliv. 4.

This I take to be a clear, confiftent view of this famous paffage, and agrees exactly with what EZRA fays, chap. ix. 9. &c. and chap. x. 2. &c. who did not *rend his mantle and garment, and pluck the hair off his head*

---

* We find that thefe idolatrous women laid a fure foundation for this, by bringing up their children in the knowledge of the heathen tongues of their feveral countries, fo that they could not underftand the language of GOD'S law. See Neh. xiii. 23, 24.

and

and beard, and sit down astonished, because the people did what their fathers ABRAM, JACOB, DAVID, &c. had done without the *least reproof*, and had been constantly, openly, avowedly praised by the holiest of their forefathers, without the least * scruple on their part, or condemnation on GOD's part—but because they had married *heathen* women, and, as appears by *Mal.* ii. 14. had *dealt treacherously* against the *Jewish lawful* wives, by *putting them away* in order to do it.

As to the notion expressed by *commentators*, in their apparently misconceived ideas of this text of MALACHI—that because GOD created but *one man* and *one woman* at first, therefore he intended that " no man should have more " than one wife at a time ever after," I do humbly conceive, that, if GOD had *meant* so, He would somewhere have *said* so, and not have left it to the wisdom of men to put their † interpretations on what He was pleased

to

---

* When *Joseph* was solicited by *Potiphar*'s wife, he answered with abhorrence—*How can I do this great wickedness, and sin against* GOD ? Gen. xxxix. 9. latter part.—But when *Abraham*'s wife *Sarah* proposed her husband's taking *Hagar to wife*, Gen. xvi. 2, 3. he does it without the least objection. So *Jacob* took *Rachel* after *Leah*, there being then no law against marrying a *wife's sister*. This, and the many other instances, clearly prove, that the wisest and best of GOD's saints never dreamt of *polygamy*'s having any relation to the sin of *adultery*.

† As to putting our construction on any acts of GOD, so as to draw them into *precedents*, unless clearly instructed by Him so to do, it would in many cases be attended

to do; for *who hath known the mind of the* LORD, *and who hath been his counsellor?* Rom. xi. 34. Some may argue, that becaufe it was faid—" *A man shall cleave to his wife,* not " *wives,* therefore it is unlawful for a man " to have *two* or *more wives* in * fucceffion,

tended with great mifchiefs—for inftance: Suppofe we were to argue for *brothers* and *sisters* intermarrying, becaufe this muft have been the cafe among the immediate children of *Adam and Eve?* the creation of only *one man* and *one woman,* would at leaft be as good an argument *for* inceft, as *against* polygamy. But it can have no weight in either cafe, becaufe GOD, by a pofitive law, (Lev. xviii. 9.) prohibited the *first,* and by as pofitive a law (Deut. xxi. 15—17.) allowed the *second.* It pleafed GOD, that the whole *human nature* fhould refide in one common *fœderal head,* who was to be the common *representative* of all his fubfequent naturally-engendered offspring; and by *one woman* taken out of *himself,* to convey that nature which was in him to his own immediate children, and by them to his pofterity, to the end of the world. Let any one read *Rom.* v. with attention, and confider in what refpects *Adam* was a *figure of Him that was to come* (ver. 14.) and then it will be feen, that no man who ever *was,* or *will be* naturally engendered of the offspring of *Adam,* can have been, or be in the fame circumftances and fituation that *Adam* was. Wherefore a precedent againft *polygamy* is no more to be drawn from him, than againft natural generation from *Eve*'s being made out of *one of his ribs,* or from his own being immediately formed out of the *dust of the earth.*

* There was a time in the *Christian* church, when this was looked upon as only " a more fpecious and de- " corous kind of *adultery,*" and reckoned *infamous.*

The *Montanists* affirmed *second* marriages to be as fcandalous and *sinful* as *fornication.* In the *three* firft ages of the *church* " *second marriages* were reputed *scan-* " *dalous,* nay they were *condemned* by fome perfons." *Dupin,* Eccl. Hift. vol. i. 182. Engl. tranfl. But more of this hereafter.

" and

"and can only have *one* so long as he lives, because *Adam* had but *one*." This sort of conceits is like supposing that GOD forbad the wearing cloth, or silk, or linen, because He *cloathed* our first parents *with skins*. Gen. iii. 21; or supposing, like those mad *heretics* of the *second* century, who called themselves *Adamites*, that *Christians* are to meet together stark *naked* without any *shame*, because it is said (Gen. ii. 25.) ADAM and EVE *were naked, and were not ashamed*. If we take upon ourselves to interpret this or any act of GOD merely by our imaginations, we take upon us what does not belong to us. We are told, Deut. xxix. 29. SECRET THINGS *belong unto the* LORD *our* GOD, *but those things which are* REVEALED, *to us and our children for ever, that we may do all the words of His law*.

That GOD might have created 10,000 *men*, and as many *women*, is certain. Why He did not, He hath no where told us, any more than why He created only *one man* and *one* * *woman*. This and all things else are to be resolved

---

* *Milton* represents *Adam* as saying——
—— —— O why did GOD,
Creator wise, that peopled highest heav'n
With spirits masculine, create at last
This novelty on earth, this fair defect
Of Nature, and not fill the world at once
With men as angels without feminine,
Or find some other way to generate
Mankind? Par. Lost, B. 10.
We may presume that GOD made the rest of the animal creation by *pairs*, the *male and female*—Comp. Gen. i. 20—25. with Gen. vi. 19. Gen. vii. 2, 3, 9, 14—16:

resolved into His *own good pleasure, and the counsel of his own will*. Eph. i. 11. Rev. iv. 11. Our attempting to account for any of His holy acts or dispensations, any farther than the revelation of His word expressly authorizes us, is to be wise *above what is written*, to involve ourselves in endless mazes of error, till—*professing ourselves wise, we become fools.* Rom. i. 22.

God's *bringing the woman to the man*—that solemn denunciation—*therefore shall a man leave father and mother, and cleave unto his wife, and they shall be one flesh*—form a conclusive argument against wanton and causeless *divorce*; and are expressly made use of by Christ for that purpose in His dispute with the *Pharisees*, Matt. xix. 4, 5; but it is no where, in the whole scripture, made use of as an argument against *polygamy*. There

---

14—16: therefore, to draw arguments against *polygamy* (which, by the way, the scriptures have no where done) from a similar creation of the human species, would, if pursued to the utmost, prove *too much*, and of course prove *nothing*. So when God was about to destroy the earth by the *deluge*, he commanded *Noah* to come into the *ark*—" *Thou and thy sons, and thy wife, and thy sons* " *wives with thee*," in all *eight persons* (see 1 Pet. iii. 20) " and of *every living thing of all flesh*, TWO OF EVERY " SORT—*they shall be male and female*—*seven pair* of " the *clean*, and two *pair* of the *unclean*, the MALE " AND HIS FEMALE."—איש ואשתו—*Virum & uxorem ejus*. Mont. So that in the preservation of the *brutal*, as well as of the *human* species, we read of them in *pairs*—and these *pairs* are described by the same *Hebrew* words, which, in other parts of the scriptures, we render—*a man and his wife*.—For the *exact words* of these abridged *passages*, see the scriptures above referred to.

were,

were, doubtless, opportunities enough in the *antediluvian*, as well as the *postdiluvian* world, to have given occasion for it, had any * such thing been intended.

The first instance of *polygamy* which is recorded, we find Gen. iv. 19. *And* LAMECH *took unto him two wives, the name of one was*

* One weighty reason for the creation of only *one man* and *one woman* at first, may perhaps be gathered from Acts xvii. 26. where it is said—*He hath made of* ONE BLOOD *all nations of men, for to dwell on all the face of the earth.* Had more men and women than *Adam* and *Eve* been created at first, this strict affinity of relationship *by blood* could not have existed; but this was wisely and graciously contrived, as a reason for, and cement of, brotherly love—as a means of hiding pride, and boasting of one above another, with respect to their original pedigree; so that none, on this account, should despise or set *at nought his brother.* This thought is well expressed in that well-known epitaph:

> Nobles and heralds, by your leave,
> Here lie the bones of *Matthew Prior*,
> The son of *Adam* and of *Eve*, —
> Let *Bourbon* or Nassau go higher!

Although, in this corrupt and mixed state of things, civil government is necessary, therefore outward distinctions of men are necessary; for without these no civil polity could exist; yet, *in that day*, when the *governors* and *governed* shall appear before the *Great Governor of all*, they will be constrained to say, with *Joseph's* brethren, Gen. xlii. 11. *we are all one man's sons*;—and then will know, however little attention they may give to it now, that GOD is *no respecter of persons.* See Acts x. 34. If these humbling considerations were improved as they ought, they would furnish us with motives of humility, benevolence, brotherly-kindness, long-suffering, mercy, and charity to each other, beyond all the arguments of the wisest moralists of *Greece* and *Rome.* See Mal. ii. 10.

ADAH,

ADAH, *the other* ZILLAH. Here our commentators think they have found out the *sin* of *polygamy*—" It was one of the degenerate " race of Cain," saith one, " that first transgressed the law of marriage, that *two only* " should be one flesh." These are the words of one of the wisest and best (Mr. *Henry)* among our *English* commentators, and serve to shew how far men will go to support a popular notion, or pre-conceived opinion, even to the * *corrupting of the Bible*. There

are

---

* See *Henry* on Gen. iv. 19. When I saw the word ONLY interpolated by Mr. *Henry*, I really thought it a *corruption* worthy the *church of Rome*. In this I find I was not mistaken, for the *council of Trent* thus dogmatizes—" *Adam* did pronounce the bond of matrimony to " be perpetual, and that ONLY *two persons may be joined* " *therein*; a thing more plainly declared by CHRIST." See *Brent.* 784.—Now, here is an *interpolation* of the word ONLY, and a downright *lye* to justify it—for where does CHRIST *more plainly declare*, that ONLY *two persons* can be joined together in marriage?

Mr. *Henry* goes on to tell us, that " Hitherto *one man* " had but *one wife* at a time."—(How did he know that? See *Le Clerc* on Gen. iv. 19. and Thelyph. vol. ii. p. 161. n.)—" But *Lamech* took two—*From the begin-* " *ning it was not so*"—this he would prove from Mal. ii. 15. which is nothing to the purpose. See above p. 132—139. He then falls into the usual misapplication and perversion of Matt. xix. 8. where the words " *in the beginning it was not so*"—clearly and necessarily refer to the preceding sentence, which mentions nothing but " *putting away their wives*."

Mr. *Henry* concludes his annotation on Gen. iv. 19. with two practical inferences :—" 1. That those who " desert GOD's church and *commandments*" (which said *commandments* are, on this occasion, the entire *forgery* and *invention* of the *commentator)* " lay themselves open to " all manner of temptation.—2. That when an *ill* cus-

" tom

are no such words as "*two only*" in the law of marriage referred to.—It stands, Gen. ii. 24. *they shall be one flesh*; and, as mentioned by CHRIST, Matt. xix. 5. οἱ δυο—*they twain shall be one flesh*. So Mark x. 8. Had the words "*two only*" been there, we should not have red so frequently afterwards of GOD's countenancing, or His saints practising *polygamy*, any more than of *His* countenancing, and *their* practising *adultery*. I must here take notice of the *Evangelist*'s introduction of the words οἱ δυο—*they twain*, or *the twain*—which certainly was not done as an *addition* to the original words, or as an *interpolation*, in order to introduce some new *doctrine*, but merely as a sort of *paraphrase* to explain their import, sense, and meaning—that a *man* and *his wife*, though before marriage they were *two*—that is, separate, unconnected, independent of each other, so that they might or might not come together, yet afterwards they are *no more two*, separate, unconnected, independent persons, but as *one flesh*, εἰς σάρκα μίαν.—The words οἱ δυο—*the twain*—are not to be taken in their *numerical* * *sense*, for if they be, what

---

"tom is begun by *ill* men, sometimes *men* of *better characters* are, through *unwariness*, drawn in to follow them: *Jacob*, *David*, and many others, who were otherwise good men, were afterwards ensnared in *this sin*, which *Lamech* had begun."—N. B. This is called an *Exposition* of the scriptures of the Old Testament!

* Non *unitas essentialis*, sed unio seu *conjunctio mystica* vel *conjugalis* describitur.—Nold. Part. Edit. Tymp.

750,

what follows ver. 6.—*so that they are no more twain*—would not be true; for certainly a man and woman are as much *numerically* two *after* marriage, as they are *before* it, and therefore cannot be *numerically one;* but in the same sense in which they were spoken of as *two* before, they now become *one*, that is to say, in consideration of law.

The marriage destroys their unconnectedness, distinctness, and independency on each other, so that in all *legal* consideration they are *no more twain, but one flesh.* Therefore the consequence is proved which our blessed LORD meant to prove—it could not be *lawful for a man* απολυειν—*to divorce his wife for every cause*, or for *any* cause *except one*, which, of itself, divided their persons again, and amounted to a total dissolution of the marriage-bond: for to make a man live with an *adultress*, would be to make him father other people's children, defeat his own rightful heirs, and introduce that confusion into his family, which it was one grand object of the *seventh* commandment to prevent. For want of considering the words οἱ δυο—*they twain*, or *the twain*—in the *legal* sense above-mentioned, our commentators have jingled them in their fancies, till they have blundered into their *two only—two and no more:* thus interpolating and corrupting the words of the marriage-institution, as it stands recorded

---

750. " Not an *essential unity*, but an *union* or *conjunction mystical* or *conjugal* is described." Matt. xix. 5, 6. Mark x. 8.

Gen.

Gen. ii. 24. and what is worſe ſtill, making our *bleſſed Saviour* do the ſame, by repreſenting Him as uſing the words in their *numerical* ſenſe. This ſtamps untruth, nay, downright nonſenſe on what He ſays, ver. 6; for it is not true that a *man and his wife* are no more *(numerically) two*; and to ſay that perſons, who are *numerically two*, are yet *numerically one*, is downright nonſenſe. As the word *twain* is to be underſtood in a *legal* ſenſe, ſo *they ſhall be one fleſh*, cannot be underſtood in a *literal* ſenſe, as if by a kind of matrimonial *tranſubſtantiation* they became literally *one body* (ſee 1 Cor. vi. 16); but that they are ſo in a *legal ſenſe* is very certain; and therefore, as a man cannot ſeparate his *bones* from his *fleſh*, nor his *fleſh* from his *bones*, without deſtroying himſelf, ſo neither can a man *put away his wife* unjuſtly (who, in eſtimation of GOD's law, *is bone of his bone and fleſh of his fleſh*) without offending againſt the holineſs, and deſtroying the poſitive obligation of the marriage-inſtitution.

Thoſe, who by the legerdemain of this ſame *numerical* interpretation of the word *twain*, added to the *ſound* of the former clauſe of ver. 9. make CHRIST condemn *polygamy* as *adultery*, repreſent Him as uſing the word נאף—*adultery*—in an unauthorized unconformity to the *Hebrew* ſcripture (as our LORD doubtleſs ſpake in *Hebrew)*; for no where is that word uſed, to denote a man who had one wife, *taking another to her*, and *cohabiting*

with

with both (which I take to be the true and genuine notion of *polygamy*); nor is it used in *any* other sense, but to denote the *defilement of a married woman*. OUR SAVIOUR, who constantly appealed to the *Hebrew* scriptures for what he delivered to the people, can hardly be supposed to have advanced a doctrine so unsupported by *them*; and *that* before an audience of those very *Pharisees*, who we are told, Luke xi. 54. *were laying wait for him, seeking to catch something out of His mouth, that they might accuse Him*. Again—by making CHRIST declare *polygamy* to be *adultery*, they charge Him with asserting a falshood, both in point of *law* and *fact*, by declaring all such *after-taken women* not to be the real *wives* of the men who took them; for if they were, *adultery* must be out of the question. Let us examine this on the footing of scripture. It is said, 1 Sam. xxv. 42, 43, ABIGAIL *became* DAVID's *wife*, and DAVID also took AHINOAM of JEZREEL, *and they were also both of them his wives*. So witnesseth the *Holy Ghost*, and this, though ver. 44. tells us, he had at that very time *another wife* living. By saying they *were also both of them his wives* (for that must be the meaning of נשים in this context) it is making each *one flesh* with him, so that he could not *divorce* either; and if either had gone to another man, she would have been an *adultress*, and the man who took her would have been an *adulterer*. I say this, taking it for granted that the *Holy Ghost* would not have called them *his wives*, לו לנשים

לנשים—*ſibi in uxores.* Mont.—unleſs they *really were ſo.* See alſo 1 Sam. xxvii. 3.

Thus, on the authority of the *Hebrew* ſcripture, an *after-taken* woman is as much a man's *wife* who takes her, as the *firſt* is—therefore it is neither true in point of *law* or *fact,* that a man having *one wife,* and taking *another,* committeth *adultery;* for which reaſon it is * impoſſible CHRIST ſhould ever ſay ſo, and thoſe who make Him ſay ſo, wreſt His words from their true meaning.——But as this portion of ſcripture will neceſſarily fall under farther conſideration hereafter, I will now return to the hiſtory of LAMECH.

Whether he did right or wrong does not appear, for it is only ſaid—LAMECH *took him two wives.* His being " of the degenerate " race of CAIN" made it not a jot the *worſe,* or a tittle the *better,* any more than the ſame thing done by JACOB made it either the one or the other, becauſe he was " of the bleſſed " race of SETH." The invention of *muſic,* which was afterwards made ſuch conſiderable uſe of in the *temple* of GOD—of *agriculture* and the *care of cattle*—of *working* in *braſs* and

---

* It is very certain that the whole law of *Moſes,* even the *ceremonial* part of it, was at this time in all its force and obligation—therefore to repreſent CHRIST, who came to vindicate its honour, and enforce the reſpect due to it, as laying down a propoſition in direct contrariety to the whole tenor of the *Jewiſh* law, is to repreſent Him as uttering a downright falſhood, and this in the face, as it were, of the whole *Jewiſh* nation, which He ſo conſtantly referred to the writings of *Moſes,* for the truth of what He ſaid.

iron,

iron, were all found out by LAMECH's children; yet I cannot conceive that they are the less innocent in themselves, or less useful to mankind, than if they had been found out by ABRAHAM, ISAAC, and JACOB. We can only say of such observations on scripture, that they are very *silly*; but if the word of GOD is to be corrupted, in order to serve as a foundation for them, they are very *wicked*. See Deut. iv. 2. xii. 32. I only mention Mr. *Henry,* but I might name others; *one* who goes so far in corrupting the text, that he represents it as the command of GOD, that " *two, and no more,* should be *one flesh,* Gen. " ii. 24." The words simply are והיו לבשר אחד—*Et erunt in carnem unam.* Καὶ ἔσονται οἱ δύο εἰς σάρκα μίαν. Matt. xix. 5. *They twain shall be one flesh.* The words ἔσονται οἱ δύο— *they two shall be, &c.*—relate to the *man* and his *wife,* mentioned in the same verse, and answer to the והיו Gen. ii. 24. which signifies *they shall be*—meaning the איש and אשתו the *man* and his *wife,* Gen. ii. 24. So that though here be a small variation between *they shall be,* and *they twain shall be,* yet it is merely *verbal* in point of quotation; the *sense* is just the same, whether, speaking of a man and woman, we say—*they,* or—*they twain:* but adding the word *only,* or *they two and no more,* is a very material alteration, so material, as to alter the whole sense of the passage, and to make every *polygamist* that ever lived, an offender against the original *institution of marriage.* Rather than fail in this,

even

even the learned *Beza* himself will condescend to talk nonsense. On 1 Cor. vi. 16. where the *apostle* cites our Lord's words— *Two shall be one flesh*—" this οἱ δυο," says he, " is not mentioned by *Moses*, but is rightly " added, as well in this place as in Matt. " xix. 5. and Mark x. 8. because there is " only mention made of a man and of *one* " *wife*, but not of *wives*; nor is it true that a " *polygamist* is *one* with each of his several " wives, when he is rather *divided into as* " *many parts as he has wives*." Though this learned man represents a *polygamist* as *Judges* xix. 29. represents the *Levite's concubine*, whom *he divided, together with her bones, into twelve parts, and sent her into all the coasts of* Israel, yet the *polygamists* which we read of in scripture were as *entire* individuals, in a *moral* as well as a *natural* sense, as those who had but *one wife*; otherwise each woman could not have called the man * *her husband*, 1 Sam. i. 8, 22, 23. nor could each woman be called *his wife*, ver. 2. Now whatever parties, being united, in God's account are *man* and *wife*, they are also † *one flesh*, therefore

---

* It is, in our law, commonly said, that each *jointenant* is seised of the land, which he holdeth jointly, *per my & per tout*—" *by the half, or by part, and by the* " *whole*." "*Et sic totum tenet, & nihil tenet*—scil.—*totum* " *conjunctim, & nihil seperatim*, says *Lord Coke*."—"And " thus he holdeth the whole, and holdeth nothing—that " is to say, the *whole jointly*, and *nothing separately*." Coke Litt. 186. a. Litt. § 288.

† This phrase, according to the *Hebrew*, denotes all relationship, whether of *affinity* by marriage, as Gen.

fore it *is true*, "that a *polygamist* is *one* with "each † of his several wives"—that is to say, in the *legal* sense above-mentioned; nor can all the reasonings of men prove them otherwise, 'till they can prove themselves wiser than He is who declares them to be so. And I do verily believe, that if a man had *seduced* any wife of a *polygamist*, and had been arraigned before the judges of *Israel* on that statute, Deut. xxii. 22. *he* must, as well as the *woman*, have been condemned to die, notwithstanding what *Beza* has said, or what all the reasoners in the world could have said on the subject of *polygamy*, in *arrest* of judgment.

But there is a text in the Old Testament, which is looked upon by some to be a direct forbiddance of *polygamy*; for it stands in the margin of our Bibles—*Thou shalt not take one wife to another*. If this be right rendering of the *Hebrew*, then the saints of old time

---

ii. 24. or *consanguinity*. See Gen. xxix. 14. Judges ix. 2. 2 Sam. v. 1. 1 Chron. xi. 1. 2 Sam. xix. 12, 13. So that the conjuration of *Beza*, and other commentators, who have found out that a man can only be *one flesh* with *one woman*, may also find out that but *one* of his relations can be of *his bone* and of *his flesh*, or be called so with any propriety. In Lev. xviii. 6. a *man's near of kin* is in the Hebrew שאר בשרו—*remainder of his flesh*. Eng. Marg. —every near relation being, as it were, a *remnant*, or remainder of the same flesh and blood of which we ourselves consist.

† Even as CHRIST, the *husband of the church* (comp. Is. liv. 5. with 2 Cor. xi. 2.) is as really *one* with every *several* believer, as with the whole church collectively; or as the *head* is *one* with *each* and *all* the members of the body. See post.

sinned

sinned against *light, knowledge,* and *law* * with a witness! But it is translated in the text—*Neither shalt thou take a wife to her sister, to vex her, in her life-time.* Lev. xviii. 18. First, I would observe, that the marginal reading—" *one wife to another*"—disunites entirely the 18th verse from the preceding context to which it belongs; this only treats of marriages which are unlawful with respect to *affinity* and *consanguinity*. The *brother's wife* had there been spoken of, ver. 16; here, most naturally, as a necessary part of the prohibition of *incest*, the *wife's sister*. Secondly, This rendering of the text is agreeable to the grammatical sense of the *Hebrew*, which the other is not. This is demonstrably

---

* Ipsos quoque *Judæos* hanc legem de *polygamia* haud accepisse, perpetua consuetudo plures sibi ex hac gente jungentium uxores ostendit. Non autem videntur tanto impetu per *vetitum nefas* ruisse, præcipuè legis divinæ cætera studiosissimi, si expresso hujusmodi mandato hac de re cautum fuisset. Tympius in Nold. p. 30, not r.

" That the *Jews* themselves did not understand this
" law as concerning *polygamy*, their constant practice of
" marrying a plurality of wives demonstrates; for it is
" not probable that they should have rushed with such
" violence into prohibited wickedness, especially those
" who were most observant of the divine law in all other
" respects, if cautioned against it by so express a com-
" mandment."

This is certainly very *improbable*, yet not so *improbable*, as that, if *polygamy* be against the original institution of marriage, and, as such, here forbidden by a *positive law*, God should no where appear to disapprove it, or enact any *judicial law* against it, on the side of the man, as on the side of the woman. See Lev. xx. 10. where the *wife* who is defiled, and the *man* who defiles her, are condemned to *capital punishment*.

shewn

shewn in *Tympius*'s note on Lev. xviii. 18. in *Noldius*, Heb. Part. אשה p. 30. But as I find the meaning of this important paſſage better explained by the learned *Biſhop Patrick* on the place, than I can expreſs it in any words of my own, I will tranſcribe the *Biſhop*'s note as it ſtands:

"There are a great many eminent writers, who, following our marginal tranſlation *(one wife to another)* imagine that here *plurality of wives* is expreſsly forbidden by GOD, and they think there is an example to juſtify this tranſlation, *Exod.* xxvi. 3. where *Moſes* is commanded to take care that the *five curtains* of the tabernacle were coupled together, *one to its ſiſter*, as the *Hebrew* phraſe is, meaning *one to another*; which, if it were true, would ſolve ſeveral difficulties: but there are ſuch reaſons againſt it, as that I cannot think it to be the meaning. For as *more wives than one* were indulged *before* the law, ſo they were *after*. And *Moſes* himſelf ſuppoſes as much, when he provides, a man ſhould not prefer a child he had by a *beloved wife*, before one he had by her whom he *hated*, if he was the *eldeſt ſon*; which plainly intimates an allowance in his law of *more wives than one*."

Here, by the good and learned *Biſhop*'s leave, I would obſerve that he expreſſes himſelf rather inaccurately; for by ſaying— "MOSES himſelf ſuppoſes as much," and by calling the law he is mentioning, "*his* " (MOSES's)

"(Moses's) law,"—it looks as if Moses was speaking by his *own* wisdom, and establishing some law merely on his *own* authority; whereas Moses, under the immediate inspiration of the *Holy Ghost* (Numb. xi. 17, 25. and 2 Pet. i. 21.) is the mouth of God Himself to the people; to whom He says, *Deut.* iv. 5. *Behold, I have taught you statutes and judgments, even as the* Lord *commanded me, that ye should do so in the land whither ye go to possess it.* The only instance in which Moses acted by his *own* authority, was in the matter of *divorces.* When our Saviour is mentioning this, *Matth.* xix. he does not say —God *suffered,* but—Moses, *because of the hardness of your hearts, suffered you to put away your wives; but from the beginning it was not so*; plainly intimating that such *divorce* was not of God's ordaining, but merely of Moses's *permission,* as an expedient to obviate the mischiefs of his enforcing the letter of the law in every instance, by compelling them to retain their wives; thus subjecting them to their ill treatment and brutality, even to the beating and perhaps killing them. So that, in this *toleration* of *divorce* for, or upon account of, the *hardness of their hearts,* Moses might say as Paul, 1 *Cor.* vii. 12. *To such speak I,* not *the* Lord—but as to other things, not I, but the Lord, ver. 10.—The *Bishop* proceeds—" And so we find expressly their
" *kings* might have, though not a *multitude,*
" *Deut.* xvii. 17; and their *best king,* who
" red God's law *day and night,* and could
" not

" not but understand it, took *many* wives
" without any reproof: nay, GOD gave him
" more than he had before, by delivering his
" (late) master's *wives* to him, 2 Sam. xii. 8.
" And besides all this, MOSES, speaking all
" along in this chapter of *consanguinity* and
" *affinity*, it is reasonable, as *Schindlerus* ob-
" serves, to conclude he doth so here, not of
" *one woman to another*, but of one * *sister to*
" *another*. There being also the like reason
" to understand the word *sister* properly in
" this place, as the words *daughter* or *mother*
" in others, ver. 17, and chap. xx. 14.
" where he forbids a man to take a woman
" and *her mother*, or a woman and *her daugh-*
" *ter*, as *Theodoric Hackspan* sufficiently notes.

" The meaning therefore is, that though
" *two wives at a time*, or *more*, were permitted
" in those days, no man should take two
" *sisters* (as JACOB formerly did, before there
" was any positive law against it) begotten of
" the *same father*, or born of the *same mother*,
" whether legitimately or illegitimately,
" (which, though it may seem prohibited
" before, because the marriage of a *brother's*
" *wife* is forbidden) yet it is here directly
" prohibited, as other marriages are which
" were implicitly forbidden before; for
" ver. 7. the marriage of a *son* with his *mo-*
" *ther* is forbidden, and ver. 10. the marri-
" age of a *father* with his *daughter*."

* It is to be observed that אחות is used *four* times in other parts of the chapter, and necessarily signifies, as our translators have rendered it—*a sister*. So Lev. xx. 17, 19.

To

To the above remarks of the learned and judicious *Bishop Patrick*, I will venture to add a conjecture of my own, the solidity of which must be submitted to the *reader*'s determination. It is very certain that at ver. 16. the marriage of a *brother's wife* is forbidden, and as the *wife's sister* is thereby virtually or implicitly forbidden to marry the *sister's husband*, it might be supposed that there was little occasion to mention the *wife's sister* in direct terms afterwards, ver. 18. But the necessity of this is apparent, when we recollect the precedent of JACOB, which the *Jews* would probably have urged against an *interpretative* prohibition of such a thing, at ver. 16. It was certainly *no sin* in JACOB, because there was *no law* against it; but after this positive law, it could not be done *without sin*, for—*sin is the transgression of the law.*

As there was but *one* man and *one* woman at first, the peopling of the world must have been carried on between much nearer relations, and therefore there could be no law to forbid marriages of this sort. So after the flood, when but *eight persons*, and those all of one family, were left of mankind, we find, for many ages, no laws enacted against marrying within those degrees of relationship, which were afterwards expressly prohibited. But when the * *reason* ceased, the *thing itself*
was

---

* After the *Exodus*, the *Israelites* were restrained from marrying within certain degrees of consanguinity, which had been, till then, permitted, to prevent their taking wives

was to cease, as demonstrably appears by GOD's enacting the positive laws against marrying within certain degrees of *consanguinity* and *affinity*; subject nevertheless, like all other of His general laws, to such exceptions, restraints, or qualifications, as He in his infinite wisdom should see expedient. Some of them carry their own reasons with them, others do not, but doubtless all equally wise, as equally the dispensations of *Omniscience*.

By the way, I cannot help observing it as a very extraordinary thing, that the *Christian* churches should adopt one part of the law respecting marriages, and pay no regard to the rest of it. They have made the *eighteenth* chapter of *Leviticus*, from ver. 6 to ver 18, inclusive, a part of our religion; so Exod. xx. 14. and some other passages of the law. But why this, and not the rest of the whole law of GOD, where marriage, as His ordinance relating to all mankind, is concerned? Is not this proceeding of *Christian churchmen*, like that of the *Jewish*, *Mal.* ii. 9. where GOD complains—*Ye have not kept my ways, but have been partial in the law?* The man who

---

wives from among the idolatrous nations with whom they lived.

This was the reason which *Abraham* gave, for chusing a wife for *Isaac* from his own kindred, *Gen.* xxiv. 3, & seq. and his descendents for following his example, *Gen.* xxviii. 1, & alib. but which was now entirely ceased, by their being so multiplied; so that they could easily find wives, without being necessitated to marry their near relations, or to contract marriages with the *heathen*. See Ant. Univ. Hist. vol. iii. p. 140.

renders

renders a solid reason for adopting *Exod.* xx. to ver. 17, inclusive, and Lev. xviii. from ver. 6 to ver. 18, inclusive, as well as many other parts of that chapter, and at the same time rejecting *Exod.* xxii. 16. and *Deut.* xxii. 28, 29, as touching the *moral* intendment of them, will perform a very difficult task, unless he can prove that marrying *a wife's sister*, for instance, is a greater crime, and of more evil tendency to mankind, as well as more inimical to the interests of *civil society*, than *enticing a virgin—debauching* her—and then * *abandoning* her to *infamy* and *prostitutution*; or, that though this was a *sin* in the days of *Moses*, yet it is *no sin* now, and therefore the positive commandments which GOD enacted to prevent it, are no longer to be considered of any force or obligation.

It is true, that we do not keep *precisely* the † *seventh day*, as the *Christian Sabbath*, looking

upon

---

* This is what the *Jews* do not suffer to be done to this hour—if a *single man* debauches a virgin, he is obliged to *marry her*—if a *married man* does so, he is obliged to maintain her as long as he lives. This in countries where *polygamy* is not allowed; in others, where it is allowed, he must *marry her*. Surely, in this respect, they may *rise in judgment against this generation, and condemn it*.

† I have lately seen a MS. of that laborious calculator and chronologist, *Mr. Kennedy*, in which he would prove, that what we call *Sunday*, is the true original *Sabbath*. This is very clear, that the *week* was divided into *seven days*, so early as at the creation of the world (see Gen. i.); that each day is distinguished by the works which GOD wrought therein; that the day on which GOD is said to

rest

upon the *fourth* commandment, in that respect, as ceremonial, typical, or prefigurative of something else (whether rightly or no does not come within my present design to consider); but as to the *moral* part, which sanctifies a given *portion* of our time for the public worship of Him to whom we stand indebted for *all*, we very rightly look upon this as the bounden duty and service of *Christians*, as well as *Jews*, till time shall be no more. So with regard to the sum of *fifty shekels*, or the dower according *to the dowry of virgins*, (see *Exod*. xxii. 16. *Deut*. xxii. 29.) this may be set down among the ceremonial or temporary observances of what may be called, to this purpose, the *Jewish* law. But with respect to the *moral* intendment of those laws in *Exodus* and *Deuteronomy*, which was to establish, ratify, and confirm the *marriage-ordinance* in the fullness of its obligation—*they shall be one flesh*—to prevent men from abandoning women to whoredom and prostitution, and all the bitter consequences of seduction and dereliction, those laws ought to be as binding on the consciences of mankind, as the *morality* of the *fourth*

---

rest from all His work that He had made, is called the *seventh day*, which he *hallowed and sanctified* on that account; that the fourth commandment recites all this, as the reason for its being kept holy; that the *Jews* have at all times observed our *Saturday* as the *seventh* day or *Sabbath*; that its Greek name Σαββατον, and its Latin name *Dies Sabbathi*, always denoted the *Jewish* SABBATH; and that the day we call *Sunday*, is in the New Testament called Μια Σαββατων, the *first day of the week*—ergo, it cannot be *the seventh*.

commandment, or of any other law of God whatsoever. To these purposes they are as much *moral* laws as *any* of the *ten commandments*. If this be not the case, why do we waste the time of public worship in causing these chapters to be red over to the people? *Deut.* xxii. is our first lesson for the *evening*-service every 4th of *March*; as is *Exod.* xxii. for every 8th of *February* in the *morning*. But it would be very strange if the *minister* was to preface with—" Good people, ye are
" assembled here to hear the word of God;
" but ye are not to mind what ye hear, be-
" cause the protection of females from the
" lust, villainy, treachery, and cruelty of
" men, is no longer an object of the
" laws which I am going to read to you.
" They bound the *Jews*, but *we Christians*
" have nothing to do with them." Dreadful as such language would be to hear, it says no more, than every man does, who contends for the obsoleteness and abolition of these wise, holy, and salutary provisions for *female* security.

With respect to the New Testament, the subject of *polygamy*, simply considered, is not so much as mentioned, either as good or bad. The more I have searched, the more I am convinced that it is not to be found, unless incidentally in the epistles to *Timothy* and *Titus*, and there only hinted at as the possible situation of certain people. Nor is there the least occasion it should be mentioned, as it was amply explained and deter-

Vol. I. M minately

minately settled in the *law which was given by Moses* (see John i. 17.); where we do not find it said, that *one law* was given by *Moses*, and *another law* by *Jesus Christ*; but Ὁ νόμος, THE LAW—which, in the connection it stands, must signify the *whole law*—*all* the law which GOD ever ordained or revealed to mortals—*was given by* MOSES; *Grace*—to pardon the transgressions of that law; *Truth*—to fulfil and answer every demand of its *moral* requirements, as well as every ceremonial prefiguration—*came by* JESUS CHRIST. *Heb.* ix. 15. Col. ii. 17. So that CHRIST *is the end of* THE LAW *for righteousness to every one that believeth.* Rom. x. 4.

However, as it is almost universally taken for granted, that " though *polygamy* might " be *allowed* under the Old Testament, yet " it is forbidden under the New Testa- " ment;" and as this opinion is as prevalent as that of *transubstantiation*, and the worship of the *Virgin Mary*, are in the church of *Rome*, and for centuries were in the church of *England*, let us proceed farther to examine the foundation upon which it stands.

In the first place, I cannot find, or even conceive, an instance in which the writings of the *apostles* of CHRIST contradict those of MOSES and the PROPHETS. If there could be such a thing, *both* must be *rendered suspicious*—*one* must be *false*—both sides of a contradiction cannot be *true*. The *adversaries* of revelation have long *tried*, as they have earnestly wished, to find such a thing, but

but in vain! God forbid that its *friends* should even imagine it possible! If it be true, that the scriptures of the Old Testament are *able to make us wise unto salvation* *, 2 Tim. iii. 15. it must be because they contain the *law* and the *gospel*; for no man can be *wise unto salvation* without the knowledge of these. They certainly contain *both*—the *gospel was preached unto* ABRAHAM, *Gal.* iii. 8; to the ISRAELITES under the Old Testament, as *well as to us* under the New Testament. Heb. iv. 2. We have *the same spirit of faith*, 2 Cor. iv. 13. and doubtless the same *object of faith*, 1 Cor. x. 4. *Numb.* xxi. 9. with *John* iii. 14, 15. Wherefore it is not to be conceived, that GOD should leave the *heirs of salvation* in a state of ignorance touching the *original* institution of marriage, or of the meaning of those *positive* laws which were to enforce it (and this after the giving of the law for 1500 years together) any more under the Old Testament than under the New Testament. It must be as necessary for a *Jew*, in order *to be wise unto salvation*, to know GOD's mind and will on these interesting and important subjects, as for a *Christian*. Each must be *judged* by the *same law*—each *saved*, though under different dispensations of it, by the *same gospel*.

---

* The Apostle adds—διὰ πίστεως τῆς ἐν Χριστῷ Ἰησοῦ —*through faith which is in* CHRIST JESUS, *i. e.* believing Him to be the MESSIAH. For want of believing which, the apostate *Jews* were not made *wise unto salvation* by the scriptures of the Old Testament.

As little probable is it, that He should allow His own beloved children to fly in the face of His authority, and live in the breach of His *positive law*, for so long a period, without the least check or reproof, when part of His gracious covenant runs in these words, Pf. lxxxix. 30. *If his children forsake my* LAW, *and walk not in my* JUDGMENTS; *if they break my* STATUTES, *and keep not my* COMMANDMENTS; *then will I visit their offences with the rod, and their sin with scourges.* There are instances enough of this for other things—witness DAVID's *broken bones*, Pf. li. 8. for his *adultery* with BATHSHEBA, and murder of URIAH. But where is there one instance of it for *polygamy?* Wherein did GOD ever punish it? DAVID died as really a *Christian believer* as St. PAUL did; witness his *last words*, 2 *Sam.* xxiii. 5; and yet, amidst all the explicit confessions he made in the most solemn hours of his *repentance*, he does not once * bewail the *polygamy* he lived in; nay, almost the last act of his life was an act of *polygamy*, in taking ABISHAG

---

* Which is very extraordinary, and indeed *unaccountable*, if to have more than *one wife at a time* be a *mortal sin*. The character also which we have of *David*, 1 *Kings* xv. 5. has, upon this principle, a degree of *obscurity*, which must render it wholly unintelligible—for how can it be said of a man, who lived and died in an open, avowed, wilful, and continued course of deliberate iniquity, *that he did that which was right in the eyes of the* LORD, *and turned not aside from any thing that He commanded him all the days of his life*, *save* ONLY *in the matter of* URIAH *the* HITTITE?

the

the *Shunamite* to *lie in his bosom*, his wife BATHSHEBA being then living. For though it be said, 1 Kings i. 4. that *he knew her not*; yet it plainly appears, by what SOLOMON said, 1 Kings ii. 22, 23. that she was so *betrothed* or *espoused* to DAVID, as to be looked upon as *his wife* *. Accordingly she belonged to the crown; was to be at the disposal of the *successor*; and therefore ADONIJAH, who was elder than SOLOMON, by asking for ABISHAG, the late king's widow, to wife, is treated as having a treasonable design against the crown itself, and is put to death as a *traitor*.

Is it then conceivable that *polygamy*, allowed of GOD uninterruptedly through so many ages and generations with impunity and even approbation, should all of a sudden start up into a *mortal sin*, by the *seventh* commandment's receiving a construction which it never before had—which was never before given to the words in which it was conceived? How could our lives and properties be secure, if time could alter the meaning of our penal statutes?—who will draw the line, and say how much or how little time is necessary to effect this? But if such can be the case with the *moral* law of GOD, then was the *Psalmist* mistaken in calling it *perfect* (Ps. xix. 7.) for it is *changeable*.

---

* Comp. Deut. xxii. 23, 24. where a *betrothed* virgin is called the man's *wife*, so as to make it *adultery* to defile her.

Then is it less to be depended on than the laws of the *Medes* and *Persians*. *Esth.* i. 19.—less sacred than the decree of an *earthly monarch*. *Esth.* viii. 8. *Dan.* vi. 15. If this be the case, what man can have any security for his *peace?*—In order therefore to avoid something *worse* than *absurdity*, we must conclude, that the original *institution of marriage*, and the *seventh* commandment of the *decalogue*, mean neither more nor less, where *Christians* are concerned, than where the *Jews* were—or, in other words, they mean precisely *one* and the *same* thing under the New Testament as under the Old Testament.

By taking texts here and there in the New Testament, and detaching them from their reference to and connection with the Old Testament, many *heresies* have arisen; as *Arianism*, *Socinianism*, and perhaps most others. *Ye do err, not knowing the scriptures.* So with regard to *marriage*—because CHRIST said—*Some make themselves eunuchs for the kingdom of heaven's sake: he that is able to receive it, let him receive it* (Matt. xix. 12.); and St. PAUL, 1 Cor. vii. 1. and in other parts of that chapter, speaks in favour of a *single life*, with respect to the then *distressed* state of the church (ver. 26) there were multitudes of people, in the early * ages of *Christianity,*

---

* " There arose in the *church* from *antient times*, sects
" of *heretics*, who condemned wine, and the use of ani-
" mal food, and *marriage*; and not only *heretics*, but
" the *orthodox* also, ran into extravagant notions of the
" same

tianity, who took these things in a wrong sense, and found out that "marriage was a "*carnal* thing, and forbidden by the New "Testament, as unbecoming the purity of "that dispensation:" little reflecting, that the command of *increase and multiply*, and the institution of *marriage* as the means thereof, were the dispensations of GOD Himself to our *first parents* when they were in a state of perfect innocence, and therefore could not be incompatible therewith.

That venerable man *John Trapp*, on 1 *Cor.* vii. 8. says—" The blemish will never be " wiped off some of the antient * *fathers*, " who, to establish their own idol of I know " not what *virginity*, which they themselves " had not, have written most wickedly and " basely of marriage." To say truth, I cannot conceive any man's conscience to be more *taken captive by the devil* (2 Tim. ii. 26) than

---

" same kind, crying up *celibacy* and a *solitary life* be-
" yond measure, together with rigid and uncommanded
" austerities and macerations of the body. (*Jortin*,
" Rem. vol. i. 278.)—*Christ* therefore, as we may con-
" jecture, was present at a *marriage-feast*, and honoured
" it with the miracle of turning *water* into *wine*, that it
" should stand in the *gospel* as a confutation of these
" foolish errors, and a warning to those *who had ears to*
" *hear*, not to be deluded by such *fanatics*. St. *John*,
" who records this miracle, lived to see these false doc-
" trines adopted and propagated." Ib.

* " *Jerom*, *Ambrose*, and other *fathers*, have de-
" claimed against matrimony, and recommended monk-
" ish abstinence almost as much as *Manes*, and have
" employed almost as insignificant arguments." Id.
vol. ii. p. 69.

his is, who is brought under a perfuasion that *celibacy* is more *pure* and *holy*, and, as such, more acceptable to GOD than *marriage*. Such a one, who, under this perfuasion, abstains from marriage, lives in perpetual * opposition to that command which was given with a *blessing* from GOD—*increase and multiply, and replenish the earth*, &c. This was at the original creation of *male* and *female* upon earth. Gen. i. 27, 28. And again, at the renewal of the earth after the deluge, this commandment stands, Gen. ix. 1, 7. repeated *twice*. Now can an opposition to so positive, so express, so reiterated an ordinance of Heaven, be reckoned a constituent part of *righteousness* and *true holiness*? What is this, but to fly in the face of the *divine wisdom* and *goodness*, and to esteem ourselves *wiser* and *holier* than the LORD of all? So those who

---

* Dr. *Alexander*, Hist. Wom. vol. ii. p. 269. introduces what he there says on the subject of *emasculation* on a religious account, with this pertinent and sensible observation:

"The two sexes were evidently intended for each other, and *increase and multiply* was the first great command given them by the Author of Nature. But suppose no such command had been given, how it first entered into the mind of man, that the propagation or continuation of the species was criminal in the eye of Heaven, is not easy to conceive. Ridiculous, however, as this notion may appear, it is one of those which early insinuated itself amongst mankind, and plainly demonstrated, that reasoning beings are most apt to deviate from nature; and not only to disobey her plainest dictates, but, on pretence of pleasing the Author of Nature, to render themselves for ever incapable of obeying them."

prefer

prefer a life of *solitude* to matrimonial connection, as *holier* and *better*, how much *holier* and *better* do they make themselves than Him who said—*It is* NOT GOOD *for man to be alone?* It is remarkable that the reiterated command for the propagation of the species stands, Gen. ix 7. in direct connection, as it were, and immediately following after the positive law against *murder:* as *privation* of life is an offence against this, *prevention* of life is something very like it, and therefore fitly placed near it in the sacred code.

Some of the fathers were wild enough to say—*hoc dictum, ratione multitudinis liberorum, pertinere ad tempora ante* CHRISTUM, *non ad nos qui alio vivimus ævo—mundum jam non desiderare* ILLUD CRESCITE ET MULTIPLICAMINI. " This command, by reason
" of multiplying children, belonged to
" the *times before* CHRIST, not to *us*, who
" live in another age—the world does not
" now want that same—*Be fruitful, and mul-*
" *tiply.*" Such were the delusions of *Jerom*
—*Tertullian*—*Chrysostom*—*Cyprian*—*Oecumenius*, &c. Bernard, in Cant. Serm. 59. thus glosses on the words—*The voice of the turtle is heard*, &c.; which he says is " the preach-
" ing of *continence*, respecting those who cas-
" trate themselves for the kingdom of hea-
" ven. At *the beginning* that voice was not
" heard, but rather *increase and multiply*; for
" barrenness was subject to a curse; *poly-*
" *gamy*

" *gamy* was * allowed," &c. His words are
—" *Vox turturis audita eft,* quæ eſt predicatio
" continentiæ, eos, qui ſe *caſtrant* propter
" regnum cœlorum, ſpectans ; cum ab initio
" vox iſta non ſit audita, ſed magis—*creſcite*
" *& multiplicamini,* ſterilitas etiam maledic-
" tioni fuit ſubjecta, *polygamia* conceſſa," &c. ;
but all this is now at an end, " quia hodie,
" repleto mundo, non tam ſit neceſſaria
" quam olim"—" becauſe now, the world
" being filled (with people) it is † not ſo ne-

* This ſame *St. Bernard,* abbot of *Clairval,* from whom the *Ciſtertian* monks derived the name of *Bernardins,* was one of the moſt eminent among the Latin writers of the 12th century. He was a man of genius, taſte, and judgment, in ſome reſpects, in others weak and ſuperſtitious. See Moſh. vol. i. 591. A pretty clear proof of the latter part of his character lies before us. His confining the command—*Be fruitful and multiply*—*to the days of the Old Teſtament,* is certainly a maſter-ſtroke of folly and weakneſs—however, his acknowledgment of the allowance of *polygamy* as a concomitant of that command, is much more ſcriptural and conſiſtent, than the comments of ſome more modern expoſitors (or rather *expoſers*) of the ſcriptures, who contend for the obligation and permanency of the command itſelf, but deny the permanency and obligation of thoſe laws which the divine wiſdom enacted for its regulation.

† De liberis ferendis non ita folliciti erant *Chriſtiani,* ut ob id ſolúm ducendæ uxoris neceſſitatem ſibi imponerent ; ideo quod finem feculorum de proximo inſtare ſuſpicarentur. *Tertull.* de *Monogamia. Creſcite & redundate evacuavit extremitas temporum.* See Pole Synop. in 1 Cor. vii. 1. " The *Chriſtians* were not ſo ſolicitous concern-
" ing the propagating children, as if, on that account
" alone, they were to lay a neceſſity on themſelves to
" marry, becauſe they might ſuſpect the end of the
" world was very near. *Tertull. de Monogamia.* The
" (ſuppoſed approaching) end of the times vacated the
" command of—*increaſe* and *multiply.*" See *Pole* Syn.
1 Cor. vii. 1.

" ceſſary

"cessary as formerly." If the reader has a mind to see how far folly and enthusiasm can carry people on these subjects, let him read *Tertullian*'s epistles to *Eustachius*—to *Gerontius*—and against *Helvetius*; *Tertullian* on Chastity; *Chrysostom* on Virginity; *Cyprian* on the discipline of Virgins; and *Oecumenius* on 1 Cor. vii.—then he will begin to find out how MARRIAGE ITSELF was vilified, and of course what gave rise to the condemnation of *second* marriages of all sorts, therefore of *polygamy*, in the *Christian church*, till the church of *Rome* had the impudence to *anathematize* the man who should say, that " it was *not forbidden by the law of* GOD," (see *Brent*. Coun. Trent. p. 784) " just as they " did those who should affirm, that for a " *priest* to marry was *allowed* by the law of " GOD." Ibid.

The consequences of all this unnatural plan of *celibacy* are too many to enumerate, too * *horrible* to particularize. It fared with numbers

---

* It is an observation of the excellent *authors* of *the History of Popery*, vol. i. p. 359. that " the first law " against a certain *unnatural vice* in *England* was by *Anselm* Archbishop of *Canterbury*, in the days of *William Rufus*; which said *vice* seems not to have been heard " of here till *priests* were forbidden marriage. However, " they treated it very gently, leaving it less penal in a " *priest*, than to enjoy his lawful wife.——*Secular* men, " guilty of this crime, were to be absolved only by the " *bishop*; but the *monks* and *priests*, it seems, might ci- " villy absolve *each other*. Yet even this *canon*, such as " it is, was soon after recalled, and never published." BERNARD, *Cent*. 12th, said, *that sin* was *frequent* among
the

numbers of the *Christians*, who did not like *to retain* the *divine command* in their practice, as it did with the *heathens*, who did *not like to retain* God *in their knowledge—*God *gave them up to uncleanness, to dishonour their own bodies between themselves:* who changed the *truth of* God *into a lye*, &c. *For this cause* God *gave them up* * *to vile affections*, &c. See Rom. i. 24—28. When we endeavour to stop the course of a river by laying a dam across the stream, the effect must be, that it will either make its way, bearing down all before it, or it will make a passage over its banks, and overflow and destroy the country. Such is the effect of endeavouring to stop the natural course of those desires which the Creator hath implanted in us for the purpose of carrying His *primary command* into execution. They will bear down all before them, or be turned out of their course; and then follows what the history of the *Popish* celibacy abundantly acquaints us with. As this is a subject too indelicate to dwell upon, I will only refer the reader to those books which treat thereof; such as *Fox's Martyro-*

---

the *bishops* in his time, and that this, with many other abominations, was the effect of prohibiting marriage. Burnet *Hist.* of *Reform.* vol. ii. p. 91, 3d edit.

* A thousand instances of which might be given—*sed ab uno disce omnes*—Pope *Sixtus* V. on the petition of *Peter Ricu*, cardinal and patriarch of *Constantinople*, of *Jeronymo* his own brother, and the cardinal of St. *Luce*, permitted " unto them and every of them, *sodomy*, with " this clause—fiat ut petitur—Let it be done as it " is desired," *History* of *Popery*, vol. ii. 292.

logy—

logy—The *Packets* from *Rome*, collected and published in *two volumes* quarto, by a *set of gentlemen*, 1735, under the title of *The History of Popery*, vol. ii. p. 431. A work this, which is too valuable to be lost to the public; and therefore, as I fear it is near out of print, it were to be wished it should be reprinted in as handsome an edition as that above referred to. See also *Burnet Hist. Ref.* vol. i. p. 191.

As for those men who have the *gift of continency*, they, as it appears from the scriptures, and all experience, are probably *very few*, at least comparatively; and those who received it in the days of *our* LORD and His *apostles*, seem to have received this for the particular purpose of keeping themselves *disentangled from the affairs of this life*, during the infancy and persecution of the church, 1 Cor. vii. 7, 17. Such do not want *cloysters* and *cells* for their security. As for those who have * it not, locking them up together in

---

* These certainly constitute the bulk of mankind, as all experience throughout all ages sufficiently shews. The natural structure of the human body, its natural secretions, &c. which are carried on daily, not by any contrivance or management of the creature, but by the power of infinite wisdom, impressed, we know not *how*, on the wondrous mechanism of every part, afford us such *physical* reasons for this, as to amount to demonstration of the necessity of marriage in the generality of men. This observation is abundantly verified by the manner of OUR SAVIOUR's expression, Matt. xix. 11, 12. where He speaks of a power of total abstinence as the immediate and *special gift* of heaven, and this for a *special purpose*, unless

in

in such places, and depriving them of the remedy which GOD *commands* in *marriage*, has been attended with a two fold wickedness; 1. in living contrary to the ordinance of Heaven; 2. in gratifying their desires contrary to the course of nature, or at least in some way which the *divine law* hath prohibited. Therefore the *Apostle* doth not say—if *they cannot contain*, let them shut themselves up, or pray that the order of nature may be inverted; but—*let them marry*; it is better *to marry than burn :* as if he had said—" One or " *other* of these must be the consequence." So, when married persons have separated for a while or *season*, on some *religious occasions*— come together again, saith he, lest *Satan tempt you for your incontinency*.

From all which it may be gathered, that *celibacy* is not an ordinance of GOD, but a snare of *Satan*—that marriage *is* the ordinance of GOD; therefore, that a man who *may* marry, and doth not, has no more * warrant from GOD's word to expect that he shall be kept from *vice*, than that he would be

---

in the cases He puts of *accidental* imbecillity, arising, in some, from a defect in their constitution, being *born eunuchs*; in others, from external violence by the hands of men.

* For, *continence* being none of those graces that are promised by GOD to all that ask it, as it was not in a man's power, without extreme severities on himself, to govern his own constitution of body, so he had no reason to expect GOD should interpose, when he had provided another remedy for such cases. *Burnet* Hist. Ref. vol. ii. p. 91, 3d edit.

kept

kept from *starving*, if, instead of *eating* and *drinking*, he was to pray that the appetites of *hunger* and *thirst* might be totally annihilated.

The indiscriminate † and total prohibition of *polygamy*, as it has *no warrant* from the word of GOD, may also be the means of plunging many into the mischiefs of uncommanded *celibacy*; for many men there are, who very early in life marry, perhaps without all the consideration which ought to be exercised in so momentous an undertaking—many things may happen which may be very reasonable, and indeed unavoidable, causes of separation from their wives; as for instance—incurable disease of mind or body, unconquerable violence of temper, perpetual refractoriness * of disposition, levity of behaviour—

† If the enacting part of 1 Jac. c. 11. had gone no farther than the preamble, and its severity been confined to—" divers evil-disposed persons, who being married, " run out of one county into another, or into places " where they are not known, and there become to be " married, having another husband or wife living, to " the great dishonour of GOD, and utter undoing of di- " vers honest men's children, and others"—it would have been a wholesome law, and highly justifiable in its penalty on such miscreants; who are undoubtedly guilty of one of the vilest and most injurious frauds that can possibly be committed. It seems to fall within the equity of Exod. xxi. 16. for such persons are a sort of ἀνδραπο-δίςαι, or *man-stealers*.

* It is to be feared, that there are not a few females, who (like other monopolists) take the advantage of the poor husband's situation, to use him as they please; and this for pretty much the same reason why the *ass*, in the fable, insulted and kicked the poor *old lion*—because it is not in their power to *resent* it as they *ought*.

The

viour—which, though not amounting to such proof as to be the ground of utter *legal* divorce, yet such as may destroy the whole comfort

The advice which king *Ahasuerus* received from his wife men, the seven princes of *Media* and *Persia*, upon queen *Vashti*'s disobedience, would have an excellent effect, could it be followed. Many an high-spirited *female* would have too cogent a reason against the indulgence of a refractory disposition, not to suppress it—her *pride*, which is now the husband's *torment*, would then become his *security*, at least in a great measure; for *pride* is a vice, which, as it tends to *self-exaltation*, maintains uniformly its own principle—not to bear the thoughts of a *rival*. See *Esther* i. 10, &c. As things are with us, the poor man must grind in *mola asinaria* during life.

It is certain, that nothing can be a release from the bond of marriage itself but *death*, or an act of *adultery* in the wife. But that a man is at all events bound to maintain the *external* bond, by cohabiting with a woman, who, instead of being an *help meet for him* (as we say) becomes, by the violence and perverseness of her temper and disposition, a constant and increasing torment, and this after the most friendly, tender, and kind admonitions—is not consonant either to scripture or reason.

Some will tell us, that such a thing must be looked upon as happening by the will of Providence, as a chastisement or visitation from Heaven, and therefore must be submitted to and endured.

So is sickness from the hand of God; so are afflictions of all kinds, and certainly to be submitted to with patience and resignation; yet to use means of recovery from sickness, and of deliverance from trouble and affliction, are apparent duties; and why not in the other case? The great *Milton* has some excellent and scriptural observations on these points in his *Tetrachordon*; to which I refer the reader.

It was proposed in the *book* for *reformation* of the *ecclesiastical law*, 1552, that " Desertion, long absence, capital
" enmities, where either party was in hazard of their life,
" or constant perverseness, or fierceness of an husband
" against his wife, might induce a divorce"—this fell to
the

comfort of a man's life. By these and many other means, an husband may be reduced to the situation of an *unmarried* man, harrassed by the same desires, subject to the same temptations; yet his condition is ten-fold worse; the one may *marry*, the other can-

the ground by the death of Ed. VI. Burnet Hist. Ref. vol. ii. p. 198.

The whole analogy of scripture agrees with that saying of the *Apostle*—*Let not the wife depart from her husband*; and again—*Let not the husband put away his wife*—*1* Cor. vii. 10, 11. But then these things must be construed agreeably to the analogy of that *wisdom which is profitable to direct*—Eccl. x. 10. They cannot mean, that *a wife is not to depart from her husband,* who threatens or endangers *her life*—nor that an husband may not separate from a wife who obstinately sets herself to be the plague and torment of *his*. Surely all this is within the equity of 1 Cor. vii. 15. and that persons are not *under bondage in such cases.*

This kind of things falls under a sort of *necessity,* which must always interpret the law in favour of self-preservation. *Thou shalt do no murder*—constitutes a capital offence in the man who wantonly or maliciously kills another—but if a man slays another in his own defence, it is an excusable homicide: this from the necessary care which every man has a right to take of his own life. The *ship-master* to whom I intrust my goods, is wicked and base, if he wantonly cast them into the sea; but if a storm arise, and he cast them out to save the ship from sinking, he is highly justifiable. I would therefore argue from *necessity* on the point of *separation*; for I cannot find any privilege conferred on one creature to make another wretched, and that without remedy. Of this *necessity* every person must judge at his peril; for—as the old *proverb* says—*None can tell where the shoe pinches, so well as he that wears it:* but then be it remembered—that *every man shall give an account of himself to* God. Rom. xiv. 12. If this were considered as it ought to be, it would certainly be the best means of binding both parties over *to their good behaviour,* in all conjugal disputes.

not: fo he muft remain hopelefs and helplefs, or plunge into *vice* and mifery, becaufe he is debarred of the remedy which GOD hath provided, ftripped of that undoubted privilege with which GOD and nature have invefted him, by the lyes and forgeries of *fathers and councils*, &c. The *Romifh* church indeed, at the *council of Trent*, ANATHEMATIZED all who fhould fay, that "thofe who "have not the gift of chaftity might marry, "in regard that GOD doth not deny the gift "to him that doth demand it." This *antifcriptural* decree, which directly gives the lye to the *Apoftle*, 1 *Cor.* vii. 9. is founded upon a *fallacy*, which many fall into, from arguing without the neceffary diftinction between what GOD *can* do, and what He *will* do. That He *can* do every thing is without a doubt; but that we are warranted to expect He *will* do what He hath no where promifed, is not true. GOD *could* certainly have made us to live upon the *air*; but He hath not: meat and drink are abfolutely neceffary for our fubfiftence; it would therefore be the higheft prefumption, nay even the madnefs of *enthufiafm*, for any man to pray that the natural appetites of *hunger* and *thirft* might ceafe, and that for the future he might live, not on meat and drink, but folely by refpiration of *air*. So, to pray to Him whofe command is—*Be fruitful and multiply, bring forth abundantly in the earth, and multiply therein* (Gen. ix. 7.) that the natural defire which is to lead to this may be annihilated, and the effect of it deftroyed,

is

is to *petition* againſt the *divine wiſdom*, to arraign the *divine holineſs*, and to remonſtrate, in effect, againſt having any ſhare in an obedience to the *divine command.*—Where *is* there —where *can* there be a promiſe, to warrant ſo unhallowed a proceeding? Surely no where, but in the imaginations of thoſe who have fallen themſelves, and who want to lead others into the *ſnare of the devil*. When we pray againſt what GOD hath *forbidden*, no doubt we ſhall, in His own way and time, *obtain grace to help in every time of need*; but when we pray againſt what He has *commanded*, we tempt Him to deliver us up to the deluſions of our own minds, and *our end will be according to our works*—what that end is likely to be, the hiſtories before hinted at very ſufficiently declare.

That there may be ſituations, and particular circumſtances, under which it is not only *lawful*, but *duty*, to pray for *continence*—I mean for entire ſubduction of, and power over, our natural deſires—there can be no doubt; as where they would lead us to forbidden enjoyment: but then we muſt judge of this by the ſcriptures, not by the prejudices, folly, and ſuperſtition of men like ourſelves: for, at this rate, we may be praying that GOD would alter His mind, change His will, and vacate His commands, in order to make way for our oppoſition to them. Whereas, *this is the confidence that we have in Him, that if we aſk any thing* ACCORDING TO HIS WILL, *He heareth us*. *And if we know*

that

that He hear us, whatsoever we ask (i. e. AC-
CORDING TO HIS WILL) *we know that we
have the petitions that we desired of Him.* 1 *John*
v. 14, 15.

For a man to pray that he might never
again feel the appetites of *hunger* and *thirst*,
or, at least, be enabled to refrain entirely
from satisfying them, would be deservedly
reckoned madness—but to pray to be kept
from *gluttony* and *drunkenness*, and all forbidden indulgence and excess, would be asking
according to the will of GOD, and the man
would have a *scriptural* ground and warrant
to expect an answer of peace.

So, if a man takes it into his head, that
those other *desires*, which GOD hath, for the
wisest purposes, implanted in our nature, are
sinful in themselves, and, on *this footing*, prays
against them, he is under a sad delusion, and
every petition he utters is no less than an arraignment of the *wisdom* and *holiness* of the
great *Creator* of all. Yet the *Popish* histories
are replete with miracles wrought by *Christ*
and the *Virgin Mary*, in answer to such petitions; and no doubt but these *lyes* are most
devoutly believed by thousands, who make
men's * *traditions*, and not GOD's *word*, the
rule of their faith.

Besides

---

* Among the fooleries of the *sixth century*, an entire
abstinence from marriage was held the surest way to Paradise. Women were not even suffered to approach the
altar, nor touch the pall which covered it, unless when,
by the *priests*, it was delivered to them to be washed.
The *eucharist* was too holy to be touched by their naked
hands,

Besides the evils which have been noticed as the consequences of our *superstition* on the subject of *polygamy*, the utter *extinction* of *families* might also be mentioned; whereas, sooner than this should be the case in *Israel*, we find GOD enacting a peculiar *positive law*, in order to prevent it; which said law was certainly a virtual command of *polygamy* in many, perhaps in most, cases, as it was very rare to find an *unmarried* man among the *Jews*. The law to which I allude, is that of Deut. xxv. 5. where the *husband's brother* was to marry the widow of the deceased, if he died without children—*that his name might not be put out of Israel*. Though all the reasons of this law do not now subsist, therefore the law itself, as far as those reasons have ceased, hath itself ceased; yet it serves to shew us that GOD did certainly allow *polygamy*, and even *command* it, sooner than suffer inheritances to fail by the *extinction of families*.

The end of marriage, say some, is *society* and mutual *comfort*; but they are rather an *effect* of marriage, none of the *principal* end,

---

hands, they were therefore ordered, by the *canons* of the church, to have a white linen glove upon the hand in order to receive it. See Alexander's Hist. of Wom. vol. i. p. 166. The council of Auxerre, ann. 578, decrees, that *women* communicate with their *dominical*, which some suppose to have been a linen cloth, wherein they received the *species*, as not being allowed to receive them with the bare hand.

See *Burnet* Hist. Ref. vol. ii. p. 76. 3d edit. Also *Chambers*—sub voc. *Dominical*.

which is *procreation of children*, and so the continuance of mankind, according to the first institution, Gen. i. 28. As for *comfort* and *society*, they may be between man and man, woman and woman, and therefore no *proper* end of marriage. That *conjunction* which cannot answer the great end for which marriage was ordained by GOD, should not prevent or hinder that which *can*, nor does it appear from scripture that it was ever intended it *should*.

Frigidity, or perpetual *impotency of generation* on the man's side, is held by our laws, a cause of divorce *a vinculo matrimonii*; therefore it is but reasonable, that a perpetual *impotency of generation* (which at a certain time of a woman's life may be ascertained) in the woman, should be allowed as a reasonable and justifiable ground for *polygamy*. Folly and superstition may set up an objection to this, but *nature*, *reason*, and *scripture*, all unite in their suffrage for the truth of the position. See Gen. xvi. 2, 3. Gen. xxx. 1—9.

Among us, if a man be married to a *barren* woman, he cannot take another wife while she lives, but must content himself with letting his nobility, titles, honours, and family be annihilated, and his estates escheat to the crown, under pain and penalty of being adjudged a *felon* if he marries a *second wife* (living the first) who might be the means of continuing and transmitting all these things to a long and numerous posterity.

This

This foolish superstition is like that of the *Jews* in the days of *Mattathias*, who suffered themselves to be slaughtered by the enemy without resistance, because it was the *sabbath-day*, 1 Mac. ii. 32, 38; or like that of the *Carthusians*, who live entirely on *fish*, and would not eat a piece of *other flesh* (see 1 Cor. xv. 39.) even to save their lives.

The modern *Jews* are wiser, for though they in general coincide with the government where their lot happens to be cast, so that they are *polygamous* or *monogamous*, according to the laws of the country they live in; yet if a *Jew* be married *ten years* to a woman, and has no child by her, he is at liberty to take another, that he may have an heir to his substance; and in so doing he certainly is justified by the law of GOD; which law we have set aside, and established our own superstition in its place, which not only tends to the annihilation and extinction of families, and of course to *depopulation*; but is, as elsewhere is more fully observed, the source of endless ruin and destruction to the *weaker sex*, whose *seducers*, if married men, are totally exempt from making them that amends, and doing them that justice, which GOD's law commanded, and which, among *us Christians*, is looked upon as *duty* to withhold, or rather, as a *mortal* * *sin* to comply with.

As

---

* *Bellarmine*, that great champion for *The Man of Sin*, saith—Lib. 4. de Rom. Pontific, " Si Papa erraret præ- " cipiendo

As these points are fully treated in other parts of this book, I will now proceed to shew, that the wild notions about marriage, which were introduced into the church, bear an earlier date than the days of *Tertullian*, and those other fathers mentioned before.

"There were others," says Mr. *Brough-ton*—Hist. lib. tit. *Marriage*—"who simply
"exclaimed against marriage as *unlawful*
"under the *gospel*. This doctrine was first
"taught by *Saturnilus*, a scholar of *Simon*
"*Magus* and * *Marcion*, but afterwards bet-
"ter known amongst the † *Encratites*; to
"these may be added the *Apostolics* or *Apo-*
"*tactics*, the *Manichees*, *Severians*, and many
"others. The church had great struggles

"cipiendo vitia, & prohibendo virtutes, teneretur ec-
"clesia credere vitia esse bona, & virtutes malas, nisi
"vellet contra conscientiam peccare."
"If the *Pope* should err in commanding *vices*, and in
"prohibiting *virtues*, the church would be bound to
"believe that vices are good, and virtues evil, unless
"she would sin against conscience." And again, *Cont. Barcl.* c. xxxi. "In bono sensu dedit CHRISTUS *Petro*
"potestatem faciendi de peccato non peccatum, & de
"non peccato peccatum." "In a good sense—
"CHRIST gave *Peter*" (and of course the *Pope*) "a
"power of making that no sin which is sin, and to
"make that to be sin which is not a sin." What better principle do we proceed upon in the matters here mentioned?

* *Marcion* prescribed to his followers an express *prohibition* of *wedlock*. See *Mosheim*, vol. i. p. 110. edit. *Maclaine*. One of *Marcion*'s abominable tenets, which he laid down to his followers, was, that they should "renounce the precepts of the GOD of the Jews." Ib.

† See *Newton* on the Prophecies, vol. ii. 442—3.

"with

" with thefe antient *heretics,* who inveighed
" bitterly againſt marriage under the *goſpel-*
" *ſtate,* and wrought upon many weak minds,
" to be guilty of great irregularities, under
" pretence of a more refined way of living.

" The church had alſo another conteſt
" with the *Montaniſts* and *Novatians,* about
" *ſecond* marriages, theſe *heretics* rejecting
" them as utterly unlawful."—And indeed
the eccleſiaſtical hiſtories inform us, that this
madneſs (for I can call it nothing elſe) was
carried ſo far, as that *ſecond* marriages were
ſtyled no better than *whoredom;* and *eccleſiaſtical* perſons were forbidden to be preſent
at them on pain of *excommunication.* This
in the very face of the ſcriptures of GOD,
which declare juſt as much for *ſecond* marriages as for *firſt.* Rom. vii. 2, 3. 1 Cor.
vii. 39. By all this we ſee what work may
be made with the ſcriptures, when the imaginations of men are let looſe, inſtead of *comparing ſpiritual things with ſpiritual,* and making GOD the interpreter of His own word.

As for the practice of *polygamy* among the
firſt *Chriſtians,* it was probably very * frequent;

---

* So it ſhould ſeem to have been in times long after them, not only among the *laity,* but the *clergy* alſo; for Pope *Sylveſter,* about the year 335, made an *ordonnance,* that every *prieſt* ſhould be the *huſband of one wife* only.

So in the ſixth century, it was enacted in the canons of one of their councils, that if any one is married to *many wives,* he ſhall do penance. See Alex. Hiſt. Wom. vol. ii. 217, 272.

The caſe of *Philip* Landgrave of Heſſe, as determined by the *ſix reformers,* is well known. But all theſe things
prove

quent; if not—why did PAUL (1 Tim. iii. 2. and Tit. i. 6.) recommend the choice of *Bishops* and *Deacons* from amongst those who had but *one wife?*—What occasion for this caution of the *apostle's*, if none had *more than one?* That the election was to be made from amongst the *Christian believers*, there can be no doubt, that is to say, of such as had been admitted to *baptism* and the *Lord's supper*, and were enrolled as *members* of the *Christian* church. To suppose that none of these had more than *one wife*, is to suppose the *apostle* giving a needless rule in the election of *Bishops* and *Deacons*. To suppose that any who had *more than one wife*, should be admitted to *baptism* and the *Lord's supper*, if CHRIST had forbidden *polygamy* as *adultery*, is to suppose a greater absurdity still, and that the great *apostle of the Gentiles* was less faithful to his trust, than those *Jesuits* who refused to admit the King of *Tonquin* into the CHRISTIAN church, unless he would put away *all his wives but one:* for which these *pseudo-apostles* were very justly driven out of the country.

The learned *Selden* has proved, in his *Uxor Hæbraica*, that *polygamy* was allowed, not only among the *Hebrews*, but among most other nations throughout the world; doubt-

---

prove nothing, with respect to the lawfulness or unlawfulness of the matter in the sight of GOD: I only mention them, to shew that *Christians* have, by no means, thought always alike on the subject. The *opinions* of an inspired *apostle* are certainly good evidence—to *these* let us attend.

less among the inhabitants of that vast tract of *Asia*, throughout which the *gospel* was preached by the great *apostle of the Gentiles*, where so many *Christian* churches were planted, as well as in the neighbouring states of *Greece;* yet in none of Paul's *epistles*, nor in the seven awful *epistles* which St. John was commanded to write to the *seven churches* in *Asia*, is *polygamy* found amongst the crimes for which they were reproved. Every other species of *commerce between the sexes*, is distinctly and often mentioned, this not once, except on the *woman's* side, as *Rom.* vii. 3; but had it been sinful and against the law on the *man's side*, it is inconceivable that it should not have been mentioned on *both* sides equally.

When St. *Paul* says that a *Bishop* or *Deacon* is to be the *husband* of *one wife*, it certainly carries with it a tacit allowance of *polygamy*, as to the *lawfulness* of it with regard to * all *other* men; not that it was *sinful* in one more than in another; but this was a prudential caution in that distressed and infant state of the *church*, that those who were to have the management of it,

---

* Cardinal *Cajetan*, who disputed with *Luther* at *Augsburg*, and who is said to have given a brief, but judicious exposition of the *Old* and *New Testament*, writes thus—" Pluralitatem uxorum nusquam a Deo prohi-
" beri; adeoque *Paulum* cum *Episcopum* vetet habere
" *plures uxores*, reliquis concedere." " A plurality of
" wives is no where forbidden by God: so that *Paul*,
" when he forbids a *Bishop* to have *many wives*, allows
" it to others." Rainold de lib. Apoc. tom. i. præl. 4.

should

should have as little avocation and distraction as the nature of things would admit of. PAUL does not say that a *Bishop* or *Deacon* should not be *married*, as the church of *Rome* says, but that he should be the *husband of one wife*; for however those who had *more* could find time to manage their *own* affairs, they could not be supposed to have leisure enough to attend the *church*, and its embarrassed and various concerns, as they ought. Upon this principle he seems to give the preference to those who had *no wife*, 1 Cor. vii. 32, 33. *I would have you without carefulness. He that is unmarried careth for the things that belong to the* LORD, *how he may please the* LORD: *but he that is married, careth for the things that are of the world, how he may please his wife.* This certainly relates to all *Christians*, but especially to *ministers*. The *heretics* of old took it so strongly in the *former* sense, that they held marriage *unlawful* to *Christians*—the *Papists* take it so strongly in the *latter*, that it is one of the authorities on which they forbid their *clergy* * to marry at all.

There

---

* The celibacy of the *clergy* was among the errors of very early date, for *Paphnutius*, a venerable *confessor* and *prelate*, who assisted at the *Nicene* council, which was held ann. 325, where there was a dispute, whether " *ecclesiastics* should not separate from their wives, " which they had married while *laymen,*" said—Satis esse ut qui in clerum fuissent adscripti, juxta *veterem ecclesiæ traditionem*, jam non amplius uxores ducerent.—" It was sufficient that they who were inrolled
" among

There are some who interpret the above passages (1 Tim. iii. 2. and Tit. i. 6.) to mean, that a *Bishop* or *Deacon* should, if a *widower*, have had but *one wife*, or have been but *once married*; and this upon the ground of what is said, 1 Tim. v. 9. concerning the *women* who were to be chosen to the office of *Deaconesses*—*Let not a woman be taken into the number under sixty years, having been the wife of one man*. There are also those, who, on the authority of these passages, hold it unlawful for a *minister* * to marry a *second* time on the loss

" among the clergy, according to the *antient tradition of*
" *the church*, should no more marry." *Clerical celibacy*, and the condemnation of *polygamy*, stand on one and the same *footing*, and that a very *lame* one; that is to say, on the *antient tradition of the church*; so did the religion of the *Scribes* and *Pharisees*, and so do the *superstitions* of the *church of Rome* to this day.

Paphnutius's speech on the occasion is to be found in Jortin, Rem. vol. ii. p. 249. Though what *Papchnutius* says may rather apply against the *clergy* marrying a second time, yet those to whom he spake must be supposed to have holden it unlawful for the *clergy* to marry at al, else how could they be for their separating from the wives they took when *laymen*?

However, even the partial prohibition of wives to the *clergy* did not ripen into a *decree*, 'till about fifty years after, when *Siricius*, bishop of *Rome*, ordained, that if a *clerk* married a *widow*, or a *second wife*, he should be divested of his office. For many hundred years this was not observd, 'till Gregory VII. called *Hildebrand*, by cruel decree of excommunication, deprived ministers of their *lawful wives*, and compelled the clergy to the vow of *continency*. *Hist. of Popery*, vol. i. 21.

* Whether any carry this point so far as the anonymous answerer to Luther, Tr. *de digamia Episcoporum*, I cannot say; but he declares—" Mortaliter peccant qui
" bigamos (sacerdotes scil) ecclesiæ stipendio sustentant"—

loſs of his ‡ wife, and unlawful alſo for *any* woman to *marry again* on the loſs of her huſband.

" tant."—" They ſin mortally who ſupport clergymen that have been twice married, with the allowance or ſtipend of the church."——Again—" Peccant qui ſcientes ex bigami ore verbum Dei pollui audiunt."—" They ſin, who knowingly hear the word of GOD polluted, by the mouth of a miniſter who has been twice married."——Again—" Bigamus cenſendus eſt, non ſolum is qui duas duxit virgines, ſed & viduam aut aliter corruptam."—" He is to be reckoned a *bigamiſt*, not only who has married two *virgins*, but alſo he that hath married a *widow*, or a *woman* otherwiſe corrupted."

His concluſion breathes the true ſpirit of ignorance, ſuperſtition, and blind zeal.——" In ſummâ—quicunque proprias voluptates, & luxuriæ exactionem, *apoſtoli* verbis & *patrum* honeſtis præponit decretis, non tamen ſacerdotis aut eccleſiaſtico ſtipendio cedere dignum putat, is non ſolum tolerandus non eſt, ſed ad corvos abigendus, quò non ovis morboſa totum corrumpat ovile, & tam laudabilem, bonam, & longævam conſuetudinem peſtilenti ſuo defædet exemplo."—— ' In fine, Whoſoever prefers his own pleaſures, and the requirements of luxury, to the words of the *apoſtle*" (we muſt here ſuppoſe 1 Tim. iii. 2. and Tit. i. 6. to be meant) " and to the decent decrees of the *fathers*, and yet doth not think proper to depart from the miniſtry, or his eccleſiaſtical ſtipend, is not only not to be tolerated, but to be driven away to the crows" (we ſhould ſay, *thrown to the dogs*) " that one ſcabby ſheep might not mar the whole flock, and defile, by his own peſtilent example, ſo laudable, good, and antient a cuſtom."

‡ WILLIAM WHISTON, of famous memory, who, in an early part of the preſent *century*, was the great reviver and patron of the *Arian* hereſy in this country, and might be called *Dr.* CLARKE's *maſter*, in this branch of *blaſphemy*; has left us ſome very remarkable matters on record.

One

husband. These ridiculous opinions owe their birth to the before-mentioned cause, of taking

One is, that the *New Testament* is the only rule of *faith*, and criterion of *truth* among *Christians*—and this to be interpreted by *apostolical tradition*.——Another is, a *lesson* to all *Clergymen*, who are so profligate as to subscribe the doctrine of the *Trinity*, as held by the Church of *England*, though they do not believe it; and this, that they may gain admission to those preferments, which, on such terms, they have no right to hold—for *Whiston*, very fairly and honestly, gave up his professorship at *Cambridge*, sooner than dissemble, or give up his opinions; for which he is to be *honoured*, as an *honest* man, however mistaken he might be in his religious notions. Dr. *Samuel Clarke*, his pupil, died *Rector* of the *valuable* living of *St. James's*.

Another matter which *Whiston* left behind him, seems to be a *bone* for the *Clergy*, which those would do well to *pick*, who, with the ingenious *William Whiston*, are for setting up a new *Christian law*, or *law of the gospel*, of which *Christ* and *St. Paul* are the *legislators*.

Whiston's words are as follow—" It may not be amiss,
" here to take notice of that *Christian law*, for the mar-
" riage of the clergy but *once*; which is now so fre-
" quently broken by *Protestants*, and gives the *Papists*
" a great handle against them, as observing no rules for
" *restraining* their *inclinations* of that kind. I say, the
" *Protestants* do allow their clergy, not only to *marry*
" more than *once*, but to act as *Clergymen* after such
" *second* marriages, without the least permission under
" the *gospel* for so doing. Now, though the *law of*
" *Christianity* be plain, not only from copies of those
" laws of *Moses*, which oblige *Christians*; but from the
" present *New Testament*, the *apostolical constitutions*, and
" the known interpretation and practice of the *four first*
" *centuries*, that *Bishops*, *Priests* and *Deacons*, are allowed
" to *marry but once*; yet am not I sure, but they might
" marry a *second* time without reproach, if they volun-
" tarily degraded themselves, and reduced themselves
" among the laity; in whom *second* marriages were not
" condemned; though I confess, I do not remember one
" example

taking words by the *sound*, instead of the *sense* —the usual consequence of detaching scripture from scripture, not comparing it with itself, by taking the whole together. By this, men may prove—*quidlibet ex quolibet*—" what " they please from what they please;"—and this is the sheet-anchor of error, as well as of many monstrous practices, and so has been in all ages; they can be maintained no other way. The whole doctrine of *transubstantiation*, absurd as it is in all its parts, is held together by the sound of *Hoc est corpus meum*

" example of such voluntary degradation and reduction
" in all *Christian* antiquity. I am confident our great
" men are, with *Grotius*, too good critics; and know
" *Christian* antiquity too well, to pretend that *St. Paul*'s
" ordinances, that a *Bishop*, a *Priest*, and a *Deacon*, must
" be the *husband* of *but one wife*, signifies but *one wife at*
" *a time*; as some of our *weaker* authors are willing to
" interpret it. Nor was this constitution so severe then
" as the moderns imagine; for almost all the *bishops*
" were originally *fifty* years of age, e'er they were or-
" dained. The next order seem to have been in general
" considerably above *fifty*; which their very name *pres-*
" *byter*, i. e. *elders* of the parish or diocese, directly sig-
" nifies: and as for the *deacons*, they were, by parity of
" reason, to be supposed between *thirty* and *forty*; which
" ages, for these three orders, when we once restore, the
" objections of the *moderns* against this law will come to lit-
" tle. I mention this here, because I had once a discourse
" with *Dr. Clarke* upon this head, who looked upon that
" latter interpretation as ridiculous. Nor had he any thing
" else to alledge for the modern *Protestant* practice, but
" that this command might be supposed peculiar to the
" *first age of Christianity*: which yet, I dare say, was a
" secret to all those *first ages of Christianity*; which, so far
" as I have observed, always esteemed every *law of the*
" *gospel* to belong equally to all under the *gospel*, from
" the first 'till the *second coming of* CHRIST, our *legislator*."
See WHISTON, Life of CLARKE, p. 140—142.

—This is my body.—The *sound* of *hæreticum devita*, in a Latin verfion of Tit. iii. 10. has authorized the moft barbarous murders of thoufands, who have been burned alive by the inquifition, under the denomination of *heretics*. It has been made to fignify *hæreticum de vitâ—an heretic from life*; that is—*put him* from life—*kill him*.—Thus, by feparating the word *devita*, and turning the laft two fyllables into the fubftantive *vita*, the prepofition *de* juft anfwered the purpofe. A lefs *tragical* confequence of this method of interpretation is related by *Erafmus*. He tells of a friar preaching from thofe words of Christ, Luke xvii. 17. which ftand in fome *Latin* verfions—*Nonne decem facti funt* * *mundi*—who began to prove there are *ten worlds*. An arch fellow ftanding by, ftopped his mouth with the following words—*Sed ubi funt novem?—But where are the nine?*

It is faid of *St. Francis*, that from the words, *Go you into all the world, and preach the gofpel to every creature*, he thought himfelf bound to preach to *beafts* and *birds*, and accordingly did it very often, and with *wonderful fuccefs*, as they tell us in the legend of his life. Perhaps it was much on a like principle that *St. Anthony* of *Padua* went and preached to the *fifhes*—whofe difcourfe to them may be found in *Broughton* Hift. Lib. vol. i. p. 53.

* I would juft acquaint the *unlearned* reader, that the fubftantive *mundus* fignifies *a world*—the adjective *mundus* fignifies *clean*.

Dr. *Hammond*, in his note on 1 *Tim.* iii. 2. says—" What is the meaning of μιᾶς γυναικὸς ἀνὴρ—*the husband of one wife*—both here and ver. 12, and *Tit.* i. 6. and of ἑνὸς ἀνδρὸς γυνὴ—*the wife of one husband*—chap. v. 9. will not easily be resolved." But surely all difficulty vanishes, when the whole is taken together; and it is observed from the *original* in what different *tenses* the verbs γινομαι and ἐιμι are used. This shews that the *apostle*, 1 Tim. iii. 2, and Tit. i. 6. was describing the situation of the men he was then speaking of, as what *it then was*—and in 1 Tim. v. 9. that of the *widows*, as to what *it had been*. 1 Tim. iii. 2. Δεῖ ᾖν τὸν Ἐπίσκοπον ΕΙΝΑΙ μιᾶς γυναικὸς Ἄνδρα—A *Bishop ought to* BE (not to HAVE BEEN) *the husband of one wife*; and Tit. i. 6. Ἐί τις ΕΣΤΙΝ μιᾶς γυναικὸς—*if any* BE (IS) *the husband of one wife*. Ἐςιν being of the present tense, can signify only what a man *is* at *the time spoken of*: whereas the expression concerning the *women*, 1 *Tim.* v. 9. is widely different. The woman is called Χηρα, a *widow*; and it is observable, that the verb is not expressed as before, either in the infinitive or indicative mood of Ἐιμι, *to be*, but by the participle of the *præteritum*, or *past time*, of the verb γινομαι, *to be* or *become*.—It is γεγονυῖα—which we have rightly rendered—*having been*—that is— in *time past having been*, or *become the wife of one man*—a *widow*, who never *had been* but once married; not—that had not had *two husbands* at a time; such a thing was hardly

ever heard of, as lawful, even amongst the *heathens* * themselves. I would therefore harmonize and paraphrase the whole as follows :—" Forasmuch *as all things are to be*
" *done decently and in order*, (1 Cor. xiv. 40.)
" but this cannot be, unless *some* proper
" form of government be established; it is
" necessary that proper officers be appointed
" to administer that government. Some who
" are to be—'Επισκοποι—overseers of the
" whole; others Διακονοι—*deacons*, or infe-
" rior serving *ministers* under them. The
" first order of men are to *overlook* the *clergy*,
" as well as the *laity*—to *preach the word*—
" administer the *sacraments*, and to have
" power to censure *evil doers*, even as far as
" *excommunication*, the *church* agreeing there-
" to. 1 Cor. v. 4, 5. Such an office should,
" doubtless, be filled with men of irre-
" proachable characters, and of such con-
" duct and dispositions as to be in all respects
" *blameless*, not only for the better mainte-
" nance of their *authority*, but also for the

---

* Never among *Jews*, or even *Turks*, was it permitted that the woman should have more than one husband at once. Only among the *barbarians* there is mention of the Πολυανδροι, a people so called, because the wife among them had *many husbands*. So among the *Medes*, that dwelt in the mountains, it is said a woman was married to *five husbands at once*. See *Hammond* on 1 Tim. iii. 2. *Montesquieu* mentions the tribe of the *Naires*, on the coast of *Malabar*, where the women have many husbands. Sp. of Laws, vol. i. p. 374, octavo. But all this is as contrary to nature itself, as the custom of some of the *Indian* women's drowning their children in the *Ganges*, or exposing them to wild beasts to be devoured.

" influence

"influence of their *example*. As such an
"office must moreover require great atten-
"tion, those should be chosen, who are en-
"tangled as little as possible in the *affairs of*
"*this life*. 2 Tim. ii. 4. Therefore, though
"for this reason *single men* might in general
"answer the purpose best, (1 Cor. vii. 33.)
"yet it may be expedient, in some instances,
"to chuse *married men* into the offices of
"*Bishops* and *Deacons*. Where this is the
"case, the election should not be made of
"such of the *Christians* as have more than
"*one wife*, as such a situation must necessa-
"rily involve the person in more *worldly*
"*care*, than can be consistent with a due at-
"tention to that *care*, which must *come upon*
"*them daily*, respecting the *church*. There-
"fore, the having more than *one wife* should
"always be considered as a bar to a man's
"election, either to the office of a *Bishop* or of
"a *Deacon*, (1 *Tim*. iii. 12.); for though these
"last may not have so extensive a jurisdiction,
"yet, what with preaching the word—assist-
"ing the *Bishops* and *elders*—visiting the
"sick—and distributing the *church*'s alms to
"the poor—*one wife* and family is as much
"as can be at all considered consistent with
"any tolerable diligence in the duties of a
"*Deacon*'s office.

"But as the sick are to be visited and at-
"tended, as well as the poor relieved, it
"may be necessary also to appoint *women* for
"these purposes, especially as to attending
"and nursing the poor of their *own sex*.

"These

" These may require many offices highly
" improper for *men* to be engaged in;
" though the nursing *sick men*, or visiting and
" relieving them, may very properly fall also
" under the care of *women*. These *women*
" may also be called Διάκονοι τῆς ἐκκλησίας (see
" Rom. xvi. 1.) *servants* or *ministers of the*
" *church*. Those who are to be deemed
" proper for these offices, must not be
" young, raw, unexperienced girls; nor
" *married women*, whose attention belongs to
" their husbands and families, 1 Cor. vii. 34;
" nor the *younger widows*, who are not arrived
" at a time of life suitable to such employ-
" ments, 1 Tim. v. 11: let these *marry*, to
" keep themselves out of mischief, ver. 12,
" 13, 14. The only *women* who are fit to
" be chosen as *servants* or *ministers* of the
" church in the respects above mentioned,
" should be far advanced in years; that is to
" say, not less than *threescore years old*, who
" having buried their husbands and *brought*
" *up their children*, 1 Tim. v. 10. have time,
" as well as inclination, to devote themselves
" to the offices of the church. They should
" also be *sober* and discreet persons, who, by
" their conduct in their younger years, have
" shewn their temperance and sobriety, by
" having contented themselves with *one hus-*
" *band*, and who, ever after the death of that
" husband, have secluded themselves from
" any further worldly engagements of that
" sort, so as to be justly styled *widows indeed*;
" *though desolate, yet trusting in* God (1 Tim.

O 3 v. 5.)

" v. 5.); and like Anna, *Luke* ii. 36, 37. " *continuing in supplications and prayers night* " *and day.*"—This I take to be a consistent and clear view of these passages taken together. As we may from hence infer, that there were women in the church younger than *sixty years*, by the Apostle's express exclusion of those *under* that age from those offices to which women were to be chosen; as also that there were many who had been *twice married*, by his designing those who had been but *once married* for the aforesaid offices; so we may as fairly conclude, from his saying *a bishop*—δεῖ εἶναι—*ought to be*—and again, if any, ἐςιν —*is or be* the *husband of one wife*—that there were many *Christians*, not who *had had*, but at that *present time* actually had *more than one wife*. If this had not been the case, it would have been as much out of the question to have mentioned the having but *one wife*, as to have said, that none should be chosen but those who had but *one head* or *one body*, when it was not to be supposed that any man had more.

As to the conceit, that, " what the *Apostle* " says about the *bishops* and *deacons*, is to " prove that no *minister* may marry a *second* " time," it is all but as bad as saying, with the church of *Rome*, that he *ought not* to *marry at all*.

With respect to the business of *polygamy*, as to the thing itself, nothing that is here said proves it to be more or less sinful in one man than in another; that depends wholly on the law

law of God delivered by Moses. Therefore the *prudential* reasons, for which he evidently excepted against *polygamists* being elected to *church-offices*, no more affects the matter of *polygamy*, than the excepting against *women* under sixty years old, proves it *sinful* in a woman to be *younger*, or that, because no woman was to be chosen to the office of a *deaconess* who had been *twice married*, therefore it was sinful for the woman to marry again after the death of her husband, contrary to 1 Cor. vii. 39. and to the express advice of the *Apostle*, 1 Tim. v. 14.

As to the supposed unlawfulness of *second* marriages, or the notion, that if a man lost his wife, it was *sinful* to marry again; this began very early in the church, and spread itself even to this country. We find in the time of *Ed.* I. * about the year 1276, the parliament adopted a constitution made by the *Pope* at *Lyons*, to exclude *men* that had been *twice married* from all *clerks privilege*. So that if a man was convicted of *felony*, who would otherwise have had *his clergy*, and it appeared that he had been *twice married*, he was to be *executed like other lay-people*. A statute of 18 Ed. III. mitigated the rigour of this law with respect to clerks, by making a suggestion of *bigamy* triable by the *ordinary*, before the *justices* could proceed. But all were delivered from the bondage of such laws by 1 Ed. VI. c. 12. § 16. which enacts, that

* See Burnet Hist. Ref. vol. ii. p. 323.

—" every

—" every person, who by any law or statute
" of this realm ought to have the *benefit of*
" *clergy*, shall be allowed the same, although
" he hath been *divers times married* to any
" single woman or single women, or to two
" wives or more, or to any widow or wi-
" dows."

Among the six famous articles proposed by Henry VIII. to the *parliament* and *convocation*, one was—" whether *priests*, that is to
" say, men dedicate to GOD by priesthood,
" may, by the law of GOD, marry after or
" no?"—" After great, long, deliberate,
" and advised disputation and consultation
" had and made concerning the said article,
" as well by the consent of the *King's High-*
" *ness*, as by the assent of the *Lords spiritual*
" *and temporal*, and other *learned* men of his
" *Clergy* in their *convocations*, and by the
" consent of the *Commons*, in this *present*
" *parliament* assembled, it was and is finally
" resolved, accorded, and agreed — that
" *priests*, after the order of priesthood re-
" ceived as afore, *may not* * *marry by the law*
" *of*

---

* In the *eighth century*, some monks pretended, that the angel *Gabriel* had brought *twelve* articles from heaven, one of which was, that *ecclesiastics* must not *marry*. See Jortin Rem. vol. ii. p. 43.

In the *ninth century*, *Pope Nicholas* I. made a decree to restrain *priests* from marrying. The bishop of *Augsburg* wrote a pathetic letter to the *Pope*, setting forth the sad and mischievous consequences of taking their wives from the *priests*. The letter is at large in *Fox*, vol. ii. p. 392. and well worth reading. He tells Pope *Nicholas*, that his predecessor *Saint Gregory* (i. e. Gregory

"of God. The enacting part of 31 Henry
"VIII. c. 14. goes on and says—If any
"person shall preach—teach—or obstinately
"affirm and defend, that any man, after the
"order of priesthood received, may marry
"or contract matrimony, he shall be ad-
"judged to suffer death, and forfeit lands
"and goods as a felon; and if any priest do
"actually marry or contract marriage with
"another, or any man that is or hath been
"a priest do carnally use any woman to
"whom he is or hath been married, or with
"whom he hath contracted matrimony, or
"openly be conversant or familiar with any
"such woman, both the man and the wo-
"man shall be * adjudged felons."

That gory IV.) made such a decree, but repented of it on this occasion; to use the old bishop's words as they are there translated—" Upon a certain day, as *St. Gregory* "sent to his fish-pond to have some fish, his servants "drained it, and found at the bottom 6000 infants "heads, which were brought to him. Upon this he "did greatly repent in himself his decree touching the "single life of the *priests*, which he confessed to be the "cause of that so lamentable murder." The letter in *Fox*, as above cited, is in Latin; the translation is referred to p. 393, as having been before inserted; which the reader may turn to. Whether the above letter was written by the *bishop of Augsburg*, according to Crit. Hist. *of England*, p. 83. or by *Volusianus bishop of Carthage*, as *Fox* seems to think, is very immaterial.

* How ought the *clergy* of the church of *England*, some of whom are not only *married* men, but, having lost a *first*, are now living in comfort, honour, and reputation with a *second wife*, (see before, p. 190. n.) to bless the day when men *dared* to attack the reigning *superstition* of the times, and in the face of all manner of
reproach,

That all this was contrary to the law of GOD is apparent; for the *priests* and *Levites* under the Old Testament, and the *apostles* and *other ministers* under the New Testament, who were respectively the *clergy* of the time, might marry, and many of them were actually married men. I therefore mention these things, to shew how we may be led into error, even to *putting men to death, thinking we do* GOD *service* (John xvi. 2.) when once the word of GOD is left for the inventions and *traditions of men*; and how far men may believe things which are *contrary* to scripture are *right* and *good*, and things *agreeable* to

reproach, and even of the danger of *death* itself, boldly vindicate those rights of mankind, with which the LAW OF GOD had invested them, but of which they had been deprived by the insolent tyranny of men like themselves?

It little concerned *Luther*, and his fellow *champions* for the honour of the DIVINE LAW—that they were called *antichrists—scandals to religion—revivers and propagators of the laws of Mahomet*—or that the Popish *Cerberus*, with his *three heads* of IGNORANCE, SUPERSTITION, and BLIND ZEAL, threatened to tear them to pieces. They *persevered*—they were *successful*—and what they sowed in times of *darkness* and *persecution*, we are reaping in days of *light* and *liberty*.

Thank GOD, the aforesaid *Cerberus* is chained up. He now will *bark*, and *bark* he may 'till he be *hoarse*; the man who minds him can have but little else to do.

The *author* of this book pretends not to be a *prophet* —but judging from what *has been* to what *may be*, he entertains not the least doubt, that, a *century* hence, the world may either wonder at the *man* who had WILDNESS enough to attack the *present system* of things with regard to *marriage*, or that there were found people who were ABSURD enough to abuse him for it.—This to THOSE WHOM IT MAY CONCERN—VERBUM SAT.

scripture

scripture are *wrong* and *abominable*—that this may become the *creed* of a *whole nation*, nay of a *whole church* including *many* nations, so as to gain the sanction of public *statutes*, the solemn opinions of *lawyers*, the most awful determinations of *courts of justice*. The condemnation of *polygamy* is equally an human device, and has no more authority from scripture for making a man *a felon and to suffer death* (see 1 Jac. c. 11.) for having *two wives*, than the stat. 31 Henry VIII. above mentioned, had for hanging a *priest* and the *woman* he had married. All these things are equally the inventions of men, or rather of * SATAN *transformed into an angel of light*; but the scriptures are the true *Ithuriel*'s spear, the *touch* of which alone can make him appear in his own shape, of *a lyar and a murderer from the beginning*.

The first public † law in the empire
against

---

* *Luther* saith well—" Satanæ commentum est, peccatum fingere ubi nullum est, & justitiam negare, ubi vera est."—" It is an invention of *Satan* to feign *sin* where there is none, and to deny *righteousness* where it truly is."

† In the year 324, Christianity was by *law established*, when *Constantine*, after the death of *Licinius*, reigned, without a colleague, sole lord of the *Roman empire*. However favourable the protection of the *civil magistrate* was at that time, as well as in after times, to the *Christian religion*, yet from hence we must date the misfortunes which have attended the interference of human power, in the establishment of *human systems* of *faith* and *ceremony*; the *former* of which have often been contrary to GOD's word, the *latter* utterly subversive of it. The advancement of the clergy in dignities, riches, and
honour

against *polygamy* was at the latter end of the *fourth* century, about the year 393, by the emperor *Theodosius*; this was repealed by the emperor *Valentinian* about *sixty* years afterwards, and the subjects of the empire were permitted to marry as *many wives* as they pleased; "nor does it appear (says *Chambers*, "tit. *Polygamy*) that the *bishops* made any "opposition to this introduction"—(he should have said *restoration*; for if it had not existed before, no law would have been made against it by *Theodosius)*—" of *polygamy* into "the empire." After all, no * human authority can decide upon the matter, as this has evidently given its suffrage *both ways* upon the same questions. But can the determinations of the *all-wise* GOD be thus precarious and contradictory? Can the Old Testament and New Testament be at as great a variance as the 31 Henry VIII. c. 14.—

honour, under this *emperor* and his successors, proved so many pernicious baits to sacerdotal ambition, avarice, and pride; and introduced those scenes of vice and profligacy among the clergy, which occasioned it to be said —Mundus *per ostium*, pietas per *fenestram*—The *world* entered in at the *door*—*piety* flew out at the *window*.

* For which reason, I forbear to lay any stress on the decisions of our chief *reformers*, Luther—Melancthon—Bucer—Zuinglius, &c. who, after a solemn consultation at *Wittemberg*, on the question—" whether for a man " to have *two wives at once*, was contrary to the *divine law?*" answered unanimously, " That it was not"— and, on this authority, *Philip* the *Landgrave of Hesse* actually married a *second wife*—his *first* being alive. This proves *what they thought*, but, by no means, that they thought *right*.

which

which makes it *death* for *both the man and woman*, in the case of a *priest*, to marry, or even to contract matrimony, or to affirm it lawful so to do—and the 5 and 6 * Edw. VI. c. 12. which declares the marriage of *clerks* to be as lawful as the marriages of *other* men?— Had the scriptures forbidden *polygamy*, all the human laws that ever could be enacted, and all the human authorities that ever could be produced, could not make it *lawful in the sight of* GOD—for that were to place men above GOD. On the other hand, if GOD hath not forbidden it, but even *allowed* it, all the men upon earth, though joined with all the *angels* in heaven, cannot make it *sinful* —for this were also to set the creatures above *their* MAKER. Judging and determining on the matter either way, but on the authority

---

* The preamble to this law affords a most striking proof of the power of *superstition* and *error* over the minds of men: for though 2 and 3 Edward VI. c. 21. had made it lawful for *priests* to *marry*, yet far the greater number of people held such marriages "to be "inconsistent with the law of GOD, and only to have "been *tolerated*" by the former statute, "like *usury* and "other unlawful things, to avoid greater inconvenience "and evils," insomuch that they "accounted the "children of such marriages to be *bastards*, as born in "unlawful wedlock, and would hardly attend the or- "dinances of the church, if administered by *married* "*priests*." Our prejudices against *polygamy* arise from the same source of error and superstition, and are equally unwarranted and groundless, as the *law of* GOD no more forbids *this* than it does the *other*. *Forbidding to marry*, where GOD has not forbidden it, is *the doctrine of devils* (1 Tim. iv. 1, 3.) however *holy*, *pure*, and *pious* it may be deemed, whether by *Protestants* or *Papists*.

of God's law, is a much more serious thing than is usually imagined; for there are as many *woes* pronounced on those *who call good evil*, as on *those who call evil good*. Is. v. 20.

The learned Grotius, in his book *De Ver. Christian. Rel.* lib. ii. § 13. note 12, seems to intimate, that 1 Cor. vii. 4. is to be relied on as a *text* full in point to prove the unlawfulness of *polygamy* amongst *Christians*; for that it was lawful amongst the *Jews*, he not only allows, but brings many authorities to prove, in *note* 7. on *lib.* ii. *sect.* 13. But there is another text, at ver. 2, which, as it has been looked upon as a conclusive argument against *polygamy*, I will first consider, and then proceed in order to the following verses, from ver. 2 to ver. 5, inclusive. The words of the text alluded to are —*Nevertheless, to avoid fornication, let every man have his own wife, and every woman her own husband.* The strength of the whole argument drawn from this passage consists in a sort of * quibble upon the word *wife*, that, as well as the word *husband*, being in the *singular number*—*wife*, not *wives*. But sup-

---

* I have elsewhere observed, on the danger of this method of interpretation, we have but to rely on the *sound* of words, and *all second* marriages are directly forbidden, ver. 27. *Art thou loosed from a wife? seek not a wife.* Again, the method of establishing doctrines by mere words or sentences detached from the context, might furnish us with as direct a prohibition of marriage to *Christians*, as ever was contended for in the primitive churches; for no words can be plainer than μὴ ζήτει γυναῖκα—*seek not a wife.*

pose

pose it had been said, "Let every man have his *own* servant, and every servant his *own* master," would it afford a conclusive proof, that because *no man can serve two masters*, therefore no master could have *more than one* servant?

However, as this text has been, and is, looked upon as a direct proof of the unlawfulness of *polygamy* among *Christians*, let us give it a thorough consideration. In the first place, let us restore it to its own genuine words; for our *translators* have introduced something which is not in the *original*. The words in the *Greek* are—Διὰ δὲ τὰς πορνείας—the verb *to avoid* is not there—the words τας πορνειας, which we translate *fornication*, are *plural*, not *singular*, and should be rendered *fornications*, or *the fornications*—they being in the *accusative* case, are governed, not by the verb *to avoid*, which *is not* in the text, but by the preposition διά, which *is*. This preposition διά has various meanings, according to the case it governs. Sometimes it governs a *genitive*—sometimes an *accusative*, and then it may signify—*for*;—so *Dr. Hammond* renders it here—*but for fornications*;—also—*with respect to*—*as to*—*with regard to*—*quod attinet ad*:—so ver. 26. διὰ την ενεστωσαν αναγκην, may be rendered, *with respect to (in respect of*—Dr. Hammond*) the present necessity*. Many authorities might be cited for this use of the word, both in sacred and profane writers; and it so suits with the subject-matter of the verse

verse in question, that I conceive this to be the sense of διὰ in this place.

The *context* shews very plainly, that what *St. Paul* says, is in answer to some *questions* put to him *by letter*, and sent to him at *Philippi*, where he appears to have been when he wrote the answer; and if we may judge of the *questions* by the * *answer*, which is surely

---

* This, in the instance before us, is the only way by which we can judge, as we have not the *Corinthians* letter itself to inform us of its contents; for want of which, there are some passages in the chapter *dark and hard to be understood*. Still a meaning they certainly must have; and our judgment, with respect to that meaning, should be directed—first, by a consideration of the manners, customs, dispositions, and characters of the *writers*, also of their situation with regard to time and place—secondly, of the character, situation, and office of the *answerer*; whose holy zeal, and consummate knowledge of the *divine law*, must render it impossible for him to write a syllable which doth not exactly harmonize with the Old Testament.

Both these I have endeavoured to keep in view, while I have been setting down my thoughts on this passage of scripture.

When the *Apostle* saith, ἕκαστος τὴν ἑαυτῦ γυναῖκα 'ΕΧΕ'ΤΩ, he certainly uses the verb ἔχω in a larger sense than merely *having*.—This verb signifies to *possess*, *retain*, which is to *continue the possession of*. So it is apparently used, Matt. xiv. 4. where *John the Baptist* tells *Herod*, concerning *Herodias his brother Philip's wife*, whom *Herod* had taken to himself—Οὐκ ἔξεστί σοι 'ΕΧΕΙΝ αὐτὴν. So *Mark* vi. 18. Οὐκ ἔξεστί σοι 'ΕΧΕΙΝ τὴν γυναῖκα τοῦ ἀδελφοῦ σε—where the *Baptist* cannot be supposed *merely* to condemn *Herod's having* her at first, but also to declare the unlawfulness of his *retaining*, or *continuing the possession of* her. So here—let every man *retain*, *continue the possession of*—γυναῖκα, *the wife*—τὴν ἑαυτῦ, of *himself*—i. e. who is his own property—and not suffer her to go to other men,

surely a very fair way of judging, they probably concerned a very infamous, but common practice, that of *married men* lending out

as the custom was, nor take other men's wives to himself.

The Apostle proceeds—καὶ ἑκάςη τὸν ἼΔΙΟΝ ἄνδρα ἘΧΕΤΩ.—Here is an evident variation in the phraseology, on which we shall take occasion to observe hereafter. At present, let it be noticed, that the introduction of the word ἼΔΙΟΝ, must affect, and materially, the meaning of the word ἘΧΕΤΩ, and make also the word ἄνδρα to be taken in an exclusive sense—as thus—*Let every* (wife) retain, possess (i. e. *keep to,* as we say) the man or husband *appropriated* to her *exclusively of all other men*.

Thus both parts of the verse are in the strictest analogy with the *divine law*, and equally contribute to reprobate the breach of it by "community of women," which was a *Gentile*-custom.

As for the conclusion against *polygamy*, which is drawn from the word *wife*, as well as the word *husband*, being in the *singular* number, it will not hold; for the scriptures plainly shew us, that *wife* must frequently be understood in a *distributive* sense. A remarkable passage of this sort is in 1 Tim. iii. 12. Let *the deacons be the husbands of* ONE WIFE—μιᾶς γυναικὸς ἄνδρες. But can any body suppose, that there was to be but *one wife* amongst them all?—So in the tenth commandment—*Thou shalt not covet thy neighbour's* WIFE—This (like *ox, ass, house, servant*) must be taken in a *distributive* sense, and mean any *married woman* or *women* whatsoever. So Exod. xxi. 33, 34. *If a man dig a pit, and not cover it, and an ox or an ass fall therein—the owner of the pit shall make it good,* &c. Are not *pits,* and *oxen,* and *asses,* to be here understood? So in the text, the word *wife* means any *woman* or *women* who may be married to the man.

The word *husband* must be understood in an *exclusive* sense, because the whole *Bible* shews that a woman could have but *one husband*—here well expressed by the Ἴδιον ἄνδρα. In short, this scripture, like all others, must be interpreted according to the *analogy of the faith*, by taking a view of the *divine law* in all its parts, and not by con-

or even *marrying* their *wives* to other people, and of courſe the *married women* going from their *own husbands* to *other* men. That this was the caſe in *Corinth*, may well be taken for granted, when we conſider that there were ſo many ſources from which ſuch practices were ſo eaſily derived. The *Corinthians*

fining ourſelves to mere literal conſtruction of a ſingle word—or text—or paſſage; for, by this means, we might be brought into all the errors of the *church of Rome*, or into all the *hereſies* that have been invented; not one of which is without ſome *text* of ſcripture for its ſupport, which being *wreſted* from all the reſt, has been *wreſted* from its meaning, and made to ſignify juſt what the fancies of men have applied it to. It is very truly obſerved by an antient writer, " *Turpe eſt* " *tota lege non inſpecta, vel perlecta, de lege judicare.*" " To judge of the law, without reading over and ex- " amining *the whole*, is ſhameful."—He proceeds—" Ita " turpe etiam *theologo textum originalem* in ſcriptura ſa- " cra non inſpicere, aut illum ſtudio præterire, & tamen " ſcripturam explicare velle."—" So it is ſhameful in a " *theologiſt* not to inſpect *the original text* in the ſacred " ſcripture, or purpoſely to paſs it by, and yet pretend " to explain the ſcripture." If this ſentiment had had its due weight, it would have leſſened the numbers of *expoſitors* and *commentators* on the BIBLE, in no inconſiderable degree.

The interpretation which the *Rhemiſts* give to this 1 Cor. vii. 2. is by no means to be deſpiſed—I will here ſet it down; for—

——— *Fas eſt & ab hoſte doceri.* ———

" Let every one *have*, *keep*, or *uſe* his own wife, to " whom he was married before his converſion; for the " Apoſtle here anſwereth to the firſt queſtion of the *Co-* " *rinthians*, which was not—whether it were lawful to " marry? but—whether they were not bound, upon " their converſion, to abſtain from the company of " their wives married before in their infidelity? as ſome
" did

thians were a people lewd and * debauched to a proverb—Κορινθιαζειν, to *Corinthianize,* or play the *Corinthian,* was a *phrase* which expressed a man's being abominable:—add to this the fondness of the *Greeks* for the maxims of the *divine* PLATO, as he was called, one of which was—κοινας μεν γυναικας, κοινας δε ειναι παιδας, that "women and children "ought to be common:"—add to this the sect of the *Gnostics,* those early *heretics,* who held "a community of women, and that all "marriage was of † the devil;"—these spread their errors far and wide among the *Christian* churches:—and lastly—the horrid practice of *men's lending their wives to others,*

"did persuade them they ought to be." This would seem a good exposition of the place, if the *Apostle* had not so expressly treated *this point* in the following *verse.*

* See 1 Cor. vi. 11. former part. *Strabo* writes, that there was at *Corinth* a temple of *Venus,* so rich, that it maintained above a thousand harlots sacred to her service, ιεροδουλους έταιρας, which were consecrated both by men and women to that goddess. See the advantage and necessity of the *Christian* revelation, by *J. Leland,* D. D. vol. i. p. 174. Others say, that the number of prostitutes in honour of *Venus* at *Corinth* was 2000. See *Lett. of Jews* to *Voltaire,* vol. ii. p. 53.

Strabo, Geog. lib. xii. speaking of the temple of the *moon* in *Comana* of *Cappadocia,* where all manner of the most horrid *impurities* were committed, as parts of *religious worship,* calls it—" *a little* CORINTH."

† Among the errors of the famous *Manes* or *Manichæus,* in the third *century,* this principle is found—he taught, that "all marriage is of the devil, invented by "him to tie the souls to the flesh, and to retard their "return to heaven." See *Jortin's Remarks,* vol. ii. p. 50.

was even a fort of ‡ law in *Greece*; this originated firſt in *Sparta,* that famous city of *Peloponneſus,* on the edge of which *Corinth* ſtood; from thence it ſpread itſelf into the reſt of the cities of *Greece, Corinth,* no doubt, as well as others. The following account of this vile cuſtom is to be found in *Plutarch*'s life of the celebrated *Spartan* lawgiver *Lycurgus.* " He *(Lycurgus)* next bethought
" himſelf how to prevent that wild and wo-
" maniſh paſſion of *jealouſy,* by making it a
" matter of reputation, not only to baniſh
" from matrimony all violence and diſorder,
" but alſo to allow men the freedom of *im-*
" *parting the uſe of their wives* to deſerving
" perſons, that ſo they might have children
" by them. And he laughed at thoſe who
" think the violation of the marriage-bed
" ſuch an inſupportable affront, that they
" revenge it by murders and cruel wars.
" *Lycurgus* thought a man not to be blamed,
" who, being in years, and having a young
" wife, ſhould recommend ſome virtuous
" handſome young man, that ſhe might
" have a child by him, who might inherit
" the good qualities of ſuch a father, and

‡ *Grotius,* ſpeaking of the *Jewiſh divorces,* faith—
" Quod et hodie uſurpant *Mahumetiſtæ,* & olim *Græci*
" ac *Latini* tanta licentia, ut & uxores ad tempus uten-
" das aliis darent *Lacones* & Cato." Which the *Mahometans often practiſe at this day, and formerly the Greeks* and *Latins, with ſuch licentiouſneſs, that they could grant the uſe of their wives to others for a* GIVEN TIME. *This was the caſe among the Lacedemonians, and Cato alſo did the ſame.* See Grot. de Verit. lib. ii. § 13.

" this

" this child the good man loves as ten-
" derly as if he was his own getting.—On
" the other hand, a worthy man, who was
" in love with a *married woman* upon ac-
" count of her modesty, and well-favoured-
" ness of her children, might, without for-
" mality, *beg of her husband a night's lodging*,
" that he might, like slips of a fine tree,
" planted in a goodly garden, have children
" of a good race, and well related. For *Ly-
" curgus* was of opinion, that children were
" not so much the propriety of their parents,
" as of the *whole commonwealth*; and there-
" fore he would not have them begotten by
" the *first comers*, but by the best men that
" could be found."

This custom was far from being reckoned *criminal* * or *adulterous*, it was applauded greatly;

---

* The *community of wives* cannot be conceived to have escaped the lewd *Corinthians*, when we consider how it spread far and wide among the *Gentiles*. This is said to have been the custom of the Troglodytes, Agathyrsi, the Massagetæ, and Scythians, of whom *Strabo* saith—
" they had their *wives in common*, agreeably to the laws
" of *Plato*."

The natives of *Russian Lapland* were confusedly known to the antients under the name of *Troglodytes* or *northern pigmies*. They are, for the most part, not above *four feet* and *an half* high, and dwell in caverns; they are just the same people they were formerly—they are said to intreat strangers to lie with their wives and daughters, as an *honour* done to them, and from a desire of amending, by their means, the defects of their own race. See *Volt.* Works. Transl. by *Franklin*, vol. xxviii. p. 10, 12.

Puffendorf has given a long list of other nations, which had the same custom among them, such as the antient inhabitants of *Britain*, the *Sabeans*, those of the

greatly; and "so far were women from that scandalous liberty which has been objected to them, that they knew not what the name of *adultery* meant."—"A proof of this we have in *Geradas*, a very antient *Spartan*, who, being asked by a stranger what punishment their law had appointed for *adultery?* answered—"My friend, there are no *adulterers* in our country." "But, replies the stranger, suppose there were one, how would you punish him?" He answered—"The offender must pay to the plaintiff a bull, with a neck so long, that he might drink out of the river *Eurotas*, from over the top of mount *Taygeta*." "Why, 'tis impossible to find such a bull, said the man." *Geradas* smiling replied— "'Twas just as impossible to find an *adulterer* in *Sparta*." It is endless to observe on the total blindness of such people, with respect to the *law of* GOD: but when the *Corinthians* were awakened to a sense of *divine* things, though, as well as others in that part of *Greece*, they had been * infected with this

kingdom of *Calecut*, the antient *Lithuanians*, &c. See *Leland*, vol. ii. p. 129, note r.

Diogenes, whom *Epictetus* celebrates with the epithet of *divine*, held that " *women ought to be common*"—looking upon marriage to be nothing; "that every man and woman might keep company with whom they liked best, and that therefore children ought to be in common." Ib. 132. So the *Stoics* held that *women ought to be in common* among the wise, 133.

* *Lycurgus* established his laws in *Lacedæmon* almost 900 years before CHRIST, so that they had full time to circulate and grow into customs, not only in *Greece*, but also in many other parts of the world.

Spartan leaven, and followed the *practices*, as they had imbibed the principles of their *neighbours*; yet neither custom, example, nor prejudice of education, could silence, or any longer satisfy their consciences, and therefore they seem to have written to the *apostle*, to know his sense of the matter; which he clearly gives them in the words of the text, and which evidently reprobate this horrid * custom. Having, in the preceding *chapter*, discussed at large the subjects of *whoredom* and *fornication*, and lewdness in general, he begins this seventh *chapter* with an answer to the *particular* questions proposed to him in the letter which he had received from them. The passage may be thus paraphrased:—*Now concerning the things whereof ye wrote unto me*—" I say, first in general,
" though not for the reasons which some of
" your *philosophers* have given, nor for those
" which the *Gnostics* have suggested, as if
" marriage was *wrong* or *sinful in itself*, but
" for *prudential* reasons, arising from the si-
" tuation of things at this time (ver. 26.)
" *it is good*, καλὸν, *useful, profitable* (ver. 8
" and 26.) *for a man not to touch a woman*—

---

* By the manner of *St. Paul*'s expressing himself, 1 Cor. v. 1. he seems to insinuate, that, one man's taking or *having another's wife*, was a matter by no means *unheard of amongst the Gentiles*; though a man's having *his father's wife* was.

See an instance of this sort of degeneracy among the *Jews*, Amos ii. 7.

" to have no dealings with the *other* † *sex.*
" (See Matt. xix. 11, 12.) *But with respect*
" *to the * fornications* you mention, and con-
" cerning which you desire to know my sen-
" timents; I answer, conformably to the
" law of God, which ordains, that a man
" *shall cleave to his wife,* &c. (Gen. ii. 24.)
" and that no woman shall *depart from her*
" *husband,* and *go to another man* (see Rom.
" vii. 1, 2, 3). *Let every man have his*
" *wife*—την γυναικα εαυτε—the woman who
" belongs to him—and not lend her out, or

---

† Μη απ]εσθαι γυναικα is construed by some learned men, by *ducere uxorem*—*to marry a wife*;—but I rather think our translation right—*not to touch a woman*—for, as the word ανθρωπω denotes *man* in a *general* sense, so, to make both parts of the sentence correspond with each other, the γυναικα seems to be general also. The word απ]εσθαι answers to the Hebrew נגע, which sometimes means to *touch* or *meddle with,* in a *carnal* sense. See Gen. xx. 6.

* There is no necessity to restrain the word πορνειας in this place, as our translators seem to have done, to the idea of what is usually meant by that term, that is to say, *commerce with harlots*; for it is a general word, expressive of *adultery,* as well as what is called *fornication.* Thus the *apostle* uses it but a little before in this very *epistle,* chap. v. 1. to denote not only *adultery,* but also *incest.* It is used as signifying *adultery,* Matt. v. 32. xix. 9; for though it may there signify lewdness committed before marriage, but not found out till afterwards, yet it must necessarily also be understood to mean such acts done after marriage; for our Lord cannot be supposed to mean that the *former* was a just cause of *divorce,* and not the *latter*—so that the word πορνεια must include *both.* Πορνειας being plural, well denotes the complicated crimes of the husband's lending his wife to another man, and the wife's going to another man besides her husband, including also the crime of him who took her.

" suffer

"suffer her to marry another, nor let him
"take a woman who is not γυνη εαυτȣ, *his*
"*wife*, but another man's, to himself. So
"*also let every* married *woman have her own*
"proper *husband*—τον ιδιον ανδρα—the man
"appropriated to her, exclusively of all other
"men upon earth, and not depart, or suffer
"herself to *lent* or *given* to any *other* man."

I would here observe, that there is a very remarkable difference of expression, which though preserved in many other translations, is not in ours. We render the two clauses just alike, whereas they are not so in the original, but—την 'ΕΑΥΤΟΥ γυναικα, and τον ΙΔΙΟΝ ανδρα. The *Latin* translations preserve this difference of expression—*suam uxorem*—*proprium virum*. Leusd. ex Mont. So the old and new translations in *Beza*'s Testament, and *Barker*'s Eng. Test. 1615, and the *Geneva*, 1557. *Let every man have* HIS WIFE, *and every woman her* OWN *husband. If all scripture be given by inspiration of* GOD, (2 Tim. iii. 16.) and holy men *spake as they were moved by the Holy Ghost*, (2 Pet. i. 21.) I cannot but think that there is some weighty reason for the difference of expression, in giving the epithet 'Ιδιον to the *husband*, with respect to the *wife*, and not to the *wife*, with respect to the *husband*. This is observable, not only in this place, but in * many others.

Leigh,

* Rom. viii. 32. we meet with a very material proof of the *emphatical* import of the word 'Ιδιος, to denote CHRIST's being GOD's *own proper son*, in such a sense as no creature is or can be. So, in the passage under consideration,

Leigh, Crit. Sac. observes this, as occurring every where in the sacred writings of the New Testament—*uxoribus sui* ιδιοι ανδρες *tribuuntur passim in sacris*. Leigh sub voc. ιδιος. Eph. v. 24, 25. τοῖς ἰδίοις ἀνδράσιν, *their own husbands*—τὰς γυναῖκας ἑαυτῶν, *your wives*;— and ver. 28, τας ἑαυτων γυναικας, *their wives*— την ἑαυτȣ γυναικα, *his wife*.—Again, *Col*. iii. 18, 19. τοῖς ἰδίοις ἀνδρασιν— *propriis viris*—*their* OWN *husbands*—τὰς γυναῖκας, *your wives* (ἑαυτῶν being understood). *St. Peter, who was the apostle of the circumcision*, uses the same mode of expression, 1 Pet. iii. 1. *Let the wives be subject*, τοις ἰδιοις ἀνδρᾶσιν—*propriis viris*—*to their* OWN *husbands*. Comp. 1 Pet. iii. 5. The word ἰδιος has certainly an emphatical meaning wherever we find it, therefore must have its emphasis in this place, as well as in others. It seems to denote such an *appropriation* of the *husband* to the *wife*, as that she could not *have*, or *go to any other man*. This idea may be illustrated from Rom. xiv. 4. *Who art thou that judgest another man's ser-*

---

deration, the word Ιδιος denotes that the man is the woman's husband, in such a sense as no other man is or can be. CHRIST, John v. 18, is said to call GOD Ιδιον Πατερα—His *own proper father:*—this must be in a sense as exclusive of *all other beings*, as the ιδιος ἀνηρ is exclusive of *all other men*.

So 1 Cor. xv. 38. *God giveth it a body as it pleaseth Him, and to every seed*—το ιδιον σωμα—*his* OWN *body*, i. e. so peculiarly appropriated to that sort of grain that it can pass into no other.—Thus hath GOD given to every WIFE—τον ιδιον ἀνδρα — *her own — peculiar — appropriated*—HUSBAND—so that, *while he liveth* (Rom. vii. 3.) she can *pass* to no other man.

vant?

vant? τῷ ἰδίῳ κυρίῳ—*proprio domino*—*to his* OWN *master he standeth or falleth*. Here ἰδιος is used as an epithet to the *master* with respect to the *servant* (as 1 Tim. vi. 1. Tit. ii. 9.) and must denote such an *appropriation* of the master to the servant, as to exempt the servant from the authority, power, controul, command, or service of any other, but that *of his own* (ἰδιɛ) master; for, as was observed before, *no man can serve two masters*, though the master may have *many servants*; nor is any of his servants the less so, because he has others. So here, 1 Cor. vii. 2. and the other passages referred to, the husband is styled ἰδιον, to denote, that *no other* man can have any power, propriety, or interest whatsoever in the society of the wife, but the ἰδιος ἀνηρ, the proper and appropriated, peculiar husband. I own that I can account for this difference of expression in no other way, than by supposing the *scripture* consistent with itself, and that the distinction so evident in the Old Testament was to be preserved throughout the New Testament—that though a man might have *more than one wife*, yet a woman could have but *one husband*; had she more, neither could be styled properly ἰδιος ἀνηρ, for she would be as much the property of one as of the other, or rather be *in common* between, or among them, according to their number; whereas, doubtless, though a man has *two wives*, each may be properly styled γύνη ἑαυτοῦ—*his wife.

* The propriety of this can hardly be disputed, when we reflect that it is the constant language of the Old Testament.

No man may be said to have an *exclusive* property in, or appropriation of himself to, a person or thing, which others may share with him: therefore the word ἴδιος is peculiarly adapted to denote the *exclusive* appropriation of the *husband to the wife* to be, like the *exclusive* appropriation of the *master* to the *servant*, such a one as gives to him *alone*, exclusive of all others, the whole *attention, obedience*, and *service* of the party, so long as the relation which requires these shall continue. Whereas γυνη, *wife*, is never found with the *exclusive* ἴδιος, but coupled only with the pronoun possessive ἑαυτȣ. To illustrate what has been said, we may observe as to *Jacob* and his two wives, *Leah* and *Rachel*, *Rachel* as well as *Leah*, with respect to *Jacob*, was γυνη ἑαυτȣ, *his wife* (Gen. xxx. 26. xxxi. 50.) and he the ἴδιος ἀνηρ, the *husband*, exclusively of all other men, *appropriated* to *both*, insomuch that *neither* could have gone to any other man, without being an *adulteress*: but we no where find *Jacob*, nor any other *polygamist*, stigmatized as an *adulterer* or *fornicator*, on account of his having *two wives*. That such a custom as *Plutarch* shews to have originated from the famous lawgiver of *Sparta*, should reach *Corinth*, which stood at the edge of *Peloponnesus*, is not at all surprizing, when we find it had even reached to * *Rome*. *Numa Pompilius*, the

---

* In short, this custom of *lending* wives to each other was so common among the *Gentiles*, that it is inconceivable such a practice should not be among the *Corinthians*.
Cæsar

the famous succeffor of *Romulus*, anno 715 before *Chrift*, eftablifhed this horrid practice among the *Romans*. He was a great reformer of *religion*, and improver of the *laws*, in which he is faid " to have had a particular " regard to the preferving of *modefty* in wo-
" men. Neverthelefs, he permitted huf-
" bands to lend their wives, after they had
" had children by them. This was a kind
" of temporary *divorce*, in favour of thofe
" men whofe wives were barren; but the
" hufbands ftill continued to have the fame
" power over them, and could call them
" home, or lend them to others, as they
" pleafed." Ant. Univ. Hift. vol. xi. p. 298.

That this practice long continued at *Rome*, there can be little doubt; for, about 700 years afterwards, we find, that *Cato* of *Utica* actually gave his wife *Marcia* to his friend *Hortenfius*, and himfelf affifted at the wedding.

The words of the text clearly apply to the forbidding fo monftrous a breach of the law of marriage, and apply equally to *polygamy* as to *monogamy*. *Abigail* and *Ahinoam*

Cæfar tells us of the antient *Britons*—" *Ten* or *twelve* " of them have wives in common amongft them—but " every woman's children are accounted his, who firft " poffeffed her when a virgin; fo many men, having " each of them married his proper wife, afterwards " agreed upon that friendly way of poffeffing them." De B. G. lib. v. Much more to the fame purpofe may be found in *Puffendorf*, book vi. c. 1. § 15.

were,

were, with respect to *David*, each of them γυνὴ ἑαυτȣ, *his wife*—for the *Holy Ghost* faith, 1 Sam. xxv. 43. *they were both of them his wives:* and therefore he was the ἴδιος ἀνηρ, the peculiar, proper, appropriated husband to both. If DAVID had taken *another man's wife*, or either of them had been lent out or given to another man, this would have fallen directly under the interdict of the *apostle*, who here says no more than is exactly consonant with the *law of Moses*.

Saying that this text forbids *polygamy*, because the word *wife* is in the singular number, is mere trifling; as much so, as contending that a man is to love but *one* * *neighbour*, because it is said, *Thou shalt love thy neighbour as thyself*; not *neighbours*; or that he shall keep but *one servant*, because it is said,

---

* We meet with numberless passages in the scripture, where the *singular* is not to be understood *exclusively*, that is, so as not to include the *plural*, but *distributively* so as to include it. Witness the passages referred to, as also the *fourth* commandment—" Thou shalt do no " manner of work, thou nor thy *son*, nor thy *daughter*, " nor thy *man-servant*, nor thy *maid-servant*, nor the " *stranger* that is within thy gates." Are we to gather from hence, that a man is to have but *one son*, *one daughter*, *one man-servant*, *one maid-servant*, &c.? So the ninth commandment—" Thou shalt not bear false wit- " ness against thy *neighbour*."—Endless are the examples of this sort, which might be brought, to shew that, in many instances, the *singular* number cannot be confined to an *exclusive* sense, but must, of necessity, be extended *distributively*, so as to include *many*, and indeed *all* of the kind which is spoken of: and in this sense the word *wife* must be understood, 1 Cor. vii. 2, in order to make the text harmonize with the Old Testament.

Rom.

Rom. xiv. 4. *Who art thou that judgeſt another's man's ſervant*, in the *ſingular* number, not *ſervants*, in the *plural*: or to argue for *polygamy*, becauſe it is ſaid, 1 Cor. vii. 29. *they that have wives*, and not *every one that has a wife*. All ſuch literal or verbal criticiſm is mere *word-catching*, far below the dignity of fair argument, and deſerves nothing but contempt.

Thoſe who repreſent the *apoſtle* as addreſſing himſelf to *ſingle* perſons, and adviſing them to marry, *to avoid fornication*, make him guilty of evident *tautology*—for the eighth verſe is expreſſly addreſſed to the *unmarried* and *widows*. After wiſhing that all, like himſelf, could live *unmarried* (that they might have leſs diſtraction in their attendance on the ſervice of God, ver. 35.) he adds —*but if they cannot contain let them marry, for it is better to marry than burn*—πυρουϲθαι, to *be fired*, to be *on fire*—(comp. *Cant*. viii. 6. *Hoſ*. vii. 4.) that is, with *luſt*, or unchaſte deſires, by which they might be driven into the commiſſion of *fornication*, and all *manner of uncleanneſs*;—which is, in effect, ſaying the ſame thing over again, as ſome would have him to ſay at the *ſecond* verſe, the very terms of which ſhew it to be addreſſed to *married perſons*; for how could the *apoſtle* ſay to a *ſingle man*—*let him have*—ἐχετω, *retain* —γυναικα ἑαυτȣ, *his wife*; or to a *ſingle woman*—*let her have*, i. e. *keep to*—τον ἰδιον ανδρα, *her own huſband?* The immediate connection of this verſe with the three following,
which

which can belong to *married people only*, is another strong argument for the truth of this observation. Besides, if we understand the ἑκαστος, *every man*, and the ἑκαστη, *every woman*, to relate here to any but the *married people*, it may seem to make the *apostle* command *every one to marry*, whether they chuse it or not, contrary to ver. 7, 8. The word ἑκαστος is certainly *relative*, and must agree with some *masculine* substantive understood: this can be, (agreeably to the rest of the verse) nothing but ἀνηρ, which, in the last clause, must signify *husband*—τον ιδιον ανδρα, *her own husband*, and so in the *four times* it is used in the two *following* verses. The word ἑκαστη is also *relative*, and must agree with some *feminine* substantive understood; this can be no other than γυνη, which, in this verse, is rendered *wife*; and so the *four times* it is used in the following verses. If the ανηρ and γυνη which are *understood*, had been rendered as they are uniformly in the rest of the *context*, all difficulty in understanding, and all disputes about, the *apostle*'s meaning had been saved, and the *evil alluded to* reprobated in as plain terms as the *apostle* intended it should; for the verse would have stood thus—*Let every husband* (or married man) have *his wife*—γυναικα ἑαυτȣ, the wife that belongs to him—*and every wife* (or married woman) have *her own husband*.

When he addresses himself to *single persons*, and advises them to *marry* to *avoid fornication* (which is certainly the meaning of

ver.

ver. 9.) he does not use a *doubtful* * *periphrasis*, but speaks the matter in the common usual phrase—γαμησάτωσαν—*let them marry*. There is something remarkable also at the tenth and eleventh verses, where, in answer to some questions put to him in the *Corinthians* letter, probably about *married persons*, who were in a state of *separation*, he says—*Let not the wife depart from her husband, but if she depart*—μενέτω ἄγαμος—*let her remain unmarried*. Comp. Rom. vii. 3. and 1 Cor. vii. 39. This is said to be the *command of* God, ver. 10; how is it that it is not extended *to the husband?* It is only said—*Let not the husband put away his wife*. Had he construed Matt. xix. 9. by the *sound* instead of the *sense*, he most probably would have said of the *husband* also, μενέτω ἄγαμος—*let him remain unmarried*, in case of *her departure*, or of his *putting her away*.

But as those *false apostles, deceitful workers, transforming themselves into the apostles of* Christ, 2 Cor. xi. 13. had, by their *erroneous* and monstrous doctrines, saying, "that all marriage was of the *Devil*" (for such was the doctrine of the *Gnostics)* sadly distressed the consciences of weak people, and led them to think, that, as *marriage* was a *sinful* thing, therefore all conjugal inter-

---

* Which seems not conformable to the *idiom* of the *Greek language* itself, for I do not recollect, that, in any *Greek author*, any more than in the *scriptures*, ἔχειν γυναικα, or ἔχειν ἄνδρα, ever signifies to *marry*, or stands as a phrase for γαμειν or γαμηθηναι.

course between married people must be * _sin-ful_ too, we find the _apostle_ proceeding, ver. 3. to answer that part of the _letter_ which related to their distress on this account. But, so far from deeming the intercourse of married persons wrong, he says—" Let the husband ren-
" der unto the wife _due benevolence_, Ὀφειλο-
" μενην ἐυνοιαν (which answers to the ענה of
" _Moses_, Exod. xxi. 10. and which we de-
" cently render _duty of marriage)_ and like-
" wise _the wife unto the husband. The wife_
" _has not power over her own body_, so as to
" withdraw herself entirely from the _con-_
" _jugal debt, but the husband_ may, as a mat-
" ter of right, have access to her at all pro-
" per times and seasons. Likewise _the hus-_
" _band has not the power_ (ȣκ ἐξȣσιαζει) _of his_
" _own body_, so as to withdraw from the con-
" jugal intercourse with his wife, _but the_
" _wife_, as a debt due from the contract
" which the man is under to her, by the
" very terms of their union, has a right to
" his _society_.

" Therefore, _defraud ye not one the other_—
" μη ἀπογερειτε ἀλληλους—do not _deprive_ or
" _wrong_ each other in these respects, under
" a false notion of its being sinful to come
" together as man and wife. There may
" be _times_, indeed, when both may find it

---

* In the 4th century there were a set of people who censured _matrimony_, and said, that " wives and husbands " _cohabiting_ together cannot be saved." These were condemned by the council of _Gangara_, anno 369. _Jortin_ Rem. vol. iv. p. 43.

" expedient,

" expedient, and therefore both consent to
" separate for a while; as on occasion of
" particular abstinence and devotion: but
" let not even this exceed the bounds of
" prudence, lest, if it should, *Satan* should
" take the advantage of you, and tempt
" you to gratify, in an unlawful way, those
" desires which may lawfully be satisfied
" between married persons. However, I do
" not insist upon the matter of your parting,
" even for a season, by way *of commandment*,
" κατ' επιταγην, but by way of *permission*,
" κατα συγγνωμην." See 2 *Cor.* viii. 10.

I take the Ὀφειλομενην ἐυνοιαν of *Paul* to answer exactly to the word ענה, which is rendered *duty of marriage*. This is mentioned by *Moses* to be still due to the *first wife*, though a man take a *second. Exod.* xxi. 10. Therefore this passage of *St. Paul* no more concludes against *polygamy*, than that of *Moses*, which actually supposes it. The root ענה, means to *act upon some person or thing*—and, in *Kal*, to *lie with a woman*, Gen. xxxiv. 2. Deut. xxi. 14. Deut. xxii. 24, 29: so that by comparing scripture with scripture, we shall find one part explain the other. There is a similarity of expression between *Moses* and *Paul*, which, I own, makes me think that the *latter* copied the sentiments of the *former*, upon the subjects before us. *Moses* saith וענתה לא יגרע—*her duty of marriage he shall not withold—subtract—withdraw—keep back from* her. *Paul* says—*let the husband render to the wife due benevolence*—Ὀφειλομενην

Ἐυνοιαν

Ἐυνοιαν—which is saying the same thing, in other words indeed, but with the same meaning. To *render* to another their due, is not to *withold* it; and not to *withold* it, is to *render* it. *Paul* says, μη ἀποϛερειτε—*Moses* says לא יגרע, which the LXX actually translate ἐκ ἀποϛερήσει. This is the very identical verb which we translate *defraud* not. גרע signifies to *subtract* or *withdraw*—to *withold* or *keep back*;—the Greek ἀποϛερεω has the *same meaning*—so that *Paul* may be said to translate, just as the LXX have done, the גרע of *Moses*. The only shadow of difference between the *Jewish law-giver*, and the *Christian apostle*, consists in the explicitness of the *latter*, and concisenes of the *former*. *Moses*'s words imply what *Paul*'s declare, and, *vice versâ*, *Paul* declares what is implied by *Moses*. If the *husband* is not to withold the *marriage-duty* from *the wife*, this must imply that the *wife* is not to withold it from the *husband*. There must be a parity of reason in both cases. Neither *husband* nor *wife* can *have any such power over their own bodies*. This is plainly *said* by *Paul*, and, in consistence with the *law of marriage*, must evidently be *meant* by *Moses*. For my own part, I as much believe that *Paul* had the doctrine in Exod. xxi. 10. in his mind, when he * wrote

* On looking into *Pole* Syn. in 1 Cor. vii. 3. I find him of the same opinion—" Respexit hic *Paulus* locum " illum, Ex. xxi. 10. ibi enim idem quod hic marito " præcipitur." " *Paul* here looked back to that place " in Exod. xxi. 10. for there the same thing is com- " manded to the husband as here."

that

that part of the answer to the *Corinthians* letter, wherein he solved their difficulties about the *intercourse* of married people, as it is now in my mind, while I am writing these words; and thus, upon good authority, even that of the mind of GOD as delivered by *Moses*, he could be so peremptory in declaring that *such intercourse* was *duty* on both sides, and therefore could not (as the *Gnostic* doctrine might have led them to suppose) be a *sin*.

St. Paul, who, before his conversion, *had profited in the Jews religion above many his equals in his own nation*, Gal. i. 14. could hardly, after his conversion, be ignorant of the law of *Moses*; so far from it, he was, undoubtedly, a most accomplished teacher of it. Witness the masterly manner in which he explains the sense and meaning of the *moral* law, and unfolds the whole design of the *ceremonial* law. By the first, he demonstrated the necessity of the *gospel* for salvation—by the *second*, he shewed the *gospel* to have been one and the same, though under different dispensations of it, from the fall of *Adam* to the coming of *Jesus Christ*. Now to set *Paul*, as a law-giver, in *Moses'* seat, and to represent him as condemning that which was not condemned by the *law of Moses*, is to make him act inconsistently with his own declaration, Rom. iii. 31. *Do we make void the law through faith?*—GOD *forbid! yea—we establish the law.* It is to make him transgress the law, by despising that solemn sanction, which equally forbad *adding to it, or dimi-*

nishing from it; and to put him in much the same situation with those, whether *men or angels*, who preached *any other gospel* than *that which he preached*; for to preach any other law than that *which was given by* Moses, is as great an offence as to preach any other *gospel* than that which *came by* Jesus Christ. This we may learn from the very words of the law itself. Deut. iv. 2. xii. 32.

Dr. *Whitby*, a very laborious and learned commentator, in his comment on—*the husband*, ἐκ ἐξουσιαζει, *hath not power of his own body, &c.* says—" Here is a plain * argument " against *polygamy*." That here is a plain argument to prove that he shall not withhold the *duty of marriage* from the wife, and that, in this respect, *neither* shall *defraud* or withold from the other, on proper occasions, the *conjugal debt*, is very certain. But as what is here said, is founded in the very *nature* and *essence* of the *marriage-relation*, it must equally concern all that ever have married, or shall marry, to the end of the world, as

* " Sane *patres Tridentini*," saith one, " si adhuc in
" vivis essent, ipsis immortales agerent gratias, quod a
" scripturis anathematis in polygamos vibrati justitiam
" atque æquitatem defenderint, eaque præstiterint quæ
" ipsi ne quidem audere voluerint."
" Truly the *fathers* of the *council of Trent*, if they
" were yet alive, would give immortal thanks to those
" who should defend, out of the holy scripture, the
" justice and equity of their *curse* brandished against *po-*
" *lygamists*, and who should do that, which they them-
" selves would not even dare to attempt."

well

well under the Old Testament as the New Testament; it bears equally hard, if it be an argument against *polygamy*, on the man who, having *one* wife, *took another*, in the days of *Moses*, as on any one who should do so at this hour (for certainly the marriage-relation must always be the same) and will prove much more against certain *distinguished characters* under the Old Testament, than I dare say the author meant it should. For this we have his own word—" Nor can I think" (says he) " that *Abraham*, *Jacob*, *David*, and other " pious men, would have had *more wives*, or " *wives* and *concubines*, had this been a plain " violation of the *law of nature*; nor would " God have so highly approved of them, " had they lived in *adultery*." Note on *Matt.* xix. 7, 8.

When learned and pious men find out " plain arguments" against things which are not mentioned, or even hinted at, in the *text*, it is a shrewd sign that * *prejudice*, and not
judgment,

---

* How this learned man's *prejudices* warred against his *judgment* (like many others who want to support a preconceived opinion, against the *truth* which would overturn it) may be seen from the concession he falls into, in his note on Mark x. 11. in the following words— " Since to commit adultery is to violate the bed of " another person, he that commits adultery against his " wife, must violate her bed, which no husband can do " only by doing that which an husband lawfully might " do. Since then a right to *polygamy*, is a right to mar- " ry more wives than one, he that hath this right, can- " not violate the bed of his first wife, by assuming an- " other to it. It *therefore must be acknowledged*, either
" that

judgment, dictates the *comment.* The *Corinthians* had a very " plain argument" against their fears about married persons *cohabiting* together ; and if they compared this scripture, ver. 3, 4, with what *Moses* so positively laid down, Exod. xxi. 10. the *polygamists* among them were no more to forsake the company of *their wives,* so as to withold the *duty of marriage,* than those who had but *one wife* were to withdraw themselves from *her society* in the *same* respect.

That there were many *polygamists* among the *Gentile* converts, as well as among the *Jewish,* there can be but little doubt ; for, as * *Grotius* observes—*Inter Paganos paucæ gentes una uxore contentæ fuerunt.*—" Among
" the

" that the husband, under CHRIST's institution, and by
" the original law of matrimony, had no such right,
" or that he that marrieth another cannot, by that,
" commit adultery against his first wife." Here is a fair ISSUE IN LAW joined—and must be tried by THE LAW— for CHRIST made no *institution* whatsoever on the subject of *marriage,* but only *declared, explained,* and *inforced* those already made and recorded in the LAW *which was given by* MOSES. This LAW, like all other RECORDS, is to be tried by ITSELF—taking the WHOLE TOGETHER.

* *De Verit.* lib. ii. § 13. So *De Jure,* lib. ii. cap. 5. § 9. he says—" Sed & apud *Græcos,* CECROPS primus,
" teste *Athenæo,* μιαν ἐνι ἐζευξεν, *unam fœminam uni ma-*
" *rito attribuit :* quod tamen ne Athenis quidem diu
" observatum Socratis & aliorum exemplo docemur."
But among the Greeks, CECROPS *first,* as *Athenæus witnesseth,* allowed *one woman to one man ;* which, *nevertheless, was not long observed, even at* ATHENS, *as we are taught by the example of* SOCRATES *and others.*

Παλαι γαρ ειωθεισαν και—Ελληνες, και Ιυδαιοι, και δυο η τρισι, η πλειοσι γυναιξι νομῳ γαμειν κα]α ταυ]ον συνοικειν. Theodoret—cited by *Whitby,* on 1 Tim. iii. 2.
" *Formerly*

"the *Pagans*, few nations were content with one wife;" and we do not find the *apoſtle* making this any bar to *church-memberſhip*, though he expreſsly does to *church offices*. See before, p.   It can hardly be ſuppoſed, that if *polygamy* were ſinful, that is to ſay, an offence againſt the law of GOD, the great *apoſtle* ſhould be ſo liberal and ſo particular, in his epiſtle to the *Corinthians*, in the condemnation of every other ſpecies of illicit *commerce between the ſexes*, and yet omit this in the black catalogue, chap. vi. 9, &c. or that he ſhould not be as zealous for the honour of the *law of marriage*, and of the *ſeventh commandment*, which was evidently to maintain it, as *Ezra* was for that po-

---

"Formerly the *Jews* and *Greeks* were wont to be married to TWO or THREE, and even MORE *wives together*."

Stanley, Hiſt. of Philoſophy, Tit. Socrates, p. 53, ſays—that " the occaſion whereupon the *Athenians* (who from the time of *Cecrops* had ſtrictly obſerved ſingle marriage) allowed *bigamy* in the time of *Socrates*, was, that in the ſecond year of the 87th Olympiad, and the 3d of the 88th, *Athens* was viſited extremely by the *peſtilence*, which, attended by war and famine, occaſioned ſo great ſcarcity of men, that they made an edict, for any that would, to take *two wives*. *Euripides* made uſe of this indulgence, and that *Socrates* alſo did ſo, is atteſted by *Satyrus* the *Peripatetic* and *Hiernonymus* the *Rhodian*, who recorded the order; to which *Athenæus* imputes the ſilence of the comic poets in this particular, who omitted no grounds of reproach."

However, it is much to be doubted, whether *Cecrops* did any more than inſtitute *marriage* itſelf among the *Grecians*, who, before his time, lived promiſcuouſly, and coupled as their fancy led them. See Ant. Univ. Hiſt. vol. vi. p. 175.——After all, as CECROPS is ſuppoſed to have been *cotemporary* with MOSES, it is not very probable, that we ſhould meet with any accounts of him, which can be depended upon.

ſitive

sitive law of Deut. vii. 3, against the marrying with *heathens*. *Ezra* made the *Jews put away the wives* which they had illegally taken, and even the very *children* which they had by them; How is it that *Paul*, if *polygamy* was sinful, did not make the *Gentile* and the *Jewish* converts put away *every wife*, but the *first*, and annul every *polygamous contract?* Why not say, that being the *husband of one wife* was as necessary to the being a *Christian*, as to be chosen a *Bishop* or *Deacon?* for it certainly was, if *polygamy* be *sinful. John the Baptist*, at the expence of *his liberty*, and afterwards of his life, honestly, openly, in words that it was out of the reach of all commentators to sophisticate, or give more than one meaning to, told *Herod*, with respect to *Herodias*, his brother *Philip's wife—It is not lawful for thee to have her*. But how could *Paul*, with truth, say to the *Ephesians*, the *Corinthians*, or any other people amongst whom he ministered— I *have not shunned to declare unto you*, πασαν την βουλην, ALL (the whole) *counsel of* GOD —if *polygamy* were a sin, and he did not as openly and plainly declare against it, as he did against every other fleshly transgression of GOD's *pure and holy* law? That he has no were done this, I may say—*res ipsa indicat*.

As for taking a *text* here or there, detaching it from the *context*, and the *context* itself from the rest of the *Bible*; then chusing out a single *sentence*, or *word* in a *sentence*, this too without any reference to the original *Hebrew* or *Greek*, and because it seems to *sound that way*, to make it a proof of some opinion we have

have been taught to hold; it is that fort of criticifm which may make the fcripture prove any thing, and every thing, juft as fancy leads, and, in fhort, muft render the fcriptures themfelves as vague and indeterminate as the minds of men are.

Wetftein, Prol. p. 146, fpeaks of " certain " *doctors—qui, neglecta connectione contextus* " *facri, fingulas pericopas tanquam fingulas fen-* " *tentias, & quafi totidem aphorifmos confide-* " *rant; ut ita liberius fuæ phantafiæ indulgere,* " *atque quidlibet ex quolibet efficere poffint.*"— " Who neglecting the connection of the " facred context, confider all the feveral ver- " fes, as fingle fentences by themfelves, and " as fo many *aphorifms*, or general maxims, " fo that they may the more freely indulge " their own fancy, and make what they " pleafe from what they pleafe."

Whoever has red the hiftory of that *renowned* worthy, Alderman *Whittington*, whofe *biographer* tells us that he was twice *Lord Mayor of London*, may recollect a circumftance in that *great* man's life, which affords an exemplification of the aptnefs which poffeffes the human mind, to interpret *founds* into that particular *fenfe* which its own prejudices, however imbibed, wifh to put upon them. It is faid that *Whittington*, being an apprentice in the *city*, left his mafter with an intent to go into the *country*. It being about the time of evening, he fat himfelf down fomewhere in the fkirts of the town; his ear was caught with the ringing

of

of *six bells*, he listened attentively to them, 'till at last he persuaded himself that they proclaimed his future greatness in the following *sounds*:

   1 2 3 4 5 6
 " Turn again *Whittington*,
   1 2 3 4 5 6
 " Lord Mayor of *London*."

He was so captivated with the conceit, that he not only imagined the *bells* * said this to him, but that all who heard them must give their *peal* the same interpretation; and, no doubt, under such a prepossession, it would have been almost impossible to have persuaded him to the contrary.

So, when men have been brought up under the prejudices of *vulgar opinion* and *common error*, and have their minds swayed and biassed by long custom to one certain train of thinking, they have but to meet with a text in scripture which seems to echo to their *sense* of things, that *sense* will immediately chime in with the *sound*, and both together, almost beyond the power of conviction to the contrary, confirm them still more strongly in their sentiments. What these may happen to be, makes very little difference—

---

* " We have an homely English proverb, which says
" —' As the fool thinks, the bell clinks'—A proverb
" applicable, in our opinion, to all arguments founded
" on the *sound*, and arbitrary meaning of words." Lond.
Review for 1778, p. 75.

             whether

whether it be *tranfubftantiation*—praying to faints—worfhipping images—the doctrine of *purgatory*—or, " though *polygamy* was *allowed* " under *the law*, it is forbidden *under the* " *gofpel*"—or, in fhort, any other popular prejudice: they will always act towards fcripture as *Whittington* did with *the bells*, till that liberality of mind, which ought to poffefs us, as the privilege of thinking and reafonable beings, opens the way to *free enquiry*—then, and not till then, we fhall be *noble* like the *Bereans*, Acts xvii. 11. who would no longer be led by their own prejudices, or prejudiced by other people's opinions, but *received the word of* GOD *with all readinefs of mind, and fearched the fcriptures daily, whether thofe things* (which they heard preached by *Paul) were fo*. The fcriptures which thefe *Jews* at *Berea* fearched fo *diligently*, muft have been the fcriptures of the Old Teftament; no others, if written, could then have come to their hands; but they compared the New Teftament as preached by *Paul*, with the Old Teftament of *Mofes and the prophets*, that they might judge whether the things he declared to them were of divine authority, anfwerable to former revelations of GOD's mind and will, or not. This is the method which I have endeavoured to obferve throughout this book, and which I moft fincerely recommend to every reader, as well as to every perfon who wifhes to *know* and to *do* the will of GOD. If once we detach the

New

New Testament from the Old Testament, there is not a single *heresy* that will not find something to say for itself, perhaps more than we may be able very easily to answer. But let us carry what we hear to the Old Testament; if it exactly * tallies with that, we may be sure it is a right interpretation of the New Testament; if otherwise, it must be false, because the mind and will of GOD can never vary, disagree with, or contradict itself. I do not say these things with regard to any particular doctrine of the New Testament, but with respect to the whole.—The doctrine of a *Trinity in unity*—the *incarnation*—*birth*—*life*—*teaching*—*miracles*—*sufferings*—*death*—*burial*—*resurrection*—*ascension*—*glorification,* and *intercession* of *Jesus Christ*, together with the aspect these things bear towards the salvation of mankind, if only related in a book, no single article of which was ever heard or thought of for *four thousand* years together, would challenge little more of my assent or belief, than the *Koran* of *Mahomet*, the *Zend*, or *Zend-avesta* of *Confucius*, or the *Shaster* of the *Bramins*. But when I compare these things with what is contained in the Old Testament, to which the New Testament so often refers for their truth, I then can no

---

* " The gospel is the best comment upon the *law,* and
" the *law* is the best expositor of the gospel: they are
" like a pair of indentures, they answer in every part:
" their *harmony* is wonderful, and is of itself a convic-
" tion. No human contrivance could have reached it."
Leslie's Works, vol. i. p. 75.

more suppose them to be false, than I can suppose it possible for men to see into futurity, exactly delineate what is to happen ages before it comes to pass, and so exactly, as that the event shall be a literal fulfilment of all that is foretold, unless *He* who is *perfect in knowledge* hath made a revelation or discovery of things which no mortal wisdom or foresight could have ever otherwise been acquainted with. Therefore, when we compare the New Testament with the Old, we may be assured that it is as impossible to be false, as that a *dozen dice* should be thrown the same number for a * million times running; no hazard or casualty could bring such a thing within the most acute calculation of chance; therefore I conclude, that nothing short of *infinite wisdom* and *divine contrivance* could ever first *declare*, and then *fulfil*, the wondrous things which are written in *Moses* and the *prophets*. When therefore I hear of a doctrine as taught in the New Testament, I am certain, if it be true, it must accord with the scriptures of the Old Testament. Thither I carry it; if I find it does not exactly *tally* with what I find there, I am certain it is false, and must arise from some misconception, and, of course, some misinterpretation of the passage where it is supposed to be found. I am told that *sin is a transgression of the law*; when I hear it asserted that *polygamy* is *sinful*, I consult *the law*; if it be forbidden *there*, I agree to the *sinfulness* of it;

---

* For which reason, AN INFIDEL may be styled, the most CREDULOUS OF MORTALS.

if

if not forbidden there, but † *allowed*, I find myself reduced to this *dilemma*—either the asserter of such a proposition, who says he takes it from the New Testament, is *mistaken*, which is *probable*, or the New Testament must *contradict the law*, which is *impossible*.

With respect to what is frequently urged against *polygamy* among *Christians*, that "tho' it was allowed by the *law of Moses*, yet it is *forbidden by the law of Christ*"—by which CHRIST is made a repealer of the *old*, and a giver of a *new law*—it so affects His character as the *Messiah*, as to render Him, if it be true, *not* the person which *Moses* and the *prophets* represent Him, or what He represented Himself to be. The discussion, therefore, of this *horrid position* requires, and shall have, a *chapter* by itself.

At present, I will advert to an argument taken from the New Testament, to prove the unlawfulness of *polygamy* among *Christians*, though *allowed* to the *Jews* under the Old Testament. St. Paul, * Eph. v. 31, 32. and in some

---

† "*Lex Hebræa omnem spurcitiem inhibet, sed plures uni concedit uxores.*" GROTIUS.——" The *Jewish* law restrains all filthiness, but allows a plurality of wives to one man."

* That *marriage* may be looked upon in a *typical* view, with respect to the union of CHRIST with the church, appears very clearly from this scripture, and the others referred to—but in this view of the matter, *polygamy* and *monogamy* were equally *typical*—the *former*, of the *church*, as consisting of *Jews* and *Gentiles*, and of the many and various individual believers among them—the *latter*, of the whole company of *believers*, collectively considered,

some other passages, represents marriage as a figure or representation of *Christ* and *His church*, which is but *one:* whereas, having *more wives* than one at a time, destroys the *analogy* which the marriage-state bears to Christ *and His church*. In answer to which, I would ask, If Christ *and His church* were not as much *one* under the Old Testament as under the New Testament? Is. liv. 5. *Thy Maker is thine husband, the* Lord *of Hosts is his name; the* God *of the whole earth shall He be called.* See also Jer. iii. 14, 20. The *church,* taken *collectively*, is but *one*; but *distributively*, it consists of *many.* Rom. xii. 5. *We being many, are one body in* Christ—and 1 Cor. xii. 12. *For as the body is* one, *and hath many members, and all the members of that one body being many, are one body, so also is* Christ. So that the argument against *polygamy*, taken from the *union* and *unity* of Christ and *His church*, rather leans the other way; unless, contrary to scripture and fact, it could be proved that the *church* consisted but of *one member*; whereas it consists of *many*, and yet is but *one body*—*one houshold*—Eph. ii. 19. *One family*, even though the *saints in heaven* be also taken into the account. Eph. iii. 15. The *bride* or *spouse* of Christ is but *one*— i. e. *one church*; yet every member of that church is as distinctly the *spouse* of Christ, as really *married to Him that rose from the*

---

as making but *one body*, of which Christ is the head. Comp. Rom. xii. 5. 1 Cor. xii. 2. with Eph. i. 23. ii. 21, 22.

dead (Rom. vii. 4.) as the *whole* is, collectively confidered. Surely thefe fcriptural illuftrations of the nature of the marriage-bond, afford a complete anfwer to that queftion, " If a man hath *two wives*, how can " he be *one flefh* with *both*—or *each one flefh* " with him ?" See Eph. v. 30.

We alfo read not only of the *church of* CHRIST in the *fingular* number, but of the *churches of* CHRIST in the *plural*, about forty times in the New Teftament; which, by the way, is at leaft as conclufive an argument for *polygamy*, as the other is *againft* it.

From the making CHRIST and *His church* an emblem of *marriage*, or *marriage* an emblem of CHRIST *and His church*, fome have looked upon it as a *facrament*. There is certainly an *outward fign* of fomething *fpiritual*; but as there wants that which is effentially neceffary to make it a *facrament*, which is GOD's own appointment of it as fuch, the more fcriptural profeffors of *Chriftianity* reject it. For the fame reafon I would reject thofe arguments againft *polygamy*, which are drawn from the *union of Chrift and His church*, becaufe GOD has no where eftablifhed their authority, (that I can find) either in the Old Teftament or the *New*. Thefe arguments would have been juft as conclufive under the *former* as under the *latter*. The *church* is called the *married wife*. If. liv. 1. Her REDEEMER, *the* LORD *of hofts*, is called *her Husband*, ver. 5; but never did *Ifaiah*, nor any other of the *prophets*, ufe this as an argument

ment against the *polygamy* of the people. If this was not done, or so much as hinted at, under the Old Testament, why are we to conceive it to be done under the *New*, when the same things and persons are equally represented under both?

Had *polygamy* been intended to have been condemned under the New-Testament dispensation, I should humbly suppose that our Lord would have put the matter out of question by words too plain to admit of the least dispute: that He *whose loins were girt about with faithfulness* (If. xi. 5.) would have been at least as *faithful* to His hearers of *the lost sheep of the house of* Israel, to whom He was so immediately sent (Matt. xv. 24.) and spoken to them in as *plain* and *unequivocal* terms as *John the Baptist* did to *Herod*, upon the subject of *his brother Philip's wife* (Matt. xiv. 4.) There cannot be the least doubt, that numbers of our Lord's *multitudes of hearers* were *polygamists*—all in *principle*—many in *practice*; nor can it be doubted, that if this was against the *law of marriage*, the law of the *seventh* commandment, or any other *positive law* of God, it must be a mortal, damnable * sin, involving the *man* as well as the *woman* in

---

* *St. Augustine*, lib. xxii. c. 47. against *Faustus*, says of *polygamy*—" *Quando mos erat crimen non erat.*"— " When it was a custom, it was no crime."—How this great man could be capable of such an absurdity is astonishing.—The idea of a *sinful act* losing its *criminality* from *custom*, or the frequency of the commission of it, leaves little room for God's command, Exod. xxiii. 2.

in destruction and perdition. *Paul* could declare openly, that if *a woman, living her husband, be married to another, she shall be called an adulteress*, and vouches the *law of* God for

Thou shalt not follow a multitude to do evil. Nunc propterea crimen est, faith he, *quia mos non est*.—" Now it is a " crime, becaufe not cuftomary."

St. *Chryfoftom*'s account of the matter is much more confiftent with fcripture and common fenfe, when, fpeaking of *Abraham* and *Hagar*, he fays—ὐδέπω γαρ ταυ]α το]ε κεκωλυ]ο—*Thefe things were not then forbidden.* Indeed *Auguftine*, in other parts of his writings, fpeaks much in the fame manner. " There was (fays he) a " *blamelefs* cuftom of one man having many wives—for " there are many things which at that time might be " done in a way of *duty*, which now cannot be done but " *licentioufly*—becaufe, for the *fake of multiplying* pofte- " rity, *no law forbad a plurality of wives.*" See Grot. de Jur. vol. i. p. 268. note ʰ.

St. *Auftin*, like others of the fathers, feem to have fuppofed that the command, *Be fruitful and multiply*—and the allowance of *polygamy*, as a means of fulfilling it, went hand in hand together:—that as that command— " Ratione multitudinis liberorum, pertinuit ad tempora " ante Christum: non ad *nos* qui alio vivimus ævo— " quia hodie, repleto mundo, non tam neceffarium fit " quam olim—mundum non defiderare illud *crefcite & " multiplicamini*"—therefore the allowance of *polygamy* ceafed with the neceffity of the *command* which it accompanied.

Thus, as is ufual, one abfurdity begat another. Thofe who could be perfuaded, that the command for the propagation of the human fpecies was only obligatory on former ages, might very confiftently fuppofe, that even marriage itfelf had very little to do with *Chriftians*, and that therefore *polygamy* became an *evil*, which they allowed to have been a *lawful* thing, and even *duty*, in times paft. Such are the γραωδεις μυθοι—the *aniles fabellæ*— the *old women's ftories*—which the *fathers* told, till they believed them, and, on their authority, they are believed to this hour!

his

his authority, *Rom.* vii. 1, 2, 3. How is it that Christ did not openly fay the fame thing on the part of the man?—Becaufe, if He had, He could *not* have *vouched the law of* God for his authority; and for the fame reafon, that he could not *fay* it, he could not *think* it, for God's *law was within his heart,* Pf. xl. 8. and no *thought* could ever be in the *pure* and *perfect* heart of Christ, but what was exactly conformable, *in all things,* to the *pure and perfect law of* God. Let us then carry what our Lord faith againft *divorce,* Matt. xix. 9. to the *law and to the teftimony,* and it can no more conclude againft *polygamy,* fimply confidered, than it concludes againft *bigamy,* or a man's marrying a *fecond* wife after the death of his *firft,* and being *twice married.* Some of the primitive fathers cited it, to prove that *every fecond marriage was adultery;* but here their learned and pious advocate, *Dr. Cave,* does allow, that " they ftretched " the ftring till it cracked again."

I might alfo obferve, that, if *polygamy* was a fin, and even a *national* fin, an *epidemical* tranfgreffion of the law of God, it is very extraordinary that our Lord's *fore-runner, John the Baptift,* who came to *preach repentance,* fhould not mention, nor even hint at it; for his commiffion ran thus—Luke i. 17. *To turn the hearts of the fathers unto the children, the difobedient to the wifdom of the juft; to make ready a people prepared for the* Lord. It is faid of him, Matt. xvii. 11.

that he should *restore* or *reform* (ἀποκαταςησει) *all things*.

No man could have a fairer opportunity to bear his testimony against a *national sin*, than the *Baptist* had; for it is said (Matt. iii. 5.) *Then went out to him Jerusalem, and all Judea, and all the region round about Jordan;* and among the numbers *who were baptized of him in Jordan, confessing their sins* (ver. 6.) there were *many harlots* (chap. xxi. 32.) So that it is evident he did not spare to inveigh most sharply against the sin of *fleshly uncleanness*; had *polygamy* been of this kind, he doubtless would have preached against it, which, if he had, some trace would most probably have been left of it, as there is of his preaching against the sin of *whoredom,* by the *harlots* (ἀι * πορναι) being said to *believe on him*; which they certainly would not have done, any more than the *Scribes* and *Pharisees* (Matt. xxi. 32.) if the preacher had not awakened them to a deep and real sense of their guilt, by setting forth the heinousness of their sin. He exerted his eloquence also against *public grievances,* such as the extortion of the public officers of the revenue—the *publicans*—τελωναι —*tax-gatherers*—likewise against the oppressive methods used by the *soldiery,* who made it a custom either to take people's goods *by violence,* or to *defraud* them of their property,

* The word πορναι may signify *lewd women* of all sorts.

by

by extorting it under the terror of *false accusation*. These were *public grievances*, against which the *Baptist* bore so open a testimony, that the *publicans* and *soldiers* came to him, saying—*What shall we do?* This being the case, is it conceivable that a man of the *Baptist*'s character, who was so zealous for the honour of the law, as to reprove even a *king* to his face for *adultery*, should suffer, if *polygamy* be *adultery*, a *whole nation*, as it were, of public *adulterers*, to stand before him, and not bear the least testimony against them? I do not say this is a *conclusive*, but it is surely a very strong presumptive argument, that in the *Baptist*'s views of the matter, *polygamy, whoredom*, and *adultery* were by no means the same thing.

Having finished, for the present, what I had to say on the subject of *polygamy*, as supposed to be condemned by the New Testament, I must return back to the Old Testament, to shew that *polygamy* was not only *allowed* in *all cases*, but in some *commanded*. The first instance of this which I shall mention, is with respect to the law, Deut. xxv. 5—10. *If brethren dwell* * *together, and one of them die, and have no child, the wife of the dead shall not marry without unto a stranger: her husband's brother shall go in unto her, and take her to him to wife, and perform the duty of an husband's*

---

* They are said to *dwell together*, not only who were in the *same family*, but in the *same country*. Gen. xiii. 5, 6.

brother unto her. And it shall be that the first-born which she beareth, shall succeed in the name of his brother which is dead, that his name be not put out of Israel, &c.

This law must certainly be looked upon as an *exception* from the general law (Lev. xviii. 16.) and the reason of it appears in the law itself, viz. " To preserve inheritances in " the families to which they belonged." Therefore all lands which had been mortgaged, were to return back to the owner at the year of *jubilee.* See Lev. xxv. 25, 28. See also a special provision against the alienation of lands from the tribe to which they belonged, Numb. xxxvi. 2—9. This was of the utmost consequence in the designs of *Providence* respecting the MESSIAH, whose *genealogy*, with respect to his being of *the seed* of *Abraham—the tribe of Judah—the family of David*, was not more ascertained by his lineal descent, than by the preservation of *Bethlehem Ephrata* in the *tribe of Judah*, and *family of David.* By which it came to pass, that the prophecy concerning the very *place* of the MESSIAH's *birth* was literally fulfilled (Comp. Mic. v. 2. with Matt. ii. 4, 5, 6, and Luke ii. 3, 4, 5, 6, 7.) The *Jewish* [*] *doctors*, as Mr. *Selden*, in his *Uxor Hæbraica*, and others after him, observe, made several ex-

---

[*] Their comments on the *Old Testament* are about as much to be depended upon, in general, as the *Popish* comments upon the *New.* See *Fulk* on *Rhemish Testament*—per tot.

ceptions

ceptions to this law; but as the *text* makes *none*, I know not that we are warranted in making *any*. Bishop *Burnet* seems to have had a right view of the matter, in his observation on the *generality* of this law. His words are—" Yea, *polygamy* was made, in
" some cases, a *duty* by *Moses*'s law; when
" any died without issue, his brother, or
" nearest kinsman, was to marry his wife,
" for raising up seed to him; and *all were*
" *obliged* to obey this, under the hazard of
" infamy if they refused; neither is there
" any exceptions made for such as were mar-
" ried; from whence I may faithfully con-
" clude, that what God made *necessary* in
" some cases, to any degree, can in no case
" be *sinful in itself*, since God is holy in all
" his ways. And thus far it appears that
" *polygamy* is not contrary to the law and
" nature of marriage."

I am indebted for the above quotation to the * before-mentioned reverend *Dean*'s book on *polygamy*, wherein the *Dean* seems a little comforted by the *Bishop*'s having said, that
" he was at a distance from his books and
" papers, when he gave his opinion on this
" point."—" This," adds he, " was the best
" excuse that could be given for so rash a
" decision, which it would have been for
" the honour of his reading to have re-
" tracted, and which, I sincerely wish he

---

* See before, p. 116.

" had

"had retracted, when he returned to his books."

The good *Dean*, in his zeal against *polygamy*, don't give himself time to consider the soundness of the learned *prelate's* opinion.

As there was *no law* against *polygamy*, there was nothing to exempt a *married man* from the obligation of marrying *his brother's widow* on this account; for if so, things might have been so situated, that *Bethlehem* might have gone away into some other family than that of *David*, into some other tribe than that of *Judah*, and, of course, *Joseph and his wife Mary* have gone elsewhere to *be taxed*; for this might evidently have been the consequence of the *widow and the inheritance* going into the hands *of a stranger*. But God says —*The wife of the dead shall not marry without unto a stranger—her husband's brother shall go in unto her*, &c. Here is a *negative* clause, positively declaring whom she shall *not* marry, and an *affirmative* clause, as positively declaring whom she *shall*. Now let us suppose, that not only the *surviving brother*, but all the near *kinsmen*, to whom the marriage of the widow, and the redemption of the inheritance belonged, were *married men*; if that exempted them from the obligation of this law—as they could not *redeem the inheritance*, unless they *married the widow* (Ruth iv. 5.)—the end of this important law must in many cases be defeated—the widow

dow be tempted to marry a stranger—to put herself and the inheritance into his hands—and the whole reason assigned for the law itself, that of *raising up seed to the deceased*, to preserve the inheritance in his family, that *his name be not put out of Israel*—fall to the ground. For which *weighty* reasons, as there was evidently no law against *polygamy*, there could be no exemption of a man from the positive duty of this law *because he was married*. As we say—*ubi eadem ratio ibi idem jus*.

But the learned *Dean*, in order to overthrow all the *Bishop*'s reasoning on the subject, observes from *Selden*'s Ux. Heb. that " the *Chaldee* paraphrast, the *Midrash*, and " *Josephus*, agree, that this was the reason " why *Mahlon*'s next kinsman refused to re- " deem *Ruth*, his widow, viz.—Because it " was *not lawful for him to marry her*, having " *a wife of his own*." That people should invent reasons for men's actions, where none are given, is not so surprizing as overlooking the reasons that are given, and substituting others which do not appear to be so much as thought of by the parties themselves. This is the case here—*Mahlon*'s next *kinsman* is applied to, as by law he ought to have been, to buy *Mahlon*'s inheritance, and to marry *Ruth* his widow: his answer is neither more nor less than this—" I cannot redeem it for " myself, *lest I mar my own inheritance*."—How these words relate to the *lawfulness* or *unlawfulness*

unlawfulness of the matter, was reserved for the ingenuity of modern interpreters to make out—that they may, and most probably do, relate to the *expediency* or *inexpediency* of such a step, the *kinsman*'s present circumstances considered, may be easily inferred from the *words* of the *reason* given. The *kinsman* might be married, perhaps have many children, and but a small provision for them—therefore, when he hears of not only disbursing the redemption-price for *Mahlon*'s parcel of land, but that this could not be done, without marrying a very poor young woman, by whom he might have another numerous family of children, which he could not maintain, educate, or provide for, out of the small parcel of land which was * *Elimelech*'s, but must diminish his own inheritance of which he was possessed, to the damage of his other family, he prudently declines the *kinsman's part—lest*, said he, *I mar mine own inheritance.* Such a sense as this the words will most certainly bear; but as to their meaning that the man would not marry *Ruth*—" because it was not lawful " for him to marry her, *having a wife of his* " *own*"—it is a conceit, fetched even farther than, one would think, the utmost unfairness of prejudice itself could reach.

---

* *Elimelech* was the father of *Mahlon*; therefore the land is called *Elimelech*'s, it descending to *Mahlon* from him.

Since I wrote the above, I have looked into *Bishop Patrick*, on *Ruth* iv. 6. who mentions the passage alluded to in the *Chaldee paraphrast*, and *the Midrash*; and so far from their appearing to say what the *Dean* would make them, there is not a word of any such thing; they put quite a different sense upon the words. As for *Josephus*, I would almost venture to affirm, without looking into the book, that he cannot so grossly contradict himself; for when he is writing that part of the *History of David*, where he speaks of his polygamy, he says—δοντος δε αυτω και γυναικας ας δικαιως και νομιμως ηγαγετο —(God) " giving " him *wives*, which he *justly and lawfully* " *married.*" However, having consulted *Josephus* on the subject, I find no such reason assigned by the *kinsman*, for refusing to redeem *Mahlon's* land, and to marry his widow, as the *Dean* asserts.—*Josephus*, Antiq. lib. ix. c. 5. § 4. speaking of the *kinsman*'s refusal, says, that he rejected the offer— Ἐιναι δε και γυναικα λεγων αυτω και παιδας ηδη· " Saying, he had already a wife and chil- " dren;" but not a word that it was " un- " *lawful to marry another woman.*" Not that *Josephus* represents the matter as the *Bible* does, any more than the learned *Dean* rightly represents the sentiments of *Josephus*. It might not be expedient for the *kinsman* to marry *Ruth*, as he was circumstanced; but this has nothing to do with the *lawfulness* or *unlawfulness* of the matter, with respect to

the

the law of God. *Lawfulness* and *expediency* are very distinct and different considerations. See 1 Cor. vi. 12. 1 Cor. x. 23. As for Mr. *Selden*, he, in the very passage which the *Dean* quotes, resolves the *kinsman*'s refusal to marry *Ruth* into a matter of *prudence*, and that for much the same reasons which I have assigned above.

The law itself on which we have been discoursing, was only a *local* and *temporary* institution, and, in the very nature of it, could only concern the *Jews*, and that only with regard to their peculiar situation before the coming of the *Messiah*, when so much depended on the clearness of *family descent* and *inheritance*. It is observable that this law, though not reduced to writing and published till the time of *Moses*, yet existed among the *patriarchs*, as we learn from Gen. xxxviii. 8.

I now shall observe on some laws of more extensive import, the obligation of which must concern *every man*, and that at all times and places, because the evident purpose for which they were ordained, and the reasons on which they are apparently founded, must equally concern all mankind. The *laws* I mean, are those already spoken of, as made for the preservation of the *female sex* from *ruin and prostitution*, by compelling every man to marry the *virgin* he *lies with*. The first of them is to be found *Exod.* xxii. 16; the other *Deut.* xxii. 28, 29. These *laws*
must

muſt in ſome caſes * *command polygamy*, and therefore, in ſuch caſes, make it a *duty*; for they are ſo framed as to admit of no other conſtruction, conſiſtently with the terms in which *Moſes* hath recorded them. The terms in which theſe laws are enacted, with reſpect to the *men ſeducing* or *taking virgins*, &c. are as *indefinite* as words can poſſibly be: *If a man*, ſays our tranſlation.—This muſt, *ex vi termini*, mean *any man* whatſoever, be his ſituation what it may—which is exactly the ſenſe of the *Hebrew* כי איש—As the right underſtanding of this comprehenſive and unlimited word איש is of the utmoſt importance to the point in queſtion, I will lay a full and clear explanation of it before the reader.

 איש " This word has no relation to *kind* or
   " *ſpecies*, though, according to its dif-
   " ferent genders, it has to *ſex*; but is
   " applied to almoſt any diſtinct *being*
   " or *thing*; as, for inſtance, to *man*.
   " &c." See *Parkhurſt*'s Heb. Lex.
   ſub voc. ישה—" which," ſaith he,
   " denotes *exiſtence, ſubſiſtence, reality*."

---

* Luther, de Digam. Epiſcoporum, § 65, ſays—" *Nota ſunt jura Moſaica de fratris defuncti uxore, & filia corrupta invito patre, quæ cogunt plurium uxorum eſſe virum.*"—" The Moſaic laws concerning the wife of a deceaſed brother, and concerning a daughter defiled againſt the father's conſent, are well known, which *compel* a man to have a *plurality of wives*."

I will next subjoin the interpretation of *Calasio*, who, in his valuable *Hebrew Concordance*, gives us some *hundreds* of *texts* in which this word occurs.

איש " *Persona, creatura*—nomen generale
" quod essentiam rei non distinguit"
—A *person*, a *creature*—*a general name, which doth not distinguish the essence of the thing spoken of.*

איש " Homo generaliter complectens mas-
" culum & fœminam." MAN *generally, including male and female.*

איש " Quis—quilibet—aliquis—unusquisque
" —quisque—alter."—*Who*—*whosoever—any one—* every one—* every man—any other*—
" *unus   ullus*"
 some one   any one.

איש " Sexus masculus in qualibet animan-
" tium specie" cum " mentio fœmi-
" næ additur." Ut Gen. vii. 2. (xxiv. 16.) The MALE SEX *in any species of animals where the female is also mentioned.*

איש " Vir—maritus—si cum uxore confe-
" ratur." Gen. iii. 6. *An* HUSBAND, *a* MARRIED MAN, *where joined with* WIFE.

* Thus it is rendered, Job. xlii. 11.

The reader has now before him the meaning of the word איש, wheresoever it may be used, as applicable *to*, or significant *of*, mankind; and by this may see the use of it throughout the Bible where *man* is mentioned. He may also see that the phrase כי איש—*If a man*, &c. so far from carrying any exception with it, as to a man's situation of being *married* or *unmarried*, excludes all exception whatsoever wherever we meet with it; therefore as much in the texts of *Exodus* and *Deuteronomy* as elsewhere. Let the *reader* take the *Hebrew*, or even the *English* concordance, and try the experiment: he will find that כי איש in *Hebrew*, and *If any man* in *English*, are in the scriptures, as in every other book I ever met with, as *indefinite* as words can be, with relation to the subject in question.

But if no exception as to the *situation of the man* is *expressed*, is it not *implied?*—So far from that, the *Holy Ghost* (in this passage particularly) has demonstrably guarded against any such implication, and this by adding the words *not betrothed* to the description of the *virgin* or *damsel*, which is done in both places. *Expressio unius est exclusio alterius*—the *expressing* an *exception* with regard to the *woman*, but *none* with respect to the *man*, proves, as far as the soundest rules of construction of all laws can prove, that *none* was intended.

Had any restriction of this law with regard to the *situation* of the *man* been intended, it might easily have been expressed, by only add-

Vol. I.   S   ing

ing some *restrictive* expression or * epithet to the description of the *man* as to that of the *damsel*. But, instead of any thing of this sort, we find the indefinite איש; and therefore our translators have rightly rendered it *a man* indefinitely;—so the LXX—ἐὰν δέ τις—*but if any man*;—the Latin—*si vir*—*if a man*;—the French of D. Martin—*si quelqu'un*—*if any one*. Though all the *translators* of the *Bible* which I have met with, have modestly, humbly, and faithfully represented the mind of God as He has been pleased to reveal it, yet some expositors have ventured to interpret כי איש—*if a man*—by—*If an unmarried* man—thus

* The restrictive description of the *damsel* is לא ארשה —*non desponsata*—*not betrothed*. But no איש is added to the *description* of the *man*. And it is very remarkable, that though *betrothing* is used so often in the *Bible*, it always relates to the *woman*, never to the *man*, as the *person betrothed*. The *man* is said to *betroth* a *woman*, as Deut. xxviii. 30. Deut. xx. 7. & al.—so when *betrothing* is figuratively used, as Hos. ii. 19, 20. But in neither sense is it once used in all the scriptures *passively on the man's side*.

This distinction is also maintained in the New Testament. See Matt. i. 18. Luke i. 27; ii. 5. 2 Cor. xi. 2. This can make no difference with regard to DIVORCE; but it seems to make a *considerable* one in certain other respects.

Agreeably to the above remarks, *Gronovius* on *Grot. de Jure.* lib. ii. c. 5. § 8. n. 20. observes, that where *Grotius* speaks of the woman's contracting herself to the man, there is " tacitly implied, that the contract on the man's " side is not by *nature*, but from *positive institution.*" See before, p. 22. n. This must mean *human institution*, for there is no trace of such a thing in the *Bible*, as the confinement of the word איש to the side of the woman sufficiently demonstrates.

corrupting

The reader has now before him the meaning of the word אִישׁ, wherefoever it may be used, as applicable *to*, or fignificant *of*, mankind; and by this may fee the ufe of it throughout the Bible where *man* is mentioned. He may alfo fee that the phrafe כִּי אִישׁ—*If a man*, &c. fo far from carrying any exception with it, as to a man's fituation of being *married* or *unmarried*, excludes all exception whatfoever wherever we meet with it; therefore as much in the texts of *Exodus* and *Deuteronomy* as elfewhere. Let the *reader* take the *Hebrew*, or even the *Englifh* concordance, and try the experiment: he will find that כִּי אִישׁ in *Hebrew*, and *If any man* in *Englifh*, are in the fcriptures, as in every other book I ever met with, as *indefinite* as words can be, with relation to the fubject in queftion.

But if no exception as to the *fituation of the man* is *expreffed*, is it not *implied?*—So far from that, the *Holy Ghoft* (in this paffage particularly) has demonftrably guarded againft any fuch implication, and this by adding the words *not betrothed* to the defcription of the *virgin* or *damfel*, which is done in both places. *Expreffio unius eft exclufio alterius*—the *expreffing* an *exception* with regard to the *woman*, but *none* with refpect to the *man*, proves, as far as the foundeft rules of conftruction of all laws can prove, that *none* was intended.

Had any reftriction of this law with regard to the *fituation* of the *man* been intended, it might eafily have been expreffed, by only adding some *restrictive* expression or * epithet to the description of the *man* as to that of the *damsel*. But, instead of any thing of this sort, we find the indefinite איש ; and therefore our translators have rightly rendered it *a man* indefinitely;—so the LXX—ἐαν δε τις—*but if any man*;—the Latin—*si vir*—*if a man*;—the French of D. Martin—*si quelqu'un*—*if any one*. Though all the *translators* of the *Bible* which I have met with, have modestly, humbly, and faithfully represented the mind of GOD as He has been pleased to reveal it, yet some expositors have ventured to interpret כי איש— *if a man*—by—*If* an *unmarried* man—thus

* The restrictive description of the *damsel* is לא ארשה —*non desponsata*—*not betrothed*. But no ארש is added to the *description* of the *man*. And it is very remarkable, that though *betrothing* is used so often in the *Bible*, it always relates to the *woman*, never to the *man*, as the *person betrothed*. The *man* is said to *betroth* a *woman*, as Deut. xxviii. 30. Deut. xx. 7. & al.—so when *betrothing* is figuratively used, as Hos. ii. 19, 20. But in neither sense is it once used in all the scriptures *passively on the man's side*.

This distinction is also maintained in the New Testament. See Matt. i. 18. Luke i. 27; ii. 5. 2 Cor. xi. 2. This can make no difference with regard to DIVORCE; but it seems to make a *considerable* one in certain other respects.

Agreeably to the above remarks, *Gronovius* on *Grot: de Jure*. lib. ii. c. 5. § 8. n. 20. observes, that where *Grotius* speaks of the woman's contracting herself to the man, there is "tacitly implied, that the contract on the man's "side is not by *nature*, but from *positive institution*." See before, p. 22. n. This must mean *human institution*, for there is no trace of such a thing in the *Bible*, as the confinement of the word איש to the side of the woman sufficiently demonstrates.

3   corrupting

corrupting the passage by an interpolation, not only unwarranted by the *Hebrew text*, but by every translation of it extant. This method of interpreting scripture, not by scripture, but by our own prejudiced imaginations, is making the word of GOD to mean *any* thing and *every* thing which fancy may invent; and rendering it—instead of a *sure word of prophecy, to the which we do well to take heed, as unto a light that shineth in a dark place*, 2 Pet. i. 19.—a sort of *ignis fatuus*, by no means to be depended on for a director and guide, in so awful a concern as therein is proposed to every man to whom that word shall come.

The only shadow of excuse for such an interpretation, or rather *corruption* of the passages above mentioned, is the being able to produce some *positive law* against a man's *having more wives than one at a time*; and then, in order to make GOD's laws agree together, it may be thought reasonable to restrain the indefinite expression כי איש—*if a man*, in *Exodus* and *Deuteronomy*, to *unmarried men only*. But as the *first* is impossible, the *second* is without, and indeed against, all authority from the law of GOD; for that it allowed *polygamy*, is just as clear as that it allowed *marriage*. Therefore the consequence is, that the expression in question being *general*, without *limitation* or *exception* with respect to the situation of the man, as *married* or *unmarried*, it must in some cases command *polygamy*, and therefore make it a *duty*. This consequence must be *allowed*, if we let scripture

ture speak for itself; it could not be avoided by any other means than a *man's* refraining entirely from the *other sex*, or, if he married, contenting himself with *one wife*. If a man went farther than this, he must take the consequence.—But as GOD would not suffer *a whore of the daughters of Israel*, so he made these laws to prevent their being exposed to prostitution by men's *taking* them, and then *putting them away*. This was just as likely to be the case where *married* men were concerned, as where *others* were; therefore positively forbidden as to *both* alike.

That there were some ingredients in these laws, of the ceremonial, local, or temporary kind—as the payment of *the fifty shekels to the father*—we do not deny; but that the *morality* of these laws must survive as long as *morality* itself exists, is as clear, as that exposing a woman to *prostitution* and *ruin* must at all times be equally hateful in the sight of GOD, and therefore at all times equally provided against by these humane and salutary laws.

In confirmation of what is here said, I would lay it down as a rule in all cases, that wherever a *moral* intendment appears to be involved in the words of a *ritual, ceremonial,* or *local* and *temporary* institution, there, though the *letter* of the law itself can have no place among us, yet the *spirit* and *moral intention* must survive as long as the world endures. For instance, it is written, *Deut.* xxv. 4. *Thou shalt not muzzle the ox when he treadeth out the corn.* By this we must suppose, that it

was

was the custom in *those days*, and in *that part* of the world, to lay the *sheaves on the floor*, and to get the *corn* out by the *treading* or trampling of * oxen. We get the corn out of the *sheaves* by *threshing* with *flails*; therefore the *letter* of the law above mentioned has nothing to do with us. But the *spirit* of this law being of a *moral* nature, and to teach us, that *those who labour in the word and doctrine* are to *live of their labours*, for that *the labourer is worthy of his reward*—this law is itself quoted by *St. Paul*, 1 Cor. ix. 9. 1 Tim. v. 18. as a 'proof that *they who preach the gospel should live of the gospel*. 1 Cor. ix. 14. From whence, as from other instances which might be mentioned, I infer, that though a *law itself*, or *some part* of it, may have vanished as to the *letter*, yet it *may*, or rather *must*, survive as to the *spirit* of it.

Shall we say, that we must construe the words—*if any man*—to mean *unmarried* men only, 'because, though God's laws do not forbid *polygamy*, yet *ours* do? To imagine that our laws are to controul the laws of God, is a blasphemous arrogance, in comparison of which, Cardinal *Wolsey*'s—Ego et Rex Meus—is *humility* itself in the very abstract. The law of the land is such, that a *married Englishman* cannot publicly and openly marry *the virgin he has seduced* or *taken*; he cannot

---

* *Kolben* tells us, that this practice is observed at the *Cape of Good Hope*, (vol. ii. p. 73) and adds—" 'tis most
" certain, that corn is much more expeditiously got out
" of the ears by the treading of *horses* or *oxen*, than it is
" by *threshing*. A team of *eight horses* or *oxen* will tread
" out more corn in a few hours, than a dozen men can
" thresh out in a whole day."

obey the *letter* therefore of these laws of GOD, as the *Jews* could have done; but he can and ought to make them the law of his conscience; and if he has *taken a virgin,* &c. he can, according to the *spirit* of these laws, *maintain, protect,* and *provide* for her, and, if he survives his present engagement, marry her publicly in preference to all other women upon earth.—Thus would one great end of this law be answered, and millions be preserved from destruction. If indeed the woman is profligate enough to forsake the man, and voluntarily unite herself with another, she is guilty of transgressing these laws of GOD, as in other cases of *adultery;* for, the same reason which is given why the man *shall not put her away all his days,* viz. *because he hath humbled her,* goes to what is also said of the woman—*she shall be his wife*—she certainly therefore *is his wife* in GOD's sight, and *whosoever toucheth her shall not be innocent,* Prov. vi. 29.

I some time ago met with two sermons, which were preached, and afterwards printed, on occasion of passing the *marriage-act.* The learned author, speaking of *polygamy,* expresses himself as follows:—" We find like-
" wise in those early times, and afterwards,
" that *polygamy* was partly indulged, but
" only upon certain *typical* occasions, and
" then only among the *patriarchs* and some
" of the *kings,* who were all express types of
" CHRIST in their several marriages; and in
" this respect they each typified and pre-
" figured CHRIST's marrying the *Jewish*
                                    " church,

"church, and the several churches of the
"*Heathen* nations, which, under the gospel,
"were all designed to make but *one church* or
"one *spouse*; therefore, under the *gospel*, po-
"lygamy ceases, and but *one wife* is allowed."

If this author will examine his *Bible* a little more closely, he will find himself mistaken both in his *premises*, and in his *conclusion*. In the first place, it cannot be true that " *polygamy* was partly indulged, only
" upon some typical occasions, and then only
" among the *patriarchs* and some of the
" *kings*."—This appears from the law, Deut. xxi. 15. which was enacted after the *patriarchal* age had ceased, and many ages before there was a *king in Israel*. That law is framed in *general* terms, so as to include *any* and *every* man—that has *two wives:*—it does not say, if a *patriarch* or *king* hath *two wives*—but—
כי תהיין לאיש שתי נשים—literally—" *if*
" *there be to a man*"—or—as we translate it
—" *if a man have*—*two wives*" See Taylor Concor. sub voc. היה, N° 82. It is apparent, then, that the law being *general*, it was meant to regulate a *general* practice. It is also *untrue* in point of *fact*, that " *polygamy*
" was partly indulged only to *patriarchs* and
" some of the *kings*;" witness *Elkanah*, who was neither *patriarch* nor * *king*, but a *Le-*

---

* So it is said of *Gideon*—*He had seventy sons of his body begotten, for he had many wives*. Judg. viii. 30. Of *Jair*, he had thirty sons. Judg. ix. 4. *Ibzan of Bethlehem had thirty sons and thirty daughters*. Judg. xii. 9. *Abdon* had forty sons, ver. 14. These were neither *patriarchs* nor *kings*, but all *judges* of *Israel*, and must, by the numbers of their children, be concluded to have been *polygamists* as well as *Gideon*.

vite, defcended from *Kohath*, the fon of *Levi*, 1 Chron. vi. 27, 28; and yet we find, by his hiftory, 1 Sam. i. 1, &c. that *polygamy* was *indulged* to him as evidently as to any *patriarch* or *king* that ever lived. From all which it appears, that our *author*'s conclufion— " therefore, under the *gofpel, polygamy* ceafes, " and but *one wife* is allowed"—falls to the ground. But let us look back again to Deut. xxi. 15.—That law was evidently made to regulate the difpofal of a man's *inheritance* who had *two wives*, and to prevent the *difherifon* of the *firft-born* through favour and affection towards the child who was not fo, becaufe born of the *favourite wife*. This could not concern the *patriarchs*, who had all been long dead—nor (immediately at leaft) the *kings*, who did not exift till near *four hundred* years afterwards—nor the *priefts* and *Levites*, who could have *no inheritance* to difpofe of. *Numb.* xviii. 20, 21. Deut. x. 9. xii. 12. latter part. Deut. xviii. 1, 2.—If then it did not concern the *people at large*, it was *nugatory*, for it concerned *nobody* at all.—This is furely a very fufficient proof that *polygamy* was an allowed practice of the *Jews* * in general.

---

* The modern *Jews* forbid *polygamy* among the people, and this from the authority of fome paffage in the *Talmud*; but the reafons affigned to me, on difcourfing with a learned *Jew* on this fubject, were of the prudential kind; fuch as the people in general being too *poor to maintain more than one wife, the quarrels it occafioned*, and the like.—I afked him if he looked upon it as forbidden by the law of God?—" No, God forbid," replied he earneftly; " what then muft be the cafe of *Abraham*, " *Jacob*,

neral. The *all-wife* GOD cannot be suppoſed to enact ſo poſitive a law, if there were no perſons who could be objects of it; and this law to regulate *certain circumſtances* which did not exiſt; nor is it eaſy to imagine, that if thoſe *circumſtances* were *ſinful*, they would not have been as explicitly *condemned*, as they are here plainly allowed and regulated. What has been obſerved above, concerning the law of *Deut.* xxi. 15. holds equally true of *Exod.* xxi. 10. which had as little to do with *patriarchs* and *kings* as the other had.

I cannot conclude this part of my ſubject without mentioning a caſe, which thoſe would do well to conſider, who confound *polygamy* with *adultery*, and plead the authority of the *great* and infallible *interpreter* of GOD's *mind* and *will* for ſo doing; I mean the caſe of *Abimelech*, King of *Gerar*; who, having already a *wife of his own*, ſent and took *Sarah* the wife of *Abraham*, Gen. xx. 2. *But* GOD *came to Abimelech in a dream by night, and ſaid to him*—*Be-*

"*Jacob, David*, &c.?" He likewiſe told me, that this prohibition was "not *univerſal*, for that in ſome coun-
"tries *polygamy* was ſtill practiſed among the *Jews*." He added, "that even *here*, if a *Jew* married a woman, and
"had no children by her, after *ten* years he might marry
"another *wife*." So, where a man defiles a *virgin*, "*ſhe
"ſhall be his wife*, agreeable to Exod. xxii. 16. and Deut.
"xxii. 28, 29." I take the truth to be, that the *Jews*, as to the buſineſs of *polygamy*, uſually conform to the cuſtom of the country where they live. "As for the
"modern *Jews*," ſays *Leo Mutinenſis*, "thoſe of them
"who live in the *Eaſt*, ſtill keep up their antient
"practice of *polygamy*; whereas in *Germany* they are not
"allowed this privilege, and in *Italy* very rarely, and
"only in caſe a man hath lived *ten* years with his wife
"without iſſue." See *Puffend.* book vi. ch. 1. § 16.

hold,

hold, thou art but a dead man, for the woman which thou haft taken—for fhe is a man's wife. Here GOD plainly fet forth *His* thoughts of *adultery*, or *taking a man's wife*; that it is a *fin* to be punifhed with *death*.—However, *Abimelech* had not actually *defiled* her, and fhews that, if he had not been deceived by *Abraham's* faying that *Sarah* was *his fifter*, he would not have taken her at all.—*Said he not unto me, She is my fifter? and fhe, even fhe herfelf faid, He is my brother. In the integrity of my heart, and innocency of my hands, have I done this.* And GOD faid unto him in a dream, *Yea, I know that thou didft it in the integrity of thine heart, for I alfo witheld thee from finning againft Me, therefore fuffered I thee not to touch her.* The fin of *adultery* is certainly marked very ftrongly, but here was a fair opportunity to have as ftrongly marked *polygamy*, if that was a fin alfo. How could *Abimelech*, having a wife, ver. 17, take *any other woman innocently?* and yet GOD allows this to have been done, in his anfwer to the plea of *Abimelech*. Though he was innocent as to an intentional *adultery*, being ignorant that *Sarah* was *Abraham's* wife, yet *Abimelech* muft know that he had a *wife of his own*, and therefore could not *innocently*, and in the *integrity of his heart*, take any other woman of any kind, if *polygamy* was a *fin*. But fuppofing this poor * *heathen* was *ignorant*, and

---

* " It appears by this whole hiftory of *Abimelech,*
" that he was a man of great virtue in thofe days; not
" an *idolater*, but a worfhipper of the *true* GOD, as *Melchizedeck*, the *high-prieft* of that country, was." *Patrick* on Gen. xx. 7.

therefore

therefore said this knowing no better, yet God could not be *ignorant* of His *own mind and will*, when he said—*Yea, I know that thou didst this in the integrity of thine heart, for I also witheld thee from sinning against Me.* Rather, why did he not say—" Thou wicked " wretch, how canst thou dare to talk of the " *innocency of thine hands*, and of the *integrity* " *of thine heart?*—supposing thou didst not " know *Sarah* to be *another man's wife*, yet " the taking *any woman*, as thou hast already " a *wife of thine own*, is against the *law of* " *marriage*, and therefore a *mortal sin.*" Instead of this, God allows his plea, and the moment *Abimelech* restored *Sarah* to her *husband*, God graciously removes every mark of his displeasure, ver. 17, 18. *So* Abraham †

prayed

† Who was himself at that hour a *polygamist*. See Gen. xvi. 3, 4. It is likewise to be observed, that *Abraham* was a *Christian* believer, as much so as *Paul* was, who tells us, *the gospel was preached to Abraham*—that he *believed it*—*was justified by faith*—and that they which *be of faith, are blessed with faithful Abraham*, who is (spiritually) *the father of all believers* in Christ. Comp. Rom. iv. 16, &c. with Gal. iii. 9, 14. and John viii. 56. *Abraham* would have been exceedingly puzzled, to have found out what the *gospel which was preached to him* (and in which he *believed* and *rejoiced*) had to do with polygamy, or to have accounted for the possibility of *the children of his faith*, in future ages, finding out that it was the same thing with *adultery*; when *Abraham*'s own *eyes* and *ears* were witnesses of there being put as great a difference between *polygamy* and *adultery*, as could possibly exist between any two things in creation; and this, by the determination of *that* God, who afterwards gave the law to *Moses* at *Mount Sinai*—and who bore testimony concerning *Abraham*—that he had *obeyed His voice*—*kept His* charge—His commandments—His statutes—and His laws. See Gen. xxvi. 5.—But how is this

consistent

prayed unto GOD, and GOD *healed* ABIMELECH, *and his wife, and his maid-servants*—ואמהתיו (which seem to have stood in the same relation to *Abimelech*, as the אמה—*Hagar* (See Gen. xxi. 10. Comp. Judges viii. 31. with ix. 18.) did to *Abram*, chap. xvi. 3, 4.) *and they bare children*—וילדו—*pepererunt*, Mont.—*they brought forth: for the* LORD *had fast closed up all the wombs of the house of* ABIMELECH, *because of* SARAH, ABRAHAM'S *wife.* It should seem by the context, that GOD had *witheld Abimelech from sinning against Him*, in a criminal access to *Sarah*, by inflicting a *judicial disability of* some kind upon him; also, to mark the more strongly His holy indignation against him, for taking *another man's wife*, He rendered *Abimelech*'s wife, then *great with child*, (as also such of his *maid-servants*, who it should seem, from what is said, ver. 17, 18, were probably his *concubines*, and some of them also *great with child)* unable *to bring forth*—but when *Sarah* was restored, *Abimelech* was restored to his own women, and they to him.—All this by the *immediate* hand of GOD.

I would only say, that any person who can attentively consider the several circumstances of this history of the divine interposition, and talk of the sinfulness of *polygamy* in the sight of GOD, even putting it on the same footing with *adultery*, will appear to differ very

consistent with *truth*, if *Abraham*'s polygamy was an open and continued violation of GOD'S *primary law of marriage?* or if, as St. *Ambrose* speaks—he was living in *adultery* ?

widely,

widely, in his judgment of the matter, from this authentic record of the *mind* and *will* of the Most High.

How early an abhorrence of the sin of *adultery* was impressed on the minds of men, and of the *punishment* which awaited it, may likewise be gathered from the history of *Isaac* and *Abimelech king of Gerar*, which is recorded Gen. xxvi. particularly at ver. 10, 11.

It is to be remarked also, that throughout the whole scripture, the same approbation; many like circumstances which evidenced that approbation; also, like *answers to prayer*, and like *miracles*, in token of that approbation, attended equally on a *second*, or *after-taken wife*, under a *polygamous* contract, as on a *first* or *only* wife. This may be said to be uniformly the case, as may appear from the following

PARADIGM.

Sarai was barren—she had no child—Gen. xi. 30.

And *Abram* said, Lord God, what wilt thou give me, seeing I go childless?—Behold to me thou hast given no seed.—And He brought him forth abroad, and said, Look now towards heaven, and tell the stars, if thou be able to number them; and He said unto him—So shall thy seed be. Gen. xv. 2, 3, 5.

And God said unto *Abraham*, As for *Sarah* thy wife, I will bless her, and give thee

And *Sarai* said unto *Abram*, Go in unto my maid; and she gave *Hagar* to her husband *Abram* to be his wife. And he went in unto *Hagar*, and she conceived—and the angel of the Lord said, I will multiply thy seed exceedingly, that it shall not be numbered for multitude. Gen. xvi. 2, 4, 10. Yea,

God said, As for *Ishmael*, behold I have blessed him, and will make him fruitful,

thee a son of her. Yea I will bless her, and she shall be a mother of nations; kings of people shall be of her. Gen. xvii. 15, 16.

God said—*Sarah* thy wife shall indeed bear thee a son, and thou shalt call his name *Isaac*. Gen. xvii. 19.

And *Sarah* conceived and bare *Abraham* a son in his old age—and *Abraham* called his name *Isaac*. Gen. xxi. 2, 3.

Isaac was forty years old when he took *Rebekah* to wife—and *Isaac* intreated the Lord for his wife, because she was barren; and the Lord was *intreated of him*, and *Rebekah* his wife conceived. Gen. xxv. 20, 21.

Manoah's wife was barren and bare not; and the angel of the Lord appeared unto the woman, and said unto her, Behold, now thou art barren and barest not, but thou shalt conceive and bear a son—and the woman bare a son, and called his name *Samson*; and the child grew, and the Lord blessed him. Judg. xiii. 2, 3, 24.

fruitful, and multiply him exceedingly; twelve princes shall he beget, and I will make him a great nation. Gen. xvii. 20.

And the angel of the Lord said unto *Hagar*, Behold thou art with child, and shalt bear a son, and shalt call his name *Ishmael*.

And *Hagar* bare *Abram* a son, and *Abram* called his son's name, which *Hagar* bare, *Ishmael*. Gen. xvi. 11, 15.

Jacob took *Leah* and *Rachel*—but *Rachel* was barren. Gen. xxix. 31. And she gave him *Bilhah* her handmaid to wife; and *Jacob* went in unto her; and *Bilhah* conceived and bare *Jacob* a son. And *Rachel* said, God hath judged me, and hath also *heard my voice*, and hath given me a son. Gen. xxx. 4, 5, 6.

And *Bilhah*, *Rachel*'s maid, conceived again, and bare *Jacob* a second son, and *Rachel* said, נפתולי אלהים נפתלתי " By the " agency (Heb. twistings) " of the *Aleim* I am in- " twisted with my sister— " *i. e.* my family is now " interwoven with my sis- " ter's, and has a chance " of producing the pro- " mised seed." See Park. Heb. Lex. פתל.

When *Leah* saw that she had left off bearing—she took *Zilpah* her maid, and
gave

[271]

From henceforth all generations shall call me bleſſed. *V. M. Luke* i. 48.

There was a certain *prieſt* named *Zacharias*, and his wife's name was *Elizabeth*—and they had no child, becauſe *Elizabeth* was barren, and they both were well ſtricken in years. And the *angel* ſaid unto him, Fear not, *Zacharias*, for thy *prayer is heard*, and thy wife ſhall bear thee a ſon, and thou ſhalt call his name *John*—and he ſhall be great in the ſight of the LORD, &c. And his wife *Elizabeth* conceived, and ſaid—Thus hath the LORD dealt with me in the days wherein he looked on me to take

gave her to *Jacob to wife*. And *Zilpah, Leah*'s maid, bare *Jacob* a ſon. And *Zilpah, Leah*'s maid, bare *Jacob* a ſecond ſon. And *Leah* ſaid—Happy am I, for the daughters will *call me bleſſed.*

And GOD hearkened unto *Leah*, and ſhe conceived and bare *Jacob* a fifth ſon. And *Leah* ſaid, GOD hath given me my hire, *becauſe I have given my maiden to mine huſband*. And GOD remembered *Rachel*, and GOD *hearkened to her, and opened her womb*, and ſhe conceived and bare a ſon, and ſaid, GOD *hath taken away my reproach*. And ſhe called his name *Joſeph*, and ſaid, The LORD ſhall add to me another ſon. Gen. xxx. 24. See alſo Gen. xxxv. 9—12.

There was a certain man of *Ramathaim Zophim* (a *Levite* of the family of the *Kohathites*, ſee 1 Chron. vi. 33, 34, &c.) and his name was *Elkanah*. And he had *two wives*—the name of one was *Hannah*—and of the other *Peninnah*.—*Peninnah* had children; *Hannah* had no children—the LORD had ſhut up her womb.—And her adverſary alſo provoked her ſore for to make her fret, becauſe the LORD had ſhut up her womb. And ſhe was in bitterneſs of ſoul, and *prayed* unto the LORD, and wept ſore—and
ſhe

take away my reproach among men. And she brought forth a son, and his name was called *John*, &c. Luke i. 5, 7, 13, 25, &c.

she vowed a vow, and said, O Lord of Hosts, if thou wilt indeed look upon the affliction of thine handmaid, and remember and not forget thine handmaid, but wilt give unto thine handmaid a man-child, I will give him unto the Lord all the days of his life—&c. Then *Eli* (the *high-priest*) answered, and said—Go in peace, and the God of *Israel* grant thee thy petition that thou hast asked of Him, &c. Wherefore it came to pass, when the time was come about, after *Hannah* had conceived, that she bare a son, and called his name *Samuel*, saying, Because I have *asked* him of the Lord, &c. And *Hannah* said — For this child I *prayed*, and the Lord hath given me my petition that I *asked* of Him. 1 Sam. i. 1, &c. See also chap. ii. 20, 21, 26.

Song of the Virgin Mary.

My soul doth magnify the Lord, and my spirit hath rejoiced in God my Saviour.

For he hath regarded the low estate of his handmaiden.

He that is mighty hath done to me great things, and holy is his name.

And

Hannah's Song.

Mine heart rejoiceth in the Lord, mine horn is exalted in the Lord, my mouth is enlarged over mine enemies, because I rejoice in thy salvation.

There is none holy as the Lord.

He

And His mercy is on them that fear Him from generation to generation.

He hath shewed strength with His arm, He hath scattered the proud in the imagination of their hearts.

He hath put down the mighty from their seats, and hath exalted them of low degree.

He hath filled the hungry with good things, and the rich He hath sent empty away.

He hath holpen His servant *Israel*, in remembrance of his mercy, &c.

He will keep the feet of His saints.

The bows of the mighty men are broken, and they that stumbled are girt with strength—the wicked shall be silent in darkness.

The adversaries of the LORD shall be broken to pieces—the LORD maketh poor and maketh rich, He bringeth low and lifteth up.

They that are full have hired themselves out for bread, and they that were hungry ceased.

He shall give strength unto His king, and exalt the horn of His anointed.

The conclusion of all which appears to be, that either we do not worship the same GOD which the *Jews* did, or the GOD we worship doth not disallow nor * disapprove *polygamy*. Miraculous blessings bestowed of GOD, in answer to the prayers of people living in open breach of His law, are totally contradictory to the whole scripture-character of GOD. *The way of the wicked is an abomination to the* LORD, *but the prayer of the upright is His delight.* PROV. xv. 9. *He that turneth away his*

---

* To say that He once did not disallow or disapprove it, but that He has *changed His mind* upon the subject—is one of those assertions which are diametrically opposite to the attribute of *unchangeableness*, so strongly marked out in scripture, and which *is*, and must be, of the very *essence* of an ALL-PERFECT BEING.

ear from hearing the law, even his prayer shall be abomination. Prov. xxviii. 9. Comp. Pf. lxvi. 18, 19, 20.

In what has been said on the subject of this *chapter* on *polygamy*, I should think arguments enough have been brought to prove that it was *not sinful* in the sight of GOD, under the Old Testament, and that the *blessed* GOD, by *becoming man* (1 Cor. xv. 47.) and condescending to appear on earth for us men, and for our salvation, *in the likeness of sinful flesh*, Rom viii. 3; *made of a woman made under the law*, Gal. iv. 4; *came not to destroy the law*, by lessening the *security* which it was evidently made to afford the *weaker sex* against the *stronger*. That the *treachery* which was so positively forbidden, and so amply provided against, among the *Jews*, should be *allowed* to *Christians* (who are *children* of the same *Heavenly Father*, *subjects* of the same *Almighty King*) and even *commanded* them in some cases, is a monstrous supposition!—repugnant to the positive institution of GOD, *They shall be one flesh* —contradictory to all *sound* reason—and abhorrent from every *generous, honourable*, and *humane* principle. Whatever the *situation* of the *man* may be, the danger arising to the *woman* from the consequences of *seduction* and *dereliction* is *equal*, therefore *equally* provided against by the law of GOD.

How *polygamy* became reprobated in the *Christian church* is easily accounted for, when we consider how early the reprobation of

marriage

marriage itself began to appear. The *Gnostics*, whom *Epiphanius* derives from *Simon Magus*, condemned *marriage* in the moſt ſhocking terms, ſaying that it was " *of the Devil*;" but this was to ſupport themſelves in their horrible tenet, that " *all women ſhould be common* amongſt them." Better people ſoon afterwards condemned marriage as *unlawful to Chriſtians*, and this under a wild notion of greater *purity* and *perfection*, in keeping from all intercourſe with the other ſex. This opinion divided itſelf into many ſects, and gave great trouble to the *church* before it was diſcountenanced. Still *ſecond marriages* were held *infamous*, and called no better than *lawful whoredom*. Nay, they were not aſhamed to write, that, " *a man's firſt wife being dead, it was* adultery, *and not* marriage, *to take another*." Amidſt all this, *polygamy* muſt neceſſarily receive the ſevereſt *anathema*—for if it could be ſuppoſed *unlawful for Chriſtians* to marry *at all*, and then ſo deteſtable to marry a *ſecond time*, after the death of a wife, the having *two at once* muſt be, *a fortiori*, accounted more horrible than all the reſt. All theſe ſeveral opinions had texts of ſcripture preſſed into their ſervice, by the *ingenious zeal* of their ſeveral abettors: the Old Teſtament was of no authority in the matter; the New Teſtament was made to *ſpeak* what it did not *mean*, concerning what it *does* mention; and conſtrued ſo as to condemn what, when rightly underſtood, it *does not* mention. The two first of these conceits about marriage have been long exploded, except with respect to the *Romish clergy*, who, to this hour, are *forbidden to marry*. But *polygamy* throughout the *Christian church*, the *western* part of it at least, is looked upon as a sin against the *seventh* commandment, though there is not a syllable in the *whole Bible* which makes it so. When I mention *polygamy*, I would always be understood to mean on the *man's side*, for on the *side of the woman*, the whole scripture shews it to be a *capital offence*.

Why this distinction should be made, HE best knows who made it; but, in part, we may suppose, from the consequences attending on *one side*, which cannot be on *the other*; these are finely touched by the strong and masterly pen of the *son of Sirach—Ecclus* xxiii. 22, 23. Having spoken of the *adulterer*, he saith, (agreeably to Lev. xx. 10.) *This man shall be punished in the streets of the city*, (see also *Deut.* xxii. 24.) *and where he suspecteth not he shall be taken*. He then proceeds—*Thus shall it go also with the wife that leaveth her husband, and bringeth in an heir by another—For*, first—*she hath disobeyed the law of the Most High*—secondly—*she hath trespassed against her own husband*—and thirdly—*she hath played the* whore *in* adultery, *and brought children by another man. She shall be brought out into the congregation, and inquisition shall be made of her children.—Her children shall not take root, and her branches shall bring no fruit. She shall leave her memory to*

be

be curfed, and her reproach fhall not be blotted out. Though thefe be the words of an *apocryphal* writer, they deferve the higheft regard, becaufe they are exactly confonant with the law of God. But it is very extraordinary, that in a difcourfe againft *fornicators, whoremongers,* and *adulterers* (which commences, ver. 16. and is continued to ver. 26. inclufive) not a word fhould be faid againft *polygamifts,* if *polygamy* were a fin as much on the *man*'s fide as on the *woman*'s.—He moft likely would not have paffed it over in filence had there been *any law* againft it.

His defcription of the *adulterefs* is very fine, and the aggravations of her offence, by bringing forth a fpurious iffue, ftrongly marked; but they are fuch as cannot exift on the man's fide, and therefore hence, in part at leaft, arifes the difference.

What he fays of the *adulterer* is alfo remarkably ftriking, and evidently taken from *Job* xxiv. 15. We lofe much of its propriety, from our mif-tranflation of Ὁ Ἀνθρωπος παραβαινων ἀπο της κλινης ἀυτȣ—*A man that breaketh wedlock,* we call it; but this is not a tranflation of the words—they literally are —*the man who tranfgreffeth from out of his bed*—like the *murderer,* Job xxiv. 14. *who, rifing with the light, is in the night as a thief*— So the *adulterer.* Saith *Job*—the eye of the *adulterer waiteth for the twilight, faying, No eye fhall fee me, and difguifeth his face.* The fon of *Sirach* reprefents the adulterer as " *leaving his bed,* ftealing out of it, as it " were,

" were, to execute his plans of wickedness,
" at a time when he thinks the unseasonable-
" ness of the hour, and the darkness of the
" night, will conceal him from the eyes of
" all." This man is, in *Job*, called נאף—an *adulterer*, or *defiler of other men's wives.*—That the same character is meant by the son of *Sirach*, is evident, from comparing *Ecclus* xxiii. 18. with *Job* xxiv. 15; and the punishment said to await him, *Ecclus* xxiii. 21. with that assigned to *adulterers*, Lev. xx. 10. Deut. xxii. 22, 24.

Another reason of the difference, that is to say, why *polygamy* should be allowed to the *man*, and no such liberty belong to the *woman*, arises also from the *inferiority* evidently stamped upon the *woman* by the GOD *of nature*, by whom she is placed under the absolute *power* of *her husband*, so that she cannot dispose of her *person*, on any occasion, or to any purpose whatsoever, to any other but to himself, as may appear from Gen. iii. 16. She is not at liberty to make any *contract* whatsoever, without her *husband's* consent—even *religious vows* are utterly void; she cannot *perform* them if the *husband* disagreeth thereto. Numb. xxx. 8. *The wife is*—ὑποτασσομενη τω ἰδιω ἀνδρι—*subjected to her own proper husband*, 1 Pet. iii. 1. The apostle *Paul* uses the same expression, when he says, Rom. xiii. 1. *Let every soul be subjected* (ὑποτασσεσθω) *to the higher powers*. But none of these things are said on the *side* of the *man*—even in teaching in the congregation, the *apostle* marks out the woman's *inferiority*—1 Tim. ii. 11. *Let the woman learn*

in

in silence with all subjection—I suffer not a woman to teach, nor to usurp authority over the man, but to be in silence. Again, the same *apostle* saith—*The head of the woman is the man—the man is not of the woman, but the woman of the man; neither was the man created for the woman, but the woman for the man.* 1 Cor. xi. 3, 8, 9. It appears then from the *nature of things,* as constituted by the *Creator* himself, that the *man* hath powers which the *woman* hath not, and therefore may use a freedom of action which the * woman cannot. The *apostle's* saying, *the man was not created for the woman, but the woman for the man,* reminds me of the manner in which CHRIST vindicated his disciples, when they were accused by the *Pharisees* of breaking the sabbath, because they plucked some ears of corn on the sabbath-day—*He said unto them, The sabbath was made for man, and not man for the sabbath, wherefore the Son of Man is* LORD *also of the sabbath.* The reader may transfer this argument, by parity of reason, to the other subject which we have been speaking of; and it furnishes a proof, by no means inconclusive, why a *man* may be a *polygamist,* but a woman not.

But we may go farther, and observe, that

---

* Besides all this, it may be said, that the more wives a man hath, the more children he is likely to have; but this cannot be on the woman's side; for she cannot breed the oftner by having more men than one.—Such a mixture is known to be even destructive of *conception,* so that the more men a woman may have, the less likely is she to breed at all. This surely affords a strong proof that *polyandry* (as it is called) is contrary to nature.

without *this difference,* the grand ends of GOD's *moral government,* with respect to the *commerce of the sexes,* would not have been provided for. The very *laws* themselves, which were made to secure *those* ends on *both* sides, must have become mere *cyphers.* If *polygamy* had been *permitted* on the *woman's side,* what must become of that law—Deut. xxii. 22. *If a man* (כי איש—*if any man whatsoever) be found lying with a woman married to an husband, then they shall both of them die, both the man that lay with the woman, and the woman. So thou shalt put away evil from* IsRAEL? If the having *more wives* than one at a time had been *forbidden the man,* what, in numberless instances, must have become of Deut. xxii. 28, 29. *If a man* (כי איש as before—*if any man whatsoever) find a damsel that is a virgin which is not betrothed—and lie with her—she shall be his wife ; because he hath humbled her, he may not put her away all his days ?* The *first* of these laws (as that of Lev. xx. 10.) was apparently to secure the man against the *treachery* of the *woman*—the *second* (as *Exod.* xxii. 16.) to secure the woman against the *treachery* of the man—and *both* to secure the world from that confusion and mischief which must be brought upon it (and are daily brought upon it by our disregard of these laws) by the *treachery* of either.

As the *woman* had the business of *parturition* allotted to her, she must necessarily be looked upon as the *repository* of those bonds and cements of human society, without which

it

it cannot * fubfift; fuch as family defcents, pedigrees, genealogies, inheritances, and all communications and diftinctions of relationfhip. Therefore the *Creator* did, in his infinite wifdom, fet bounds to the *commerce of the fexes*, on the part of the *woman*, which could not be paffed under pain of death.

Whoredom and *fornication* are, for the fame reafons, alfo inimical to thofe *bonds* of human fociety above-mentioned, introductory of all manner of confufion and wickednefs, incon-

---

* The *rabbinical* explanation of the word נאף—in Exod. xx. 14. has fomething very ftriking in it. *R. Levi* faith, that " this word, abfolutely and fimply, denotes
" *congrefs* with *the wife of another man*. Nor is it ufed
" but where a *married woman* is concerned. The reafon
" of this precept is, that the world fhould be peopled
" agreeably to the will of God. The bleffed God
" willed, that all creatures of the world fhould bring
" forth fruit according to their refpective fpecies, and
" that one fpecies fhould not be mixed nor confounded
" with another. He willed that the fame fhould obtain
" with refpect to the human offspring, that it might ap-
" pear whofe child every man was, and that the feed of
" *one* fhould not be confounded with that of *another*.
" Moreover, many corruptions are found in *adultery*,
" which occafion the breach of many commandments.
" God commanded to *honour parents*; but in cafe of
" *adultery* they cannot be known. So we are forbidden
" any intercourfe of marriage with *fifters*, and *other rela-
" tives*; but *adultery* tends to deftroy thefe laws; for,
" where this is, men cannot know their own relations."
Thus fpeak the *Rabbins*, agreeably to the fcriptures, and matter of fact, therefore are worth attending to in this point. The *reader* muft furely fee, very evidently, reafons for the *feventh* commandment on the *woman's* fide, which cannot apply on the *man's*, and why *adultery*, or *defiling a man's wife*, was made fo *penal* to *both parties* concerned.

fiftent

fiftent with the law of marriage, and the probable caufes of ruin and deftruction to the *female fex.*—Therefore, as *feduction* and *dereliction* muft, in the very nature of things, lead to thefe, the pofitive law of GOD forbids *any man* to take *a virgin*, and then abandon her.

As to what has been faid touching the harmony of the *Old* and *New Teftaments*, and the perpetual obligation of the *moral law* as to its *immutability*, fo that what it once *forbad* it always *forbids*, and what it did *not forbid* can never be *forbidden*—it is a point of fuch infinite confequence, as to deferve a recapitulation—and as I cannot fum up the matter in words more clear and forcible, than our *church* has done in her feventh *article*, I will introduce the conclufion of this *chapter* with that found and fcriptural account of the matter:—

" The *Old Teftament* is not contrary to the
" *New*; for both in the *Old* and *New*
" *Teftament* everlafting life is offered to
" mankind by CHRIST, who is the only
" mediator between GOD and man.
" Wherefore they are not to be heard,
" which feign that the *old fathers* did
" only look for *temporary* promifes.

" Although the law of GOD, given from
" GOD by *Mofes*, as touching *ceremonies*
" and *rites*, do not bind *Chriftian men*;
" nor the *civil* precepts thereof ought,
" of neceffity, to be received into any
" commonwealth—yet, notwithftand-
" ing, no *Chriftian* man whatfoever is
" free

" free from the obedience of the com-
" mandments which are called *moral.*"

No one can confider aright the *divine inftitution of marriage*, and not fee that it is founded in the very *nature of things*, and that by the GOD of nature. This is as felf-evident, as that if mankind were to *increafe and multiply, and replenifh the earth*, there muft be an appointed means by which this was to be brought to pafs. Therefore the laws concerning *marriage* cannot be reckoned a mere object of thofe *rites and ceremonies* which were to *vanifh away*. Heb. viii. 13.

Nor can they be reckoned among the objects of that *civil polity*, which was only calculated for the government of a *particular* people, in a *particular* part of the world, and that under *particular* circumftances, fuch as never were or can be known to any other people on the earth—unlefs *marriage* itfelf can be fuppofed to be confined to them, and not equally to concern the whole human race.

The *moral* law hath therefore *marriage* as its object, as concerning, in the higheft and moft material points, the *moral* actions of men. This clearly appears, not only from the very nature of the thing itfelf, but from the very words of the *feventh* commandment—*Thou fhalt not commit adultery*; and again of the tenth—*Thou fhalt not covet thy neighbour's wife*. Thefe are *moral* laws, equally binding at *all times*—in *all places*—over *all perfons.* And as the *feventh* commandment is a *moral* law

law founded on the divine inſtitution of *marriage itſelf*, ſo are all the expoſitions of it which are to be found in the ſcripture, unleſs we can be abſurd enough to imagine, that the *letter* of a law can be of a *moral* nature, and that the ſenſe, meaning, and intendment of it are only of a *ceremonial* or *civil* tendency.

What is meant by the word נאף—*adultery*, is not to be determined by the conceits, inventions, cuſtoms, or laws of men, but by the mind and will of GOD, as revealed to us in the *precepts* and *examples* which are recorded in *His word* for our inſtruction; and eſpecially from the uniform and unvaried idea annexed to the uſe of that word throughout the writings of *Moſes* and the *prophets*. If theſe have failed in giving us the true ſenſe of it, then is it not true that their writings *are profitable for doctrine, for reproof, for correction* (ἐπανορθωσιν — the amendment of what is wrong) for *inſtruction in righteouſneſs*, ſo that *the man of* GOD (i. e. the believer) *might be perfect, thoroughly furniſhed* (both as to *knowledge* and *practice*—nothing *leſs* can be the ſenſe of ἀρτιος) *unto all good works*, 2 Tim. iii. 16, 17. The ſcriptures which are ſpoken of in this paſſage are the ſcriptures of the Old Teſtament, or *thoſe holy ſcriptures* which TIMOTHY *had known from a child*—before a ſingle line of the New Teſtament was written, ver. 15. If therefore *polygamy* does not ſtand recorded as a *ſin* againſt the law of GOD, either by *Moſes* or the *prophets*, but as a matter

owned,

owned, blessed, allowed of God, we must say, unless we pretend to be wise above what is written, that it is *no sin,* for *sin is the transgression of the law.* As to the common notion, that it was made sinful by some *new law* of Christ, and absolutely forbidden in the New Testament, it is one of the *three pious* * *lyes* which owed their invention to the *ignorant zeal* of some professors and writers in the very early ages of *Christianity.* One was " —that marriage was a carnal thing, incon-" sistent with the purity and perfection of

---

* " It was a maxim avowed in the 4th century, that
" —it is *an act of virtue to deceive and lye, when, by that*
" *means, the interests of the church might be promoted.*—
" This horrible maxim was indeed of long standing,
" and had been adopted for some ages past, to the un-
" speakable detriment of that glorious cause in which
" they were employed. And it must be frankly con-
" fessed, that the greatest men, and most eminent saints,
" were more or less tainted with this corrupt prin-
" ciple. We would willingly except *Ambrose* and
" *Hilary, Austin, Gregory Nazianzen,* and *Jerome* ; but
" truth, which is more respectable than these venera-
" ble fathers, obliges us to involve them in the general
" accusation." See *Mosheim,* vol. i. p. 200.
" Though the primitive *Christians* (says *Moyle*) lived
" up to the full rules of their religion with the utmost
" probity and innocence of manners, yet it is too cer-
" tain, there were some persons among them, who,
" through a mistaken zeal, made no scruple of *lying* for
" the sake of their religion. Their fictions found an
" easy reception in a credulous age, and were conveyed
" down to posterity as certain truths." See *Jortin,*
Rem. vol. i. p. 299.
Du Pin owns, that *St. Hilary* seems to think " a lye
" necessary upon some occasions." Vol. ii. p. 76.

" a *Christian,*

"a *Christian*, and therefore ‡ unlawful under the gospel."—Another was—that "if a man, on the death of his wife, married again, it was no better than *adultery*."—The *third*, begotten between the other two, was—that "*polygamy*, though allowed to the *Jews* under the Old Testament, is forbidden to *Christians* under the *New*." The two first (among the *Protestants* at least) *are come to nought*—the *last* is as generally believed among *Christians* of all sorts, as the lye of *transubstantiation* is in the *Romish* church. And there can be little doubt, but that a man who has *two wives*, under whatever circumstances they might be taken, would be looked upon to be as *impious*, and as much a *child of the devil*, among us, as a person would be among the *Papists*, who *wickedly* refused to give up his outward senses, and to believe that a small piece of *wafer*, after certain words said over it by a *priest*, is the body, flesh, blood, and bones, of a man six feet high—or as a *priest*, *bishop*, or *pope*, who married at all.

As these things will be farther considered under the head of *Superstition*, I will now

---

‡ *Epiphanius*, Hæres. 58, speaks of the *Valesians*, who castrated themselves, and also their *guests*, that by this means they might introduce them into the kingdom of "heaven—" Se & hospites suos castrârunt, ut ita secum "introducerent in regnum cælorum."—They held that "none but *eunuchs* could be saved.

Nisi quis eunuchus fieret, salvari non posse.

hasten

hasten to the examination of a *notion*, which I fear is *too common* among us, and on which what is usually said and thought on the subject of *polygamy*, is for the most part built; I mean that of representing CHRIST as appearing in the world, as "a *new lawgiver*, "who was to introduce a *more pure and perfect* "*system of morality*, than that of the *law which* "*was given by* MOSES."—This horrible blasphemy against the *holiness* and *perfection* of GOD's law, as well as against the truth of CHRIST, who declared that *He came not to destroy the law, but to fulfil it*—this utter contradiction both of the *law* and the *gospel*—was the foundation on which the heretic *Socinus* built all his other abominable errors. From whence he had it, will appear in the sequel. In the mean time, I cannot help stopping a while to lament the progress which *Socinianism* is daily making among us—with many, among the *Dissenters* especially, it is called *new light*—but, thank GOD! there are yet some remaining, who call it by its true name —*old darkness*—and as such oppose it.—As it is coincident with the main subject of the following *chapter*, it will fall in my way to say something, which I hope will thoroughly apprize the *reader* of the mischiefs which must result from *Socinianism* in all its shapes. —In the course of what I shall have to say, it will appear, that, so far from CHRIST's ever condemning *polygamy*, which, as a *new lawgiver*, he is supposed to have done, He never mentioned it during the *whole course of His*

His ministry, but left that, as He did all other *moral* actions of men, upon the footing of that law under which *He was made*, and to which He, for *us men*, and for *our salvation*, became not only *subject*, but even *obedient unto death*. Phil. ii. 8.

Upon the whole, I take the truth to be, that the first *general institution of marriage*, accompanied with the first *general blessing*, is to be found in those words of Gen. i. 28, *Be fruitful, and multiply, and replenish the earth.—* The special manner of this, together with the indissolubility of the obligation created by it between the parties, is revealed, Gen. ii. 24. where it is said—*A man shall be joined*—דבק —προσκολληθησεται—agglutinatus erit—to *his woman*—and *they*, as in consequence thereof, *shall become one flesh*, i. e. *inseparable* from each other. Gen. iii. 16. reveals the entire subordination and subjection of the *wife to the husband*—and the rest of the *Bible* shews us, that *virgins* could not be *seduced*, and *taken* as *appetite* might *prompt*, and then abandoned and forsaken as licentiousness might *incline*— but that *monogamous* and *polygamous* contracts were equally valid and binding, equally lawful as to the inheritableness of the issue, and all other marks of legitimacy, that is to say, on the *man*'s side; but that, on the *woman*'s, polygamy was, for the most apparently-wife reasons, forbidden under pain of death.

While this system was reverenced and observed, we read of no *adultery*, *whoredom*, and *common prostitution* of women among *the daughters*

ters of Israel: no *brothels, street-walking,* * *venereal disease:* no CHILD-MURDER, and those other appendages of female ruin, which are too horrid to particularize. Nor were these things *possible,* which, since the revocation of the divine system, and the establishment of human systems, are become *inevitable.* The supposing our *blessed Saviour* came to destroy the *divine law,* or alter it with respect to marriage, is to suppose Him laying a foundation for the misery and destruction of the weaker sex; whereas no *being* less wicked than *Satan* himself, could ever have devised the almost total departure from GOD's LAW, which, from even the earliest ages of *the church,* since the Apostles' times, is to be found among the *Christians.*

I now put an end to this long chapter; in which *polygamy,* divested of all the nonsense of human reasonings, is set in its true *scriptural* light, as not *sinful in itself,* but, in some cases, highly *expedient*—in others—*duty;* and

---

* Much has been said concerning the antiquity of this disease. The subject is ably handled, and indeed exhausted, in that learned and laborious work of *Johannes Astruc,* de Morb. Ven. lib. i. I will only here observe, that as the *divine law* punished *adultery,* or the defilement of another's wife, with death in both parties—and *whoredom* was, on the part of the woman, also a *capital offence*—the consequences of *prostitution* must of course be prevented, by the prevention of the thing itself. Besides, the almost universality of marriage among the *Jews* (for *celibacy* was a disgrace) and the fixing the *virgin* on the man who first *took her,* so that he could not *put her away all his days,* left little room for *prostitution,* had their laws been even less severe against it.

in this last view of it, forming one *link* in that divine chain of *heavenly legislation,* on which the security and protection of the *weaker sex* is suspended; it being, upon the footing of God's law, as highly criminal for *one man* as *another,* to *seduce* and abandon to prostitution and ruin, those who have a most indefeasible claim upon him for their safety and support.

If among us, as among the *Jews,* and as formerly in *France,* and now in some other parts of the world, a *single man,* be his rank and station what they may, was constrained to * marry publicly the woman he seduces; and if the *spirit* of the *divine law* was so far complied with, as to compel the *man already married,* to give security for the maintenance and provision of such woman as he seduces, and, if his present *engagement* shall determine, to *marry publicly* her whom, in God's account, he has *married privately*—it would be such a check upon the licentiousness of mankind—

---

* In the book for the *reformation* of the *ecclesiastical laws,* in the time of *Edward* VI. it was proposed, " that " those who corrupted *virgins,* were to be excommuni- " cated if they did not *marry* them, or, if that could not " be done, they were to give them the third part of their " goods, besides other arbitrary punishments." See Burnet, Hist. Ref. vol. ii. p. 198. This, and many other salutary proposals, fell to the ground by the death of that excellent young *Prince, Edward* VI.—Had *Queen Elizabeth* paid attention enough to the mischiefs accruing to her sex from the want of some such regulation, to have had it passed into a *law,* it might justly have been reckoned one of the glories of her *reign.*

such a restraint upon what is called *gallantry*—such a security for female chastity—and such a preservative against *prostitution*, as might make those who live to see it say—

Jam redit & virgo, redeunt Saturnia Regna.
VIRG.

Now *Justice* and the *Golden Age* again return. Doubtless, *irregularities* there always *were*, and always *will be*, while *human nature* is *human nature*. Still, a vast difference there must be found, between a *system* which is formed as a check to the lust, treachery, and cruelty of mankind, and *one* which, in *numberless* instances, lets them loose to act without controul.

APPENDIX to CHAP. IV.

SINCE the preceding *chapter* went to the press, the *author* has been favoured with a transcript from a tract in the *British Museum*, which contains the whole of * *Bishop Burnet*'s opinion on *polygamy*. The *reader* has before seen it partially quoted; but the whole is here inserted *verbatim*.

" IS *polygamy* in any case *lawful* under the
" *gospel?*
" For ANSWER. It is to be *considered*, that
" *marriage* is a *contract* founded upon the *laws*

---
* *Bishop Berkely* thought *polygamy* agreeable to the *law of nature*. See Lond. Mag. for *June* 1754, p. 267.

" *of nature*, its end being the *propagation of*
" *mankind*; and the *formality* of doing it by
" *churchmen*, is only a supervenient benedic-
" tion, or pompous solemnizing of it; and
" therefore the *nature of marriage*, and not
" any *form* used in the celebration of it, is to
" be *considered*. It is true, the case is harder,
" when any is married by such a † *form*, as
" binds

---

† The *Bishop* here doubtless alludes to that part of our *form*, where the priest is to ask the man—" Wilt thou
" have this woman to thy wedded wife—&c.—and,
" forsaking all other, keep thee *only unto her*, so long as
" ye both shall live ?
" *The man shall answer*,
" I will."

Here is no *decent* qualification, as in the *ordination* of ministers—" I will endeavour so to do, the LORD being
" my helper"—" I trust so"—" I think so"—" I have
" so determined, by GOD's grace"—or the like; but, with the peremptoriness and confidence of a *Stoic*, who held—ἐφ' ἡμιν ἐςιν ὁσα ἡμετερα ἐργα—" *all our own actions*
" *are in our own power*"—ill suited to a frail and fallible creature, who knows *not what a day may bring forth*—(see *Prov.* xxvii. 1. comp. *Jer.* x. 23.) the *answer* is to be—I WILL—I—REX DOMINUSQUE MEI—I WILL.

The man is afterwards to take her—" *for better and*
" *for worse*"—but, be she ever so much *worse* than he *took her for*, short of actual *adultery*, still he is to groan under the sore bondage of what is called HIS VOW; which his fellow-creatures have just as much right to impose upon him, from any authority in scripture, as another set of people had, to make a man *vow* voluntary *poverty*—perpetual *chastity*—and implicit *obedience* to a fellow-mortal—on becoming a *monk*.

There was a time when, if *such a one* had *married*, the *law* (see 31 Hen. VIII. c. 14.) would have sent him to the *gallows*, and no doubt the *church* would have sent him to the *devil*. TEMPORA MUTANTUR—well if we could say—as touching *all* the foolish and unscriptural *snares*,
which

"binds him to one *woman,* than where he is
"bound only by the *tie of marriage,* con-
"ceived in *general terms.*

"The *case* of mankind, since the *fall,* varies
"very much from what it was in *innocence;*
"for then the soundness of their *bodies,* and
"purity of their minds, did keep out of the
"way all the hazards of *barrenness, sickness,*
"*uncleanness,* or *crossness* of *humours,* which
"made the former law not so proper for
"mankind; yet still a *single* marriage was the
"perfecter, as being * nearer the original.

"Before the flood, we find *Lamech* a poly-
"gamist; such were *Abraham* and *Jacob* af-
"ter it; not that this was not indulged by
"*Moses;* for all that he did relating to these
"affairs, was only to allow a DIVORCE, which
"was a *proviso* for the hardness of the hearts
"of the *Israelites.* Every man was bound to
"maintain whom he had first married; lest,
"therefore, such as designed another wife,
"and could not maintain a *former,* might
"use *indirect* ways to be rid of them, this
"*fair one* of *divorce* was allowed † by GOD;
"and

which mankind have invented, and laid for one another's
consciences—ET NOS MUTAMUR IN ILLIS. We may
observe that the aforesaid *vow,* exacted by the *priest* in
the marriage ceremony, is a *corruption* of Gen. ii. 24.
—*Therefore shall a man leave his father and his mother, and
shall cleave unto his wife.*

* See *Burnet* on the Articles of the Church of *England,*
3d edit. fol. p. 288.

† I just take the liberty to observe, that it is best to
keep to the expression of scripture. Our BLESSED SA-
VIOUR doth not say, that GOD *allowed divorce*—but—*Mo-*

"and their *polygamy* was practised, without
"either *allowance* or *controul*, as the *natural*
"*privilege* of mankind. Neither is it any
"where marked among the *blemishes* of the
"patriarchs; David's wives, and store of
"them he had, are termed by the prophet,
"God's *gift to him*: yea, *polygamy* was made
"in *some cases* a duty by *Moses*'s law;—when
"any died without issue, his brother, or
"nearest *kinsman*, was to marry his wife, for
"raising up seed to him; and all were
"obliged to obey this, under the *hazard* of
"*infamy*, if they refused it; neither is there
"any exceptions made for *such as were mar-
"ried*. From whence I may *faithfully* con-
"clude, that what God made *necessary* in
"some cases to any degree, can in *no case be
"sinful in itself*; since God *is holy in all His
"ways*.

"But it is now to be examined, if it is
"*forbidden* by the gospel. It is certain, that
"our Lord designed to raise mankind to the
"highest degrees of purity and chastity; and
"therefore our Lord and St. Paul do pre-
"fer a *single life* to a married state †, as that
"which qualifies us for the kingdom of
"heaven, and was loaded with the fewest

---

ses allowed or *permitted* it;—so the Bishop expresses himself a few lines higher.

† " This was meant only with respect to *particular*
" persons in *particular* circumstances, such as an *apostle*;
" which is the reason why St. *Paul* applies it chiefly to
" himself." 1 Cor. vii.

"incumbrances;

" incumbrances; and by this rule, a *single*
" marriage being next to none at all, was
" certainly more suitable to the *gospel,*"
[he means the times of the *gospel.*] " But a
" simple and express *discharge* of *polygamy* is
" no where to be found.

" It is true, our LORD discharges *divorces,*
" except in the case of *adultery*; adding, that
" whosoever *puts away his wife* upon any
" other account, commits *adultery:* so St.
" *Luke* and St. *Matthew* in one place have it
" —or *commits adultery against her:* so St.
" *Mark* has it—or *causes her to commit adul-*
" *tery:* so St. *Matthew* in another place.

" ' If it be *adultery* then to take another
" ' woman after an *unjust divorce,* it will fol-
" ' low that the *wife* has *that right* over the
" ' *husband*'s body, that he must *touch no*
" ' *other.*'—This is indeed *plausible,* and *it is*
" all *that can be brought from the New Testa-*
" *ment,* which seems convincing; *yet it will*
" *not be found of weight.*

" For it is to be considered, that if our
" LORD had been to *antiquate polygamy,* it be-
" ing so deeply rooted in the men of that
" age, confirmed by such fashions and *unques-*
" *tioned* precedents, and riveted by so long
" a practice, he must have done it *plainly* and
" *authoritatively,* and not in such an involved
" manner, as to be *sought* out of his words by
" the *search* of *logick.*

" Neither are these *dark words* made more
" clear by any of the *apostles* in their *writings:*
" words are to be carried no farther, than
                                         " the

"the *design* upon which they were written will lead them to; so that our LORD being, in that place, to strike out divorce so *explicitly*, we must not, by a *consequence*, condemn *polygamy*; since it seems *not to have fallen within the scope* of what our LORD does there disapprove.

"Beside, the term *adultery* may be taken in general, for such a *breach* of *wedlock* as is equivalent to *adultery*; and such is an *unjust divorce*. This may be the importance of the phrase used by St. *Mark*, viz. —*he committeth adultery against her*; or all may be better explained by the phrase St. *Matthew* uses about it, in one place—*he causes her to commit adultery*; since he that *exposeth* or *tempteth* to sin, shares in the *guilt* with the person that succumbs: and from this it appears, that *polygamy* is not declared *adultery*, neither in the place cited, nor any other that I know of.

"'But it is true that *polygamy* falls short of the intendment of marriage, in *innocency*, to which state, we that are *under the gospel* must return *as near as it is possible*.'—It is to be confessed that *polygamy* was much condemned by the ancients, though I think I have met with something about it, that is little noticed; but of that I can adventure to say nothing at this ‡ distance from my books and papers.

"But

---

‡ How unfairly *Dean Delaney* represents this passage in the *Bishop*'s paper, may be seen before, p.   where

"But all that being granted, it is to be
"considered that the *antients* were *unjust* and
"*severe* against *marriage* (itself), and did ex-
"cessively favour the *celibate*, or single (life);
"so that in some places, they who married a
"*second* time, were put to do *penance* for it;
"and, indeed, both *Jew* and *Gentile* had run
"into such *excess* by their free commixtures,
"that it is no wonder if the holy men of
"those ages, being provoked to a just zeal,
"against such unjust practices, must have
"been carried, through immoderate swaying
"of the counterpoize, into some extremes on
"the *other hand*.

"Therefore, to conclude this *short answer*,
"wherein many things are hinted, which
"might have been enlarged into a volume, I
"see nothing so strong against *polygamy*, as
"to balance the *great* and visible *imminent*
"hazards that hang over so many *thousands*,
"if it be not *allowed*."

The *author* cannot help expressing the highest satisfaction in finding, that in what he has written on the subject, he has had the honour of coinciding in so many points,

we are to suppose his *Lordship* making "the best excuse
"he could, for giving a *rash opinion*—whereas, he seems
to give the circumstance of being at "a distance from
"his books and papers," as a reason for not producing
testimonies from the *antients* "little noticed," but which,
if produced, would tend to shew, that some of them
thought as his *Lordship* did upon the subject.

with

with the sentiments of this learned, judicious, and excellent *Bishop*. But, on the other hand, he must express his sorrow, that his *Lordship* was so far " distant from his books and pa-
" pers," otherwise, it is most probable, that he would have produced some valuable testimonies from the *antients*, concerning what he hints at as—" *little noticed.*"

Another thing is also to be lamented, which is, that the good *Bishop* did not proceed to explain what he meant by those " great and
" visible imminent hazards," mentioned in the last paragraph.

If so small and inconsiderable a person as myself may venture to guess at the meaning of so considerable and great a man as *Bishop Burnet*, I should suppose, that his *Lordship* has here a reference to his observation before made, concerning the difference between the state of *innocency*, and that of mankind since the *fall*, and to those *evils* which he mentions as the consequences of the *latter*—which could not exist during the *former*. Such as
" *barrenness, sickness, uncleanness, or crossness*
" *of humour.*" What " great, imminent,
" and visible hazards hang over *thousands*," from these causes, has been observed before, p.   To vindicate, therefore, the lawfulness of *polygamy* is, as the world is now constituted, in *such cases* at least, to act as a good *citizen of the world*, by vindicating the
" natural privileges," and necessary *rights* of mankind; and it is, at the same time, to
act

act as a sincere believer of *divine revelation*, to set forth, openly and without disguise, that HEAVENLY SYSTEM, by which those *rights* are established and secured. To vindicate also that *universal law*, which had the good of the WHOLE for its object—to shew that its *wisdom* and *beneficence* are too VAST to be confined to a *single people*, or a single period of *particular dispensation*—to free it from that obscurity which *monks* and *priests*, and other *enthusiasts* and *fanatics*, have involved it in, to the distress and destruction of millions—is a task reserved *alone* for those, who, for the sake of *truth*, are willing to sacrifice their ease and *reputation* to the malevolence of *ignorance* and *prejudice*.

CHAP. V.

CHRIST *not the Giver of a new Law.*

MOSHEIM (Eccl. Hist. *Maclaine's* edit. quarto, vol. i. p. 295) very justly observes—" When once the *ministers* of the " *church* had departed from the antient simplicity of religion, abuses were daily multiplied; and *superstition* drew, from its " horrid fecundity, an incredible number of " absurdities, which were added to the doctrine of CHRIST and his apostles."—This is very true, and very strikingly exemplified in that learned and accurate writer's history of the *Christian church*, both with regard to *ceremonies* and *doctrines*. Among other absurdities in point of *doctrine*, is the notion that " CHRIST's mission upon earth, was to " exhibit to mortals a *new law*, distinguished " from all others by its unblemished *sanctity* " and *perfection*." In vol. ii. p. 277, this is represented as one main article of the *Socinian* creed, and it is to be wished that it never had been adopted but by the immediate followers of *Socinus*. Yet this is the language we hear daily, and is at the bottom of that extravagant notion expressed by *Gronovius* on *Grotius* de Jure, tom. i. p. 274, octavo, 1735 —maintained

tained by many learned men, and even adopted as an axiom by the generality of Chriſtians, as much as the *Pope's* ſupremacy and infallibility were before the *Reformation*—namely, that —" Lex naturæ & veteris fœderis concedunt " *polygamiam*"—*The law of* * *nature and of the* " Old

* By *lex naturæ*, or *law of nature*, I underſtand, for my own part, as far as I can make ſenſe of the expreſſion, or reconcile it to *truth*, that *lex non ſcripta*, or *unwritten law*, given of GOD to *Adam*, and from him derived by *tradition* to the people of GOD till the time of *Moſes*, when the *lex ſcripta*, or *written law*, was *given by Moſes*. See *John* i. 17. *former part*, and *Rom*. v. 13. Both theſe *laws* are in ſubſtance *one* and the *ſame*. The *moral* obligation of *each* demanded the *ſame obedience*; the *ceremonial* inſtitutions of *both* pointed out the ſame ſacrifice and atonement for ſin. Neither of theſe *laws* forbad *polygamy*, therefore it was practiſed by *Abraham*—*Jacob*, and doubtleſs many others who lived under what is called the *patriarchal* diſpenſation—as well as by the *Jews* under the *Moſaical* diſpenſation. As for what is generally underſtood by the *law of nature*, the offspring of what is called the *light of nature*, or the *mores communes naturali rationi conſentanei*—GROT—by which I ſuppoſe we are to underſtand—" Common rules of *moral action*, which are con- " ſonant to every man's *natural reaſon*"—thus making men their own *lawgivers*, as to what is *morally good* and *evil*; this, notwithſtanding all the learned *lumber* that has been written upon the ſubject, is a definition not unlike that of the ſtate of *Iſrael*, when they had no *king*, *but every man did that which was right in his own eyes*. Judges xvii. 6. A *law of nature*, which is to ſpring from, and be agreeable to every man's *natural reaſon* in this *corrupted* ſtate, is a ridiculous *chimæra*, that may bear as many forms as there are men in the world.—It is *Atheiſm* at bottom (for there is but ONE LAWGIVER—compare Iſ. xxxiii. 22. James iv. 12.) and is beſt deſcribed by——

Monſtrum, horrendum, informe, ingens, cui lumen ademptum.

Let

"*Old Testament, allow polygamy, but it is forbidden*—" Lege Christi"— *by the law of* Christ. This appears to be the opinion of *Grotius* in that place on which *Gronovius* comments: for he says—" Ex Christi lege ir-
" ritum est conjugium cum eo qui maritus sit
" alterius mulieris, ob jus illud quod Chris-
" tus fœminæ pudicitiam servanti dedit in
" maritum."—*By the law of* Christ, *a marriage with a man who is the husband of another woman, is void and of none effect, by reason of the right which* Christ *gave to the woman, who preserves her chastity, over her husband.* Here then Christ is set up to exhibit to mortals a *new law*, and that, in opposition to *the law of nature*, and of the *Old Testament*, as

---

Let those who think I carry this matter too far, consult Rom. i. 21, &c. which passage of *holy writ* may be looked upon as a summary of what is said in the Old Testament, of the depravity, blindness, ignorance, and wickedness of the *fallen human nature.* This is abundantly confirmed by all history, and daily experience. *Dr. Alexander,* Hist. of Wom. vol. i. p. 169, says, very truly—" Man, in that rude and uncultivated state in
" which he originally appears in all countries, before
" he has been formed by society, and instructed by ex-
" perience, is an animal, differing but little from the
" wild beasts that surround him." Here let me once more recommend to the *reader*'s perusal, Dr. Leland's *Advantage and Necessity of the Christian Revelation.* There he will see a very authentic account of what man is,
" though formed by society, and instructed by expe-
" rience," without the *light* of divine *revelation.* This, not as it respects the *vulgar* and *illiterate*, but those also who are handed down to us, as most eminent for *wisdom, learning,* and *philosophy.* — The world by wisdom knew not God, 1 Cor. i. 21. Comp. Job xi. 7, 8.

Gronovius

Gronovius expresses it. How this idea harmonizes with the *heresy* of *Socinus*, may appear from the short view which we have of the *Socinian theology, Mosh.* vol. ii. p. 276.—
"God, who is infinitely more perfect than man, though of a similar nature in some respects, exerted an act of that power by which He governs all things, in consequence of which an extraordinary person was born of the *Virgin Mary*. That person was Jesus Christ, whom God first translated to heaven, and having instructed Him fully there in the knowledge of His will, counsels, and designs, sent Him again into this sublunary world to promulgate to mankind a *new rule of life, more excellent than that under which they had formerly lived,* to propagate the truth by His ministry, and to confirm it by His death." Thus blasphemed *Socinus* against the excellence, purity, and perfection of the law of Jehovah, as well as against the glory and divinity of the *Son of* God! However, this notion about a *new law* given by Christ, is not * to be called the invention of *Socinus,* who

* *Eusebius,* the famous bishop of *Cæsarea,* one of the most learned *Greek* writers of the 4th century, whose eminent talents and acquisitions were accompanied by many errors and defects (see *Mosheim,* Eccl. Hist. vol. i. p. 286—7) says, in Demonst. Evang. lib. i. c. 1. that "the law of *Moses* was given only to the *Jewish* nation, and that only while it remained in its own country:" from whence he infers, "Οτι διὰ τῦτο ἑτέρε προφήτε καὶ ἑτερε νομε προσεδένοε." "That on this account there "was

who lived so late as the 16th century; it was a doctrine of the *Koran*, when the impostor * *Mahomet* set up his religion; for we are there informed, that, " of 224,000 *prophets* " which have from time to time been sent " into the world—among whom 313 were " *apostles*, sent with special commissions to " reclaim mankind from infidelity and su- " perstition—*six* of them brought *new laws* " for that purpose, which successively *abro-* " *gated the preceding*. These were, 1. *Adam*, " 2. *Noah*, 3. *Abraham*, 4. *Moses*, 5. *Jesus*, " 6 *Mahomet*." See Broughton, Hist. Lib. tit. *Mohammed*.

It was fundamentally necessary for *Mahomet's* plan, to have it believed that GOD had sent several prophets into the world; who had successively abrogated the laws of those who had gone before: for as *Mahomet's* intention was to appear as such an one himself, he very artfully kept his followers from looking after the credentials of his mission in the writings of the *Old* and *New Testaments*; for had he appealed to these himself, or referred his followers to *their* evidence of his mission from GOD, He must have appeared as great an

---

" was a necessity for *another prophet*, and *another law*." See *Barbeyrac*, Fr. notes on Grot. de Jure. liv. i. c. 1. § 16. note 1.

* Earlier still—" *Lactantius* considers CHRIST's mis" sion as having *no other* end, than that of leading man" kind to virtue, by the most *sublime precepts*, and the " most *perfect example*." *Mosheim*, vol. i. 188, note h, century 4th.

impostor

impostor in their eyes, as doubtless he was in his * own.

The *blessed Jesus* proved the reality of His mission, by a course directly contrary to this, for, in all His *teaching*, He constantly appealed to the *law* and the *prophets*—" *It is* " *written,*" was His warrant for all He said and did—He founded all His claim to the character of the MESSIAH, on the writings of the † Old Testament, and all His *miracles* were a constant appeal to what was there foretold concerning him. So far from assuming to Himself the authority of abrogating that holy, perfect, and spiritual *rule of life,* which was contained in the law given from GOD by *Moses,* He began His public ministry with the most solemn protest against such a supposition. Therefore, to contend for his enacting any *new law,* contrary to the *law of nature, and of the Old Testament,* is to call in question His veracity, and to place Him in a rank of *imposture* even below *Mahomet* himself. *Mahomet* professed ‡ to reform,

* *Mahomet* was too cunning not to be sensible of this. Therefore he got rid of all danger from their authorities, by making it believed that the *pentateuch, psalms,* and *gospels* were so altered and corrupted, that little credit was to be given to them—That GOD had promised to take care of the *Koran,* and to preserve it from any *addition* or *diminution. Koran,* c. 15.

† So His fore-runner, *John the Baptist,* appealed to the Old Testament for the truth of his mission. See Matt. iii. 3. Luke iii. 4—6, with John i. 22, 23.

‡ This adventurous impostor declared publicly, that he was commissioned by GOD to destroy *Polytheism* and *Idolatry,*

form, but in truth to deſtroy, the *law and the prophets*, as they had deſtroyed all *preceding ſyſtems:* whereas CHRIST moſt ſolemnly declared—that *heaven and earth could ſooner paſs, than one jot or tittle paſs from the law*—*Think not*, ſaid He, *that I am come to deſtroy the law or the prophets; I am not come to deſtroy, but to fulfil*. So far from abrogating the *law*, or *rule of life*, which had been delivered by the hand of *Moſes*, or ſetting up a *new law* in oppoſition to it—He came into the world to be ſubject to it in all things, and ſo to fulfil the *whole righteouſneſs* of it. Matt. iii. 15. *To magnify and make it honourable*. Iſ. xlii. 21. even by *His obedience unto death*. Speaking in the *ſpirit of prophecy* (Pſ. xl. 8.) He ſays—*Lo*—*I come*—*in the volume of the book it is written of me*—*I delight to do thy will, O my* GOD; *yea,* THY LAW *is within my heart*. And in His public miniſtry, how uniformly doth he ſpeak the ſame thing? How does He diſclaim the imputation of abrogating the law of GOD, and of ſetting up any *new law* of His own, in oppoſition to it? *He whom* GOD *hath ſent*, ſaid He, *ſpeaketh the words of* GOD. *John* iii. 34.—*My doctrine is not* MINE, *but His that ſent me*.

Idolatry, and then to reform, firſt the religion of the *Arabians*, and afterwards the *Jewiſh* and *Chriſtian* worſhip. For theſe purpoſes he delivered a *new law*, which is known by the name of The *Koran*, or *Alcoran*, &c. Moſheim, Part i. c. 2. § 2. Cent. 7.—*Mahomet* calls *Jeſus* the *Reformer* of the *Law of Moſes*. See *Turkiſh Spy*, vol. ii. p. 116. edit. 1691.

John vii. 16, 17.—*If any man will do His will, he shall know of the doctrine, whether it be of* GOD, *or whether I speak of* MYSELF. John viii. 28.—*I do nothing of* MYSELF, *but as my Father hath taught me I speak these things.* John xii. 49, 50.—*I have not spoken of* MYSELF, *but the Father which sent Me, He gave Me a commandment what I should say, and what I should speak. My meat is to do the will of Him that sent Me, and to finish His work.* John iv. 34.—This is not the language of one who came to abrogate GOD's *law,* as delivered by *Moses,* and to set up a *new law* of His own, contrary to the *rule of life* revealed in the Old Testament, but of one who came to fulfil the *righteousness* of the law, every *precept* of which He revered, whose every *commandment* He perfectly obeyed.

Let the reader turn to his *Bible,* and consider what is said of the law of GOD—Pf. xix. 7, 8, 9, 10, 11, and throughout the whole long 119th *Psalm,* and surely he must say, that the idea of a more *excellent law,* or *rule of life,* than is therein set forth, is as replete with *folly,* as it is with *blasphemy.* The same testimony which the Old Testament bears to the *perfection* of the *divine law,* is also borne in the New Testament. When CHRIST delivers that summary of it, *Mark* xii. 30, 31, under the two heads *of the love of* GOD *with all the heart*—and the love *of our neighbour as of ourselves*—He says—*There is* NONE OTHER *commandment greater than these.* So *Paul,* (Rom.

(Rom. vii. 12.) *The law is holy, and the commandment holy—juſt—and good.* And again (ver. 14.) The *law is ſpiritual.—Enter not into judgment with thy ſervant,* O Lord, ſaith the Pſalmiſt, *for in thy ſight ſhall no man living be juſtified.* Pſ. cxliii. 2.—For *by the deeds of the law there ſhall no fleſh be juſtified in his ſight,* ſaith the *apoſtle,* Rom. iii. 20. And again, Rom. iii. 19. *Whatſoever things* THE LAW *ſaith, it ſaith to them, that are under* THE LAW, *that every mouth may be ſtopped, and all the world become guilty before* God. After all this, to talk of " a more excellent " law—a more pure and perfect rule of life," goes beyond *folly,* it borders upon *madneſs.*

But as *madneſs* is uſually allowed to be ſo far conſiſtent with itſelf, as to *argue right,* though from *wrong principles,* we muſt obſerve that this ſcheme of abrogating the *old law,* and of introducing a *new one,* was a neceſſary and conſiſtent part of the *Socinian* plan—to ſuffer a *rule of life* to remain, which, from its *purity and holineſs,* concluded all men under *ſin,* and condemnation, ſo that *no fleſh could be juſtified by it*—and, at the ſame time, to deny the neceſſity of a *vicarious ſatisfaction and atonement* (which is the very marrow of the *Socinian* hereſy)—was to render the ſalvation of man *impoſſible. Socinus,* therefore, to eſtabliſh a conſiſtent plan, abrogates the *divine law* as delivered by *Moſes,* by which man cannot be ſaved, and introduces a *new law* (called the *law of* Christ) by which he might

might be saved. This made way for the rest of the * *Socinian* scheme, so that the divinity of CHRIST's person—His *vicarious obedience—sufferings—atonement—*and *satisfaction—*being rendered unnecessary, were all struck out of the *Socinian gospel.* Thus the pride of fallen man's reason, or rather the reasonings of his pride, are made to triumph over the wisdom of GOD. But as in all wickedness there is *folly*, so in this; for if no man *could be justified* by a law *less excellent, pure,* and *perfect*, how could he be saved by one that is *more* so? This has been seen by the *Socinians;* therefore—*sincerity* is their gospel obedience, and if they fail here (as fail they must) a *sincere desire to obey* will serve the turn.— Thus ends the *Socinian,* with the *Mahometan,* in the destruction both of the *law and the gospel:* and CHRIST, like *Mahomet,* is to annihilate *Moses* and the *prophets!*

If we attend to our *Saviour*'s preaching, and especially to that heavenly discourse delivered from the *Mount,* we shall find Him a most zealous advocate for the law of GOD, as delivered by *Moses.* We shall find Him stripping it of the false glosses, by which the Jewish *rabbies* had obscured or perverted its

---

* The *Turkish Spy*, Vol. ii. Lett. 15. writing to the *Mufti* concerning different *Christian* sects, says, " There
" is a sect which they call *Socinians,* who seem to preach
" out of the very book of glory, (i. e. the *Alcoran*) de-
" nying the divinity of *Jesus* the son of *Mary,* the
" *Christian's Messias;* even as our divine *Law-giver*
" does, in several chapters and versicles of the *Alcoran.*"

meaning, and restoring it to that purity and spirituality by which it reacheth even to *the thoughts and intents of the heart*. For instance, when He is about to enter upon a faithful exposition of the *moral law*, lest his hearers should imagine, that what he was about to say, was contrary to the law of the Old Testament, being so different from the teaching of the *Scribes* and *Pharisees*, He prefaces his discourse with those remarkable works—Matt. v. 17—20. *Think not that I am come to destroy the law or the prophets, I am not come to destroy, but to fulfil; for verily I say unto you, till heaven and earth pass away, one jot or one tittle shall not pass from the law, till all be fulfilled.* So far from abrogating the *old rule of life* delivered from GOD by *Moses*, no *one* single *part* of it, not a *sentence*—a *word*—a *letter*—a *bit of a letter*, was to be destroyed. *Whosoever, therefore, shall break one of these least commandments,* and shall teach men so, *he shall be called the least in the kingdom of heaven*; but whosoever *shall do and teach them, the same shall be called great in the kingdom of heaven.* What *commandments* were these? The sequel shews that they were the commandments of the *moral law*, or *rule of life*, delivered from GOD by *Moses*. *For except your righteousness* (or conformity to those commandments, which ought to be *internal* and *spiritual*) *exceed the righteousness of the Scribes and Pharisees* (which was merely *outward* and *formal*) *ye shall in no case enter into the kingdom of heaven.* He then enters upon

an

an exposition of the *sixth* commandment, which He vindicates from the bare, outward, literal construction, received by *old tradition*, and taught by the *Scribes* and *Pharisees*—*Ye have heard that it was said by them of old time, Thou shalt not kill, and whosoever shall kill, shall be in danger of the judgment*—but I say unto you, that *whosoever is angry with his brother without a cause, shall be in danger of the judgment: and whosoever shall say to his brother, Raca, shall be in danger of the council: but whosoever shall say—Thou fool—shall be in danger of hell-fire.*—This—" *I say unto you*"—does not imply that CHRIST meant to abrogate GOD's *law* against *murder*, and to set up a *new law* of His own instead thereof—but to shew the people, that what they had been taught by the *Scribes* and *Pharisees*, after the *tradition of the elders*, namely, to look upon the *sixth* commandment as reaching only to the *outward act* of *murder*, was false, for that, in the *spiritual* view and intendment of *that law*, it forbad every temper which resembled it, or could lead to it; such as violent, causeless, unprovoked anger, or any malicious inclination of the heart, breaking forth and shewing itself in opprobrious and injurious language; these are as contrary to the *law of the second table—Thou shalt love thy neighbour as thyself*—in their nature and tendency, as *murder* itself. So 1 John iii. 15. *He that hateth his brother is a murderer, and ye know that no murderer hath eternal life abiding in him.*

CHRIST then proceeds to explain the *seventh* commandment. *Ye have heard that it was said by them of old time, Thou shalt not commit adultery. But I say unto you, that, whosoever looketh upon a woman to lust after her, hath already committed adultery with her in his heart.* This—"*but I say unto you*"—does not imply that CHRIST meant to repeal the *seventh* commandment, but to explain it, as he had done the *sixth*, and to shew that it not only meant to forbid the act of *defiling another's wife* (γυναῖκα) but even indulging in the heart an *evil desire* towards her. Whereas the *Scribes and Pharisees*, after the *tradition of the elders*, stuck to the *outward letter*, and taught, that nothing but the *outward act* was a *breach of this law*. What *our* LORD said here was no *new* commandment, but what was implied in the *tenth* commandment—*Thou shalt not covet* (lust after) *thy neighbour's wife.* So Prov. xxiv. 9. *The thought of foolishness is sin.*

Again. *Ye have heard that it has been said by them of old time, Thou shalt not forswear thyself, but shalt perform unto the* LORD *thine oaths. But I say unto you, Swear not at all, neither by heaven, for it is* GOD's *throne, nor by the earth, for it is His footstool,* &c.—but let your communication be *yea, yea, and nay, nay; for whatsoever is more than these cometh of evil.* OUR LORD, by His—" *but I say* " *unto you*"—doth not enact any *new law*, but explains and restores the honour of the *third* commandment—*Thou shalt not take the name*

name of the LORD *thy* GOD *in vain.* This evidently forbids all vain and rash swearing, and the use of GOD's holy name (לשוא) *in vain, to no purpose,* in men's communication with each other. Even swearing by the *creatures,* is an interpretative breach of this commandment; for, as OUR LORD shews, there is no *creature* but hath some *relation* to GOD.

Ye have heard that it hath been said, An eye for an eye, a tooth for a tooth; but I say unto you, that ye resist not evil, but whosoever shall smite thee on the right cheek, turn to him the other also, &c. This refers to *Exod.* xxi. 24, where the law of *retaliation* was enacted, to be administered by the *judges of Israel* in a judicial way, on the lawful conviction of offenders: but the *Jews*, who were taught to abuse every thing, made this a rule of proceeding in their own *private acts of revenge* upon one another. Such a temper and disposition as this was very *sinful* to indulge, much more so to gratify; OUR LORD therefore checks this, by teaching patience and forbearance, and doing good to, rather than injuring, *their enemies.* But still here is no *new law,* the Old Testament taught the same. Exod. xxiii. 4, 5. *If thou meet thine enemy's ass or his ox going astray, thou shalt surely bring it back to him again. If thou see the ass of him that hateth thee lying under his burden, and wouldst forbear to help him, thou shalt surely help with him.*—Prov. xxiv. 17. *Rejoice not when thine enemy falleth, and let not thine heart be glad when he stumbleth, lest the* LORD *see it,*

and

and it displease Him.—Prov. xxv. 21. *If thine enemy* * *hunger, give him bread to eat; if he be thirsty, give him water to drink.*—Lev. xix. 17, 18. *Thou shalt not hate thy brother in thine heart—thou shalt not* † *avenge, nor bear any grudge against the children of thy people, but thou shalt love thy neighbour as thyself. I am the* Lord. All this is but saying what Christ says in other words.—This doctrine is inforced by *example,* as well as taught by *precept,* in the Old Testament. See 1 *Sam.* xxiv. 17, 18, 19, with Pf. vii. 4. But what a bright example have we, of rewarding *evil with good,* in the character of *Joseph?* Gen. xlv. &c.

Give to him that asketh thee, and from him that would borrow of thee turn thou not away. This is the very language of Deut. xv. 7, 8, 10.

Ye have heard that it hath been said, Thou shalt love thy neighbour and hate thine enemy: they certainly had heard such a doctrine *from the Scribes and Pharisees,* but it was false; the law said, *Thou shalt love thy neighbour,* but

---

* We find the prophet *Elisha* preaching this very doctrine to the king of *Israel,* with respect to his enemies the *Syrians,* who were captivated at *Samaria,* during the war with the kings of *Syria.* See 2 Kings vi. 22.

† Mr. *Bate,* on this place, well observes,—" It is " wonderful, that they, who read these commandments, " can talk *of the spirit of the law's* differing from that of " the gospel, as if the Spirit of God could differ from " Himself, and the same love were not required of the " *Jew* as is of the *Christian;* when, on the *love of* God " and *our neighbour,* hang all the law and the prophets, " according to both the Old and New Testament."

in no part of it, *Thou shalt hate thine enemy—* directly the contrary, Lev. xix. 18. Yet what numbers of people are there, that believe it did allow *hatred to enemies,* and that the *forgiveness* of them, and *doing them good*, was never known till CHRIST preached it! The *apostle* tells us—*Love worketh no ill to his neighbour, therefore love is the fulfilling of the law.* Rom. xiii. 10. What law is meant, appears ver. 8, 9; not a *new law of* CHRIST, but the *old law* delivered from GOD by *Moses.* As *there is but one lawgiver* (James iv. 12.) so there is but *one law* *.

More instances of the truth above contended for might be adduced, but I will refer the reader to but one more on this part of the subject, wherein, if CHRIST could ever have had the least intention of abrogating the *old rule of life,* given from GOD by *Moses,* and setting up a *new one* of *his own,* he had a fair opportunity of declaring it.—Matt. xix. 16. *One came unto him, and said, Good master, what good thing shall I do, that I may have eternal life? He said unto him, If thou wilt enter into life, keep the commandments. He saith unto Him, Which?* JESUS *said, Thou shalt do no murder—thou shalt not commit adultery—thou shalt not steal—thou shalt not bear*

---

* Nothing can be clearer upon this point, than our SAVIOUR'S *summary* of all He had been saying on the subject of relative duties, throughout the whole of His divine discourse. *Therefore, all things whatsoever ye would that men should do to you, do ye even so to them, for* —THIS IS THE LAW AND THE PROPHETS.

false

false witness—honour thy father and thy mother—and—thou shalt love thy neighbour as thyself. The young man saith unto Him, All these things have I kept from my youth up: what lack I yet? Jesus said unto him, If thou wilt be perfect, sell that thou hast, and give to the poor, and thou shalt have treasure in heaven; and come and follow me. The use which I would make of this scripture, is to shew that every necessary requisite for *entering into life*, as far as the *second table* of the law is concerned, is here set down—but we find not a syllable of any *new law*, or one *jot or tittle* subtracted from the *old*. Comp. Luke x. 25—28. The *old law* is repeated word for word, and summed up in its spiritual sense and import in the last sentence, which occurs in the Old Testament in just the same words. See Lev. xix. 18. *Thou shalt love thy neighbour as thyself.*—The proof which our Lord required of this man's *sincerity*, that of *giving to the poor*, was as much a duty under the Old Testament as under the *new*. See Deut. xv. 7—11, and Pf. xli. 1. The *following* Christ was so far from being a *new law*, that it was the *only way to heaven* which God ever revealed since *the fall of man*. Comp. Deut. xviii. 15, with Acts iii. 22, 23, 24, and Matt. xvii. 5.

But it hath been urged, that Christ declared Himself to introduce a *new law*, *John* xiii. 34. where He saith, *A new commandment give I unto you.* The context runs thus: *A new commandment give I unto you, that ye love*

love one another; as I have loved you, that ye also love one another.—By this shall all men know that ye are My disciples, if ye have love one to another. It surely cannot be meant, that, by the term " *new commandment,*" we are to understand the introduction of some law totally *new in itself,* as to the matter of it, without evident *inconsistency,* and absolute *contradiction:* for OUR LORD says, Matt. xxii. 39, 40. *To love our neighbour as ourselves,* is one of the *two great commandments, on which hang* ALL THE LAW AND THE PROPHETS. And St. John speaks of *our loving one another,* as an *old commandment which we had from the beginning.* Comp. 1 *John* ii. 7, 8. with 2 *John* v. 6. *St. Paul* saith, *Rom.* xiii. 8. *Owe no man any thing, but to love one another—he that loveth another fulfilleth the law. For this— thou shalt not commit adultery—thou shalt not kill—thou shalt not bear false witness—thou shalt not covet—and if there be any* OTHER COMMANDMENT, *it is briefly* comprehended in this saying—*Thou shalt love thy neighbour as thyself. Love worketh no ill to his neighbour,* therefore LOVE IS THE FULFILLING OF THE LAW. Comp. 2 John 5, 6. So James ii. 8. *If ye fulfil the* ROYAL LAW (νομον βασιλικον) ACCORDING TO THE SCRIPTURE, *Thou shalt love thy neighbour as thyself* (See *Lev.* xix. 18.) *ye do well. But if ye have respect to persons* (See *Lev.* xix. 15. *Prov.* xxiv. 23. xxviii. 21.) *ye commit sin, and are convinced* (ελεγχομενοι, convicted) OF THE LAW *as transgressors. For whosoever shall keep the whole*

whole law, and yet offend in one point (or *instance*—ἐν ἑνί) *is guilty of all*—i. e. "He is as truly a *sinner*, and as *truly* subject to punishment, though not so severely, as if he had actually been guilty of all possible transgression against GOD's laws." See *Parkhurst*'s Gr. & Eng. Lex. sub voc. ενοχος. For *He that said, Do not commit adultery;* said *also, Do not kill. Now, if thou commit no adultery, yet if thou kill, thou art become a transgressor of the law,* ver. 11.—i. e. by offending against the authority of the LAWGIVER. Whether in one or more instances this be done, the *whole law*, considered as one entire rule of obedience, is violated, and the offender of course liable to punishment. Comp. *Gal.* iii. 10. See a very sensible paraphrase on *James* ii. 8—12. in *Guyse*'s Paraphrase on the New Testament.

St. *James* addresses this epistle to the believing *Jews*, but holds forth no other rule of obedience to them, than the ROYAL LAW delivered from GOD to *Moses*, and recorded in the Old Testament. For the perfect *law of liberty*, see chap. i. 25. and chap. ii. 12. See *Guyse*'s Paraphrase on the New Testament, note on *James* i. 25. and on *Rom.* iii. 27.

Demonstration cannot be clearer, if these passages be duly considered, that CHRIST could not mean, by a *new commandment*, one that had never before existed, but to establish the *old commandment* among His disciples, not only on the footing of its *general* obligation as they were *men*, but also on that *special* consideration of their relation to *Him*, and to one another, as His difciples, fo as, if need were, to *lay down their lives for each other*. The inforcing this by a *new* ‡ *example*—on *new obligations*, on *new motives*—feems to be the meaning of Christ's calling the *law of brotherly love* a *new commandment*. So his difciple *John*, (1 *John* iii. 14.) *We know that we have paffed from death unto life, becaufe we love the brethren;* and ver. 16. Hereby perceive we the *love of* God, *becaufe he laid down His life for us, and we ought to lay down our lives for the brethren*. Something like this intenfe affection we read of in the Old Teftament. From what other motive could *Mofes* fpeak, when he faid, on the behalf of his *offending brethren* (Exod. xxxii. 32.) *Oh this people have finned a great fin, and have made them gods of gold!* (ver. 31.) *yet now, if Thou wilt, forgive their fin, and if not,* blot me, *I pray thee, out of thy book which thou haft written.* See alfo 2 Sam. xxiv. 17, where *David* pleads with God for the people, *when he faw the angel that fmote them,* and faid — *I have finned, I have done wickedly; but thefe fheep, what have they done? let thine hand, I pray thee, be againft me, and againft my father's houfe.* How were both thefe great men eminent *types* of *the good Shepherd, who laid down His life for the fheep!* John x. 11. Here we may alfo obferve the amiable and affectionate conduct of *Abigail,*

---

‡ Which may be inferred from the words—" *as I* " *have loved you.*"

when,

when, on the behalf of her churlish husband *Nabal*, she ventured forth to meet the angry *David*, and *his men*, 1 Sam. xxv. 18, 22, 23, taking *his* fault upon *herself. Upon* ME, said she, *my lord, let this iniquity be, and let thine handmaid, I pray thee, speak in thine audience, and hear the words of thine handmaid:* then follows, to ver. 32. one of the most *noble*, though *simple* instances of the perfection and persuasiveness of eloquence that we meet with, even in the *sacred writings:* one would almost think that *Virgil* had this transaction and that of *David*'s in his view, when he wrote the speech of *Nisus* to the *Rutulians*, on the behalf of *Euryalus*, as much as that he had the prophecy of *Isaiah* before him, when he wrote his *Pollio*.

> *Me, Me, adsum qui feci, in Me convertite ferrum;*
> *O Rutuli, mea fraus omnis; nihil iste, nec ausus*
> *Nec potuit—Cœlum hoc & conscia Sydera testor.*
> *Tantum infelicem nimium dilexit amicum.*

> " Me, Me, he cry'd, turn all your swords alone
> " On me; the fact confess'd, the fault my own.
> " He neither could or durst, the guiltless youth—
> " Ye moon and stars bear witness to the truth!
> " His only crime (if friendship can offend)
> " Is too much love to his unhappy friend."
>
> DRYDEN.

So in the friendship between *David* and *Jonathan*—1 Sam. xviii. 1.—where it is said —*the soul of Jonathan was knit with the soul of David,*

David, *and Jonathan loved him as his own soul:* and ver. 3.—*then Jonathan and David made a covenant, becaufe he loved him as his own foul.* And we actually find *Jonathan* interpofing with *Saul* on the behalf of *David*, even at the rifque of his own life. 1 Sam. xx. 32, 33. So *David*'s affection to *Abfalom*—*Would to* GOD *I had died for thee, my fon!* 2 Sam. xviii. 33. And, to the fhame of *us Chriftians* be it fpoken, this heroic and difinterefted friendfhip is even to be found among the *Heathen* (in notion at leaft) witnefs the fine and beautiful ftory of *Nyfus* and *Euryalus*. Virg. Æn. ix. l. 427, &c. Even *Epicurus* could fay, " that a wife man " will fometimes die for his friend." See Leland, vol. ii. p. 96.

We muft readily allow, that the REDEEM-ER's love to his people furpaffeth all human conception, as to the full and adequate knowledge and comprehenfion of it, and leaves, at an immeafurable diftance, all the inftances of the moft difinterefted *love* and *friendfhip*, that ever did, or can exift among mortals. This is finely touched by the pen of infpiration, Rom. v. 7. *For fcarcely for a righteous man will one die: yet peradventure* (ταχα, perhaps) *for a good man fome would even dare to die.* But GOD *commendeth his love to us, in that while we were yet finners* (and therefore—*enemies*, ver. 10.) CHRIST *died for us.* Well then may the fame APOSTLE (Eph. iii. 19.) call it—Υπερ-βαλλουσαν της γνωσεως αγαπην τȣ Χριȣυ—*the love of* CHRIST *which paffeth knowledge.* Thefe confiderations may fuffice to fhew, that OUR

Lord's—καθως ηγαπησα υμας—*AS I have loved you*—is not to be taken in any other sense, than as directory for the *motives* of their affection towards each other, or to describe the *manner* of that love which they were to bear each other *as his disciples*, and for *his sake*. This was a *new commandment*, not as to the *matter* of it (for *love is the fulfilling of* THE LAW) but as to the *manner* and *measure* of it, grounded on the *new principle* of their relationship *to him*, and to each other *in him*.

A like sentiment occurs Luke vi. 36. *Be ye therefore merciful*, AS (καθως) *your Father is merciful*; where GOD's *mercy* to man, is made the rule of our dealings with each other. What is there, in all this, contrary to, or inconsistent with, *Moses* and the *prophets*?

"But we meet with the very expression—
"the law of CHRIST, Gal. vi. 2.—*Bear ye one
"another's burdens, and so fulfil the law of
"CHRIST.*"—By *bearing one another's burdens* (a metaphor taken from easing another by carrying a burden for him, or assisting him in carrying it) I should apprehend that we are to understand, what the *Apostle* expresses—Rom. xii. 15.—by *weeping with them that weep; i. e.* so to be affected with *their sorrows*, as even to make them *our own*, and to be as assiduous in their removal, or alleviation, as we should be *were they our own**. But is this a *new law* of CHRIST, in opposition to,

---

* This sympathetic tenderness is finely touched by the *Apostle*, 1 Cor. xii. 25, 26.

inconsistent

inconsistent with, or differing in the matter of it from, the law of the Old Testament? Rather, doth not this fall under—*thou shalt love thy neighbour as thyself?* Compare Gal. v. 14. This was to be observed under the Old Testament, as well as under the *New*; we find this exemplified in those familiar instances put Deut. xxii. 1—4. Nor was this to be confined to *friends* only, but to be extended to *enemies*. Exod. xxiii. 4, 5. Though the *letter* of these laws expressed only things comparatively trivial, yet, doubtless, the spirit of them extended to matters of more serious consequence, and were rules for their conduct towards each other in whatever calamities they or theirs might be involved: a very striking instance of this appears (Psalm xxxv. 12, 13, 14.) in the behaviour *David* observed with respect to some of his ungrateful enemies—*they rewarded me evil for good, to the spoiling of my soul* (שכול—to the *depriving it of comfort.*) *But as for me, when they were sick* (or *afflicted*, as חלה also signifies) *my clothing was sackcloth—I humbled my soul with fasting—I behaved myself as though he had been my friend or brother—I bowed down heavily as one that mourneth for his mother.*

However, by the * *law of* CHRIST, may we not suppose something more to be meant than

---

* Those phrases—the *law of* CHRIST—*the Christian law*—the *law of the gospel*—the *morality of the gospel*—the *law of the New Testament*—as they are commonly used and understood, have greatly confounded the ideas of
mankind

than as to the *doctrine* which He taught in conformity to the *law of love?* May we not suppose, that here is a reference to the * *example* He set—to the *principle of action* (for so ‡ νομος sometimes is to be understood—see Rom. vii. 21.) which led Him to bear our

mankind with regard to true and genuine *Christianity*, and have added no little strength to the cause of *Socinianism*.

All this arises from a want of duly considering and understanding the *nature*, *use*, and *properties* of the *divine law*, as well as the place it holds in the œconomy of the covenant of redemption.

Its nature.—*Spiritual—holy—just—*and *good—*therefore can never save, but be the ministration of death and condemnation to us as transgressors and guilty creatures. So that which was *ordained unto life* to the *innocent*, must be *found to be unto death* to the guilty. See Rom. vii. 10, 12, 14. 2 Cor. iii. 7, 9.

Its use.—To *convince of sin—*and thus to lead the sinner to the atonement, satisfaction, righteousness, and death of CHRIST, for pardon, justification, acceptance, and life eternal. See Rom. vii. 7, 8, 9, 10. Gal. ii. 19, &c.; iii. 19, &c.

Its properties.—Being *written in the heart*, and *put into the mind*, it becomes a *rule of life* to the believer, an holy *directory* to shew him how he ought *to walk and to please* GOD; and, in the sight of the *purity*, *perfection*, and *holiness* of the *divine law*, to live under constant self-abasement, and deep humility, *looking for the mercy of our* LORD JESUS CHRIST *unto eternal life*. See Jer. xxxi. 33, 34. Eph. ii. 10. Tit. ii. 11, 12, 13. Jude 21. Phil. iii. 9.

Those who live under a *practical* view of these things, are not only *almost*, but altogether *Christians*, and can no more think of a *new law*, than of a *new gospel*. Having drank of the *old wine* of *divine truth*, they desire not *the new wine* of *human error* (Luke v. 39.) *for they say the old is better*.

* John xiii. 15. Rom. xv. 5. 1 Pet. ii. 21.
‡ See Parkhurst's Gr. & Eng. Lex. sub voc. N° iv.

burden

burden of *guilt* and *punishment*, when *He himself bare our sins in His own body on the tree*, 1 Pet. ii. 24. according to the prophecy that went before, If. liii. 4. *Surely He hath borne our griefs, and carried our sorrows. He suffered, leaving us an example, that we should follow His steps*; and in particular, by observing the same *rule* or *principle of action* towards each other as He did towards us, in bearing, alleviating, removing *each other's burdens* of affliction and sorrow, by every means in our power? The νομος—law—or rule—which Christ acted by towards us, is proposed to our imitation, with respect to the *forgiveness of injuries*, (*Col.* iii. 13.) *Forbearing one another, and forgiving one another, if any man have a quarrel against any; even as* Christ *forgave you, so also do ye.* So that when a man forgives an injury upon this principle, he may be said to *fulfil the law of* Christ in this respect, by acting agreeably to the *rule*—law—or principle of Christ towards His redeemed people. But what is there in all this inconsistent with the Old Testament, or that is not exactly conformable to it? Christ did nothing for us but what the Old Testament exactly foretold. *Acts* xxvi. 22, 23. The *Apostle*, in this passage of *Gal.* vi. 2. says only, in other words, what is said, 1 *John* iv. 11. *Beloved, if* God *so loved us, we ought also to love one another.* So our Lord, *John* xiii. 34. *That ye love one another, as I have loved you.* As it is written, If. lxiii. 8, 9. *He was their Saviour; in all their affliction He was afflicted.*

How then ought *Christians* to observe this *rule* towards each other! How ought they *to weep with them that weep*—as well as *rejoice with them that do rejoice!*—*Who is weak, and I am not weak?*—faith *Paul,* 2 Cor. xi. 29. *Who is offended, and I burn not?* Did CHRIST bear our burden—was this the νομος—the principle of action—the *rule*—the *law*—which governed Him in all He *did* and *suffered* for us? then let us *fulfil this law* towards *each other,* by interesting ourselves in each other's welfare and prosperity; so as, by our consolation, advice, and every other means in our power, to *comfort those that mourn*—*raise up them that are cast down*—*bind up the broken-hearted*—and, *in the spirit of meekness, restore those that are* * *fallen.* Thus *shall we bear each other's burdens, and so fulfil the law of* CHRIST. See Is. lxi. 1, 2, 3. Lastly, it is not improbable that the *apostle* refers to what CHRIST said, John xiii. 34, 35. xv. 12.

I have before observed, that the idea of CHRIST's setting up a *new law* in opposition to the law of the Old Testament, as more *pure* † *and holy,* is equally replete with

---

* This is the more immediate sense of the *Apostle,* Gal. vi. 2. as appears by the context; but yet I have given a larger sense to the words, as doubtless containing a rule for the conduct of *Christians* to each other under *all their burdens,* from whatever cause they may be derived.

† " At CHRISTI lex, ut res alias, ita & hanc conjugii
" inter *Christianos* ad perfectiorem redegit normam."
—" But the law of CHRIST reduced, as it did other
" things, this *law of marriage* to a more perfect rule
" among Christians." Grot. de Jure, lib. ii. c. 5. § 2.

folly

folly and *blasphemy*. This is true; for it not only carries us into the fundamental principle on which *Mahomet* founded his *Koran*, and into the very *sink* of *Socinianism*—but it sets forth CHRIST as *finding fault* with the law of GOD as delivered by *Moses*, and opposing Himself to it. This runs us, though we perceive it not, very near the borders of that monster of *heresy* CERINTHUS, and *his followers*, against whom *St. John* is supposed to have written the beginning of his gospel. They taught, that—" the Creator of this
" world, who was also the sovereign and
" lawgiver of the *Jewish* people, was a Being
" endowed with the greatest virtues, and
" derived his birth from the supreme GOD:
" That this Being fell by degrees from His
" native virtue and primitive dignity: That
" the supreme GOD, in consequence of this,
" determined to destroy His empire, and sent
" upon earth, for this purpose, one of the
" ever-happy and glorious *Æons*, whose name
" was CHRIST; that this CHRIST chose for
" His habitation the person of JESUS, a man
" of the most illustrious sanctity and justice,
" the son of *Joseph* and *Mary*, and, descend-
" ing in the form of a dove, entered into Him,
" while He was receiving the baptism of
" *John* in the waters of *Jordan:* That JE-
" SUS, after His union with CHRIST, OP-
" POSED HIMSELF WITH VIGOUR TO THE
" GOD OF THE JEWS, and was, by His insti-
" gation, seized and crucified by the *Hebrew*
" chiefs.—*Cerinthus* required of his follow-
" ers,

"ers, that they should ABANDON THE LAW-
"GIVER OF THE JEWS, whom he looked
"upon as the creator of the world; that
"they should retain *a part of the law given by
"Moses*, but should nevertheless employ their
"principal attention and care to REGULATE
"THEIR LIVES BY THE PRECEPTS OF
"CHRIST." Mosh. vol. i. p. 69. Which
said *precepts* are supposed to be the *precepts*
of one who *opposed himself with vigour* to the
GOD of the *Jewish* people, and whose disciples were to *abandon the lawgiver of the Jews*,
though they were to admit him to be the
Creator of the world!

Here then, *reader*, I have lifted up the *hive*,
and out has flown the *swarm*, not a *swarm* of
useful and industrious *bees*, but a *swarm* (ערב—
a *mixture)* like that in Ægypt, Exod. viii. 24.
which was *grievous*, and *corrupted the land*.
Here is to be seen those pestilential insects
from whence sprung * *Arianism—Socinianism
—Mahometism*

---

* The famous Dr. *Samuel Clarke*, fully asserts, that
" the *scripture*, or the known open public books of the
" *New Testament*, are the *real* and *only rule* of truth
" among *Christians.*" *Introduction to the Scripture Doctrine
of the Trinity*, p. 4. as cited by *Whiston* in the *Life of Dr.
S. Clarke*, p. 48. — *Whiston* is for removing us still farther
from the Old Testament, and insists upon it, that the *traditionary doctrines* — the *traditionary creed*, and the *traditionary preaching of the Apostles*, which are either authenticly
preserved in the *Apostolical Constitutions*, or no where, or,
however, the scriptures as interpreted according to them,
were ever in the first times owned the only certain foundations of the *Christian* settlements, &c. *Whiston*, ib. 48, 49.—
which, by the way, is no small proof, of the truth with
which I have observed the early separation of the New
Testament

—*Mahometism*—*Antinomianism*—*Neonomianism*, and all the *isms* which have plagued, harrassed, and distressed, divided, and disgraced the church ever since.

Such is the picture of the *Cerinthians*. Surely we cannot survey it attentively, without recognizing a similitude of some of the features, at least something which may be called a strong *family likeness* to the idea of " polygamy's being allowed by the law of " nature and of *the Old Testament* (that is, by " the GOD of the *Jews)* but forbidden by " the *law of* CHRIST," which is contrary to both.

If it be possible to produce a single *law of* CHRIST, which opposes the law of the Old Testament, all his claim to the character of the *Messiah* is at an end; for the *Messiah* was *to be made of a woman made under the law.* Gal. iv. 4.—*subject* to its *every precept*, *obedient* to its *every command*—and doubtless therefore to that solemn command, which, for the greater solemnity, is repeated twice over— *Ye shall not* ADD *to the word which I command you, neither shall ye* DIMINISH *aught from it.* Deut. iv. 2. xii. 32. How could the BLESSED JESUS be said to *fulfil all righteousness*, by a perfect conformity to *all things which are written in the book of the law to do them*—how say, as He doth by the Psalmist, Pf. xl. 8.

Testament from the Old Testament, and treating them as systems totally distinct from, and independent on each other.

Lo I come to do thy will—not mine own.—John vi. 38. *I am content to do it*—THY LAW *is within my heart*—if he either ADDED to the *rule of life given from* GOD *by Moses*, or DIMINISHED from it? How could he be said to observe the law in ALL THINGS—how give that holy challenge to the *Jews*, John viii. 46. *Which of you convinceth Me of sin?*—if he abrogated the *law*, the *rule* given as touching the *moral actions* of men, in any one instance, and set up a law of *his own* in opposition to it?

The *false* CHRIST of *Cerinthus* and of the *Socinian*, and the *true* CHRIST *of* GOD, are discernable by this essential difference—The first *opposed himself* with *vigour to the* GOD *of the Jews*—required that his disciples should abandon *the law given by Moses, and regulate themselves by some new precepts of his own.*— The *Holy* CHRIST *of* GOD declared—that not *a jot or tittle was to pass from the law*—*that He came not to destroy, but to fulfil it*—His whole teaching, practice, and *example, magnified the law, and made it honourable.* Therefore He exactly answered to the character given of Him in the Old Testament. *He finished the transgression—made an end of sins—made reconciliation for iniquity—and brought in* (by his sinless, perfect, and meritorious obedience) *an everlasting righteousness,* for the *justification* and *salvation* of his people to *all eternity.*

" But what shall we say of the ordinances
" of *Baptism and the Lord's supper*, are not
" these CHRIST's *own institutions*, established
" by

" by his *own authority?*"—To this I answer —that these *two sacraments* were to succeed *circumcision* and *the passover*, which were the two *sacramental ordinances* of the *Mosaic* dispensation, the whole of which was to cease and *vanish away* on the coming of *the Messiah*.

Another *priest* was to arise, not after the order of *Aaron*, but after the order of *Melchizedeck*, (Pf. cx. iv.) and this, according to the *prophecies* which went before. Now, as the excellent *Bishop Hall* observes, " some " *actions* are *prophecies*," and he instances in the history of the *brazen serpent* the truth of his position; he might have instanced in many more: and among the rest, in the history of *Melchizedeck*, of whom it is said, that *he was a priest of the most high* God, *who met Abraham returning from the slaughter of the kings, and blessed him.* Heb. vii. 1. In *Gen.* xiv. 18. it is said—And *Melchizedeck*, king of *Salem*, brought *forth bread and wine*, and *blessed Abraham*, ver. 19. In this prophetical action is exhibited a type of Christ, the *priest after the order of Melchizedeck* (see Pf. cx. 4.) exhibiting, under the sacramental *bread and wine*, his body broken, and *his blood shed, for the life of the world.* So that after the *similitude of Melchizedeck there ariseth another priest.* Now all this was foretold, because ordained to happen in the fulness of time; therefore the instituting the receiving *of bread and wine*, in remembrance of the sacrifice

fice of CHRIST, as emblems of *his body and blood*, was no *new law* of CHRIST, but as really foretold in the Old Teftament, as was the facrifice and death of CHRIST upon the crofs. CHRIST *our paſſover being ſacrificed for us* (1 Cor. v. 7.) there was an end of the typical ordinance of the *paſchal lamb*. And the *prieſt* after the *ſimilitude* of *Melchizedeck*, was to bleſs the *children of Abraham* (Gal. iii. 7.) by exhibiting *his body and blood* to their faith, under the *emblems of bread and wine*, as *Melchizedeck* (whom ſome learned men ſuppoſe to be CHRIST Himſelf appearing to *Abraham* in an human form, as he often did under the Old Teftament, in token of his future incarnation) bleſſed the *father of all the faithful*, by exhibiting to his faith the *future great ſacrifice* under thoſe emblems which were to be the appointed figures to repreſent it under the goſpel difpenfation. Thus, (as the *Apoſtle* ſpeaks, Heb. vii. 12.) as the *prieſthood* was *to be changed*, there muſt be of neceſſity alſo a change * *of the law*. But all this was pre-ordained and foretold ages before it happened, and therefore is not to be looked upon as a *mere law* of the New Teſtament, but muſt bear equal date, in the intentions and defigns of GOD, with the plan of redemption itſelf.

* It appears from the whole context, that the *moral law* is not here meant, but the *typical or ceremonial law* of *ſacrifices*, which, together with the *Levitical prieſthood*, were all to be done away on the *ſacrifice* of the *death of* CHRIST.

So

So with regard to the ordinance of *Baptism*, this was exhibited under the figure or type of *Noah's ark, wherein few, that is eight souls, were saved by water—the like figure whereunto* 'Ω 'Αντιτυπον — the antitype to which) *even baptism doth now save us, not the putting away the filth of the flesh, but the answer of a good conscience towards* God, *by the resurrection of* Jesus Christ. 1 Pet. iii. 20, 21. As the *bread* and *wine* represent the *body* and *blood* of Christ, in the Lord's Supper, so the water in *baptism* represents the cleansing of the *Holy Spirit*, and *all* exhibit to our faith, touching *what is past*, what the sacraments of the *passover* and *circumcision* represented to the faith of the Old-Testament *saints*, touching what *was then to come*; but all meet in one grand central point—Christ, *the end of the law for righteousness to every one that believeth*, Rom. x. 4. Therefore the *sacraments* of the Lord's *Supper* and *baptism*, are not *new ordinances**, in any other sense, than as appointed of God to attend on the dispensation of the *gospel of His grace*, under the *New Testament*, when those sacraments were abolished which were to attend a different dispensation of the *same gospel* under the *Old Testament*. All argue one uniform, consistent design in the blessed God, carried on in different manifestations of

---

* See the *outward visible sign* and the *inward and spiritual grace*, in the sacrament of *baptism*, beautifully set forth, Is. xliv. 3. Ezek. xxxvi. 25, 26, 27. with John iii. 5.

it, under the *Patriarchal*—* *Mosaical*—*Prophetical*, and *Evangelical* ages, but subject to no controul, opposition, or variation, as to the *matter* of any single part or atom of it. The further we follow the notion of Christ's being the giver of a *new law*, in opposition to the law of the Old Testament, the more must we see it pregnant with consequences of the most alarming and dreadful kind—because, this being the case, we are without a *Redeemer*, and of course without any *redemption*; for we are told, that Christ *died for the redemption of the transgressions that were under the* first Testament, *Heb.* ix. 15. by which first Testament we must understand the *law of* God delivered by *Moses*; but I can find no trace of any satisfaction for sins committed against any *new law* of Christ: we must look to ourselves for any *transgressions against this*: and if so—*no flesh can be saved.* Therefore some of the *old heretics*, who were maintainers of this *new-law* scheme, were perfectly consistent, in declaring, that " no sin *after baptism* could be forgiven"— against which horrible error, the 16th *Article* of the *Church of England* is very scripturally and properly levelled.—But again—this notion of Christ's abrogating the *old rule of*

---

* Those *divers washings* which we read of in the law of *Moses*, and which (Heb. ix. 10.) the *apostle* classes among the *carnal ordinances imposed till the time of reformation*, were doubtless typical of *Christian baptism*, wherein, as before under the law, the *body is washed with pure water.* Heb. x. 22.

life,

life, and enacting a *new one* in its place, as it turns us over to seek our salvation by a *new plan of obedience*, or personal righteousness of *our own*, makes void *both* Testaments. It annihilates the *law which was given by Moses*, it of course destroys the *grace and truth which came by* JESUS CHRIST. John i. 17. If we are not bound by the old *moral* law, we have no occasion to seek *redemption from its curse*, and absolution from its condemnation.—The *divinity* of CHRIST—the atonement of his precious blood—the *imputation* of His *righteousness*— His *satisfaction—merit—vicarious sufferings* and *obedience*, together with his *intercession* at the *right hand of* GOD, and all other appendages belonging and essentially necessary to his *priestly office*, by which alone we can have *redemption, even the forgiveness of our sins*, may bear as small a price in our eyes as in the eyes of *Socinus, Mahomet*, or *Cerinthus*. If the *old law* be abrogated as a *rule of life*, then have we nothing to do with —*Cursed is every one that continueth not in all things which are written in the book of the law to do them.* Gal. iii. 10. The *law* is no longer a *ministration of death*, 2 Cor. iii. 7. and *condemnation*. And, if this be the case, the whole foundation of the *redemption that is in* CHRIST JESUS is sapped and destroyed, and the whole fabric of man's *salvation*, which is *built upon it*, must fall into one dreadful and horrible union; we must reverse CHRIST's declaration—*I came not to destroy the law, but to fulfil it*—and say, that he came *not to fulfil but*

but to *destroy it*. Here we must join in the madness of the *Antinomians*, and deny the *obligation of the law*—or in the horrid errors of the *Socinians*, and renounce the *hope of the gospel*. To mention all the *appendages* to this *new-law* scheme would be endless; suffice it to say, that they are, in one shape or other, connected with every *heresy* that ever was, or can be invented; for all *heresy*, however coloured or disguised by the art and subtlety of men, or, as the *Apostle* says, Eph. iv. 14. *by the sleight of men, and cunning craftiness whereby they lie in wait to deceive*, must originate in the confounding those two distinct propositions, which are laid down in the beginning of *St. John*'s gospel as above-mentioned—*The law was given by Moses—Grace and truth came by* JESUS CHRIST.

CHRIST came, neither to set up a *new law* nor a *new gospel*, but (as the Scripture had foretold) to bear testimony to the truth of *both*, as revealed by *Moses and the Prophets*.— Thus he told *Pilate*, John xviii. 37.—*To this end was I born, and for this cause came I into the world, that I should bear witness unto* THE TRUTH: *Every one that is of* THE TRUTH *heareth my voice*. And in that most affectionate *prayer* for His *disciples*—John xvii. —He saith, ver. 17. *Sanctify them through* THY TRUTH—THY WORD IS TRUTH.

To conclude this point:—If we compare scripture with scripture in *every* instance, we shall not find a single *law*, or *rule of life*, in the New Testament, which has not its foundation in the Old Teſtament, and that CHRIST came not as a *law-giver and a judge*, when He appeared in the *likeneſs of ſinful fleſh*—Rom. viii. 3. but as a *law-fulfiller* and a *Saviour*—*I came not* (ſaid He, John xii. 47) *to judge the world, but to ſave the world.* Not to introduce any *new rule* of *right* and *wrong*, which was to change the nature of *moral good and evil*; *but for the redemption of the tranſgreſſions under the firſt teſtament, that they which are called might receive the promiſe of eternal inheritance.* Heb. ix. 15.

As a *prophet*—He opened and explained the *law*, and preached the *goſpel*. As a *prieſt* —He made *atonement* for the *guilty*.—As *king* —He eſtabliſhed the moral *law* as a *rule of life* to his *ſubjects*; leaving it as He found it —a *ſpiritual, holy, righteous, perfect* inſtitution (Pſ. xix. 7.) to which nothing could be *added*, from which nothing could be *diminiſhed*; reaching not only to the *outward* actions of the life, but to the *inward* thoughts, tempers, deſires, and intents of the heart. Were it otherwiſe, and the New Teſtament can be ſuppoſed to contain ſome *rule of life* which is not in the Old Teſtament, *Abraham's* counſel, which he adviſed the rich man's *five brethren* to follow, was very imperfect—*They have* MOSES *and the* PROPHETS, *let them hear them* —*If they hear not* MOSES *and the* PROPHETS, *neither will they be perſuaded though one roſe from the dead.* What good would *Moſes* have done them, if the *rule of life* laid down by him had been *incomplete* and *deficient*?—what benefit could have accrued to them from listening, though ever so attentively, to the *prophets*, if these had no better news to tell them, than that in the reign of *Augustus Cæsar*, a man was to come and set up a *new law?* Why refer these poor *sinners* to the writings of *Moses* and the *prophets*, if there yet remained some *new rule* of *faith* and *obedience*, not to be met with in *their writings?*—Indeed, if this was the case, it was but to little purpose for CHRIST to command the *Jews* to *search the scriptures* (John v. 39.): they might, indeed, as He says, *think they had eternal life in them*, but they were sadly mistaken, if a *new law* was to be the condition of it, and the way to it, which was not revealed and contained in those scriptures. In vain also were they * referred to the *Hebrew* scriptures, *as testifying of Him*; for not a word is there to be found of His appearance upon earth as a repealer and abrogater of the *moral* law of *Moses*, and as the enacter and establisher of a *new rule of*

---

* Very remarkable is that account which we have of OUR SAVIOUR's discourse with the *two disciples*, after his *resurrection*, as they were going to *Emmaus*—*O fools, and slow of heart* (said He) *to believe all that the* PROPHETS *have spoken!*—*And beginning at* MOSES *and all the* PROPHETS, *He expounded to them in* ALL THE SCRIPTURES, *the things concerning* HIMSELF. Luke xxiv. 25—27. And again, when He appeared to the *eleven, and to them that were with them*, (ver. 33, 36.) *He said unto them* (ver. 44.) *These are the words which I spake unto you while I was yet with you, that all things must be fulfilled which were written in the* LAW OF MOSES, *and in the* PROPHETS, *and in the* PSALMS, *concerning Me*.—Then (ver. 45.) *opened He their understanding, that they might understand* THE SCRIPTURES.

life

life in its place. When our BLESSED SAVIOUR said (Matt. v. 18.) *Till heaven and earth pass, one jot or one tittle shall in no wise pass from the law,* &c. He spake in the most emphatical manner, introducing what He said with an *Amen-verily*—and though the expressions He uses have been called *proverbial*, yet no doubt but He is to be understood *literally*. The Hebrew *jod* ' (for doubtless he expressed himself in *Hebrew*) is the smallest letter in the *Hebrew alphabet*, yet the omission of it in some words might wholly alter the sense of them.—So with regard to the κεραια, which we render *tittle*, it comes from κερας, an *horn* (Heb. קרן) and denotes those *little projections* which in *Hebrew* distinguish one similar letter from another— as a ב from a כ—or a ד from a ר. Many texts might be produced, where taking away one of these, would make a considerable alteration in the sense. Now can CHRIST be supposed to have been so watchful over the *book of the law, and all things contained therein*, as to declare that not a single letter, or the smallest part of a letter, could suffer the least diminution, and yet himself vacate, alter, change, abrogate, and repeal whole and entire statutes? And this to promulgate to mankind a *new rule of life, more excellent than that under which they had formerly lived*, hereby stamping a want of *excellence, purity*, and *holiness*, as well as of *wisdom* and perfection, on the Divine Law?

The *Apostle* says, (Gal. iii. 21.) *If there had*

had been a law given which could have given life, verily righteousness (or that by which men could have been justified) *should have been by the law*; but *the scripture hath concluded* (συνεκλεισε, hath shut up together as in a prison) *all under sin.* Again, He gives us to understand, that the justification of man is *impossible* by the law—*What the law could not do*—τὸ ἀδύνατον τῦ νομȣ—*impossibile legis*—THE IMPOSSIBLE THING *of the law*—Why so?—Because the law itself was imperfect?—No—but *because it was weak through the flesh.* Not from any defect in the law itself, but through the impediment arising from the corruption of the human nature, which has brought us under guilt, and rendered us incapable subjects of its absolving and justifying sentence. As it argues a *perfection* and *purity* of *holiness* in GOD himself, that *He is of purer eyes than to behold evil, and cannot look on iniquity* (Hab. i. 13.) so it argues a *perfection* and *purity* in the *divine law,* that it cannot *justify a sinner:* and if (according to the *new-law* scheme) CHRIST has abrogated this law, and introduced one that *can,* it must only be from a *want* of perfection and *purity* in the *new law,* which is not to be found in the *old law.* This must be attended with many certain and dreadful consequences;—amongst which, one is—*making* CHRIST *the minister of sin.* Gal. ii. 17.—Another, representing Him as defeating the *purpose* of his *own death*; for it is a maxim self-evidently true, that *if righteousness oufnefs* (or juftification) *come by the law*—by *any* law whatfoever, no matter what—CHRIST *is dead in vain.* Gal. ii. 21.

The *moral law,* or *rule of life,* delivered from GOD by *Mofes,* is founded in the very nature of *that relation* which every reafonable creature muft bear to its Creator. It is all reducible to two heads, which OUR SAVIOUR holds forth as the *two great commandments of the law. Thou fhalt love the* LORD *thy* GOD *with all thine heart, with all thy mind, with all thy foul, and with all thy ftrength;* and *thy neighbour as thy * felf*—is too *perfect* a *fyftem of morals* to admit of the leaft *addition* or *improvement:* it is *a rule of life* to *angels* as well as to *men;* and a conftant conformity to this *holy law,* conftitutes the happinefs of the *angels, principalities,* and *powers* (Col. i. 16.) of heaven. Could one of thefe ceafe from *loving* GOD with *all* its faculties; could it feel a fingle *wrong* temper, either with refpect to GOD, or to its *fellow fpirits,* it would *fin*—it would *leave its firft eftate,* and, with the other *apoftate fpirits, be caft down to hell,. and be referved in chains of darknefs unto the judgment of the great day.* 2 Pet. ii. 4. *Jude* 6.

It can therefore be no more true, that CHRIST came upon earth to give a *new law* to *mortals,* than that He afcended into heaven to give a *new* law to *angels.* He could not do either, without materially affecting the very nature of *that relation* which the intelligent

* Deut. vi. 5. Lev. xix. 18.

and reasonable parts of the creation bear to GOD and each other.

As far as the *moral* law of GOD relates to mortals, we must consider the *commerce of the sexes*, with all its various relations, consequences, and dependencies, as a most material object of it: so material, as to form a very considerable part of the *sacred code*. It naturally ranges itself under the duties of the *second table*. So the *Apostle*, Rom. xiii. 9. *For this, Thou shalt not commit adultery*, &c. and if there be any *other commandment, it is briefly comprehended in this saying; namely, Thou shalt love thy neighbour as thyself. Love worketh no ill to his neighbour.* Now, if CHRIST *forbad* that which was before *allowed*, He extended the obligation of the divine law beyond what the Old Testament had done; therefore must be said to *add* something to the *second table of the law*. This consequence cannot be avoided, if we suppose Him giving a sense to the word נאף—*adultery*—which it never had before. He certainly hereby extended the *seventh* commandment as to its *curse and punishment*. On the other hand, if He had *allowed* what the law had *forbidden* under the Old Testament, He had *diminished* from its curse and punishment, by narrowing its obligation. In this view He had *diminished* from the law. In either case, we *number Him with the transgressors* in a most awful and dreadful sense; for no positive command of the law is revealed with more solemnity than Deut. iv. 2. and Deut. xii. 32.

which

which forbad, abfolutely forbad, *both*. It is therefore as impoffible that CHRIST fhould condemn *polygamy* as *adultery*, as that He fhould allow *adultery* as *lawful commerce*; becaufe the firft was *adding* to the law, which never forbad it, the other *diminifhing* from the law, which pofitively forbad *adultery with another man's wife*. Exod. xx. 14. explained Lev. xx. 10.

To fuppofe that GOD fhould ever revoke, alter, or change thofe *moral inftitutes*, which were revealed under the Old Teftament for the regulation and government of mankind, is to fuppofe fome defect in the DEITY, fome want of prefcience to forefee mifchiefs which might arife, and which were not fufficiently guarded againft. This argues an imbecillity or weaknefs of underftanding and knowledge, like that of human *legiflators*, who make laws to remedy evils as they arife before them, but cannot *tell what a day may bring forth*; and therefore repeal at one time, the law which they made at another. When we argue for the immutability of the law, we argue for the *perfection* of it, which is, in other words, to contend for the *perfection* of HIM that made it.

When GOD *created the heavens and the earth*, He gave them a law *which cannot be broken*; by this law the material univerfe is governed, and will be governed to the confummation of all things. The leaft departure from it, either by addition or diminution, would throw the whole into diforder, confufion, and ruin,

ruin. So with respect to the *moral* world, the laws which GOD once gave for the regulation and government of this, are equally *sure* and *stedfast*; and it is owing to a departure from these, that disorder, confusion, and ruin are the portion of wretched man.

The *divine law*, as delivered from GOD by *Moses*, may be compared to a *golden chain*; the several *statutes* which compose it are the *links*. Now we know, that whichever link of a chain be broken, all that is suspended by it must fall to the ground. That the security and protection of the *weaker sex* against the deceit, violence, and cruelty of the *stronger*, depend wholly on the law of GOD, is a truth which none, who admit that GOD ever gave a law, will dispute. And shall we suppose that CHRIST came into the world to *weaken* that security, by destroying some of the *links* of the *chain* on which it is suspended? and this by introducing a *new law*, so contrary to the law *which was given by Moses*, that men, in some situations, cannot *obey the one*, without *transgressing the other?* This is making CHRIST's acts like the threatening of *Rehoboam*, 1 Kings xii. 11. *Whereas my father did lade you with an heavy yoke, I will add to your yoke. My father hath chastised you with whips, but I will chastise you with scorpions.*—But far, far be it from us, to impute such a proceeding to Him who *came not to destroy men's lives, but to save them.* Luke ix. 56.—That no such thing is chargeable upon Him, will appear still more plainly, on our taking a
nearer

nearer and more critical view of those passages of the *gospels*, in which CHRIST is supposed to condemn *polygamy* as *adultery*. The first which I shall take notice of, as introductory to the rest, is *Matt.* v. 31, 32. *It hath been said, Whosoever shall put away his wife, let him give her a writing of divorcement.* But *I say unto you, that whosoever shall put away his wife, saving for the cause of fornication, causeth her to commit adultery; and whosoever shall marry her that is divorced, committeth adultery.* Here our LORD shews that there is but one *lawful cause of divorce* in the sight of GOD, so as to set the husband entirely free from the wife. The *Jews*, on the contrary, had been taught by the *rabbies*, that a man who wanted to get rid of his wife, had nothing to do but to give * her *a bill of divorcement*, and this for *any cause* whatsoever. But CHRIST shews, that such unjust divorces had no operation on the *bond of marriage*; so that marrying such a divorced woman, was as much an act of *adultery*, as if the man had taken her while she cohabited with her husband. CHRIST

* The *Jews* themselves held, that there were two sorts of men who never could divorce their wives: First—those who failed in their proofs against them on the trial mentioned Deut. xxii. 13—19.—Secondly, those who had *laid hold on* them and *lain with them*, without betrothment or espousals, Deut. xxii. 29; for in both those cases it is especially said—*He may not put her away all his days*. As for us *Christians*, we suffer a man to *take* and *divorce* as many women as he can seduce, provided they have no *other* claim upon him, than what the *positive law* of GOD gives them.

did

did not declare this, as if it had been lawful under the Old Testament, and now made unlawful by some *new law* of His, but on the footing of the *primary institution* of marriage from the *very beginning*, as will appear when we farther consider the passage in Matt. xix. on which the conceit is founded, that " *polygamy* is forbidden by *the law* of " CHRIST." Suffice it to observe at present, that in this place of Matt. v. 31, 32. nothing is said about *polygamy*, or a man's having *two wives*.

Our LORD says—*causeth her to commit adultery*. How so?—First—by laying her under the *temptation*, which may be supposed to be not a little heightened by her resentment against her husband, who had first used her ill, and then divorced her; especially where this was done for the sake of *taking another woman whom he liked better*. Secondly—she was tempted to it by the very terms of the bill * of divorcement, which was to the following effect—

" Such

---

* The *bill* of *divorcement* was, as practised by the *Jews*, attended with so many circumstances of difficulty (as may be seen in *Selden*, Ux. Hebr. lib. vi. c. 25. p. 514.) that it seems to have been an invention rather to *prevent* divorces, than to promote them. However, it is very clear from our LORD's discourse with the *Pharisees*, Matt. xix. that they were not only *used*, but *abused*, to a very great degree.

It is remarkable that at *Rome*, from the foundation of the *republic* to the *first divorce*, there was a space of 520 years; though the men had a power of divorcing their wives almost at pleasure. This affords no small proof

of

" Such a day, fuch a month, and year, I
" fuch a one, of fuch a place, do, of my
" own free confent and choice, repu-
" diate thee *A. B.* my late wife, banifh
" thee from me, and reftore thee to thy
" own liberty, and thou mayeft hence-
" forth go whither, *and marry whom,*
" *thou wilt.* And this is thy bill of
" divorcement and writing of expulfion,
" according to the law of *Mofes* and
" *Ifrael.* Signed by two witneffes." See
Univ. Hift. vol. iii. p. 149.

The people having been taught that fuch a *bill of divorcement* was a valid diffolution of the marriage, the woman of courfe believed, that fhe, having received it, was free to *marry any other man,* as much as if her hufband had been dead; and thus was fhe *caufed,* by this deceit, to marry another, by which, in truth, and in the fight of GOD, fhe committed adultery.

of the chaftity and good behaviour of the *Roman* matrons during that period. And indeed the account we have of that *firft divorce,* need not leffen them in our efteem; for *Carvilius Ruga* did not divorce his wife for any fault in her, but becaufe he had no children by her: therefore, thinking himfelf bound by a foolifh oath, which the *Cenfors* at that time caufed people to take, he put her away, and married another. See Ant. Univ. Hift. vol. iii. p. 148. note W. and vol. xii. p. 216.

In after times, the *Roman* women grew fo debauched and profligate, that when *Severus* mounted the throne, he found on the roll of caufes to be tried, no lefs than *three thoufand* profecutions for *adultery.* He had formed a fcheme of reformation, which from that moment he abandoned as impoffible. See *Alexander's* Hift. of Wom. vol. i. 252.

The

The latter clause of ver. 32. *Whosoever shall marry her that is divorced, committeth adultery,* is wanting in the *Cambridge* manuscript. St. *Augustine* says, that some *Greek* and *Latin* copies had it not, and seems to treat it as a needless tautology; his words are these—" Explicatus hic sensus putari potuit " in eo quod superius dictum est"—"*facit* " *eam mœchari*"—" quomodo enim dimissa " fit *mœcha,* nisi fiat qui eam duxerit *mœ-* " *chus ?*"—that is—" The sense of this " clause may be supposed to be explained in " what goes before—*causeth her to commit* " *adultery*—for how could she become an " *adulteress,* unless the man who married her " became an *adulterer ?*" But when it is considered that our SAVIOUR was speaking to a people *whose ears were dull of hearing,* Matt. xiii. 15—who were taught by their *Doctors* to stand upon the mere *letter* of scripture, without entering into the *spirit* of it— it was necessary that *line should be upon line, line upon line—precept upon precept, precept upon precept*—as the *Prophet* * speaks, Is. xxviii. 10.—therefore, that our LORD should not leave them to draw conclusions from words of implication only, and thus to throw the sin upon the woman alone, because the man was not mentioned, but so express Himself as to bring the whole law on the subject into full view; as Lev. xx. 10. where both

---

* So the *Apostle,* Phil. iii. 1.—*To write the same things to you, to me indeed is not grievous, but for you it is safe.*

the *woman* and the *man* are explicitly mentioned, the one as an *adulteress*, the other as an *adulterer*. Surely then, on the analogy of scripture itself, the reading of this last clause may be retained, as it stands in our printed copies.

The next scripture to be farther considered, is Matt. xix. 9. *I say unto you, Whosoever shall put away his wife (except it be for fornication) and shall marry another, committeth adultery, and whoso marrieth her which is put away, committeth adultery.*—This is highly necessary, in order to bring into view the *whole* of our Lord's design, which was to reprobate the various abuses of *divorce*, at that time practised by the *Jews*, and among the rest, the horrid traffic, which the very *law* of *Moses*, to which they referred for their *justification, condemned*—that of *divorcing* their wives *for every cause*, and, of course, that they might *exchange* them *for a time*, and then take them *back again*;—this was expressly forbidden by Deut. xxiv. 2, 3, 4. therefore certainly included in our Lord's discourse on the subject of unlawful and unjust *divorce*. And indeed I much doubt, whether, in this place, the applying and inforcing of Deut. xxiv. 2, 3, 4. was not the *chief* object which our Saviour had in view—(see before p. 85, 86, 87.) For where a man *divorced* his wife for such a purpose (which, according to the *Hillelians* was held lawful—see before p. 82.) he became an *adulterer* in a *double* sense, as not only causing his own unjustly-divorced wife

wife to commit *adultery*, by proftituting her to another man, according to Matt. v. 32.—but alfo by taking the other man's unjuftly-divorced wife to himfelf; which, in this view of the matter, feems the true import of γαμηση αλλην in this place. We muft remember, that Chrift is arguing with the *Jews* on the footing of the *law of Mofes*, as it ftood in the * *Hebrew* fcripture, not as the *Scribes* and *Pharifees* interpreted it, or as we have tranflated it. See the learned AINSWORTH on Deut. xxiv. 1, &c. and GELL's Effay towards a New Tranflation, p. 723.

A perfon of infidel-principles was once making himfelf merry in a large company, at the expence of the fcriptures, and told his companions, that he could prove the prophet of the Chriftians (as he called CHRIST) *miftaken*, even upon the moft common fubjects. After awakening the curiofity of the company, he thus gratified it—" CHRIST fays, " that *old bottles* are not fo ftrong as *new*" (alluding to Matt. ix. 17.) " and therefore, " if *new wine* is put into *old bottles*, it will " break them—now don't every body know " that *old glafs* is juft as ftrong as *new*, for " who ever heard that *glafs* was the *weaker* " for being *old?*" A *clergyman* in company, who had been made the butt of his wit, gently reproved the ignorance and folly of

* In which the word נאף—*adultery*—in no one inftance was referred to *polygamy*, nor had any other fenfe, but the defilement of a *betrothed* or *married* woman.

this witling, by asking him if he understood *Greek* ?—" *Greek*, Sir ?—No, Sir—but what
" has *Greek* to do with it?—a bottle's a
" bottle, whether in *Greek* or *English*, every
" body knows that, and that an *old bottle* is
" just as good and as strong as a *new one*."—
" Not quite, Sir," (replied the other) " if
" they are made of *leather* or *skins*, which
" was the fact as to the bottles CHRIST speaks
" of, as their *Greek* * name imports;—and
" indeed it is so in many countries, even to

---

* Ἀσκος signifies a *leathern bottle*, or *vessel*, used to hold wine. See Josh. ix. 4, 13, where the *Hebrew* word נאדות is rendered by the LXX, ἀσκοι. They are said to be *old* and *rent*, and *bound up*. See HARM. *Obs.* on *Scripture*, vol. i. p. 131, 132.

The celebrated *M. de Voltaire*, whose malice against the scriptures could only be equalled by his ignorance of their contents, endeavours to prove, from *Prov.* xxiii. 31. that the whole book is a forgery, and not written by *Solomon*; this because כיס is rendered, in the translations before him, by the word *glass—vitrum—verre—*" whereas," says that *wise critic*, " *drinking-glasses* were not
" invented till after *Solomon*'s time," taking it for granted that כיס must signify a *drinking-glass*; whereas it denotes any *drinking-cup* which *covers or incloses the liquor*, of whatever materials the said *cup* may consist.

He is alike *happy* in his proof of 1 Sam. xxviii. (which gives an account of *Saul*'s consulting the *witch of Endor*) being a *forgery*, " because the word *Python*" (used in the *Vulgate* translation) " was not known 'till the *Jews* had
" some acquaintance with the *Greeks*, after the time of
" *Alexander*."—The Hebrew is אוב, which the LXX render by ἐγγαστρίμυθον—*ventriloquam*—a kind of *wizard*, so called from their *inward* way of speaking or muttering. But not a glimpse of *Python* is there to be found. See *Letters of Jews to Voltaire*, vol. ii. p. 275, 373. Transl. by *Lefanu*.

" this

" this day, that people use skins by way of
" vessels to contain wine."—On which side
the laughter of the company turned is not
very difficult to imagine.

Something like this *facetious* gentleman's
misconception of things is likely to be our
portion, if we form our ideas of the import
of certain passages of scripture, from the sound
of words in our *translation*, without adverting
to the *sense* of the *original*. So also, if we
interpret the scripture according to our own
conceits, without duly considering the *times*
when—the *places* where—the *occasions* on
which—and the *situations* of the *persons* to
whom they are addressed. These observations are peculiarly needful respecting the
portion of scripture now before us, especially
as we have popular mistake, vulgar error, and
of course, prejudice of education, to contend
with. Still all these cannot alter the truth
of scripture, or render it at all the more certain, that CHRIST here *condemns*, or indeed
mentions, *polygamy*.

He was surrounded at this time by a *great
multitude* of people, who, in principle, as
living under the law of the Old Testament,
were *polygamists*, and, doubtless, numbers of
them were so in *practice*—many there must
have been among this great multitude of *Jews*,
who had either married *two wives* together,
or having *one*, took *another* to her, and cohabited with *both*. Had our LORD intended to
have condemned such practices, he would
scarcely have made use of words which did

not

not defcribe their fituation, but of words that *did*. It is very plain that—*He that putteth away his wife*, by *giving her a bill of divorcement*—could have nothing to do with the man who took *two wives* together, or *one* to *another*, and cohabited alike with *both*. But we are apt, like the man and his *bottles*, to conftrue fcripture, by fuppofing perfons to whom particular things are faid, were in the circumftances *then*, in which we are *now*; but it was far otherwife: they had no municipal laws againft *polygamy*, as we have. So far from it, their *whole law* (as has been abundantly proved) *allowed* it. Which faid law, and every part thereof, was, at the time CHRIST fpake what is recorded in Matt. xix. 9, in as full force and efficacy, as at the moment after *Mofes* had delivered it to the people. He therefore could no more ftate *polygamy* as adultery by the law of *Ifrael*, than I can ftate it as *high treafon* by the laws of *England*.

It is to be obferved, that the fubject-matter in debate was the bufinefs of *divorce*, which the *Jews* had carried to a fhameful height, and this is what CHRIST is oppofing. The occafion of the difcourfe feems to be this— what He had faid in His fermon on the mount, in *Galilee*, about *divorce*, Matt. v. 31, 32, had, doubtlefs, been carried to the *Pharifees* in *Judea*, by fome of their emiffaries, who were among the *multitudes that followed Him from thence*, Matt. iv. 25. moft probably by fome of thofe *fpies*, which were fet upon all his

his *words and actions*. See Luke xx. 20. The *Pharisees* were provoked, as what CHRIST had said militated against those notions which they had received, and strenuously maintained among their disciples. On His return into *the coasts of Judea beyond Jordan*, He was also attended *by great multitudes*, ver. 2. The Pharisees thought this a fair opportunity *to entangle Him in His talk* (as Matt. xxii. 15.) and lay Him under difficulties, either that of disavowing what He had said, or, if He persisted in it, to represent Him before the multitude as an enemy to the *law* of *Moses*. Therefore we read, ver. 3. the *Pharisees also came unto Him, tempting Him*—by proposing an ensnaring question, which they supposed would lay Him under one or other of the difficulties above-mentioned, either of denying what He had said, or of appearing an adversary to *Moses*. They therefore ask Him —*Is it lawful for a man to put away his wife for every cause?* His answer to this is not founded on any *new law* of His own, but on the *original command of* GOD, delivered by *Adam*, Gen. ii. 24. The *Pharisees* then bring their design into full view, by quoting *Moses's* authority against the answer which CHRIST had given, and in defence of their own opinion. The passage which they referred to, was *Deut.* xxiv. 1, which they called a *command*; but our LORD corrects them, and calls it only a *permission*, and this—*for the hardness of their hearts*; not that it affected the matter in the sight of GOD, by vacating the marriage,

marriage, for that a man who married a *divorced woman*, was as guilty of *adultery* in the fight of GOD, as if she had not been *divorced*, and so was the *divorced* woman, who married again, *living her husband*. That this was the scope of CHRIST's reasoning upon the matter, appears from the answer which He gave to His disciples, Mark x. 10, 11, 12. when *in the house, they asked Him again of the same matter*—περι τȣ αυτȣ—about the *self-same identical* thing.—He cannot be supposed to vary His opinion upon the *same* point; therefore, in words which had the same meaning, He repeats the substance of what He had before said to the *Pharisees*.—He saith unto them, *Whosoever shall put away his wife, and marry another, committeth adultery against her;* to which He adds—*And if a woman shall put away her husband, and be married to another, she committeth adultery.*

As the *Pharisees* had referred CHRIST to the authority of *Moses*, by way of answer to what He had said, to prove the unlawfulness of *divorces*; He takes an opportunity to detect their abuse of that scripture, Deut. xxiv. 1. &c. (for this is the passage evidently referred to) and proves, on the ground of ver. 4. of that chapter, the truth of all he said upon the subject; namely, that these permissive *divorces*, which MOSES suffered (ἐπέτρεψεν) *for the hardness of their hearts*, wrought no dissolution of the marriage-bond, but that the man who thus *injuriously divorced* his wife, *caused her* to be *defiled*; and he who married her, *defiled* her; but yet, having married her, she could not * return to her *first* husband, on a *divorce* from the *second*, without a fresh act of *adultery*. Defiling a man's wife, and committing *adultery* upon her, are synonymous terms, as may appear by comparing *Prov.* vi. 29. with *Ezek.* xviii. 11, 15. Therefore our Saviour says no more in effect, than is said *Deut.* xxiv. 4; He only enlarges upon, explains, and appplies the doctrine there delivered, concerning the *defilement* and *adultery* which was the consequence of marrying a *divorced* woman, and has a view to the licentious practices of the *Jews*, under the sanction of these wanton and causeless *divorces*. The antient *Jews* had learned from the *Egyptians*, amongst whom they dwelt so long, a practice of changing their wives, and afterwards taking them again; which the law, Deut. xxiv. 1—4, was expressly made to prevent, as one of the greatest abominations in the sight of God. Still this practice prevailed in later times, as may be gathered from *Jer.* v. 8. *They were as fed horses in the morning, every one neighed after his neighbour's wife.* Their in-

* The instance of *David's* taking again *Michal*, *Saul's* daughter, after she had been the wife of *Phaltiel*, the son of *Laish*, had nothing to do with this; for she had not been *put away* from *David* by *bill of divorcement*, or any other act of his, but violently taken away by her father *Saul*, and given to *Phaltiel*. Nor was it, probably, in her power to have gainsayed the imperious commands of her tyrannical father. See 1 Sam. xxv. 44. 2 Sam. iii. 13, &c.

tercourſe with the * *Greeks* † and *Romans*, in later times ſtill, was another means of promoting this unnatural and horrid traffic. This could not be carried on among the *Jews* without the expedient of the ספר כריתת—*bill of divorcement*; without this the *adultery* had been too barefaced, but *with* it, they had been taught by their *rabbies*, ſuch as *Hillell* (who held that a man's ſeeing a woman *he liked better than his own wife*, was a juſt cauſe of *divorce*) to do as they pleaſed. They might *put away their wives for every cauſe*, therefore for this, among the reſt, becauſe they ſaw *another's* (for that may be ſignified by the word ἀλλην, as I ſhall obſerve preſently) whom they liked better than their own. Thus under theſe *divorces* they could exchange ‡ their wives. For inſtance—*A.* liked the wife of *B.*—*B.* liked the wife of *A.* —each hating his own—they agree to change —How ſhall this be done? If the wives are

* See before p. 210—13.

† How fond and eager the *Jews* were to imitate the heathen faſhions and manners, eſpecially thoſe of the *Greeks*, ſee 2 Macc. iv. 15, 16.

‡ This was ſo abhorred of God, that he made the poſitive law, Deut. xxiv. 1—4. in ſuch terms, as to prevent the man who had divorced his wife, from ever taking her again after her *marriage with another man*, not only on a *divorce* from that man, but even *after his death*. It is a grievous thing that our *tranſlation* has obſcured the whole drift and meaning of the paſſage, (ſee before p. 85, &c.) for by this it is, that the *reader* is led into the notion of Christ's making a *new law* againſt *polygamy*, while he is enforcing the *old law* againſt *unjuſt divorce*.

exchanged

exchanged without a *bill of divorce*, adultery must be acknowledged on both sides; they therefore have recourse to a *bill of divorcement*, under which the woman was held to be *legally* put away, according to the law of *Moses* and *Israel* (see before p. .) and was free to marry *whom she would*; the *bill of divorcement* being looked upon as an absolute and total dissolution of the marriage-bond. Our LORD is shewing the contrary. First, On the footing of the indissolubility of the contract, in the sight of GOD, by any human authority. Secondly, On the terms of the very law, to which the *Pharisees* referred him for their justification; which being taken *all together*, proves no more than an implied permission of *divorce* for the *hardness of their hearts*; or, as we say—*a mensâ & toro propter sævitiam*—" from bed and board by reason " of cruelty:" and this was, that women might be released from the barbarity with which their cruel husbands would have treated them, on conceiving some dislike, had they been forced to have lived with them. But yet, as *Moses* shews, the *bond of marriage* still remained; so that if a man married such a woman, he and the woman were both guilty of *adultery*, in the sight of GOD, notwithstanding the *bill of divorcement*. If this had not been the case, *Moses* could not have called the marriage of the divorced woman a *defilement* —saying, Deut. xxiv. 4.—*after she is defiled.* Our SAVIOUR, therefore, doth not by His—
I say

I say unto you, mean that He was enacting [*] a *new law*, or laying down a rule that was opposite to, or inconsistent with, the *law of Moses*—had He attempted this, he had fallen into the very snare which the Pharisees had laid for Him. But—"*I say unto you*" means here, as in the instances before related in His sermon upon the mount (see before, p. 310—313) as if He said—"Your *rabbies* teach you
"so and so, and in so teaching you they
"make void the law of GOD through their
"traditions;—but *I*, who am come to re-
"store the honour of *Moses*'s law, by restor-
"ing its true sense and meaning—I—on the
"authority of that law, which you have
"partially quoted, without taking the
"whole together—*say unto you*, though, for
"the *hardness of your hearts*, MOSES *suffered*
"*you to put away your wives*, and suspended
"any punishment which might have accrued
"for so doing, yet did he not, nor could he
"thereby dissolve the marriage itself; so
"far from it, he terms the marriage of such
"a divorced woman a *defilement*. Therefore
"I say unto you—*whosoever putteth away*
"*his wife, (except for the cause of fornica-*
"*tion*—which is the only legal cause of
"divorce) *and marrieth another*—hereby
"tempting, and even provoking the *divor-*
"*ced* woman to *marry another man*—that
"though the *personal guilt* follows the *per-*

[*] Mr. *Salmon* well observes, that "the *gospel* is a "covenant revealing *grace*, not commanding a *new mo-* "*rality*." Essay on Marriage, p. 134.

"*sonal*

" *sonal act*, with respect to her, so that if
" she, *while her husband liveth, be married to
" another man, she shall be called an adulteress*
" (see Rom. vii. 2.) yet the guilt of this
" adultery will also be imputed to him who
" was the wilful occasion of it, by *causing
" her to commit it*. And as to you, who,
" for the purpose of *exchanging your wives
" with each other* (a matter which the law of
" *Moses*, in a part of the passage which you
" refer me to, but which you don't mention,
" was particularly made to guard against *)
" have put away your wives—and to you
" who marry such divorced women—and to
" you divorced women, who think yourselves
" at liberty to marry whom ye will, when
" ye are unjustly put away from your hus-
" bands—*Moses* calls all this *defilement*, which
" is but another term for *adultery* :—there-
" fore *I say unto you*, as well as to those
" who, contrary to the law above-mention-
" ed, *take back again* the women they have
" once divorced †, after they have been mar-
" ried

* For this, saith *Abarbinel* on Deut. xxiv. 4. was to imitate the *Ægyptians*, who changed their wives, and took them again into their houses, which was the occasion of great filthiness; for, as *Isaac Arama* glosses, if this had not been prohibited, a gate had been opened unto vile men to make a trade of *changing* their wives, and thereby filled the land with *whoredom*.—See *Patr.* on *Deut.* xxiv. 4.

† Though the bill of divorcement wrought as a sort of divorce *a mensa & toro*, and as a release from the *vinculum externum*, or *outward bond*—yet nothing but *adultery* or *death* could dissolve the *vinculum internum*, which was
created

" *ried* to others—however ye may have been
" taught to abuse the toleration of divorce
" on particular occasions—that all the cases
" which I have mentioned, touching men
" divorcing their wives and marrying others,
" thereby causing their unjustly-divorced
" wives to marry other men—of men marry-
" ing divorced women—and divorced women
" marrying other men—this is all contrary
" to the law of marriage itself, as delivered
" *to* and pronounced *by* ADAM, Gen. ii. 24.
" as well as to the law of the *seventh com-*
" *mandment*, delivered *to Moses*, and *by* him
" delivered to the people at *Mount Sinai*.
" In short, these are only several * methods of

created by the special command of GOD—*they shall be one flesh*. Therefore, when a divorced woman went away from her husband, and married another man, she committed an act of *adultery* in the eye of GOD: but this dissolved the *first contract*, and made her the wife of the *second* man; therefore, if this man put her away, the first husband, of whom she had been the ἀπολελυμενη, (see Luke xvi. 18.) could not take her again without committing *adultery*;— for after her departure from him, under the *bill of divorcement*, she had become, by the husband's own act and deed, and by her act of adultery, another man's property, otherwise she could not be supposed (ver. 2.) to become *another man's wife*. The law therefore of Deut. xxiv. 1, &c. was especially made to prevent such abominable traffic.—See the preceding note.

* The reader may observe, that, in this paraphrase, I have endeavoured to lay before him every interpretation of the passage, which harmonizes with the meaning of the word נאף—*adultery*—as it is used in the *Hebrew* scripture; for it cannot be supposed that CHRIST, who is speaking of the law of *Moses*, should call any thing *adultery*, but that which is so by that law.

" incurring

" incurring the guilt of *adultery*; therefore all the *falvos* which your confciences may derive from your abufe of *Mofes*'s permiffion, with refpect to *bills of divorcement, however highly efteemed amongft men, are abomination in the fight of* God. Luke xvi. 15."—Here Christ puts the *Pharifees to filence*, by the very law which they had partially quoted, with the hope of enfnaring Him, and making Him appear as an enemy to the law of *Mofes*. We do not read of any reply which they attempted to make: this would certainly not have been the cafe, had they underftood him to have fpoken againft *polygamy* as *adultery*; the *Pharifees* could have defired nothing more to their purpofe, of reprefenting Him as an enemy to *Mofes*, as there was not a fingle paffage in the whole *law* of *Mofes* to have fupported Him againft them on that point. They were ready enough, on other occafions, to call upon him for his *authority* as to what he *faid and did*—See *Matt.* xxi. 23. *Mark* xi. 28.—but here they are totally filent: and this under the only fair opportunity they ever had, of convicting Him of a downright *falfhood*, as laying down that for *law*, which their law contradicted. It is therefore plain that they underftood Him in no fuch fenfe. Neither did His own difciples underftand Him to fpeak of any thing but *divorce*.—They are faid, Mark x. 10, *in the houfe to afk Him again of the fame matter*; His anfwer was in fubftance the fame: the conclufion which the difciples draw from it is—

If

If the case of the man be so with his wife, it is not good to marry—i. e. "If a man cannot get rid of his wife when he pleases, he had better not marry at all." This conclusion must have been made from their understanding Christ to speak of *divorce*, for it is totally foreign from the matter of *polygamy*;—How could they possibly mean that a man had better have *no wife at all*, if he could not have more than *one at once?* It must likewise be supposed, that they did not misunderstand their *Master*, for if they had, He would doubtless have set them right in his reply (Matt. xix. 11, 12) and not have there said, what clearly shews them to have understood Him aright.

Now let us consider Matt. xix. 9. still more closely, taking it in connection with his subsequent explanation of it *to the disciples in the house*. Mark x. 10, 11, 12.

I say unto you—*Whosoever shall put away his wife*—καὶ γαμήσῃ ἀλλην—*and shall marry another;* ἀλλην must here have a reference to the preceding γυναικα, which we render by the word *wife*—therefore γυναικα must be understood as following the word ἀλλην, and this may be construed in the sense of αλλοτριαν γυναικα—*another man's wife*, i. e. *a divorced woman.* We find the word ἀλλης, so used, 1 Cor. x. 29. ὑπο ἀλλης συνειδησεως—which we rightly translate — *another man's conscience.* The learned *Wetstein* takes ἀλλην in this sense, in his note on Matt. xix. 9.—His words are —"Αλλην] *i. e.* Ἀλλοτρίαν ab alio itidem viro
repudiatam

repudiatam—vel ab illo divertentem, ut *Herodias* * & *Salome*.—" *Another*] that is—an-
" other man's *wife*, who has been repudiated
" by him, or who has left her husband; as
" did *Herodias* and *Salome*." He mentions

* *Salome* was sister to *Herod* the *Great*. She is said to have been the first woman who repudiated her husband. *Herodias* left her husband *Philip*, and married the said *Philip*'s brother, *Herod Antipas*; for which *John* the *Baptist* severely reproved him, saying—*it is not lawful for thee to have her*. Matt. xiv. 4. For saying this, he had a double authority. First, as to the *incest*, Lev. xviii. 16. Secondly, with regard to her being *another man's wife*, Lev. xx. 10. *Herod*'s situation was just what our LORD condemns in the passage of Mark x. 11, 12. He had *put away his first wife*, who was the daughter of *Aretas*, king of *Arabia*, that he might take his brother *Philip*'s wife, with whom he had fallen in love; and he did this at the request of *Herodias* herself. This was *putting a way his wife, and marrying* ἄλλην, i. e. ἀλλοτρίαν, *another's*, which was *adultery*; as was *Herodias*'s leaving her husband, and marrying *Herod*. All this (except the incest) fell directly under the condemnation of the *divine law*, as explained by CHRIST to the *disciples*, and doubtless was meant by what he said before, in the presence of the *multitude*, to the *Pharisees*; and may serve as a proper illustration of the doctrine of the *divine law*, as set forth by our LORD, with respect to *unlawful divorces*, taking ἄλλην in the sense of ἀλλοτρίαν.

See also the case of *Drusilla*, a daughter of *Herod Agrippa*, who forsook *Azizus*, king of *Emesa*, and married *Felix*—(see *Acts* xxiv. 24.) also of her two sisters.—*Berenice*, the eldest, left her husband *Polemon*, king of *Pontus*, to go to others—and *Mariamne*, the youngest, was married to *Archelaus*, and forsook him to marry *Demetrius*, an *Alexandrian Jew*. Ant. Univ. Hist. vol. x. p. 643, and note E.

The above-mentioned *women* were of high *rank* and *dignity*; but doubtless others practised the same, who were of too low a degree to be subjects of the *historian*'s pen.

afterwards

afterwards a difficulty he was under from this interpretation of ἀλλην—as it seems to make the text say the same thing * *twice over*; and on επ' αυτην, Mark x. 11. he has the following note, which I will lay before the reader in *English*, referring the learned to the original.—*Against her.*] "There are some
" who interpret this to relate to the *second*
" or *latter wife, on whom* the husband might
" commit *adultery*, properly so called; which
" he cannot be said to commit if he should
" marry a *virgin*, or a *widow*, but only by
" marrying a woman who had been in like
" manner *(i. e.* unjustly) divorced by another
" man. But there is an † objection to this
" interpretation,

* This objection is at an end, if the latter clause is to be left out, as in the *Cambridge*, and many other copies. See *Mills* and *Wetstein* on Matt. xix. 9.

† Since the first edition of this book, I have considered very deeply this objection of *Wetstein*'s, as well as the ground on which it stands. He certainly, when writing on Mark x. 11, 12. had the clause of Matt. xix. 9. in his mind, insomuch as to confound it with Mark x. 12; but, on the most attentive consideration, I cannot think, with *St. Austin* and others, that the latter clause of Matt. xix. 9. viz. *He that marrieth her that is put away committeth adultery*, has the least *tautology*, even taking the αλλην in the former clause in the sense of αλλοτριαν—because the whole verse, taken together, is no other than a complete refutation of the *Jews* doctrine of divorce *for every cause*, and a full establishment of the truth which Christ is contending for—viz.—that no cause, but that of *adultery* in *the wife*, is any ground of *divorce* from the bond of marriage, so as to exempt the man who should marry her, living her husband, from the crime of adultery. In this view the whole will stand thus—viz.

—*Whosoever shall put away his wife* (except for *fornication,* which is the only thing which can dissolve the
contract,

" interpretation, which is, that by this
" method of interpreting the paſſage, the
" ſame

contract) *and ſhall marry another* (γυναικα, wife or woman
unjuſtly divorced) *committeth adultery* (upon ſuch woman
—επ αυ]ην—Mark x. 11.) no unjuſt divorce diſſolving her
contract with the man who put her away.

Thus far the firſt clauſe—on which it might be ſuppoſed, that, as the firſt man had not only *put away his
wife* by a bill of divorcement, but alſo married *another
divorced woman,* and by that committed *adultery*, ſuch
an act releaſed the firſt woman entirely from him, and
therefore any other man might innocently take her to
wife, as a woman divorced juſtly and entirely; the bond
being vacated by the huſband's *adultery.*—But our LORD
declares it to be otherwiſe ſettled by the law; nothing
but *adultery in the wife* could diſſolve the bond of marriage,
therefore, the act of the huſband above mentioned, did
not bring the wife into the ſtate of a *ſingle woman*, ſo as
that ſhe might marry again, living her huſband—wherefore CHRIST adds—that *whoſo married a woman* under
ſuch circumſtances of unjuſt and invalid divorce (απολε-
λυμενην—*that had been put away* in this manner) *committed adultery,* no act of the huſband's ſetting her free from
him.

This latter clauſe ſeems therefore as neceſſary as the
former—in order to elucidate the whole doctrine of *divorce,* and to prove, that no one real cauſe or ground of
it, ſo as to diſſolve a marriage, exiſted on the footing of
the *divine law,* but *fornication or adultery in the wife;*
which appears alſo to be clearly laid down Matt. v. 32.
with the ſpirit and ſenſe of which ſcripture, this paſſage
of Matt. xix. 9. exactly harmonizes.

In this view of the matter, this ſcripture, ſo far from
condemning *polygamy,* rather eſtabliſhes it; otherwiſe a
man's taking a *ſecond* woman, if ſuch taking was *adultery*
againſt the firſt wife, would ſet her free, and if ſo, a
man who married her would not ſin, for *adultery* is certainly a releaſe, *a vinculo matrimonii,* with reſpect to the
party againſt whom it is committed.

It may alſo be obſerved, that no poſſible caſe can be
put of a man's actually committing *adultery,* but by intercourſe

" same thing would be said *twice over*, once
" at this ver. 11, and again at ver. 12."

Here I cannot help dissenting from this learned and judicious man; for surely a man's *putting away his wife,* and marrying another *divorced woman,* and a *woman's putting away her husband, and marrying another man,* are very different ideas. In both cases adultery is committed, whether the woman be unjustly put away from her husband, or she put herself away; but when we consider, as in the case of *Herodias* and *Salome,* that this last was growing into a custom—for *Salome's* example was soon followed by others, as *Josephus* * writes—it was natural for CHRIST to condemn this in as *express terms* in one case as in the other, *both* being equally opposite to the law of GOD.

The *Jews* at this time had much intercourse with the *Romans, Judea* having been long reduced to the situation of a *Roman* province, and no doubt, in the very corrupt state in which the *Jews* universally were, the *Roman* manners easily insinuated themselves among the *Jewish* women. See before, p. 364, n. *Divorces,* though allowed very early in *Rome,*

---

tercourse with the *wife of another*; for which reason it is a solecism to talk of his committing *adultery upon* or *against* his *own wife,* in any other sense, than by *causing, tempting,* or *prevailing* on her to commit it, which is the case put Matt. v. 32.

* See Ant. Univ. Hist, vol. iii. p. 149, at the bottom of the note.

were never put in practice till about the year of *Rome* 520, which was before Christ 229 years, in the case of *Carvilius Ruga*, who divorced his wife because she was barren; after which they became scandalously frequent, as a corruption of manners prevailed in the *republic*, till the *Roman* women grew as licentious in leaving their husbands, as the husbands were in putting them away.—What was the character of the *Roman* ladies in this respect, we may learn from *Juvenal*[*], who wrote not many years after this time. In Sat. vi. he is dissuading his friend *Ursidius Posthumus* from marriage, by setting before him the monstrous practices of the *Roman women*, one of which was, leaving their husbands, and marrying other men.

Speaking of their *imperiousness*, he says, their grand argument, in all disputes with their husbands, was

>Hoc volo—sic jubeo, sit pro ratione voluntas.
>Imperat ergo viro:—— l. 222.

Then he proceeds——

---

[*] So from *Seneca*, who says—" Who is now ashamed of breaking the nuptial union, when so many ladies of eminence and quality reckon their years not by the number of *consuls*, but of *husbands*; and are divorced in hopes of marrying, and marry in hopes of being divorced." De Benef. Lib. iii. c. 16.

Puffendorf observes, Lib. vi. c. 1. § 15. that the borrowing and lending of wives among the *Romans*, is a practice much talked of by authors.

——Sed

———— Sed mox hæc regna relinquit
* Permutatque domos, & flamea conterit. Inde
Avolat, & spreti repetit vestigia lecti.
Ornatos paulo ante fores, pendentia linquit
Vela domus, & adhuc virides in limine ramos.
Sic crescit numerus, sic fiunt *octo mariti*
Quinque per autumnos; titulo res digna sepulchri.

" So will I have it—so command I still,
" And yield no reason but my sov'reign will."
Then the imperious wanton leaves her spouse,
From man to man she flies, from house to house,
Forgetful of her bride's attire, and bridal vows.
Again † she seeks her first-deserted man,
And, in *five* years, *eight* husbands crown her plan.—
Pity, but such atchievments should be known,
Engrav'd on brass or monumental stone !

* *Permutatque domos*] Ab uno viro ad alium aliumque transiens.—*Going from one husband to another and another.* Lud. Prateus.

† This line proves that they did not wait for their husbands' *death* to marry others, as does the next: for they can hardly be supposed to bury seven husbands in *five* years.

Ovid, who lived a little earlier than *Juvenal*, censures the man who makes a scruple of his *wife*'s going to others, as unacquainted with true politeness.

Rusticus est nimium quem lædit adultera conjux,
Et NOTOS MORES *non satis urbis habet.*

He that won't lend his wife's an awkward clown,
Unskill'd in the *known fashion* of the town.

Martial, cotemporary with *Juvenal*, has an *epigram* which shews the liberties which were taken by a Roman lady.

Mœchum GELLIA *non habet nisi unum,*
Turpe est hoc magis, uxor est duorum.

One spark serves honest *Gellia* at a time,
But her *two husbands* are a fouler crime.

Martial vi. 7. speaks of a woman not above *thirty* years of age, who had been married to *ten* different men.

Aut minus, aut certe non plus tricesima lux est,
Et nubit decimo jam THELESINA *viro.*

That this was a common practice, appears from l. 45, &c.

> Quid quod & antiquis uxor de moribus illi
> Quæritur? O medici! mediam pretundite venam!
> Delicias hominis! Tarpeium limen adora
> Pronus, & auratam Junoni cæde Juvencam;
> Si tibi contigerit capitis matrona pudici.

> What shall I say to him who seeks a wife
> Of antient manners, uncorrupt of life?
> Surely he's mad—come, Doctor, breathe a vein,
> And try to bring him to himself again.
> But if, by chance, a woman could be found
> Modest and chaste, through all the empire round,
> Thrice happy mortal!—to thy destin'd bed
> Let her, with thanks to all the Gods, be led.

In short, such was the profligacy of the *Roman* women, that if one could be found fit for his friend to marry, he would call her a *Phœnix* as we say:

> Rara avis in terris nigroque simillima cygno.

But to return to *Wetstein*.—" Others un-
" derstand this επ' αυτην of the *first* wife, to
" whom the husband might by his unjust
" divorce give occasion of *committing adul-*
" *tery*, or of flying to a second or adulterous
" marriage: but These do not explain what
" those words—*and shall marry another*—are
" to the purpose; since the divorced woman
" would be equally in danger of committing
" *adultery*, whether the husband who *put her*
" *away, marries another* or not. This diffi-
" culty came into my mind at *Matt.* xix. 9;
" but

"but on considering the matter again, I do
"not think those words superfluous, but so
"to cohere with the rest of the sentence, as
"to denote, that though the *unjust divorce*
"was the occasion of the divorced wife's
"*adultery*, yet the husband's *second* marriage
"was the occasion of the *divorce*. For ex-
"ample—If a man, having met with another
"woman, who pleased him better than his
"wife, should, in order to enjoy the other,
"give his wife a *bill of divorcement*, and grant
"her liberty to marry any body else, whom
"she chose, would this be any thing else
"than to expose her to an *adulterer*, and to
"commit the crime of *pimping*?" So the
Roman * laws—" To act the part of a *pimp*, is
"not

* *Wetstein* remarks, on the title of St. *Mark*'s gospel, that St. *Mark* wrote his gospel at *Rome*—*Wetstein* says farther, *In doctrina de divortio manifestè ad jus Romanum respicit.* " In the doctrine concerning divorce, he ma-
" nifestly had respect to the law of the *Romans*."
In the latter part of *Wetstein*'s note on Mark x. 12. p. 603, col. 2. he says—*Ex eo quod* Christus *de viris uxores repudiantibus dixerat, Marcus infert*—multo sceleftius esse, si mulier virum deserat. Quod & Romanis, quibus *Marcus* scripsit, licitum, & tum temporis, licentia supra modum graffante, familiare erat, postquam *Messalina Claudii* Imperatoris uxor, *Claudio* vivente, filio publicè nupserat, & ipse *Claudius* Octaviam *Cæsaris* filiam L. *Silano* a patre desponsatam *Neroni* collocaverat. Tacit Annal. xi. 27. xii. 3. 9.
" From that which Christ had said concerning men
" repudiating their wives, *Mark* infers, that it was by
" far more wicked for a woman to leave her husband."
This I do not see is deducible from the words of the *Evangelist*; however *Wetstein* proceeds—
" Which was permitted by the *Romans*, to whom
" *Mark* wrote, and at that time (licentiousness spread-
ing

"not less a crime than to make a gain by
"prostituting the body.—He who makes a
"gain of the *adultery* of his wife, whatever
"his rank or condition be, is punished as an
"*adulterer.*—If a man, in order to defame his
"wife, shall put an *adulterer* in his place,
"both the husband and wife shall, by law, be
"adjudged guilty of the crime of *adultery*."

By all this it appears, that nothing kept this learned man from thinking, with those first mentioned, that the ἐπ' αυτην relates to the *second* wife, (who, to make the man guilty of adultery, must be a *divorced* woman) but his supposing, that in this view the same matter is repeated *twice over*, which it certainly is not. See before, p. . This makes him also, on *second thoughts*, differ from his own note on *Matt.* xix. 9. and take the μοιχαται, *Mark* x. 11. in the sense of the *Hebrew* * Hiphil conjugation, as *causing her to commit*

―――――――――――――――――

"ing beyond measure) was a familiar thing, after
"*Messalina*, the wife of the Emperor *Claudius*, had
"publicly married *Silius*, in *Claudius*'s life-time, and
"*Claudius* himself had married *Octavia*, the daughter
"of *Cæsar*, to *Nero*, who had been betrothed by her
"father to *L. Silanus*."

All this may certainly account for *St. Mark*'s recording what our Lord said to the disciples in the house, touching *women putting away their husbands, and being married to other men*, which is omitted in *Matthew*.

* "Mœchatur] *i. e.* Mœchari facit illam, nempe
"priorem a se missam. ex collat. Matt. v. 32. Facere
"recté dicitur qui facto causam præbet. Et mos est
"Hellenistarum verba formæ *Hiphil* per activa exprime-
"re, ut Rom. viii. 26. Gal. iv. 6. *Pole* Synop. in
"Matt. xix. 9."

"Committeth

commit adultery, and so the husband, by *causing her* to do it, is *particeps criminis*, as an accessary before the fact, and may be said himself to *commit it*; as a man who hires, or causes another to commit a murder, is himself * guilty of murder;—as *David*, 2 Sam. xii. 9; *Ahab*, 1 Kings xxi. 19.

This interpretation is not new; for *Wetstein*, on Matt. xix. 9. mentions some copies, in which for μοιχαται—*committeth adultery*, is red—ποιει αυτην μοιχευθηναι—*causeth her to commit adultery*; and in one—μοιχαται—τατ᾽ ἐϛιν αναγκαζει μοιχευθηναι—*committeth adultery*; that is, *compels her to commit adultery*. I will conclude this point with observing, that, in all this, there is not the least hint or glance at

---

"Committeth adultery] that is, maketh her to commit adultery, to wit, the former wife which he sent away from him; comp. Matt. v. 32. He is rightly said to do it, who occasions it to be done. It is the custom of the *Hellenists*," (*Jews*, who spake or wrote in *Greek*) " to express words of the form *Hiphil* by active verbs." As Rom. viii. 26. where the SPIRIT's *making intercession for us*, is His causing us to pray in a right manner for ourselves; just as His crying *Abba, Father*, (Gal. iv. 6.) is His enabling us so to cry. Accordingly the *apostle*, Rom. viii. 15, speaks of Him as the *Spirit of adoption, whereby we cry, Abba, Father*. See *Guyse* Paraph. on Rom. viii. 26. and note.

* Many exemplifications of this doctrine, as very sensibly and properly adopted into the law of *England*, appear in our law-books; but in none more clearly, than in the case of *Lord Audley*, who was indicted for a *rape* on his own *wife*, he holding her while another *ravished* her;—he was *convicted*—and *executed*. He was likewise as evidently guilty of *adultery*, as the *ravisher* himself was. See State Try. vol. i.

polygamy, as *condemned,* or even *mentioned,* in these texts.

The learned *Grotius*, whom I have mentioned and quoted, at the beginning of this chapter, as maintaining a *new law* of CHRIST on the subject of *polygamy*, "afterwards "changed his opinion," (see note "", on Grot. de Jure, lib. ii. c. 5. § 9.) "as is "plain from his annotations on Matt. v. 32. "where he shews, that in that place, and "*other like passages* of the gospels, *polygamy* "is not condemned, but only the abuse of "*divorce*, from whatever cause it proceeds."
"Hence (adds *Barbeyrac)* in that excellent "little work—De *Verit. Relig. Chrift.*—he "only says—" The *Chriftians* follow the "usage of the * *Germans* and *Romans*, who
"were

---

* *Grotius*, in the passage here alluded to, doth not quote *Tacitus* fairly, whose words are—" Severa illis "matrimonia. Nam soli prope barbarorum singulis "uxoribus contenti, exceptis admodum paucis, qui non "libidine, sed ob nobilitatem, pluribus ambiuntur "nuptiis." Which proves, that the *Germans* were, in a degree at least, *polygamifts. On voit par les dernieres paroles, que, quoique cela fût rare parmi eux, il y en avoit pourtant des exemples; de sorte que c'etoit plûtôt une mode, qu'une chose regardée comme illicite.* Barbeyrac on Grot. de Jure, lib. ii. c. 5. note 12. Fr. transf. " One sees, "by the last words, that though *polygamy* was *rare* among "the *Germans*, there were however examples of it; so "that its *rarity* rather arose from *fashion* than from its "being looked upon as unlawful." As to the *Romans*, they were also *polygamifts*; for though they lived but with *one*, who was called *uxor*, a *wife*; yet their *libertæ*, and *ancillæ* or *servæ*, with whom they also cohabited, amounted to the same in point of fact.

" were content with *one wife*. Lib. ii. § 13;
" and in the note there introduced, he only
" refers to 1 Cor. vii. 4." This text, with the verses preceding it, we have very fully considered in the *last chapter*.

Since the first *Edition* of this work was published, I had a *book* put into my hands, the title page of which announces its being written on a popular occasion, that is to say,—" the affair of *Lord Grosvenor*'s action " against the D. of C." This book is entitled, " Free Thoughts on *Seduction, Adul-* " *tery*, and *Divorce*." The author styles himself a *Civilian*, and, by many parts of the book, seems to be an adept in his profession. His remarks are keen—his observations shrewd.—There are some things in which he may be thought to have gone too far; but there is a stricture on the subject of *polygamy*, as vulgarly supposed to be prohibited by our Saviour, Matt. xix. 9. which I will insert here, just as I find it, leaving it to my readers to make their own remarks upon it.

" It is indeed pretended, that the strictness
" of conjugal discipline, supposed to be re-
" commended by the *apostle*, is confirmed by

Suet. in *Vit. J. Cæs.* saith—that " he made a law, by " which every man, for the sake of propagating chil- " dren, might marry as many wives as he pleased." *M. Antony* had two wives at the same time. So had *Crassus*, and doubtless many more, whose names have not reached us.

" our Saviour himſelf; who is conceived
" alſo to have prohibited a man's having
" *more* than *one wife,* as well as a *wife's* hav-
" ing more than *one huſband.*

" But this ſuppoſition is groundleſs: for,
" as I before obſerved, from our *Saviour's*
" own words, *He came not to deſtroy the law
" or the prophets, but to fulfil them.* Now,
" under the law, *polygamy* was *allowed*; as
" plainly appears not only from practice but
" precept *.

" In ſaying, '*Thou ſhalt not commit adul-
" ' tery,*' the law did not ſay—*thou ſhalt not
" have more than one wife*; as it does when,
" reſpecting *idolatry,* it ſays, '*Thou ſhalt have
" ' no other gods but me.*' It is ſaid, '*Thou
" ' ſhalt not lie with another man's wife*;' it
" did not ſay—'*Thou ſhalt not lie with as many
" ' wives as thou wilt of thy own.*' On the con-
" trary, it appears to have been commonly

---

* " It were taking up the reader's time to little pur-
" poſe, to prove what is ſo generally known; the learned
" *Selden,* in his *Uxor Ebraica,* ſhews fully that a plura-
" lity of wives was not only allowed of among the *He-
" brews,* but amongſt almoſt all other nations, and in
" all ages. In the *Eaſt* it was almoſt univerſal, as it
" remains at this day. The ancient *Romans* indeed did
" not practiſe it, though it was not prohibited. *Mark
" Anthony,* I think, was the firſt who led the faſhion of
" having *two wives.* This faſhion laſted between *three
" and four hundred years,* when it was prohibited by an
" expreſs law, under the reign of *Theodoſius.* The Em-
" peror *Valentinian* however permitted it in a fuller ex-
" tent; nor did the *Chriſtian* Biſhops of theſe times
" make any oppoſition to this reintroduction of *polygamy.*
" *Juſtinian* and the latter councils put a ſtop to it.

" permitted

"permitted to have *two* or *more*. 'If a man
" 'have *two wives, one beloved and another
" 'hated*,' &c. Deut. xxi. 15. And again,
" 2 Sam. xii. 8, the prophet *Nathan*, re-
" proaching *David*, says, '—*Thus saith the*
" '*Lord God, I gave thee thy master's*
" '*house and thy master's wives into thy*
" '*bosom.*"

" It is true that, after the world became
" to be somewhat populous, and perhaps
" some communities apparently too nu-
" merous for the land they possessed, the
" * practice of *polygamy* was prohibited by
" the *civil magistrate*, for the *political* ends of
" *society*.

" According to the laws of *Justinian*, it
" was not *lawful* to have *two wives* at a time,
" nor even a *concubine* with a *wife*. The
" *canons* of the church also confirm this pro-
" hibition, under pretence of its being
" founded on the words of our *Saviour*, in
" His reply to the *Pharisees*. But if we

---

* " There are writers, indeed, who have laboured to
" prove, that *polygamy* does not tend to population. But,
" however ingeniously they have argued, they have
" contradicted all the experience both of ancient and
" modern times. If there are some countries, in which
" at this day *polygamy* is allowed, and yet they are not
" more populous than others where it is prohibited, the
" fact may be accounted for, by various other reasons.
" The desolation, occasioned by the plagues, wars, fa-
" mine, and licentiousness of those countries, would pro-
" bably have long since depopulated them entirely, had
" not *polygamy* been allowed."

" turn

" turn to the text, we shall find that no such
" prohibition is there either expressed or
" implied.

" *I say unto you, Whosoever shall put away
" his wife, except for fornication, and shall
" marry another, committeth adultery.* Matt.
" xix. 9.

" Very true, but if, without *putting away
" his wife*, he *marry another*, (as was the case
" with *Jacob*; when, after marrying *Leah*,
" he married also her sister *Rachel*) it does not
" appear that he would *commit adultery*.

" It is the *putting away* the first wife only,
" that made the marrying a second, *adul-
" tery*. Nor is even this a *direct* commission
" of that sin, but an *indirect* one; as such
" dismission of the first would naturally tend
" to make her form a *connection* with some
" other man; which would be direct *adultery*.
" This is plain from the words, in which
" the same prohibition is expressed in another
" place, by the same *Evangelist*, ' *I say unto
" ' you, that whosoever shall put away his wife,
" ' saving for the cause of fornication, causeth
" ' her to commit adultery*.' Matt. v. 32.

" It is true that some of our most learned
" *divines* have been of opinion, that the adul-
" tery lay in *marrying the second wife*, and
" not in the *putting away of the first*. But in
" this they have shewn themselves to be
" better *canonists* than *casuists*. Even *Bishop
" Cosens* says, it is not the dismission of the
" first wife that is *adulterous*, but the *mar-
" rying*

" *rying of the second.* But this is clearly a
" mistake; not only, because *polygamy* was
" allowed at the time when our SAVIOUR's
" injunction, respecting a man's *putting
" away his wife,* was promulgated; but be-
" cause the contrary appears on the very face
" of the text.

" The *Pharisees* did not ask *Jesus* about
" the *lawfulness* of a *plurality of wives*; but
" merely about *putting away their wives:* and
" though he answered them in a fuller man-
" ner than they seemed to require, he can-
" not be supposed to mistake the full drift
" and sense of their query.

" The question was, ' *Is it lawful for a
" ' man to put away his wife for every cause?*'
" The reply is, ' *Whosoever shall put away
" ' his wife, except for fornication (and shall
" ' marry another) committeth adultery.*' That
" is, indirectly, by depriving her of the pro-
" tection of a husband, and reducing her to
" the necessity of accepting that of some
" other man; agreeable to the words of the
" text before quoted, *causeth her to commit
" adultery.*

" Our *Saviour* indeed goes farther, and
" explains his meaning distinctly, in adding,
" *And whoso marrieth her which is put away,
" doth commit adultery.* But how so, unless
" the criminality depended on the incapacity
" of the first husband to *put her away?* This
" indeed made it *adultery* in the man marry-
" ing a woman thus unjustly divorced, be-
" cause

" caufe fhe was ftill the firft man's wife, and
" not lawfully feparated*.

" That this was certainly the meaning of
" our *Saviour*, cannot be doubted. *Mofes*,
" fays he, *becaufe of the hardnefs of your hearts,*
" *fuffered you to put away your wives*. Or
" rather, as the tranflators have more properly
" expreffed it in Mark x. 5. for the *hardnefs*
" *of your heart*.

" A mere *Englifh* reader might, from the
" former expreffion of *Matthew*, take occa-
" fion to fay, that the term *wives* in the plu-
" ral, is no more applicable to the individual
" than that of *hearts*; and that the former

---

* " The legality of the divorce appears evidently to
" depend on the *fornication* on the part of the *woman*,
" which *ipfo facto* diffolved the marriage; or, what
" amounted to the fame thing, gave the hufband a right
" to do it at pleafure, by giving his bill of divorce; and
" this feems to be particularly expreffed in reply to the
" queftion, ' Whether *a man might put away his wife for*
" ' *every caufe?*' and alfo to the additional queftion,
" ' *Why then did Mofes command, to give a writing of di-*
" ' *vorcement, and to put her away*; i. e. for every, or
" ' any caufe?'—It is this circumftance, viz. the fa-
" cility of men's divorcing their wives at pleafure, that
" accounts for the non-ufage of *polygamy* in countries
" where it was allowed by law. It has been already
" obferved, that the ancient *Romans* did not indulge
" themfelves in *polygamy*, though permitted; but this
" was for a good reafon: they wifely chofe not to have
" *two wives* in the houfe at the fame time, and therefore
" *repudiated* one before they took another; and this
" they did as often as they pleafed, with no other for-
" mality than that of fending a meffage to the wife by
" a flave, giving notice of their intentions, after the
" manner of the *Hebrews*."

" word,

" word, as well as the latter, muſt be meant
" of their *wives collectively*, and not of the
" *wives of each* ſeverally : but the original is
" in both places the ſame—Προς την σκληρο-
" καρδιαν υμων—*Beza* has it—*pro duritia cor-*
" *dis veſtri*—for your *hardneſs of heart*, in the
" *ſingular* number; but it is *dimittere uxo-*
" *res veſtras*—put away your *wives*, in the
" plural, conformable to the original.

" That this is the true ſenſe of the text,
" is farther confirmed by the remark which
" the diſciples of *Jeſus* made on it, in the
" ſucceeding verſe.

" It runs in the vulgar tranſlation thus :
" *If the caſe of the man be ſo with his wife, it*
" *is good not to marry.*

" But the verſion is here alſo palpably
" defective. By the *man*, may be miſtaken-
" ly underſtood, a *particular huſband*; and by
" his *wife*, may in like manner be underſtood
" his *ſole* and *only wife*; but the word *his*, is
" *foiſted* into the text; it is indeed uſually
" printed in *Italics*, to denote the *interpola-*
" *tion.* This prohibition is expreſſed, on
" the contrary, in the moſt general terms.
" *Si tale eſt hominis negotium cum uxore*, ſays
" *Beza*: conformable to the original—ει
" ϋτως εςιν η αιτια τȣ ανθρωπȣ μετα της γυναικος,
" not the particular caſe between *any one*
" *huſband* and his *ſole wife*; but the matri-
" monial commerce *(negotium)* between the
" ſexes in general; or, as *Vaſor* explains
" it, the condition or relative ſituation
" of

"of a husband respecting his *wives*. *Si ea est conditio viri*, &c.

"If any other argument were necessary, to establish the sense of this reply, which our *Saviour* gave to the designing *Pharisees*; perhaps some confirmation of it may be drawn from the question, put to him by the *Sadducees*, with a design equally sinister.

"*A woman*, say they (successively) married *seven husbands, At the resurrection whose wife shall she be?*—Had a *plurality of wives* not been permitted by the *divine law*, it would have better answered their end, if they had proposed the same problem, with a change of terms; and asked him, if a man had successively *seven wives*, to which of them, at the resurrection, would the husband belong?"

In justice to our author, I cannot conclude my quotations from him, without giving, in his own words, the *caveat* which he enters, against the practice of *polygamy*.——"But I am not pleading either for the piety or morality of *polygamy*. Under the *Christian* dispensation, and in times like these, I conceive *one wife* to be enough, if not *too much*, for any one man. Add to this, that, whether it be contrary to the law of GOD or not, it is expressly contrary to that of man; being forbidden in *England* by the written laws of the land."——Our author might have *strengthened* this part of his argu-

ment, by adding, " and by the *Canons* of the " *Church of Rome*."

To all the weight of evidence which has been produced against the notion of CHRIST's introducing a *new law*, either with respect to *polygamy*, or any thing else, I will add one more testimony, and such a one as must carry its own conviction with it, even into the bosom of prejudice itself. Let us hear our LORD *Himself*, Luke xvi. 18. *Whosoever putteth away his wife, and marrieth another,* (* ἑτέραν) *committeth adultery; and whosoever marrieth*

---

* On considering all that has been said, on *Matt.* xix. 9. *Mark* x. 11. and here on *Luke* xvi. 18, I do conclude, that if the μοιχᾶται—*committeth adultery*—be understood with respect to the second-taken wife—then the ἀλλην and ἑτέραν must signify, that she was a *married* or *unjustly-divorced* woman; for the marriage of a *maid* or *a widow* was never made *adultery* by the *law*, under any circumstances whatsoever of *precontract* on the man's side.

If μοιχᾶται be understood with reference to the *first wife*, whom the man had *divorced* in order to take *another*; and if in this sense we are to understand the ἐπ' αὐτην, Mark x. 11. i. e. with reference to the *first wife*;—we must then construe μοιχᾶται by *Matt*. v. 32, and suppose the man an *adulterer*, in the same sense as an accessary before the fact to a *murder*, is a *murderer*, by *causing* another to commit it.

The argument which has been usually drawn from Matt. xix. 9. by many learned men, is as follows:—" If " it be *adultery* for a man to marry a second woman after " he has *put away* the first, it is not less *adultery* to marry " a *second* while he *retains* the first."—

But there are several faults in this argument.

1. *Petitio principii*, or taking that for granted which is denied.

2. Using the word *adultery* in a sense not warranted by the word נאף—*adultery*—in the Hebrew scripture, where it only signifies the *defilement* of a *married woman*.

marrieth her that has been put away (ἀπολελυμενην) *from her hufband, committeth adultery.* This, fay fome, is Christ's "*new law*, by "which He forbad *polygamy*, which was "allowed under the Old Teftament."—As to the meaning of the words themfelves, as they are much the fame as in Matt. xix. 9. I will not repeat what has already been obferved on that place; but as to their conftituting fome *new law*, we have Christ's own authority to fay they *do not:* for obferve the preface at ver. 17. with which our Lord introduces them, wherein *He Himfelf* gives us to underftand, that, what He *here* fays, and of courfe what He fays *elfewhere* to the fame purpofe, is grounded upon *the law of the Old Teftament. It is eafier for heaven and earth to pafs, than one tittle of the law to fail.* Having introduced what He fays, ver. 18. with this pofitive affertion touching the ftability, unchangeablenefs, and perpetual obligation of *the law*, we muft, to be confiftent

3. A *non fequitur*, or conclufion which does not follow from the premifes, unlefs, *divorcing* the firft wife, and *retaining* her, fignify *one* and the *fame* thing.

4. A contradiction of the law of *Mofes*—an inconfiftency with the antient laws of the *Jews* as recorded in the *Pentateuch*.

5. A rendering the words *He that putteth away his wife,* which occur uniformly in Matt. v. 32. Matt. xix. 9. Mark x. 11. Luke xvi. 18.—which are all the texts on the fubject—mere *furplufage* and totally *infignificant*.

6. The mention of *the putting away*, keeps the whole anfwer in direct agreement with the queftion afked—viz.—Is it *lawful for a man to put away his wife for every caufe?*—which the other view of the text has nothing to do with.

ourfelves,

ourselves, or to make Him consistent; construe what He says, as grounded upon *that law*, which *He Himself* lays down as the foundation on which He spake. This can be no other than the *law of* GOD as * delivered by *Moses*; what that *condemned*, CHRIST *condemned* on its authority; but had He *condemned* what that *allowed*, or had He *allowed* what that *condemned*, there was an end of that law, and more than a *tittle* of it must be said to *fail*—πεσειν—to *fall*—*perish*, and *be destroyed*. It may be worth our while to take a short view of the context:—ver. 16. *the law and the prophets were until John: since that time, the kingdom of* GOD *is preached, and every man presseth into it*.

As if our LORD had said: " Till the coming of *John the Baptist*—which was fore-

---

* A strong and striking observation might here be made—viz. that at the time CHRIST held this discourse with the *Pharisees*, the whole law of *Moses* was in its full force, even the CEREMONIAL LAW *itself*; to which CHRIST was subject, and which He observed, from the hour of His *circumcision* to His *last supper*, when He ate the *passover* with His disciples. Luke xxii. 15. Nor did this law *vanish away*, 'till it had its full accomplishment in the death, resurrection, and ascension of the great and glorious *antitype*; when, *having made peace through the blood of His cross*, Col. i. 20, *He entered in once into the* HOLY PLACE, *having obtained eternal redemption for us*. Heb. ix. 12. From whence it follows, that during CHRIST's ministry on earth, no part of the law of MOSES could, consistently with the character which OUR LORD sustained, be altered in a single *jot or tittle*—for *He came not to destroy the law, but to fulfil it*—this could not be, if he revoked or altered, but more especially if he *opposed*, any part of it.

VOL. I.   C c   " told

"told, Is. xl. 3. Mal. iii. 1.—ye were under
"the teachings of the *legal* and *prophetical*
"difpenfation; but fince *John*'s coming, that
"*gofpel*, which was prefigured by the cere-
"monial and typical rites of the *Mofaic*
"difpenfation, and foretold for ages together
"by the prophets, is now openly declared.
"This is not confined, as the others were,
"to the *Jews* only; but multitudes of per-
"fons, of what nation or character foever,
"even publicans and finners of the *Gentiles*,
"fenfible of their fin and mifery, fhall be
"invited to partake of its bleffings, and will
"eagerly *prefs* for an intereft in them, though
"they be no obfervers of the rites and cere-
"monies of the *law*.

"And yet the law is not hereby made
"void;—the prophecies, types, and fhadows
"of the Old Teftament, are fully accom-
"plifhed; the *moral* law is honoured and
"confirmed, its precepts explained, and all
"its commandments eftablifhed as a law of
"My kingdom, as an eternal and unchange-
"able *rule of life* to all My fubjects. There-
"fore *think not that I came to deftroy the law*
"(καταλυσαι, Matt. v. 17.) to *diffolve* it, or
"loofen men from any of its obligations in
"point of obedience—*It is eafier for heaven
"and earth to pafs, than one tittle of the law
"to fail*—therefore, however you may have
"been taught to *make it void by your tradi-
"tions*, and efpecially with regard to your
"treatment of your *wives*, by which you
"are daily violating the *law of marriage*, in
"the

"the unjuſt and ſcandalous divorcements, which your *rabbies* have taught you to abuſe to the purpoſes of licentiouſneſs and cruelty, yet the law of GOD *changeth not*, it is the ſame now as in the days of *Adam*; and therefore—whoever *puts away his wife* unjuſtly, breaks the *law* which commands him *to cleave* to her, and *puts aſunder what* GOD *hath joined together*—and if this be done in order to *marry one you like better*, and under ſuch circumſtances of provocation, as force the wife you put away to *marry another man,* ſhe certainly ſins againſt the *ſeventh* commandment, as does the man who takes her; but yet the guilt of *adultery* is not confined to them, but lights upon you alſo, who, by your unlawful treatment of your wife, in *putting her away* unjuſtly, *cauſed her* to commit it (ſee Matt. v. 32.) You are therefore anſwerable before GOD as an *adulterer*; for there is no difference, in the eye of *His law*, between the *perpetrator* of a crime, and the *inſtigator* and *promoter* of it."

In the above paraphraſe on the context, I have endeavoured to take in the whole ſenſe of the paſſage, as agreeable *to,* and reconcileable *with,* the *law of the* Old Teſtament; for it was certainly by *this,* that our LORD regulated all His *thoughts, words,* and *actions,* on *every* ſubject, and upon *every* occaſion, as well as in the inſtance of what He ſaid, Luke xvi. 18.

Had Christ been to have introduced a *new law*, it muſt have appeared ſomewhere in *His* * *commiſſion:* we have ſeveral tranſcripts of this, relative to all His *offices*, but not a ſingle clauſe is there in any of them to † that purpoſe.

His commiſſion as a *prieſt* appears in ſeveral parts

---

* In Deut. xviii. 18, 19. it is ſaid—*I will raiſe them up a* Prophet *from among their brethren, like unto thee, and I will put* my words *in His mouth, and He ſhall ſpeak unto them* all that I shall command Him. And *it ſhall come to paſs, that whoſoever will not hearken unto* my words, *which He ſhall ſpeak* in my name, *I will require it of him.* And, ver. 15. *The* Lord *thy God will raiſe up unto thee a* Prophet *in the midſt of thee, of thy brethren, like unto me; unto Him ye ſhall hearken.* This general account of Christ's miſſion as a *Prophet*, ſeems to militate againſt every idea of His ſetting up a *new law* of *His own*. Had He done this, He had not been *like Moſes*, who received the law from God, and delivered it to the people, but like *Mahomet*, who invented a *new law* of *His own*, in oppoſition to the law of God, and impoſed it upon his followers as containing the only true religion and worſhip: whereas the *bleſſed* Jesus gave this teſt of His miſſion, John iii. 34. *He whom* God *hath ſent, ſpeaketh the words of* God—for the truth of this, His conſtant appeal was to the writings of the Old Teſtament.

I would recommend the conſideration of what is here ſaid, to thoſe, who talk of a *law of the goſpel*, more *pure and perfect* than the law of *Moſes*. So ſpake *Socinus*, and, after him, *too many* in this our *day*—I have heard this, from *more* than *one pulpit.*

† If our *bleſſed* Saviour came to overturn the law of Moses, it is a little extraordinary that he ſhould give ſo ſtrict a charge *to the multitudes, and to his diſciples*, to hear and practiſe it—(Matt. xxiii. 1, 2, 3.) *ſaying, the Scribes and the Phariſees* (who were the ordinary teachers among the *Jews*) *ſit in* Moses' *ſeat:* all therefore whatsoever *they bid you to obſerve*, (that is, all that is agreeable to the law of Moses) *obſerve and do.*

Our

parts of the Old Testament, and is thus shortly summed up, Dan. ix. 24.—*To finish the transgression—to make an end of sins—to make reconciliation for iniquity and* (thus) *to bring in everlasting righteousness.*—As a *prophet*, says he, by Is. lxi. 1. &c. *The Spirit of the* LORD GOD *is upon Me, because the* LORD *hath anointed me to preach good tidings unto the meek: He hath sent Me to bind up the broken-hearted, to proclaim liberty to the captives, and the opening of the prison to them that are bound: to proclaim the acceptable year of the* LORD, *and the day of vengeance of our* GOD; *to comfort all that mourn: to appoint unto them that mourn in Zion, to give unto them beauty for ashes, the oil of joy for mourning, the garment of praise for the spirit of heaviness, that they might be called trees of righteousness, the planting of the* LORD, *that He might be glorified.* There is nothing about a *new law* in this part of OUR SAVIOUR's commission.

As to His *kingly office,* on which He entered after His resurrection from the dead, when *He had a name given Him above every name, that at the name of* JESUS *every knee should bow, of things in heaven, and things on earth, and things under the earth, and that every tongue should confess that* JESUS CHRIST *is* LORD, *to the glory of* GOD *the Father*—His kingdom was to be administered not by any *new law,* but by that which was from the beginning,

OUR LORD does not make the least exception, nor hint at the smallest innovation, but παν]α ὁσα—*omnia quæcunque*—all things whatsoever—therefore, doubtless, relative to *marriage,* as well as to every thing else.

once written *on tables of stone,* but now to be written *on the fleshly tables of the heart,* 2 Cor. iii. 3. For thus faith the LORD—*This is the covenant that I will make with the house of* ISRAEL; *after those days I will put* MY LAW *in their inward parts, and write* IT *in their hearts, and will be their* GOD, *and they shall be my people.* Jer. xxxi. 33. Comp. Heb. viii. 10.

If CHRIST then gave a *new law,* or *rule of life,* He exceeded His commiffion, and we muſt call in queſtion His veracity, as well as His ſincerity, in that declaration of His, Matt. v. 17, 18, 19. likewiſe as to what he ſays, John xii. 49, 50. *I have not ſpoken of* MYSELF, *but the Father which ſent me* HE GAVE ME A COMMANDMENT, *what I ſhould ſay* *, *and what I ſhould ſpeak—and I know that* HIS COMMANDMENT *is life everlaſting;* (Comp. Rom. x. 5. Gal. iii. 12.) *whatſoever I ſpeak therefore, even as the Father ſaid unto Me ſo I ſpeak.* See Deut. xviii. 18, 19. In exact conformity with all this, it is ſaid, Heb. i. 1. GOD, *who at ſundry times, and in divers manners, ſpake in time paſt unto the fathers by the*

---

* If the *Father* gave CHRIST a commandment to declare *that* to be a *mortal ſin* againſt the *ſeventh* commandment, which was uniformly *allowed* as *innocent* under the Old Teſtament, this muſt infer either a *change* in the *divine mind and will,* or an *abſolute contradiction:* this laſt is uſually got rid of, as the *Mahometan doctors* get rid of the contradictions in the *Koran*—by their doctrine of *abrogation:*—for they pretend that "God commanded ſeve- "ral things in the *Koran,* which, for good reaſons, "were afterwards revoked and *abrogated.*" Thus do ſome of our *Chriſtian* Doctors treat the Old Teſtament, in order to eſtabliſh certain doctrines which they ſuppoſe to be taught in the New Teſtament reſpecting marriage.

Prophets,

Prophets, hath in these last days spoken unto us by His Son. These words are expresly and particularly addressed to the *Hebrews*; and the whole subsequent *epistle* proves the uniformity and unchangeableness of the *Divine will*, and that the *Christian* dispensation declared *none other things than Moses and the Prophets did say should come to pass.* Comp. Acts xxvi. 22.

But to return once more to our Saviour's discourse with the *Pharisees*:—Can it be imagined that Christ, so remarkable for his precision, so thoroughly accurate in all He said on every other point, should use so little in this, as not to make Himself understood by His hearers? Nay—that He should observe so little precision, as not to *describe* an offence, which we are to suppose Him to condemn? The most flagrant instances, the most obvious and palpable definitions of *polygamy* cannot be understood from what He says.—*He that putteth away his wife,* * *by bill of divorcement, and marrieth another*—does not describe *a man's taking two wives* together, *and cohabiting with both;* nor—a man's *having a wife,* and *taking another* to her, and cohabiting with *both.* Such was the Old Testament *polygamy,* not the *putting away one* in order to *take ano-*

---

* This is the sense of the word ἀπολῦσαι. Matt. xix. 7, 8, 9; and it is to be remarked, that this ingredient of *putting away,* enters into the *definition*, and therefore into the very *essence* of the offence which Christ condemns; but it is very certain that it is not of the essence of *polygamy,* nor does it enter into the definition of it.

ther.—I do not recollect a single instance in which this was ever done during the whole administration of *Moses*, the *Judges*, or *Kings*, any more than a single instance where *polygamy* was forbidden †. However the law of *Moses* forbad what our Saviour mentions, just as much as His words do. If a man once took a woman, he never (except for adultery) could *put her away all his days*; and though *Moses* suffered, in order to avoid worse consequences, *divorces* for other causes beside *adultery*, by not bringing the offenders to condign punishment in every instance, yet there never was an instance when the law of God did not condemn them. As for *polygamy*, *Josephus* says, and the Bible proves what he says to be true, that—" It was the custom of the *Jews* to live " with a plurality of wives; he calls it " πατριον—the custom of their country, deriv- " ed from their fathers."—The same historian, writing the account of God's giving the deceased *Saul*'s wives to *David*, observes, that, " God gave *David* many *wives*, which " he might *justly* and *lawfully* have." The *Pesicta*, on Lev. xviii. calls it, " *notissimum*" —a thing most *notorious*, " that He who said " it was forbidden to have *more wives than* " *one*, was entirely ignorant of the law." See Grot. de Jure, lib. ii. c. 5. § 9. in the note k.

Is it then, without the highest absurdity, to be imagined, that Christ should mention

† Unless we understand Lev. xx i. 13, 14. to forbid it in the case of the *high-priest*, as the *Jews* commonly understood it.

and condemn *polygamy* in the prefence of fuch multitudes of *Jews*, and in a fettled difpute with His bittereft foes, the *Pharifees*, who only difputed with Him to enfnare Him, and to have whereof to acccufe Him to the people as an enemy to *Mofes* (for this was their grand point in their appeal to *Mofes*'s writings) and yet that we fhould not meet with a fyllable of * reply to what He advanced, when they might have quoted the whole Old Teftament againft Him? that He fhould declare a thing to be *adultery*, without a fingle teftimony from *Mofes* to fupport Him in what he faid? and this, when He never on any other occafion taught any doctrine but on the authority of the Old Teftament, and conftantly appealed to it for the truth of what He declared?

---

* Dr. *Whitby*, in his comment on Matt. xix. 9. fays, "Here it feems evident that CHRIST prefcribes a *new law*, which had not before obtained among the *Jews*." This is the πρῶτον ψευδῶ-, the *grand miftake*, which runs through his whole comment on the paffage, as well as through the ufual and vulgar interpretation of it—But can any thing be more contradictory to every notion of *propriety*, than to fuppofe CHRIST "prefcribing a *new law*—which had never obtained among the *Jews*" in order to reftrain a practice which He proves to be forbidden by their own law, that of unjuft divorce; and to prohibit *polygamy* as *adultery*, in contradiction to the law of *Mofes*, which *allowed* it; more efpecially after declaring folemnly, that *He came not to deftroy the law*—and that *not even a jot or tittle fhould pafs from it*? To imagine CHRIST as correcting the *Jews* by a law " which had " never obtained among them," is an abfurdity of the firft magnitude; *For what the law faith, it faith to them that are under the law*, Rom. iii. 19; thofe who are not under the *law* (be *that law* what it may) have nothing to do with it.

Laftly,

Lastly. Is it conceivable, as CHRIST must be supposed to speak in *Hebrew*, that He should give a meaning to the language of the Old Testament, which, in all the writings of *Moses* and all the *prophets*, it never had? Now, wherever the verb μοιχαομαι is used in the *Greek* translation of the LXX, it constantly answers to the Hebrew נאף; and therefore there is no room to doubt, that wherever, in our SAVIOUR's discourses, as recorded by the *Evangelists*, we meet with the word μοιχαται, נאף was the very *Hebrew* term used by him: but no where, throughout the whole *Hebrew* Bible, is this word applied to a man's *marrying a second wife, living his first*, unless such *second* was either betrothed or married to another, or to any thing else, than only to the defilement of a *betrothed* or *married* * woman. This is its single idea throughout the whole. Therefore it is figuratively used to describe the people's *forsaking* GOD, and *turning to idols*. See before, p.

CHRIST said to the *Jews*, John v. 46, 47. *Had ye believed Moses, ye would have believed Me; but if ye believe not his writings, how shall ye believe My words?* It is not easy to conceive words more forcible than these, to express an absolute and unreserved appeal to the Old Testament for the truth of all CHRIST said

---

* Let any one take up an *English* concordance, and look at the word *adultery*, and he will not be able to find a single instance where it is applied to *polygamy* in any part of the Old Testament, nor in any other manner than the Hebrew נאף.

and taught in His *prophetical* character. In this character He stood before the *great multitudes* of the people and the *Pharisees*, while he was delivering, on the authority of the scriptures, the sense of those scriptures upon the matter of *unjust divorce*, and proving the criminal consequences of it to all parties concerned. He so proved His point, that His adversaries had not a word to reply. He silenced them as He did the *devil*, Matt. iv. 10, 11. by the *word of* God. But had He said *polygamy* was *sinful*, from which of *Moses*'s writings would He have proved * this? The *Pharisees* might have retorted upon Him His own declaration and appeal to the writings of *Moses*; they might have said—" Thou hast said, that if we be-
" lieved the writings of Moses, we should believe
" Thy words—Thou hast said, that if *a man*
" *having a wife, marrieth another*," (for thus they might have put it, had they understood

* *Voltaire*, in whose writings on the scripture are to be found here and there a sensible thing, among heaps of folly and nonsense; has an observation which is worth attending to, viz. " We are told in *St. Matthew*, that
" the great men, and the *priests*, and *all the council, sought*
" *false witness against Jesus, to put Him to death*.
" Now if they were obliged to seek for false witnesses,
" they could not charge Him with having preached
" openly against their law." Treat. on Tol. Franklin's transf. p. 192. vol. xxxiv. But if Christ had preached against *polygamy*, as *adultery*, He would as evidently have preached against the law of *Moses*, as if he had preached against *marriage* itself, or as a *missionary* would preach against the law of *Turkey*, who should contend for the establishment of 1 Jac. c. 11. at *Constantinople*—and this, on the authority of the *Alcoran*'s having prohibited *polygamy*.

Him

Him to have condemned *polygamy*) "he com-
"mitteth *adultery*; but where doſt Thou
"find this in *Moſes*'s writings? they are
"filled with the *allowance* of what Thou
"*condemneſt*, without a ſingle exception:
"therefore, becauſe we believe *Moſes*'s writ-
"ings, we do *not* believe *Thee*."

From all that has been ſaid, I do conclude, that CHRIST was not a deſtroyer of the *old law*, nor a giver of a *new one*—that therefore the buſineſs of *polygamy*, and all other points relative to the *commerce of the ſexes*, were fully adjuſted and ſettled by the *divine law*, ſubject to no alteration or change whatſoever, by * any power in EARTH OR HEAVEN. For thus ſaith the SPIRIT—Eccleſ. iii. 14, *Whatſoever* GOD *doeth, it ſhall be for ever, nothing can be put to it, nor any thing taken from it.*

Having now finiſhed what I had to ſay on the ſubject of this *chapter*, I ſhall next proceed, on the footing of the *divine law*, to conſider another material point relative to the *commerce of the ſexes*, which is *Divorce*.

* ZUINGLIUS, in his letter on the ſubject of King HENRY's divorce, ſays very truly—that " the *apoſtles* " had made no *new laws* about marriage, but had left " it as they found it." See BURNET, *Hiſt. Ref.* vol. i. p. 93.

APPENDIX

APPENDIX to CHAP. I.

Containing FARTHER THOUGHTS on
Exod. xxii. 16, 17.

THIS scripture is usually understood very evidently to contain a law, that he who *enticed*, &c. a young woman, should be obliged to marry * her. To understand it in any other light, is to divest the most intelligible and plain words of their certain and obvious meaning. But it is to be observed, that the *damsel* must be entirely disengaged from any *betrothment* to another man; for if she were betrothed to another, then the man who defiled her could not marry her, but both he and she, if she consented to the defilement, were to be put to death, according to Deut. xxii. 23, 24; otherwise it is here said, ver. 16. *he shall surely endow her to be his wife*, or *for a wife to himself*, as—לו לאשה—may be more literally rendered. So *Josephus*—Ὁ Φθείρας παρθένον, &c. αὐτός γαμείτω.—" He who defiles a virgin, the same shall marry her." That is, shall pay the *dowry*, and so recognize and confirm the *marriage-obligation*,

---

* I would here be understood to take the word *marry* in its *popular* sense, as denoting some outward act of public recognition of the *marriage-obligation*, such as the payment of the *dower* among the *Jews*.

which

which had been created by his antecedently taking poffeffion of her perfon.

From the 17th verfe it is ufually underftood, that, *if the father refufed to give her to him*, the man was to pay a fatisfaction in money for the injury and difgrace he had done her: and though the law, ver. 16. appointed the marriage, both as a punifhment to him that had done the wrong, and a recompence to her that had fuffered the wrong: yet that there was an exprefs refervation of the father's power (ver. 17.) if he refufed his confent, it muft be no marriage; only the money to be paid as τὴν τιμὴν τῆς ὕβρεως—a fatisfaction for her reproach, as *Jofephus* fpeaks.

The *Jewifh* doctors were very lax in their interpretation of this paffage of fcripture, who would not have it to be a command (ver. 16.) that he fhould marry her (though that was beft) but only that he fhould make fatisfaction for taking away her virginity; which was by paying fo much in the nature of *dowry* as would render her fit to be his wife if *both* of them could agree.

This interpretation of the 16th verfe, is one of thofe arbitrary expofitions of the *Talmudifts*, which by robbing the text of its plain meaning, leave us to the uncertainty of human imagination, which being various in various men, muft render the fcriptures totally uncertain as to any determinate meaning whatfoever.

The 17th verfe fays nothing of the *marriage*, whether it *fhall* or *fhall not* be *binding*, on the *father's refusal*; but only—" *If the father utterly refuse to give her unto him, he shall pay money according to the dowry of virgins.*" Here I take the words according to our tranflation—" *If,*" &c. and fuppofing it (for argument's fake) to include a refervation of the father's authority, fo that he might, even where matters had gone fo *far* as defcribed ver. 16. *invalidate* the contract, by witholding his *confent*—which, though infifted on by the *Talmudifts*, is hardly reconcileable with the peremptory and pofitive command, ver. 16.—yet this does not affect the principal point which I contend for, and which is contained in ver. 16; namely, that it is the taking *poffeffion* of the woman's *perfon* which creates the *contract*, or *marriage-obligation*. Therefore, no man, agreeably to the divine law, can entice a *virgin*, *defile* her, and then *forfake* her at his *own will and pleafure*, as is done every day among us in this *Chriftian* land, where the law of GOD is fuppofed to be the rule of right and wrong, but is, in truth and in fact, put entirely out of the queftion.

I thought fit to lay thefe feveral expofitions of this fcripture before the *reader*, that he might the better judge how far I may be right in my views of it, which are before fubmitted to his confideration, p. 25—28; and, at the fame time, form his own judgment of the matter, from that which appears to him to be moft agreeable to the context, as well as to the reft of the fcripture.

The *apostle* tells us, *Rom.* iii. 19. *Whatsoever things the law saith, it saith to them that are under the law,* therefore no *Jew*, who by *circumcision was a debtor to do the whole law* (Gal. v. 3.) could be exempt from any part of it. For a like reason, the believing *Gentiles*, who are compared to *the olive-tree wild by nature, but grafted into the good olive-tree* (see Rom. xi. 24.) and become members of GOD's church by *the circumcision made without hands* (Col. ii. 11.) are certainly *under the law* as a rule of life, and therefore subject to its *moral* precepts in every instance. From hence it ought to be concluded, that *Christians* are as much bound by Exod. xxii. 16. and Deut. xxii. 28, 29, as the *Jews* are. No reason can be given to the contrary, which will not equally apply to their exemption from the *ten commandments*; for these were at first delivered, and *immediately* and *particularly* addressed to the *Jews*, as appears from the short preface, Exod. xx. 1, 2. But can there be found a man, *mad* enough to suppose, that because they were emphatically addressed to the *people* which GOD *brought out of the land of Egypt, out of the house of bondage,* no others have any thing to do with them?

APPENDIX

APPENDIX to CHAP. II.

THE celebrated *Martinus Bucerus*, one of our excellent and learned *Reformers*, in enarrationibus ad cap. 19. *Libri Judicum*, has left us the following observation concerning *concubinage*; which seems to throw much light on the subject.

"*Concubinæ* erant *legitimæ etiam uxores:*
"sed hoc a *matronis* differebant, quod sine
"dote & sine solenni sanctificatione recipie-
"bantur: & erant ferè ex ancillis, & servilis
"conditionis: & non erant adjutoria illius
"præstantioris gradus, ut omni rerum com-
"munione gauderent sed humiliore gradu,
"& quæ haberentur humiliore loco, quod
"ad administrationem domus attinet, & ad
"filiorum successionem.—Legitimum verò
"genus concubinarum est, quum habentur
"conjunctæ copula matrimoniali, ne abjici
"temere possint: tametsi non habeant com-
"munionem plenam omnium rerum cum
"marito, ut matres-familias: nec convene-
"runt pactis dotalibus, unde & nati ex illis
"non habent successionem in hæreditate pa-
"ternâ cum natis ex matre-familias: sicut
"*Abraham* ex concubinis *veris uxoribus*, sed
"non matribus-familias, dona quædam de-
"putavit, portionem hæreditatis nullam ad-
"dixit.—Ex *legitimo genere concubinarum* fu-
"erunt concubinæ sanctorum patrûm. Et
"quia DOMINUS dignitates & patrimonia,
"quæ suis contulit, conservari vult, optan-
"dum omninò ut hoc genus uxorum, uti
"apud

" apud sanctissimos olim Patres observatum
" est, rursus apud Christianos, & maximè in
" præstantibus familiis observaretur, &c."

" *Concubines* were also *lawful wives*; but
" in this they differed from the *matrons*, that
" they were received without dowry and a
" solemn sanctification. They were usually
" from maid-servants, and of a servile con-
" dition; and they were not *help-mates* of
" that superior degree, as to enjoy a commu-
" nion of things in every respect, but in a
" lower degree, and were reckoned in a lower
" sphere, as to the administration of the
" house, and the succession of their sons.—
" They are a lawful kind of *concubines*, who
" are joined to their husbands by a *matrimo-
" nial* tie, so that they cannot rashly be put
" away; although they may not have a full
" communion of all things with their hus-
" bands, as *mistresses of the family*, nor did
" they agree [or come together] by *dowry-
" contracts*; wherefore the sons born of them
" have not a succession in the heritage of the
" father, with the sons of the *mistress of the
" house*. Thus *Abraham* gave gifts to the
" sons born of his *concubines*, who were *true
" wives*, but gave them no portion of the
" inheritance.—The concubines of the holy
" fathers were of the lawful kind. And be-
" cause the LORD wills, that the dignities
" and patrimonies which He has conferred
" on His people, should be preserved, it
" is altogether to be wished, that this kind
" of wives, as observed among the holy
" *patriarchs*, might be again observed among
" *Christians*,

" *Christians*, and especially in great and il-
" lustrious families, &c."

There is much good sense in what *Bucer* says, not only as tending to give a scriptural and proper idea of *concubinage*, but also as pointing out a convenient *medium* between men of *family* and *fortune* being obliged to match with *inferior* women whom they may happen to *take*, so as to put them upon a footing with themselves and families, and the liberty of abandoning them to prostitution and ruin.

This hint of *Bucer's*, with respect to *Christians*, seems to have been taken in some parts of *Germany*; where we are told of *wives* of a sort of *second degree*, which they call *left-handed wives*; these are indeed taken with more ceremony, but, in other respects, differ little in their situation from the antient *concubines*. See *Chambers*, Tit. HAND—and MARRIAGE.

Dr. *Alexander*, *Hist. Wom.* vol. ii. p. 267, writes thus concerning this custom in *Prussia*
" —Though their code of laws seems in gene-
" ral to be as reasonable, and as consistent
" with sound policy as any in *Europe*, yet
" we still find in it an allowance given for
" a species of that *concubinage* which has long
" since been expelled from almost all the
" *western* world. A man may there marry
" what is called a *left-handed wife*, to whom
" he is married for life, and by the common
" ceremony — the only difference is, the
" bridegroom gives her his *left* hand instead
" of his right—but with this express agree-
" ment,

"ment, that neither she nor her children shall live in the house of her husband, nor shall take his name, nor bear his arms, nor claim any dower or donation usually claimed by every other wife, nor dispose of any part of his property, exert any authority over his servants, nor succeed to his estates or his titles; but shall be contented with what was agreed on for their subsistence during his life, and with what he shall give them at his death. This privilege, however, is always in the power of the *king* to deny, and is seldom granted to any but such of the nobility as are left with large families, and, from the smallness of their fortunes, cannot afford to marry another legal wife, and rear up another family of the same rank with themselves."

There are certainly in the above very strong traces of the antient *concubinage*, which was allowed and practised under the *divine law*. If such a custom as this prevailed among us, and was inforced on men of *rank* and *fashion*, who are now turned loose on the *lower order of females*, and debauch them at *free cost*, without being under the least responsibility towards them—it would not only prove a happy check to the most mischievous licentiousness in many instances, but be also a means of preventing the utter ruin of *thousands*, who, under the present *system* of things, are seduced, abandoned, and destroyed, without any *remedy* whatsoever, or almost any possibility of escape.

END OF THE FIRST VOLUME.

www.ingramcontent.com/pod-product-compliance
Lightning Source LLC
Chambersburg PA
CBHW031228290426
44109CB00012B/199